Unsentimental Reformer

UNSENTIMENTAL REFORMER

The Life of
Josephine Shaw Lowell

Joan Waugh

HARVARD UNIVERSITY PRESS
Cambridge, Massachusetts
London, England
1997

Library of Congress Cataloging-in-Publication Data
Waugh, Joan.
Unsentimental reformer : the life of Josephine Shaw Lowell / Joan Waugh.
p.   cm.
Includes bibliographical references and index.
ISBN 0-674-93036-3
1. Lowell, Josephine Shaw, 1843–1905.
2. Women philanthropists—New York (State)—Biography.
3. Women social reformers—New York (State)—Biography.
4. Charity Organization Society of the City of New York—History.
I. Title.
HV28.L66W38   1997
361.92—dc21
[B]   97-15647

For Scott

Contents

Illustrations

Acknowledgments

More years ago than I care to remember, I began the research for a biography of Josephine Shaw Lowell. It now gives me great pleasure to acknowledge the large debts I have incurred along the way. This book started as a dissertation, and I thank Dan Howe for his invaluable assistance in formulating my thoughts about nineteenth-century society and politics. I have also benefited from the example and instruction of one of the foremost scholarly practitioners of feminist biography, Kathryn Kish Sklar. From her I have truly learned, to paraphrase Carolyn Heilbrun, how to write a woman's life. Others must be thanked as well. Eric Monkkonen offered excellent advice and a sympathetic ear throughout the years. My UCLA colleagues gave their friendship and insightful criticism, especially Joyce Appleby, Ruth Bloch, Ellen DuBois, Gary Nash, Jan Reiff, and Debora Silverman. Dawn Greeley, whose work is also on the Charity Organization Society, generously shared ideas and sources.

Institutional support was provided by a Woodrow Wilson Research Grant in Women's Studies and research awards from the Center for the Study of Philanthropy, the Graduate Center, City University of New York; the UCLA Center for the Study of Women; and the UCLA History Department. My research was facilitated by the staffs of several libraries, but I wish to especially thank the staff at the Butler Library, Columbia University, for their unfailing courtesy and professionalism.

Finally, I would like to thank the members of my family: my sons, Caleb and Joshua, who have given me the greatest possible joy and happiness, and my husband, Scott L. Waugh, my best friend and a superb critic. It is to Scott that I lovingly dedicate this book.

UNSENTIMENTAL REFORMER

Introduction

At noon on May 22, 1912, a granite fountain designed by the artist Charles Platt was dedicated in New York City's Bryant Park to the memory of Josephine Shaw Lowell (1843–1905), a brilliant philanthropist and social reformer whose career spanned forty years of New York history. The five hundred chairs arranged in a semicircle around the fountain provided a barrier between it and the curious onlookers who initially gathered to listen to the band music but stayed to hear the speeches praising Lowell's achievements. The main speaker of the day, former mayor Seth Low, singled out Lowell's founding of the Charity Organization Society of the City of New York in 1882 as her "real" memorial to the city. Then, on behalf of the committee that had established the fund for the fountain and that included Felix Adler, Maude Nathan, Reverend Henry C. Potter, Nicholas Murray Butler, Richard Watson Gilder, Augustus Saint-Gaudens, Carl Schurz, and Lillian Wald, Low presented the fountain to Mayor Gaynor, who accepted it for the city. The ceremony was witnessed by a distinguished crowd of invited guests from the worlds of charity, politics, and reform, many of whom worked closely with Lowell in the 1870s, 1880s, and 1890s.

Various speakers, as well as the newspaper reports the next day, did not fail to note that this was the city's first major public monument dedicated to a woman. Just east of the fountain a granite block was inscribed in bronze with words written by Harvard University President Charles Eliot. The words convey the high regard in which Lowell's contemporaries held her life:

> This fountain commemorates
> the strong and beautiful character of
> Josephine Shaw Lowell
> 1843–1905
> Wife for one year of a patriot soldier
> Widow at Twenty-one
> Servant of New York State and City in their public charities
> Sincere candid courageous and tender
> Bringing help and hope to the fainting
> And inspiring others to consecrated labors[1]

That Josephine Shaw Lowell achieved distinction in her life cannot be denied. And her role in history is secure: she is prominently mentioned in both contemporary and more recent historical works. Yet Lowell has never been the subject of a major biographical study. This seems especially puzzling in light of the explosion of women's history that has occurred in the past twenty-five years.[2] Why this oversight? I believe there are two interrelated reasons. The first reflects the unsavory reputation that still clings to the era in which Lowell's reputation was established, the Gilded Age. The second is the belief that late-nineteenth-century philanthropic women allied themselves more closely with men of their class than with the poor women who were the subjects of their attention.

Recent historical studies have dismissed Gilded Age reform as a conservative aberration in the great American reform tradition, and have, in Geoffrey Blodgett's words, "facilitated a swift mental passage from the grandeur of the Civil War to the excitement of the Progressive Era."[3] In this view, postwar reformers are portrayed as genteel elitists who were more concerned with defining and preserving their social status than with changing the status quo. These reformers have been singled out as agents of "social control" trying to contain an increasingly diverse and divisive society.[4]

Josephine Shaw Lowell, a representative figure of Gilded Age reform, has drawn particularly harsh criticism from a number of historians. George Fredrickson, in his *The Inner Civil War* (1965), provided the basic elements of that criticism, portraying the scientific charity movement, of which Lowell was a leader, as repressive and elitist. Fredrickson described Lowell as embodying the conservative tendencies of reform that flourished in the laissez-faire atmosphere of postwar society. The blending of professionalism and scientific principles in the field of philanthropy, he argued, placed it in the hands of elites, who, like Lowell, were "immune from the pressures of democratic politics."[5] Lowell's Civil War experiences, which so deeply impressed her contemporaries, according to Fredrickson, explained her *lack* of humanitarian sentiment. "It would not be far from the mark," he claimed, "to describe Mrs. Lowell's concept of charity entirely in patrician military terms."[6] Fredrickson remarked that Lowell demanded of the urban poor the same heroic virtues that her husband, Charles Russell Lowell, and her brother, Robert Gould Shaw, demanded of their soldiers during the war. This particular interpretation of Lowell's motives and background has been accepted and expanded upon by Paul Boyer and Lori Ginzberg.[7]

The legacy of Josephine Shaw Lowell has come to stand for a conservative charity that seemed out of place in the rapidly industrializing society of late-nineteenth-century America. Yet she believed herself to be, and other of her contemporaries believed her to be, on the cutting edge of philanthropic ideas and practice. We need to comprehend how her career—as well as the movement she led, the scientific charity movement (also called the charity organization movement), and the institution she founded and nourished, the Charity Organization Society (COS)—is now synonymous with oppression of the poor. To do this, we must examine briefly the historiography of social welfare.[8]

Before President Lyndon Johnson's "War on Poverty" commenced in the 1960s, the history of private and public charities was, with a few notable exceptions, written by its leaders and practitioners. The best institutional accounts provided a clear, concise, and critical look at the social workers of Lowell's generation.[9] They emphasized that the development of the American social welfare state, while bumpy and incomplete, was still a story of progress and achievement. In this scenario, Josephine Shaw Lowell is held to account for her "old-fashioned" ideas about individual responsibility and morality yet lauded for her other substantial contributions to philanthropy. In other words, Lowell, the scientific charity movement, and the COS are seen as flawed harbingers of a barely emerging industrial welfare system—a system whose outlines would not really begin to be filled in until the Progressive era.

This rather benign and approving view of Lowell and scientific, or organized, charity was stopped in its tracks by the new breed of activist-scholars who were influenced and energized by the national spotlight on poverty in the mid-1960s. When they looked at their own society and its welfare programs, they did not see the gentle culmination of a century of progress but rather a society content to tolerate enduring inequalities of wealth and power. The most influential work to emerge with this viewpoint was Frances Fox Piven and Richard Cloward's *Regulating the Poor*, which appeared in 1971. Piven and Cloward dismissed current welfare proposals, reforms, and policy as shockingly inadequate and further claimed that, instead of alleviating the structural conditions that led to poverty, the government's welfare programs used the power of an oppressive state to punish the poor for their own conditions.

Historians and other scholars of social welfare rightly assumed that the roots of modern attitudes toward poverty and the poor were to be found in the past. And when they examined these roots they, unlike earlier scholars, discovered that much of what passed for "doing good"—that is, public and private charity, philanthropy, and social welfare—was in reality "doing bad." How could this be possible? Piven and Cloward, now joined by a number of very fine historians, such as Michael Katz, developed and refined the theory of "social control" to explain the abuse of power inherent in a relationship that was so well defined by Lowell herself: "Charity is wishing well and doing good to those who have no legal claim upon us."[10]

It could not be stated more clearly. Inherent in the phrase "doing good to those who have no legal claim upon us" was the assumption of a prerogative by the elite to impose their standards, their morals, and their punishments on a helpless underprivileged population. Scholars who used the social-control theory to explain the development of the welfare state argued that the unequal relation of power between those who have and those who don't produced a mean-spirited and nasty benevolence. The hallmark of this type of benevolence, moreover, was that the power of the elite—and through them, private charities acting for the most part in concert with the government—was, and is, used to make the working class and the poor behave in acceptable ways, while denying them real benefits. In the mid-1960s, historians of U.S. social welfare from its origins to the present began to look at the past "from the bottom up" and found the view bleak indeed.[11]

Nowhere, according to many scholars, was welfare's oppressive tendency first more starkly delineated than in the scientific charity move-

ment and its institutional expression, the charity organization societies. Dominated by businessmen, bankers, lawyers, and patrician elites
such as Josephine Shaw Lowell, the charity organization societies personified all of the vices and few of the virtues of the earliest capitalist-
industrial response to poverty.

The evidence demonstrates that the rapid growth and popularity of
the charity organization movement in the 1880s were due to a perceived widening in the gap between rich and poor. But how to bridge
the gap? The charity organization answer was to encourage the prosperous members of the community to acknowledge the mutuality of
their existence with the poor in ways that would benefit the whole of
society. This is an old idea, and it seems relatively harmless. But the
thinking behind the idea was sinister, declared scholars. Instead of
relying on simple humanitarianism, scientific charity was cloaked in
the language of business and social science, which proclaimed a new
and enlightened way to ensure that rich and poor alike would be protected from the evil consequences of "unthinking" charity. A big part
of charity organization's self-appointed task, then, was to recast the
tough questions about poverty for the industrial age: What were people entitled to? What was the state's responsibility? What was the
private community's responsibility? Lowell and the charity organization societies were thus influential in defining the attitudes and the
ideology that set an agenda for the discussion and formulation of
welfare policy in the Gilded Age.

Fine. Poverty was being debated and defined—or in the modern
scholarly parlance, "constructed." But what most modern historians
of social welfare objected to was the combination of individualistic
uplift with moralist doctrine that, in their view, obscured the real problems of industrial society. For example, particularly offensive was Lowell's position that the "gift" of charity or aid was not the thing, but
rather the *outcome* of the gift. In other words, you cannot simply
throw money at poor people; you must consider the outcome for that
person. Relief, therefore, whether it be dispensed by an individual, a
church, a private charity, or the government, has to be just as concerned with the consequences of that act, as with the actual suffering
itself. The goal was to end dependency, and *that* was a good thing for
all of society.

It is here that many readers will find startling parallels between the
welfare debate of Lowell's era and our own. She believed "outdoor" aid

(cash or other assistance given to those in need so that they could remain at home) did not help the poor, that in fact it tended to harm their character by making them dependent on relief. She described this process from a typically Victorian concern with "character." If people were given something for nothing, they might (and in her view many did) choose the easy way out. The individual must be made to understand that relief was not a right but a highly contractual obligation with duties and responsibilities on the part of the recipient/client to improve his/her condition with the least cost to the community as possible. Today's welfare debate about reforming the twentieth century's major program of indoor assistance—Aid to Families with Dependent Children—revolves around similar issues of personal responsibility and fostering independence. If Lowell were alive today, surely she would be at the center of this highly polarized and divisive debate, just as she was in the Gilded Age.

Given her leading role in scientific charity and the negative scholarly response to it, the generally unattractive historical portrait of Josephine Shaw Lowell that has emerged is not surprising. What is surprising is her diminished role in women's history, which is the second reason Lowell has not attracted more scholarly attention. Lori Ginzberg has argued that Lowell and other elite charity women in the Gilded Age abandoned the previous generation's unique and carefully nurtured position as female social reformers outside and above the humdrum of ordinary (and male) public and political life. Instead, according to Ginzberg, they collaborated with conservative men to produce an efficient, business-oriented approach to charity that focused on class, not gender-related issues.

This type of charity resulted in an explicit denigration of the female values associated with antebellum benevolence and reform that reduced the collective power of women until it was revived in the Progressive period. And Josephine Shaw Lowell was a major force in turning the radical underpinnings of prewar benevolence "into a conservative defense of the class privilege of benevolent leaders."[12] Ginzberg removes Lowell's career from the mainstream of women's public culture (defined as women's claiming authority in the public realm through associative enterprise) by arguing that her primary attachment was to her class, not her gender. This analysis, while pointing out some important trends in philanthropy, needs to be refined and amplified by a short background discussion of women and charity in the nineteenth century.[13]

Lowell was a pioneer in the field of philanthropy in the late nineteenth century. Her achievements, however, must be located within a rich tradition of women's public activities that was available to her as she began her career in the late 1860s. As is well known, women's lives were dramatically altered in the nineteenth century as they absorbed the successive changes brought about by the market revolution, the democratization of the political system, and the rise of a powerful middle-class network of religious and reform organizations. Women played a crucial role in the latter, based on their social roles as loving, pious, and diligent wives and mothers. Middle- and upper-class American women were defined by an ideology called "The Cult of True Womanhood" that, with its emphasis on piety, purity, domesticity, and submissiveness, raised the status of all women in the 1800s even while preserving their unequal social and economic position.

By the time Josephine Shaw Lowell was born in 1843, American philanthropy had already become in part "feminized." The relatively small role that the U.S. government (compared with European nations) played in caring for its citizens left a large role for private citizens. From the early 1800s to the Civil War, women helped to shape America's welfare policies. They created and led institutions, raised money, and volunteered their time by the hundreds of thousands. From hospitals to orphanages, from asylums to prisons, women were performing an amazing variety of services—in effect helping to create a viable, if inadequate, social welfare system. Again, the foundation for American women's public role in this area was provided by their social role as the nation's moral overseers. Women were assumed to be *more* moral and religious than men, and they were given charge of protecting their families and, by extension, other people's families as well. Backed by this powerful cultural belief, women expanded their influence through participation in a dense web of voluntary associations that radiated outward from the home to the community and the nation at large.

Lowell grew up in a family that honored and participated in this philanthropic and reform tradition. Her grandfather Shaw founded a sailors' aid society and gave lavishly to charity. Her father served on innumerable boards of reform and philanthropic associations and continued the tradition of opening the family's purse to worthy causes. And, most important, all her female relations—mother, aunts, cousins, sisters—were enthusiastic contributors to the "women's sphere" of benevolent activities. For example, as a girl Lowell was encouraged to give tea and ice cream parties for the poor Irish children who lived near her parents' Staten Island estate; as a teenager she joined the local Ladies' Aid Society to help northern soldiers, who were fighting for Union and freedom; as a young woman she turned to charity to find her destiny.

There was yet another tradition for Josephine Shaw Lowell to draw on—one that did not conflict with but rather complemented the associative female world of philanthropy—and that was the example of Dorothea Lynde Dix. An intrepid crusader for the mentally ill, Dix waged single-issue campaigns to stop abuse in this area and brought herself into direct contact with the male-dominated worlds of the legislature and the press in many states, including New York, Massachusetts, and South Carolina, and in Europe as well. Dix honed her skills in the years before the Civil War as a publicist, a lobbyist, and a politician—all in pursuit of a noble cause—and her efforts must have surely influenced Lowell, who would excel in those same roles.[14]

Thus Josephine Shaw Lowell, poised in the late 1860s to make her mark in the world of philanthropy, would use both old and new ways to challenge her generation's response to the age-old question of poverty. In this book, I argue that Lowell was not simply an upper-class agent of social control who sought to isolate and punish the poor.[15] Instead, her life and career should be analyzed against the turbulent changes that were occurring within American society. Lowell's work in scientific charity, in other areas of social reform, and in politics must be judged by a whole lifetime devoted to reform stretching backward to her abolitionist origins and forward to her intense involvement in the reforms of the Progressive era. Thus I challenge and revise Lowell's historical reputation in a way that addresses the central and interrelated themes of class, gender, and politics and locates her life in a particular contextual framework.

This book considers three aspects of Lowell's career. First, it closely examines the class origins of Lowell and some of her generation who joined with her to work in the COS and related philanthropic and political reform organizations in the city. This group of reformers was drawn from a particular stratum of the American upper class—a stratum imbued with a powerful sense of social service. These women and men, who came of age during the Civil War, comprised the earliest generation of social scientists. Armed with statistics and reports, they set forth to eradicate the growing evils of urban poverty and dependency. Their motives for engaging in philanthropic and political reform were manifold and cannot be solely attributed to a drive for social control. Many, like Lowell, desired a more democratic and inclusive society and worked hard in various reform movements to achieve that aim. Chapters 1 through 3 identify the economic, religious, political, and social underpinnings of her family history and class tradition.

Second, this book demonstrates Josephine Shaw Lowell's importance to philanthropy for this period. As the issues surrounding poverty became increasingly explosive in the 1870s and 1880s, women moved to the forefront as policy-makers endowed with the legitimacy of postbellum social science. What makes Lowell particularly fascinating is her equal footing with men in the leadership of the New York State Board of Charities, the COS, and numerous other charitable and reform organizations. Lowell's relationships with male reformers reveal both the expanding horizons for women's public activity as well as the frustrating limitations still prevalent. Moreover, her work in charity and reform demonstrates that she did not reject gender-related issues. Lowell, for example, took a leadership role in advancing the opportunities for wage-earning and professional women, although, to be sure, her power and influence were sometimes limited by nineteenth-century gender boundaries.

Here is where I differ sharply from other scholars who have offered "social control" interpretations of Lowell and Gilded Age philanthropy. I believe that using the social-control theory as the sole lens with which to view this woman and her career has obscured as much as enlightened our understanding of her contribution. Too much attention has been paid to the ideological bombast of the scientific charity movement (of which there was much) and too little to the actual policies and practices as they were being worked out among groups of human beings: elites, middle-class, working-class, and poverty-stricken dependents. In Lowell's career, for example, it is clear that she and her "class" did not even come close to implementing anything like the pure ideals of the movement, and it is also clear that many of the leadership did not want to, in any event. As this book demonstrates, the actual working out of policy required much accommodation and compromise. It was a difficult business to translate ideals into reality, and the process was much too complex to be reduced to a simple formula of class oppression.

Another difference between my analysis of Lowell's life and other scholars' is in the importance accorded to gender in the charity organization movement. What is the story here? In 1882 a woman founds what would become in a few short years the flagship charity organization society. In the COS, women were in leadership positions: they developed and implemented policy, and they comprised the majority of its employees. From Josephine Shaw Lowell to the many "lady" volunteers and visitors to the paid social workers, charity organization women in the 1880s and 1890s created the foundations of the modern welfare state. Under Lowell's inspired direction, the COS built up a strong institutional base from which it conducted important research on poverty, developed and refined the "casework" approach to social welfare, and became influential in promoting the professionalization of social work. Its influence was widely felt in the university classroom, the business boardroom, and the legislative hall. How many women in the nineteenth century accomplished what Josephine Shaw Lowell did? She led a movement, founded an organization (one that, by the way, is still extant), and stuck with it, making it a true success story, if only considered from an institutional viewpoint.[16] And while it is certainly true that men also played important roles in the COS and in the scientific charity movement in general (as they have in every movement of social welfare history), I argue that gender was not brushed aside by Lowell but formed a central component of both ideology and program. Chapters 4, 5, and 6 examine her work in the charitable field as a volunteer worker for the State Charities Aid Association, as commissioner of the New York State Board of Charities, and as founder of the COS.

Finally, Lowell's biography contributes to an ongoing and much needed reevaluation of Gilded Age reform. Here the emphasis is on the dynamic connections between religion, politics, reform, and charity that existed in New York City. These connections provided an opportunity for women like Josephine Shaw Lowell to enter into mainstream political life through related reform movements. In the late 1880s, she became a force for labor activism and sought to bring the working classes and middle classes together through the Consumers' League of the City of New York, which she helped to found in 1891.

Lowell demonstrated her political mettle though repeated attempts to wrest control of the city's charitable institutions and agencies from urban "bosses" or machine politicians who would use them for their own advantage. She worked tirelessly for civil service reform, and in 1894 she founded the Woman's Municipal League, which joined with other groups to oust a corrupt, Tammany-led machine government in New York. Kathryn Kish Sklar has called Lowell "New York's most politically powerful woman," and David Hammack described the COS as part of the "de facto" government of the city.[17] With Lowell as its guiding spirit, it could hardly be otherwise. Finally, in the waning years of the century she became a dedicated anti-imperialist and contributed mightily to forming an opposition to America's overseas ambitions. Chapters 7 and 8 examine her political achievements as they intersected with charity, labor, reform, and gender issues.

Josephine Shaw Lowell emerges from this study as a major figure in American reform history. Self-consciously ennobled, but not burdened, by her distinctive family tradition, she was endowed with a capacious intellect and a rare ability to translate theory into practical programs. She was not an original thinker but a talented popularizer who was able to present effective, forceful, and clear arguments for reforms in charity, labor, and politics. And when she was wrong, she was not afraid to admit so and change her mind. She had friends and advisors from all walks of life, and with conflicting viewpoints, and from them, as well as from relevant sources, she was always seeking new insights into social problems. As a result, she advanced a markedly different agenda at the end of her career. Some may be puzzled at the young social scientist who eagerly embraced social Darwinism and eugenics in the 1870s but who in the 1880s and 1890s became a labor activist and an anti-imperialist. Lowell herself was comfortable with these anomalies, having learned throughout the years that the only way to solve injustices was to attack them on multiple levels, seeking the widest possible range of support.

Unsentimental Reformer is largely about Lowell's career. She was an intense, intelligent, and fascinating woman, and she left few traces of her intimate life. In part, this is because, unlike the vast majority of nineteenth-century women, Lowell was a very public figure, and because her work was the focus of her life, it must be the focus of this book. Carlotta Russell Lowell, her daughter and only child, wrote to a friend a year after her mother's death: "If the 'Life' [a biography of

Josephine] was to be written at all I was very anxious to have it done by someone who knew her *work*. I do not feel that without the definite work she did the public would have any right to her life at all."[18]

Indeed, if Lowell lived an "ordinary" life, she would not be a candidate for a biography. But even the most public people have a private life. Unfortunately for the curious scholar, the Shaw family had a long tradition of burning or otherwise destroying (and in some cases altering) all letters that they felt would be too revealing, too hurtful or damaging to reputations. Despite the lack of personal revelation, juicy gossip, or a scandal, there is no dearth of material on the family's activities or on Lowell's busy social/work life. In my judgment, there was little disjunction between the public and the private side of Josephine Shaw Lowell. She was what she appeared to be: an exemplary Victorian woman who dedicated her life to serving the public interest. This does not mean her life was boring or without incident. On the contrary. When we analyze what being an "exemplary" woman meant in the late nineteenth century, or define precisely which "public interest" Lowell meant to serve, we find that she lived an incredibly rich and complicated life. *Unsentimental Reformer* is a historical biography that seeks to illuminate the life of an important person who lived in a time very different from our own.

Most of all, Josephine Shaw Lowell's life and career may be summed up as an attempt to bring community to an America that was increasingly rent by division and change. While engaged in this attempt, Lowell strongly emphasized the moral responsibilities of both rich and poor, and this as well as her punitive programs for the underclass have offended the sensibilities of a new generation of scholars. Yet Lowell came to an acute appreciation of the difficulties of interpreting, administrating, and solving the problems surrounding poverty. We must recognize her growth but respect her insights into character as well. As Roy Porter has so eloquently written about Lowell's generation of Victorian philanthropists, "They had the perspicacity to recognize that problems were complex: personal but also structural, material but also moral. Poverty had much to do with the economy, but it also had something to do with the poor. Money was part of the solution, but so too was moralization."[19]

1

Beginnings

⚘ *West Roxbury, Massachusetts* ⚘

Josephine Shaw was born on the seventy-third anniversary of Beethoven's birthday, December 16, 1843, a fact that did not fail to delight her music-loving parents, Francis and Sarah Shaw of West Roxbury, Massachusetts. Josephine, or Effie, as she was fondly called by her family, was the fourth child of five and was preceded by Anna (Nan) in 1836, Robert Gould (Rob) in 1837, and Susanna (Susie) in 1839, with the youngest, Ellen (Nellie), making her appearance in 1845. The year before Effie arrived, Frank and Sarah moved from Boston, where their forebears had distinguished themselves in the worlds of finance, politics, and culture, to a large estate in the beautiful and still rural suburb of West Roxbury. At the age of thirty-two, the handsome and elegant Frank had retired from the mercantile business owned by his father, Robert Gould Shaw, to try his hand at being a gentleman farmer and to pursue his and his young wife's interests in reform. Not coincidentally, their place adjoined Brook Farm, an experiment in communal living and radical politics that briefly attracted some of the most brilliant and talented people in America, including Margaret Fuller, Nathaniel Hawthorne, Charles A. Dana, and John S. Dwight. The larger and lesser lights of the transcendental movement, of which Brook Farm was a part, flocked to the commune during its brief existence—to visit, to observe, to attend lectures and concerts, or simply to join ongoing conversations about the nature of society and how it could be positively altered.[1]

Frank Shaw was more than a good neighbor to the Brook Farmers.

He deeply believed in their attempt to provide the world with a model of communitarian life that would offer alternatives to the greedy materialism that seemed to poison relations among rich and poor Americans in the 1840s. And he, along with two brothers-in-law, George R. Russell (who also bought a country home adjoining Brook Farm) and Henry P. Sturgis, provided the major financial backing of the corporation from its inception in 1841 to its demise in 1849.[2] And so it was that Effie's earliest years were spent in a dynamic environment of both social experimentation and extreme sociability. Visitors flowed easily between Brook Farm and the Shaw home, which became a center of hospitality for Ralph Waldo Emerson, Margaret Fuller, Orestes Brownson, Bronson Alcott, James Russell Lowell, Theodore Parker, William Lloyd Garrison, and Harriet Beecher Stowe. The Shaw youngsters naturally were less impressed by the intellectual sparkle provided by the adult visitors than they were by their various offspring, as well as by the pleasing proximity of their Russell cousins. Members of the Shaw family were in constant attendance at Brook Farm lectures, costume parties, picnics, and the formal and informal conversations that played so large a part in attracting the legion of friendly visitors and curiosity seekers to West Roxbury. Dr. Codman, a boarder at the farm, remembered with pleasure the sight of "Mr. Shaw, on his horse, with his young son, a tiny little fellow, on a pony by his side," making one of his frequent visits to the farm. The Shaw children were also beneficiaries of the progressive educational system set up by the utopian community. They attended its infant school, although Rob was sent to Boston to attend Mary Peabody's grade school. Nan, Rob, and Susie also joined the West Roxbury Sunday school of their parents' friend and neighbor the Reverend Theodore Parker. There they were given basic Bible lessons while Sarah and Frank listened eagerly to Parker's eloquent sermons advocating abolitionism and other forms of Christian activism.[3]

Effie's memories of Brook Farm were necessarily hazy, for when she was four the family moved again, this time to the even more rural environment of Staten Island, New York. This move was not a precipitous one, and had been preceded by many visits by an ailing Sarah Shaw to Dr. Samuel MacKenzie Elliot, one of the foremost eye specialists of the time. Dr. Elliot, a native of Scotland, had come to the North Shore of Staten Island in 1836, where he not only established a thriving practice but founded a small settlement called Elliotsville, overlooking the beautiful Kill Van Kull River. There his more affluent invalids could reside in comfortable proximity to his ministrations. In 1847 a nearly blind Sarah was admitted to a New York City hospital under Elliot's care, while Frank tended to the children in a rented house on the island. Sarah's eyesight improved dramatically, and her overall health responded well to the bracing climate of Staten Island. In 1847 the Shaws decided to settle in Elliotsville, renting for three years prior to a European sojourn in 1851 and then building a house of their own on their return from Europe in 1855.[4]

Staten Island, New York

In those years, Staten Island had only recently emerged from its agricultural origins to become a fashionable resort for wealthy New Yorkers and southerners. Its fourteen thousand residents enjoyed an island dotted with woods, pastures, and the spectacular views that initially prompted such prominent New York families as the Winants, the Camerons, and the Van Pelts to build their estates on the unspoiled land. But Staten Island had even more to offer the Shaws by the late 1840s. A community of people from New England had moved there, and Frank and Sarah found a welcoming circle of like-minded neighbors, friends, and visitors. Indeed, a distinctly literary cast had been introduced to Staten Island, particularly on its North Shore, where the Shaws lived. This development appeared to be directly related to Dr. Elliot's impressive reputation, for it attracted some notable invalids to the island. James Russell Lowell lived there briefly as a patient of Elliot's in 1843 and returned again some years later to obtain the same benefits for his frail wife, a beloved relation of Frank and Sarah's, Maria White Russell.[5] William Emerson, a judge and brother of Ralph Waldo Emerson, settled on Staten Island, and soon it became a favorite resting place for many of the transcendentalists. Some of Elliot's other patients who became Staten Islanders included the historian Francis Parkman, the poet Henry Wadsworth Longfellow, and, from Brook Farm, Charles Dana and George Ripley. Margaret Fuller, a close friend of Sarah, fondly remembered her visit: "Often I think of your place and the woods near. I have just been staying at Staten Island and there are quite long wood-walks, and, as you go up and down them . . . you catch glimpses of the sea and of the narrows with the processions of ships gliding through."[6]

Effie's first few years on Staten Island were spent in a relaxed and festive atmosphere that was conducive to Sarah's continuing recovery and to the general well-being of the family. Staten Island was truly a paradise for youngsters, its woodlands, streams, and rich farmland offering many opportunities for play and mischief. Among the Shaws' closest island friends were John and Elizabeth Staples, whose commodious house on Shore Road was the center of many activities designed to delight the neighborhood children throughout the four seasons. The spring warming made it possible for the children to begin their instruction in horseback riding, an activity at which Anna Shaw was to excel, becoming an expert rider as a young girl. In the summer, the Staples boathouse served as the gathering place for the little people to swim, play, and participate in "crabbing parties." Berry-picking in the warmer months led to more serious explorations by Rob, Nan, Susie, and Effie of the nooks and crannies of the ravines and dense woods as the crisp air announced that fall was arriving. The cold winters had their pleasures as well. John and Elizabeth's annual Christmas party featured a huge tree decorated with homemade ornaments and was considered by the Shaws to be the highlight of the Staten Island winter season.[7] Francis Parkman, a Shaw cousin (Parkman's father was the brother of Frank's mother, Eliza Parkman), stayed with them on several occasions while under the care of Dr. Elliot. He delighted the boys of the island, especially his admiring nephew Rob, with tales of "daring" adventures on the Oregon Trail.[8]

Sarah and Frank soon gathered around them a circle of loving friends, admirers, and visitors (mostly relatives) from Boston. They never lost touch with their Boston heritage or their Boston relations. Every year there were at least several visits to and from the city. And there were plenty of visits to make: Frank was the oldest in a line of eleven children, and Sarah the eighth in a family of twelve, most of whom survived into adulthood. Nan, Rob, Effie, Susie, and Nellie had eighty-five first cousins with whom to play, share secrets, and grow up into a young adulthood shaped by the drama of the Civil War. The number of first cousins paled before the number of first cousins once removed and second and third cousins, all of whom the Shaws counted as close relations. Frank and Sarah at one time or another helped to raise as many as ten of their nieces and nephews—children whose parents, through early death or sudden incapacity, could not care for them anymore.

In their rented house on Staten Island, the Shaws hosted parties for Dr. and Mrs. Elliot and socialized with close friends and neighbors such as the Stapleses, the George Cabot Wards, the Sidney Howard Gays, and the Albert Oliver Willcoxes. Both Willcox and Gay, along with their families, were ardent abolitionists and supporters of women's rights, views strongly supported by Frank and Sarah. The Shaws were a popular couple who enjoyed entertaining and made everyone feel welcome. "I love Frank and Sarah Shaw," declared their close friend the abolitionist and writer Lydia Maria Child, "partly because they are very good-looking, partly because they always dress in beautiful colors, and partly because they have many fine qualities." Even better than that, mused Child, "they are very free from sham; for which they deserve the more credit; considering they are Bostonians and are rich."[9] High praise indeed from the fierce democrat Mrs. Child!

Life was not all parties and pleasantries for either Shaw parents or children. While living in West Roxbury, Frank's public duties included being a member of the school committee, an overseer of the poor, a justice of the peace, and the president of the first Common Council of Roxbury. His Staten Island years encompassed similar responsibilities as well as some new ones: he served as a trustee of the New Brighton Seamen's Retreat and the Staten Island Hospital.[10] Sarah, more grounded in the home with five children to supervise, was nonetheless active in several charities as well as with her activities in the abolitionist movement. Both Shaws were active in founding Staten Island's first and only Unitarian Church, where two of their daughters, Anna and Josephine, would be married. When the weather was fine, the Shaws took the ferry to the Brooklyn church of Henry Ward Beecher, whose popular and passionate sermons enthralled a generation of nineteenth-century churchgoers. Sarah's best friend, Elizabeth Staples, ran a private, informal school for some of the island's young boys and girls, which stressed the acquisition of a classical education. More than likely, it was there that Effie acquired her first real schooling. In general, girls on Staten Island were educated at home by tutors, or in nearby privately run schools, such as Mrs. Staples's. Boys, on the other hand, were usually sent off the island after their primary education was completed at local schools. This was the experience of Effie's brother, Rob, whose educational misadventures provided a bit of excitement in the otherwise peaceful existence of the Shaw family.

Rob was placed, much to his dismay, in St. John's College, a Roman Catholic school in Fordham. He promptly alerted his family to the deficiencies of the situation: "I wish you hadn't sent me here while you are on the island, because I want to be there, and now I have to stay at this old place I'm sure I shan't want to come here after vacation for I hate it like everything."[11] Rob's pleas went unheeded, and after summer vacation he was returned to St. John's only to run away from the school after a few days' residence. This defiant gesture was met with firmness on the part of both parents, and the boy was quickly escorted back to St. John's by his father. Rob's misery was to be short-lived, however, as his parents were preparing for a trip to Europe with the whole family.

✑ European Sojourn ✑

Sarah's health was still delicate, and she suffered a relapse. It was decided that the best cure for her racking cough and frail lungs would be to go to the sunnier climes of Italy.[12] An extended stay abroad was a dream long wished for by the Shaws, and this seemed like the perfect time to indulge it. Their friend Margaret Fuller preceded them by several years, just as their friends the Henry James Seniors would soon follow in their footsteps. After a stint in New York City as a journalist for the *Tribune*, Fuller continued her work in Europe, and especially Italy, from where she wrote Sarah entreating her to visit: "Come with all your children and live quietly here!"[13] The Shaws' four-year stay in Europe, beginning with their departure from New York on February 8, 1851, included extended visits to Switzerland, Italy, France, and Germany (as well as a boat trip down the Nile), where the various Shaw daughters and son attended schools and immersed themselves in European language and culture. The Shaws were part of a small but growing stream of Americans who were taking the "Grand Tour" of Europe with long stays in Rome, Florence, Paris, and London.[14] And like their more celebrated counterparts the Jameses, the Shaws eagerly embraced the opportunity to expose their children to the benefits of travel and education.

The benefits for their ten-year-old daughter were elucidated in a letter written by Sarah: "Effie is the genius of the family. She can cook, cut out things, trim hats and caps, speak French, German, and Italian, and write poetry."[15] Effie studied poetry in Paris, music in Rome and

Florence, and Shakespeare in London, which elicited this admiring comment from brother Rob: "Effie must be a bright and clever girl to be reading Shakespeare so soon."[16] Family descriptions linger on Effie's impressive linguistic abilities—a talent she shared with her father and brother. She was full of life and eager to learn and to test her imaginative and intellectual potential. Life in Europe was exciting for "the four," as their parents called Nan, Susie, Effie, and Nellie, where in a few months' time, they would be whisked from the quiet beauty of Heidelberg to the teeming, cosmopolitan streets of Paris. Josephine always remembered those early years abroad, and was especially fond of Florence, where the family spent "two winters, once in the Casa Ricasoli, now taken down, just at the corner of the Carraja Bridge, and once in the Villa Lustrini, near the Porta Romana."[17]

The Shaws brought some stability into their children's life in Europe. Settled in Rome for a winter, for example, Nan, the eldest, remained at home reading Roman history, taking drawing lessons, and learning Italian from a tutor, while sisters Effie and Susie attended a convent school on the recommendation of their Uncle Joseph Coolidge Shaw. Joseph, for whom Effie was named, converted to Catholicism in the 1830s during postgraduate study in Europe, and a few years later he became a Jesuit priest, much to the astonishment of his solidly Unitarian family. Father Joseph died shortly after the Shaws' departure for Europe, and in his will he left "To Frank's little Effie the prettiest little coral and silver rosary that can be found in my collection, with my blessing."[18] Effie, who was just one of the family members whom Father Joseph hoped (in vain) to convert to Catholicism, would cherish this keepsake. The adult Josephine Lowell refused to indulge in the prejudice that native-born Americans commonly displayed toward Roman Catholic immigrants and their church. No doubt her exposure to the religion, at home and in Europe, gave her a more sympathetic view of the Catholic Church than the one held by many of her fellow Protestant charity workers.

In their last year abroad, Effie and her sisters attended a school in Paris. It would appear, however, that "the four" were more casually educated than their brother, as was the prevalent custom. Rob was placed in a Catholic boarding school in Neuchâtel, Switzerland, where he stayed for two years before joining his family in Italy. After a year of schooling in Italy, he was sent to Hanover, Germany, at the age of sixteen to complete his European education. Thus the girls traveled *en famille* from place to place, receiving their education piecemeal, while Rob was expected to complete a sustained program of study in preparation for his entrance to Harvard on their return to America.

The elder Shaws enjoyed all the benefits of European culture by visiting countless museums, art galleries, and churches. In Rome, Florence, Heidelberg, London, and Paris, they viewed many plays and attended operas and symphonic concerts. Their daughters and son were encouraged to join them whenever school schedules allowed, so that by the end of their travels they had all "seen the best pictures, heard the best music."[19] Frank and Sarah moved easily within the American and British community in Italy, making friends, or renewing friendships, with many artists, musicians, and poets, including the sculptor William Wetmore Story. Story and his wife introduced the Shaws to the famous English poets Robert and Elizabeth Browning. Sarah and Elizabeth Barrett Browning discovered a common fascination with spiritualism and religion and began a correspondence that continued for several years.[20] One of the family's most pleasant memories was the summer of 1853 when they rented a house in Sorrento, Italy, and found to their delight that their neighbor was their old friend the diminutive actress Fanny Kemble, now separated from her wealthy husband, Pierce Butler of Georgia. Kemble was perhaps the only person they knew who had *actually* lived on a plantation and whose hatred of slavery grew out of personal experiences.[21] Little did they know as they sat at Kemble's feet listening to her horror stories of southern life on the vast Butler plantation that their son would in a few years occupy that land as a Union officer. Frank and Sarah, even though physically distant from the growing antislavery controversy in America, kept up their active interest in their country's political events through newspapers and correspondence from home.

ᴄᴏ *Homecoming* ᴏᴠ

By 1853, the Shaws were preparing for a homecoming by having a house built on property purchased on Staten Island before their departure. The plans for the house were drawn up by an architect in Paris, and the execution of the plans was to be completed by their return early in the summer of 1855. The house was a lavish one, and its scale might have had something to do with the legacy Frank received in 1853 at the death of his father, one of the richest men in Boston—indeed, in the whole country. But in 1855 the house was not quite done, and when the Shaws, minus Rob, who remained in Hanover to complete his education, set sail for home in July, their destination was the resort in Newport, Rhode Island, where they spent the remaining summer reacquainting themselves with the American scene. Shortly after, they moved into their new house on Staten Island.

It was worth the wait. The $80,000 mansion on Bard Avenue in Elliotsville was a large and elegant dwelling, especially when measured by informal island standards. Indeed, Frank and Sarah were criticized by their friends and neighbors the Wards for their departure from the more modest dwellings of the area. Mrs. Ward, reported Rob, "abused the situation of our house very much, and couldn't imagine (and said nobody else could) how Father could spend so much money on such a place."[22] Despite disapproval, the Shaws relished their new house, which contained many spacious rooms and a "sweeping staircase" that dominated the entry way. Frank and Sarah hired at least eight servants to maintain their estate, including a cook, a driver, and a gardener. Once comfortably settled, the Shaws resumed their by now well-known hospitality with a fervor, and the house was always filled with guests from at home and abroad. The grounds were also commodious, so that Anna could perfect her skills as a horsewoman. At age nineteen, Nan was a passionate advocate of all animals and wanted to dedicate her life to helping distressed and maltreated creatures, great and small. Her younger sister Effie was also an excellent rider, and could expertly wield a croquet mallet in competitive matches.

When the nearly twelve-year-old Effie returned to America in 1855, she was well educated in history, literature, and languages from her schooling in Rome and Paris, and she was eager to partake of all the pleasures and opportunities that her class, wealth, and background could offer. By all accounts, Effie was a lively, pretty, and charming girl whose evident enjoyment of life did not preclude a tender heart. Near the Shaws' new house lived a group of poor Irish families whose struggles became the object of Effie's sympathy. She started inviting the mothers and children for afternoon tea parties with ice cream and cake. These occasions were warmly encouraged by Frank and Sarah, and became a regular feature of the Shaws' public activities for years to come. Other, more serious events were pressing into Effie's privileged existence. She was becoming increasingly aware of the dangers of slavery to her country and its moral fiber. It was a hard issue to ignore in the Shaw family. Not only were her parents fervent abolitionists, but their neighborhood in Staten Island was filled with passionate antislavery reformers. One example was their close friend Sidney Howard Gay, editor of the *National Anti-Slavery Standard* from 1843 to 1857 and later editor of the *New York Daily Tribune,* beginning in 1863. The Gay house was also a center of refuge for runaway slaves, and among Gay's frequent guests were William Lloyd Garrison, Angelina and Sarah Grimké, and Lucretia Mott. Frank and Sarah often attended meetings at the house and expressed their growing concern about the political instability engendered by slavery.

Effie, like her parents, possessed a deeply idealistic nature. The family's return to America a few years before the outbreak of the Civil War would sorely test that idealism and plunge them all into the maelstrom of passion and tragedy that led to the splitting of the nation and to slavery's ultimate extinction in the war. The suffering and losses that Effie experienced in the Civil War would, as was the case with most of her generation, change her life forever. She was able to overcome her losses by dedicating her life to making the world a better place to live in. Some would say later that Lowell had an inspiring vision for her society. This vision was rooted in the public meaning that Josephine and her family bestowed upon the Civil War. The most vital lessons she drew from the war were those of public virtue, civic responsibility, and dedication to ideals, no matter what the cost. To understand the Shaws' wartime roles—as abolitionists, upper-class Brahmins, and reformers—as well as to comprehend Josephine Shaw Lowell's later career, we must look more closely at her remarkable family background.

∞ *The Shaws of Boston* ∞

In January 1844, almost a month after the new baby Effie was born, Sarah received a congratulatory letter from the transcendentalist Margaret Fuller. "I feel especially interested in the young stranger," Fuller wrote, "as it is the first that has been given you since we were acquainted. It will share (if as I believe the child represents the state of the parent preceding its birth) some of the thoughts and feelings we have had in common."[23] Because we know that the correspondence between these two women revolved around politics, social reform, and the constraints of womanhood, we may conclude that there is a kernel of truth in Fuller's belief. That the adult Effie's life also revolved around those currents, however, can be attributed less to the unique benefits of Fuller's brilliant conversation with the pregnant Sarah than to the particular social and cultural milieu into which Effie was born. Indeed, Josephine Shaw Lowell's life cannot be understood apart from its contextual underpinnings. It is very difficult to separate exactly where her parents' influence ends and her own volition begins, because of the powerful nexus of values and class characteristics that impinged upon her upbringing from the moment of her birth. Yet we can certainly isolate several elements—philanthropy, abolitionism, and transcendentalism—that would leave an indelible imprint on Josephine's mature worldview.

Both of Effie's parents came from established and wealthy Massachusetts families. Sarah Sturgis, born on August 13, 1815, was a descendant of one Edward Sturgis or Sturges from Kent who settled in Yarmouth on Cape Cod in 1646. Sturgis's occupation was listed as tavern keeper, his respectability confirmed by his election as a deputy to the General Court twice before his death in 1695. Succeeding generations of Sturgis men prospered in shipping and other commercial activities, and by 1750, Sarah's merchant grandfather, Russell Sturgis, was living in Boston on Tremont Row, where he had the distinction of having his portrait painted three times by Gilbert Stuart.[24]

Sarah's mother, Susan Shaw Parkman, could trace her ancestry to the venerable seventeenth-century Puritan divine, John Cotton. The Parkmans were mainly learned but poor country ministers until Samuel Parkman, Sarah's grandfather, arrived in Boston and made a fortune as a merchant. Parkman's daughter Susan, by his first wife, Sarah Shaw, married Nathaniel Russell Sturgis, and gave birth to twelve children, including Sarah Blake. In 1835, at age twenty, Sarah married her half–first cousin, Frank Shaw, whose mother, Elizabeth Willard Parkman, was the daughter of Samuel Parkman's second marriage, and thus a half-sister to Sarah's mother.

Effie's father, Francis George Shaw, was born on October 23, 1809, to a family that had achieved distinction in New England history. The father of the first Francis Shaw arrived from Scotland in the 1680s and married Sarah Burt, the daughter of a silversmith. Their son, Francis, born in Boston in 1721, acquired a considerable fortune through real estate speculation and other business interests. That fortune was completely wiped out in 1785, owing to a disastrous undertaking with the Boston financier Robert Gould. It was up to Francis's second son,

Robert Gould Shaw, born on July 4, 1776, to revive the family's wealth, and that he did, becoming one of Boston's merchant princes by the 1820s.

Shaw's life is a brilliant illustration of the growing power and influence of Boston's elite families, later called "Brahmins." Frank Shaw's father was part of a generation of tough and ambitious merchants whose wealth brought forth new forms of economic organization. The development and use of the corporation owed much to these early New England capitalists. "He was a real merchant," declared Frank Shaw in a memoir of his father, "loving business for its own sake."[25] Robert Gould Shaw drove himself relentlessly in pursuit of business success, and his hard work bore fruit as his influence and power increased proportionately. He helped to guide and finance Boston's spectacular growth during the antebellum years by investing in its manufacturing, banking, and transportation industries. Shaw distinguished himself as a public servant as well. He was twice elected a representative from Boston to the Massachusetts General Court, and in 1836 he was appointed U.S. commissioner and disbursing agent in charge of building a new Customs House for Boston. Shaw's staunch support of the Whig party was recognized in 1852 by his appointment as a presidential elector.[26]

The career and financial successes that attended Robert Gould Shaw's rise to prominence were nourished by his marriage in 1809 to Elizabeth Willard Parkman, daughter of Samuel Parkman of Boston and his second wife, Sarah Rodgers. Frank Shaw wrote of their courtship: "Miss Eliza Parkman was a very beautiful and highly accomplished young lady, quite gay, and fond of society, but her favored suitor proved to be plain 'Cousin Robert.' . . . They had been well and intimately acquainted from their early youth, her half-brothers and sisters being his cousins, and the acquaintance had ripened into mutual esteem and love."[27] This portrayal of Robert and Eliza's courtship demonstrates the providential nature of the elite network of extended families in which poor and deserving relatives were embraced by their wealthier relatives. Poor relations were thus given the opportunities, through marriage and job training, to realize the full potential of their families' social position. Generally, the elite families of Jacksonian America were more than eager to consolidate and preserve their fortunes through kinship and marriage. By the 1820s, the Shaws, the Parkmans, and the Sturgises were among the roughly forty interrelated families of New England comprising a formidable elite.[28] Robert and Elizabeth Shaw did their share in increasing this elite by producing eleven children, nine of whom survived to marry into other well-established families, and a tenth son who became a Catholic priest.[29]

The work ethic, family ties, and devotion to church and country were all part and parcel of Robert Gould Shaw's impressive legacy to his children and their children. A significant part of that legacy was his commitment to philanthropy. In a small publication that estimated the fortunes of wealthy Massachusetts citizens (Shaw's was put at $1.5 million), charitable contributions were considered an important aspect of a man's character. "What should Robert Gould Shaw give?" the authors asked. "Answer, fifty thousand dollars!"[30] He gave that and much more. Shaw dispensed his money generously to a wide variety of institutions and charities, and at his death he left a large fund to establish "The Shaw Asylum for Mariners' Children."[31] Both Frank and Effie would continue his tradition of "doing good" in their own lifetimes.

In his last decade the venerable merchant went beyond charity to become an ardent supporter of the antislavery and temperance movements: these two reform interests were also bequeathed to his children and grandchildren. Shaw's interest in reform movements signaled a general uneasiness with the world he and his cohorts tried to fashion for their descendants. On his deathbed in 1853, Robert Gould Shaw called two of his grandsons (one of whom was Rob) to his bedside to whisper, "My children, I am leaving the stage of action and you are entering upon it. I exhort you to use your example and influence against intemperance and slavery."[32] There is no recorded instance of Robert Gould, his namesake and Effie's adored brother, ever evincing any interest in temperance, but the fact that he went down in history as a great hero of the abolitionist movement attests to the power of family tradition.

Frank Shaw received his primary education at Boston Latin School. He entered Harvard in 1825 and left in 1828 without obtaining his degree, a pattern repeated by his son some thirty years later. That same year he joined his father's counting house and shortly thereafter embarked on a trip to the West Indies and to Europe, where he presumably polished both his business skills and his considerable linguistic talents. The early 1830s found Frank back in Boston, by now a wealthy, cultivated, and earnest young businessman whose active participation in Whig politics did not presage his decidedly unconventional future. One convention, however, that Shaw had no intention of eschewing was marriage, and on June 9, 1835, he and Sarah Blake Sturgis were joined in the bonds of matrimony. From the beginning of their courtship, it was clear that cousins Frank Shaw and Sarah Sturgis had more in common than millionaire fathers. Both came from large and affectionate families. Both at an early age showed a desire to change and improve society. Both loved music, literature, poetry, opera, theater, and travel. And both were imbued with a certain restlessness and genteel rebellion that was becoming common to their era.

There can be no doubt that Boston Brahmin society fostered a rather stuffy social and political conservatism. Upper-class Bostonians were Federalist, and later Whig, in their party affiliation and austere Unitarians in their religious beliefs. The dynamism that infused their business activities did not *automatically* flow into other areas, yet there were notable cases when it did. The young poet James Russell Lowell (the uncle of Effie's future husband, Charley Lowell) dismayed his more sober relatives with his espousal of radical abolitionism. Ralph Waldo Emerson's dramatic break from Unitarianism in 1832 and his subsequent articulation of a new philosophy called transcendentalism set a bold pattern of cultural resistance, not only for his own generation but for the next as well.

Frank and Sarah were among the many upper- and middle-class men and women who, like Emerson and Lowell, were searching for a new basis of social action. They were responding to a broad set of changes felt in every area of American society, and particularly in urban areas such as Boston. The growth of the market economy and the beginnings of industrialism brought new wealth, new opportunities, and new problems to the country. The economic engine required a constant replenishment of labor, which in the 1830s and 1840s came from Ireland. In Boston, as elsewhere, Irish immigrant workers were changing the demographic composition of the city and swelling the ranks of the Democratic party. The rhetoric of the war on privilege declared by President Andrew Jackson, whom Sarah met as a little girl, found an eager audience in the newly arrived immigrants, and their participation in popular elections posed a serious threat to Whig hegemony in New England. Periodic depressions threw many out of work and brought misery and suffering to all classes, but especially the poor. Ugly tensions between the rich and the poor were growing, and to thoughtful observers, the spirit of capitalistic enterprise was destroying the very foundations of an older traditional life based on community and caring.[33]

Many Americans relieved the anxiety and uneasiness brought about by swift social change through an embrace of religion. The early part of the nineteenth century saw increased revivalism that culminated in a spiritual earthquake known as the Second Great Awakening. Itinerant preachers such as Charles G. Finney turned away from the stern rationalism of the established churches to emphasize individual piety and the possibility of human perfection. The religious energy that fueled the revival spirit also propelled a flurry of reform activity, which one historian has colorfully labeled "Freedom's Ferment."[34] If humans were perfectible, then overcoming sin was the only barrier to enjoying heaven on earth.

The newly married Frank and Sarah joyously embraced this liberating and optimistic religion, and with it the call to reform society's evils. The young couple immediately joined the Boston Society of the New Jerusalem under the guidance of the Reverend Thomas Worcester, and thus became part of the "evangelical" wing of the Unitarian Church. These Bostonians followed the lead of the Unitarian minister Joseph Tuckerman, who used both the spirit and technique of the revivalist to urge his upper-class parishioners to intervene actively in the lives of the less fortunate. And in this case, the "less fortunate" included African Americans as well. Although far removed from the slave system of the South, the Shaws and their fellow members of the Boston Society deeply felt the sin of slavery as their own and became determined to erase it from the country. "My mother and father were among the earliest abolitionists in Massachusetts," wrote Effie proudly.[35] Her parents joined the American Anti-Slavery Society in 1838, thereby associating themselves with the more radical wing of the abolitionist movement led by their friend William Lloyd Garrison. In 1842 Frank worked with Wendell Phillips and others to lead a campaign to persuade Congress to abolish slavery and the slave trade in Washington, D.C. That same year, he became an active member of the Boston Vigilance Committee, which provided runaway slaves with the resources to live a free life.

There can be no doubt that the Shaws took themselves and their reform work seriously. Indeed, at some point during the earliest years of their married life, Frank and Sarah decided that their own, and society's, best interests would be served if he resigned from his father's business so that all of their time could be devoted to this higher work. Shaw also wished to develop his intellectual skills: he was a talented writer, linguist, and cultural critic whose creativity was being stifled by the world of commerce. Unlike his father, Frank Shaw was finding it impossible to reconcile the competing and conflicting claims of profits, philanthropy, and social reform. There is evidence to suggest that his marriage to Sarah might have been the catalyst that gave him the courage to fulfill his growing inclination to leave the family business for good. Fortunately, Robert Gould Shaw accepted Frank's decision, which came in 1842, with characteristic good grace. "He was glad to give his sons all those advantages of education of which he had himself felt that want, and permitted them to devote themselves to such pursuits as were most congenial to them," wrote a grateful son.[36] Of course, Frank Shaw's inherited wealth helped to cushion the transition period. Within five years, from 1837 to 1842, he withdrew from all political activities in the Whig party in protest over its acceptance of slavery (not to vote again in a national election until as a Republican in 1856), resigned his partnership, and moved his growing family to a new home in West Roxbury, adjoining Brook Farm.[37]

↩ Frank and Sarah at Brook Farm ↪

The change proved to be an excellent one for Frank Shaw. He truly blossomed during his stay in West Roxbury, becoming an intimate and colleague of the inhabitants of Brook Farm, and participating as a writer, critic, and translator for *The Harbinger*, the famous journal of the community. *The Harbinger*, which came out weekly, was started in June 1845 and briefly enjoyed the distinction of being the most influential socialist organ in America. It was primarily run by George Ripley and his assistants Charles A. Dana (later the editor of the *New York Sun*) and John S. Dwight, the music teacher and later distinguished critic. Among the most frequent contributors, besides Ripley, Dana, and Dwight, were Parke Godwin, Albert Brisbane, and Francis G. Shaw. The relationships forged during this time among these men prefigure their later political and social connection in New York City, where, by the 1850s, most of them lived and worked.

Frank Shaw made his deepest impression on the transcendental movement as a writer for *The Harbinger*. His first offering was a translation of George Sand's novel *Consuelo* (1845), which appeared serially in 1845 and 1846. He also translated Sand's *The Countess of Rudolstadt* (1846) and two other short works of the French author for *The Harbinger*. They were generally well received, and, as one historian noted, "It took some courage to translate and publish these two novels at a time when American critical journals were almost unanimously hostile to French fiction in general."[38] Shaw's contributions to *The Harbinger* extended well beyond translating foreign fiction for cultured Americans. His articles encompassed a wide variety of subjects, ranging from literary reviews (Alessandro Manzoni's *I Promessi Sposi* is one example) to more overtly political topics such as education, prison reform, and political economy.

Frank Shaw's thinking on political economy reflected a growing dissatisfaction with the direction of American capitalism—a dissatisfaction that must have been a powerful factor in his decision to resign from his father's firm. He wrote critically of political economy, describing it as a "science" that left out so much of the joy and meaning of human existence in its desire to place mankind solely at the service of profit. He lamented the fact that money seemed to be "the great god of our incomplete civilization."[39] Frank urged the tempering of gross materialism with a concern for social justice. One of the ways in which he provided an example of enlightened reform in action was to support Brook Farm's more explicitly political program for the reformation of society. Ripley had introduced the works of the French socialist Charles Fourier to the Brook Farmers in serious readings and discussions of socialism. The inhabitants then invited two prominent American disciples of Fourierism, Horace Greeley and Albert Brisbane of New York, to the farm to help persuade the trustees (of whom Francis Shaw was one) to write a new constitution that would be a model of socialist organization. Evidently they were persuaded, for by January 1844 a new constitution was in place, with the farm organized into a "phalanx," or Fourierist socialist cooperative.

Frank Shaw and other left-wing transcendentalists were attracted to Fourierism because of its flexibility. For example, Fourierism did not advocate violent means to achieve its stated goal of a classless society but instead "offered a peaceable solution that left private property intact but still promised to do justice to labor through a redistribution of wealth."[40] Furthermore, it provided an attractive combination of social scientific principles and the progressive impulse that also could accommodate the transcendentalist moral vision. This very early brand of social science addressed many central issues of the nineteenth century: how to foster community spirit within a capitalist system, the desirability of placing philanthropy on a scientific basis, the necessity for cooperation and efficiency in promoting humanitarian reform with the benefit flowing to all the members of society. As Carl Guarneri has written, "Fourierism was not just a communitarian program . . . but a new and penetrating way of examining American society which achieved a level of influence far beyond that of its short-lived phalanxes."[41] The adult Josephine's widely recognized ability to analyze critically a whole set of interrelated issues surrounding charity, labor, politics, and reform may well have originated in family discussions of Fourierism. Certainly her later career as a social scientist, reformer, and philanthropist revolved around advocating and implementing many of the methods first placed on the national agenda by the Fourierists.

Frank Shaw enthusiastically supported Fourierism at Brook Farm and served as vice president (with George Ripley as president) when the New England Fourier Society was formed. A reporter present at the first meeting wrote, "One of the most interesting and altogether effective speeches was made by Francis G. Shaw, a young and successful merchant, whose experience of the evils of the competitive state have led him to seek in agricultural employment a higher sphere of mental and moral culture."[42] Later, Shaw became a prominent member of the American Union of Associationists, which was presided over by Horace Greeley, editor of the *New York Tribune*.[43] Shaw had begun in earnest his search for an alternative to capitalist economic organization that would, long after Fourierism and Brook Farm had faded from the American scene, draw both him and Josephine into the orbit of Henry George, a Gilded Age reformer whose home-grown socialist remedies carried wide appeal for the disaffected at the end of the nineteenth century.

Frank Shaw's published writings advocated women's rights. He, like many other radical abolitionists, most notably his good friend Margaret Fuller, had begun to link the "slavery of sex" with the enslavement of black people. This connection was not received enthusiastically by many in the abolitionist movement who viewed the women's rights issue as a mere distraction to the main goal of eradicating slavery. Yet the obvious discrimination that women experienced as they attempted to put forth their antislavery views in the public sphere propelled several abolitionists, including the Shaws, into a broader, and gendered, critique of an unequal society. The controversy was sparked in 1837, when Angelina Grimké's speech to the Boston Female Anti-Slavery Society split the abolitionist movement into opposite camps, with those who supported a woman's right to speak in public remaining with Garrison.

Thus the parallels between the status of women and chattel slavery grew stronger for the Garrisonian faction as the movement continued through the 1830s and 1840s. Frank Shaw observed in 1846 that women would need to secure social as well as political freedom "from the bonds which do absolutely degrade them from the equal rank which is their right, and deprive them of their true position, their power to use the faculties which God has given them."[44] His advocating of equal rights for women would seem to bode well toward his own marriage with Sarah, a beautiful, intelligent, and dedicated reformer. Sarah, as strong-minded as she was attractive, shared, and to some extent directed, many of their cultural, intellectual, and social reform concerns. Her interest in transcendentalism, for example, sprang from early youth. Sarah declared that Ralph Waldo Emerson captured "my heart and *my soul*" at age fourteen, when she heard him preach at her church. She added, "As I grew older I went to all his Boston lectures and my reverence for him grew with my growth and strengthened with my strength."[45] Frank's decision to "retire" at the age of thirty-two from the world of business not only had Sarah's full support but ensured for herself a more compatible and equal place for her own work within their marriage. In other words, they enjoyed a "shared career" that challenges our prevailing notions of Victorian womanhood, with its alleged strict dichotomy of public (male) and private (female) spheres. The truth is more complex. The marriages of many American reformers demonstrated that when women acted in public ways, they often did so with their husbands' support and approval.[46]

Women, married and single, had been active in the abolitionist movement from its beginnings. Shortly after William Lloyd Garrison founded the American Anti-Slavery Society in 1831, Maria Weston Chapman created a women's auxiliary to the men's organization. Sarah became active in the organization very quickly, not only working in the annual antislavery fairs and writing the annual reports of the Massachusetts Anti-Slavery Society but also contributing her friendship and finances to one of the great female luminaries of abolitionism, Lydia Maria Child.[47] Even though Sarah was understandably bound to home and family, especially during her childbearing years, she was a well-educated and forceful woman who again and again demonstrated her eagerness to participate, with her husband and on her own, in reform activities that brought her outside of the immediate family circle. These activities, which show a certain flexibility for movement between the public and private spheres, certainly sent an important message to Sarah's four daughters, all of whom, to a greater or lesser degree, would participate in public affairs as adults.

Sarah Shaw's correspondence provides a more rounded view of her life. Letters flew fast and furious between Shaw and her female friends as already noted. But she also had warm relationships with James Russell Lowell, the elder Henry James, and Henry Ward Beecher, and their letters reveal a great respect for Sarah's opinions. From these sources, we find that Sarah was highly knowledgeable about literature, music, art, politics, and religion. She possessed a generous, spiritual, and passionate nature. Sarah Shaw was always ready to support any person or cause she thought worthwhile. One of the recipients of her help in 1846 was Sophia Hawthorne, and through her, of course, Nathaniel Hawthorne. When Sophia wrote back to thank her, Sarah replied, "Need I tell you that I am thankful for the privilege of having been able to chase one shadow from the brow of him you love so well, and shall feel more glad, if you would at any time treat me, as *angels* do each other, and tell me if I could do ought [*sic*] for your comfort."[48] One admirer described Sarah as "a woman of exceptional charm and force of character, beloved by many gifted friends, and inspiring through a long life the utmost devotion of every member of her family."[49] And as if confirming this depiction of his mother, Rob once wrote that "I have always loved her more than any one else in the world, and I think she has me, from the sacrifices she has made for me, and for which I can never repay her."[50]

Sarah Shaw took eager advantage of the educational and cultural activities that were available at Brook Farm. She attended many classes at the farm with Lydia Maria Child. Sarah also made the acquaintance of Margaret Fuller through Sophia Ripley (the wife of George), who circulated a letter in which Fuller proposed weekly meetings for interested women in order to "systematize thought, and give a precision and clearness in which our sex are so deficient, chiefly

. . . because they have so few inducements to test and classify what they receive."[51] Fuller's subsequent, and now famous, "Conversations" on topics such as "Education," "Ethics," "Culture," and "Ignorance" provided an unprecedented opportunity for the approximately fifty women who attended over the years to discuss serious subjects in a stimulating and comfortable atmosphere. Sarah Shaw was an avid participant, along with many of her friends and relations, including two of her cousins, Ellen Sturgis Hooper and Caroline Sturgis Tappan.[52] And it was Margaret Fuller—single woman, feminist, professional journalist—to whom Sarah Shaw turned when in the mid-1840s she experienced a personal crisis.

Shaw's trials are revealed in an exchange of letters to her friend Fuller, of which only Fuller's responses are extant. In 1844, Sarah had borne four children in seven years, with the fifth one arriving soon. Clearly the burdens and responsibilities of so many children in such a short time were exhausting her, and her condition was of great concern to her husband. During these years Sarah began to suffer periodic breakdowns, causing her to experience temporary blindness and other debilitating physical symptoms.[53] Her fragile health would remain a concern to her family, although eventually her constitution improved, and she lived to the ripe old age of eighty-seven. Even her privileged position could not protect her from the emotional and physical demands that a large family would necessarily make. Sarah may have been deeply frustrated that her participation in the reform and cultural activities she enjoyed so had to be sharply curtailed in order to care for her family. In the summer of 1844 it all became too much for Sarah, and her emotional outburst brought this sympathetic reply from Fuller:

I advise you not to deal too severely with yourself. There is, probably, a morbid tinge in you. . . . Treat it, as I do my headach [sic] demons, evade, rather than fight with it. Do not spend time in self-blame so much as solicit the communion of a noble and beautiful presence. No doubt you were married too young and have to bear a great deal in growing to earthly womanhood with your children. . . . You do really need some employment that will balance your life and be your serene oratory when you need one. I will talk of this when we meet. Frank asked me to come . . . and make you a little visit. I should like much to do that and then we shall say *the rest.*[54]

Sarah Shaw's condition would seem to belie the depiction of a happy family portrayed by many, including Fuller: "I shall think of all that is pleasantest, of my Sarah 'the Mother' and of her frank and loving intercourse with me. I shall think of Frank, 'the Frank,' and his wise plans for the good of injured men . . . give kisses to the gay little troop."[55] It is interesting that Fuller's description of Frank as "Frank" and Sarah not as "Sarah" but as "Mother" seems to have been at the heart of Sarah's crisis. Was Sarah desperately trying to escape the confines of her domesticity? Undoubtedly she was chafing at the bonds, and her illness might be interpreted as a physical symptom of her psychological turmoil. Women in the nineteenth century often used illness as a means to control an environment that they felt helpless to affect otherwise. When the mother was sick, the heart of the household had temporarily stopped beating. Doctors were called and consulted, patients were coddled and their wishes granted, whenever possible. When Sarah's spells of blindness began, so did the urgent visits to the Staten Island eye specialist with an anxious husband and children in tow. Within a few years the entire Shaw family had relocated to Staten Island and then on to Europe, with both moves dramatically improving Sarah's health and spirits. Then, too, it is worth considering that a stable and loving marriage and family do not prevent or preclude serious conflicts and problems. Sarah was able to claim time and space of her own, especially as the children grew older. She remained a formidable presence in her children's lives, and her influence on her famous daughter Effie can be easily inferred from their lifelong devotion to each other.

✍ A Daughter's Inheritance ✎

Family friends were struck by the similarities of character between Frank and Josephine Shaw. Joseph Choate quoted George William Curtis's tribute to the father: "The strength and simplicity and sweetness of his nature, the lofty sense of justice, the tranquil and complete devotion to duty, the large and human sympathy which was not lost in vague philanthropic feeling, but was mindful of every detail of relief; the sound and steady judgment, the noble independence of thought and perfect courage of conviction, the perfect union of sympathy and understanding, and a character which seemed to be without a flaw and to belong to what we call the ideal man." Choate then commented of the daughter: "Isn't it true that every word of that can be said with equal truth and force of Mrs. Lowell; and that it does give a just and adequate and perfect statement of her character as well as of her father's?"[56] His words forcefully convey the point that Lowell shared with her father a sense of the responsibilities that the elite—even the most conservative of Boston Brahmins—owed to the community. This paternalistic tradition of public service would be expanded by Josephine Shaw Lowell. And although her own philosophy was much tempered with the realities of a more diverse society, it would not be an exaggeration to argue that Lowell derived much of her power and prestige, so unusual for a nineteenth-century woman, from her class position. In other words, an important foundation for her social identity was established at birth, a gift from her parents, her heritage from Frank and Sarah Shaw.

Finally, from both parents Lowell received other gifts as well. From their involvement with transcendentalism came a lifelong respect for intellectual openness and a tolerance for eccentric behavior that was at odds with purists of upper-class deportment or reform politics of the 1880s and 1890s. Even more central to understanding Lowell's character and career was her inherited passion for reforming, her belief that even the most egregious wrong could be righted. If the great sin of slavery was purged from the national soul, surely the lesser evils of poverty and corruption could be similarly vanquished, if enough high-minded citizens were directing the cause. The "perfectionist thrust" so beautifully exemplified by her parents' abolitionist movement extended far beyond the Civil War. Indeed, after that conflict the former abolitionists and their children widened and expanded their reform goals to include social welfare and a host of related movements.[57] The truth is that Josephine Shaw Lowell measured almost every reform she participated in against the abolitionist movement. Sadly, she would find no comparable victory in her own generation to match that of her parents'. With this understanding of the young Effie's background in place, we can now return to the Shaw household on the eve of the Civil War.

2

First Heroes

On the evening of May 19, 1862, Effie, her sister Nellie, a cousin, Clover Hooper, and her father, Frank, were sitting in the front parlor after tea chatting excitedly about the prospect of a visit from Rob, now an officer in the Union Army. Suddenly they heard footsteps approaching on the piazza. As Effie recorded, they all said together, "Who's that?" Then, "the door opened and Rob stood there. The confusion was extreme as may be imagined, but we calmed down shortly." Rob's visit only lasted a couple of days, and Effie sadly described it as "like a dream."[1] While home, Rob was petted and praised by his admiring family circle, which had been enlarged to include a brother-in-law, George William Curtis, who had married Anna in 1856, and their two young children. The Civil War years brought many changes to the Shaw family circle. For Effie, these were years of transformation, as she grew from a girl on the brink of womanhood into, as her friend Oliver Wendell Holmes, Jr., described her, one of those "lovely, lonely women, the war widows, whose sex forbade them to offer their lives."[2]

But Effie's story cannot be told by itself. The coming of the war, the war itself, and the war's aftermath were all a part of a unique generational experience that must be examined with a wide lens. To do this, I devote this and the next chapter to interweaving Effie's life with the lives of members of her family, particularly three significant men in her life: George William Curtis, her brother-in-law; Robert Gould Shaw, her brother; and Charles Russell Lowell, her husband. All were her mentors but in different ways. And all were representative of social forces that combined to lay the foundation for the adult Josephine Shaw Lowell's worldview. George William Curtis was in the vanguard of what historian Thomas Bender calls the "Metropolitan Gentry."[3] This social group exercised a disproportionate influence over the cultural, political, and charitable institutions of New York City and, by extension, the nation. The mature Josephine would join Curtis as an important member of the Metropolitan Gentry. Effie's brother, Rob, the darling of his family, became a national symbol of New England upper-class heroism and abolitionist leadership. He willingly gave his life so that a moral cause, abolitionism, could be vindicated. Charles Russell Lowell's cruelly truncated life was embraced by his wife as a model for her own. Brilliant in mind and courageous in action, Charles posthumously offered his widow the idea of "the useful citizen," which remained permanently etched in her heart. These three men were truly Effie's "first heroes," even though as an adolescent she bestowed that honor on a dashing Civil War general. Effie's prospective brother-in-law, the well-known lecturer, writer, journalist, and cultural critic George William Curtis, appeared in her life only days after her return from Europe in 1855.

In the fall of 1856, Anna Shaw and George William Curtis announced their engagement; they were married on Thanksgiving Day of that same year. There was great excitement within the family, for the famous Curtis brought the electric aura of a celebrity to the earnest Shaw household. He quickly became a favorite with two of his three prospective sisters-in-law, Effie and Nellie, as his visits to Staten Island increased in duration and frequency. Curtis was the first of four sons-in-law for Frank and Sarah Shaw, and they had known him for many years. George and his brother Burrill were boarding students at the Brook Farm school, where they became acquainted with the Shaw family. The Curtises were the sons of a wealthy Rhode Island businessman who indulged their desires for a transcendental experience in their late teens. Both were physically attractive and gifted musicians, singers, and scholars.[4] They also worked hard at farm chores, as did everyone else at Brook Farm, but, as George later wrote, "There were never such witty potato patches, and such sparkling cornfields before or since."[5] He went abroad after Brook Farm, and traveled extensively in Europe and the East, and while in Egypt and Syria enjoyed the company of Quincy Shaw, Frank's youngest brother.[6] Curtis produced two immensely popular travel books—*Nile Notes of a Howadji* (1851) and *Lotus-Eating* (1852)—and on his return to the States found himself very much in demand as a writer, lecturer, and all around commentator on current affairs. Curtis established himself in New York City, where he shone as a star in its thriving literary community during the 1850s. He was one of the regulars at the weekly meetings at the poet Charlotte Lynch's home, where Edgar Allan Poe, Horace Greeley, William Cullen Bryant, Catherine Sedgwick, and Lydia Maria Child would gather to read from their work and engage in lively repartee. A witty, urbane man with a gift for fellowship, George William Curtis was a friend to many of the famous and talented people of his time, including Dickens, Thackeray, Longfellow, and Emerson.

Curtis's small income allowed him to enjoy Brook Farm and a European sojourn but did not provide enough to satisfy his ambitions. For them, he turned to writing, lecturing, and editing. Following the success of his travel books, he published two novels, *Potiphar Papers* (1853) and *Prue and I* (1857), which satirized New York's society life. These books established Curtis as one of America's most popular and widely read writers. In 1852, he and others founded *Putnam's Monthly*, a nationally circulated journal that featured original fiction and political opinion by American writers. A year later he took over the "Easy Chair" column in *Harper's Monthly*, where his commentaries on a wide range of topics delighted readers for almost forty years. When Curtis renewed his acquaintance with the Shaws in 1855, his growing reputation must have made it an especially pleasant occasion for his old Brook Farm friends.

Anna Shaw, who caught Curtis's eye immediately, had grown from a young tomboy "who waded through the deep snow with boy's boots and managed horses like a young Amazon" into a statuesque, poised, and lovely young woman who responded favorably to Curtis's ardent courting.[7] The handsome Curtis was thirty-two to his intended's twenty, an age gap that excited some comment among their mutual friends. Yet most seemed approving, including William Makepeace Thackeray, who wrote to his sisters that "a niece of Russell Sturgis, quite a young girl, is going to marry the cleverest and best and most gentlemanlike man in New York."[8] Anna Shaw was also extremely shy, and would remain very much in the background during her husband's long and distinguished public career. She was content to raise their children, continue her interest in horses, and act as her husband's amanuensis when needed.

After their Thanksgiving Day wedding, George and Anna Curtis moved in with the Shaws temporarily while their house, a gift from Sarah and Frank, was being built next door. During his stay, George became particularly fond of Effie, who was allowed to use his library to her heart's content, first when he was staying with his in-laws and then when the newlyweds moved into their own residence in 1859. It would be hard to overestimate the impact that Curtis had on Josephine Shaw. Certainly it did not hurt that he brought many well-known people to meet the Shaws, and that his growing reputation as a popular lecturer whose speeches drew enormous crowds excited and charmed Effie. Then, too, his interests were taking a decidedly more political bent, which pleased the Shaws. If Curtis exposed Effie and her family to a more glamorous side of New York, they reciprocated by activating a more serious side of the youthful novelist of amusing satires. "There was a time," confided Lydia Maria Child to Sarah Shaw, "when I was afraid that Mr. Curtis would waste his wealth of talent on mere externals. . . . I attribute [his moral improvement] to the healthy influence he derives from his connection with you and Frank."[9]

George William Curtis began to write and deliver antislavery lectures that placed him squarely in the middle of the growing debate over slavery in America and propelled him to the first rank of abolitionist orators, along with Wendell Phillips and Henry Ward Beecher. "Human slavery annihilates the conditions of human progress," cried Curtis in a speech given in 1856. "Its necessary result is the destruction of humanity."[10] The Shaws and all abolitionists had long agreed with his statement, but swift-moving events were beginning to make this sentiment more common to millions of northerners. The huge amount of territory acquired in the Mexican War of 1846–48 precipitated a chain of events that led to the outbreak of the Civil War in 1861. Specifically, the question raised was, Should slavery be allowed to spread in the territories (which would also include Kansas and Nebraska, part of the old Louisiana Purchase, territory still unincorporated), or would free labor prevail? And each attempted answer to the question—the Wilmot Proviso of 1846, the Compromise of 1850, the Kansas-Nebraska Act of 1854, and the Dred Scott Decision of 1857—only illuminated the difference between North and South and further polarized the nation. By the end of the decade, turmoil within the political parties reflected the great debate in the country at large on slavery and its social, economic, political, constitutional, and ideological ramifications.

The demise of the Whig party and the rise of the Republican party during the 1850s posed a serious dilemma for abolitionists. The northern public was finally reacting in disgust to the "Slave Power" of the South, but for the wrong reasons. Moral outrage on behalf of the slaves was in short supply, and was instead focused on the threat to free white men and their economic interests. As George William Curtis wryly observed, "There is very little moral mixture in the 'Anti-Slavery' feeling of this country. A great deal is abstract philanthropy; part is hatred of slaveholders; a great part is jealousy for white labor, very little is consciousness of wrong done and the wish to right it."[11] And the whole debate was being conducted in a very politically charged arena, which was not to the liking of William Lloyd Garrison and the members of the American Anti-Slavery Society, whose militant antivoting stance was a hallmark of their organizational principles.

Garrisonians believed that they could not participate in a political system corrupted by the sin of slavery without becoming corrupted as well. It was better, they thought, to remain outside and above the system, thus allowing them to retain the moral purity needed to carry on the cause. The Shaws had been members of Garrison's group since 1838 but were nonetheless very attracted to the new political wing of abolitionism. It was becoming evident to a fair number of abolitionists that continued avoidance of political commitments during these years would represent a failure of courage and of opportunity. Could one be a radical "who made no apologies for their radicalism and who crusaded . . . for immediate, unconditional, and universal emancipation and still vote for the newly established Republican party in 1856?"[12] Many abolitionists said yes, and enthusiastically worked for Republican victory, despite the party's decidedly lukewarm stance on issues of justice and equality for slaves. These abolitionists labored diligently to bring about a moral transformation of Republican party policy and, through its counsels, the nation.

Francis George Shaw and George William Curtis counted themselves among those who were political antislavery men. Frank gave money to the cause and cast his first vote since he had resigned from the Whig party in 1840 for Republican candidate John C. Fremont. Shaw and Curtis attended the Republican national convention, and both worked to ensure Fremont's nomination. Fremont set up his New York headquarters on Staten Island and after the campaign attended the Curtis-Shaw wedding. Indeed, the whole family was very much caught up in the excitement of the 1856 campaign, occurring as it did after the "little civil war" in Kansas erupted in response to the Kansas-Nebraska Act of 1854. "I never was bitten by politics before but such mighty issues are depending on this election, that I cannot be indifferent," declared Child, whose sentiments were echoed by the Shaws.[13] While their prospective brother-in-law was giving speeches to overflow crowds in lecture halls in support of the Republican ticket, Effie and Nellie declared the dashing Fremont to be their "first hero."[14] Hearing of their declaration from Sarah, Child shot back, "Isn't it too bad that [certain unworthy men] . . . should have the right to vote, while earnest souls like you and me must await the result in agonizing inaction?"[15] The resulting election of Democrat James Buchanan did not diminish the joy the Shaws felt at the Republican's good prospects for the 1860 election. (Fremont won eleven northern states.)

The Shaws' experience illustrated a notable aspect of the 1850s political scene: the increasing importance of the electoral process in the lives of Americans that began in the Jacksonian era and accelerated to unheard-of heights in the 1850s. This political culture in which popular politics played such a large part neatly excluded women, as Child pointed out in her letter to Sarah Shaw. Still, although women could not vote until 1920, their presence and influence in certain areas of the nineteenth-century public sector were great, particularly in benevolent activities and in reform movements such as abolitionism and temperance. This is because many reformers, men as well as women, relied on traditionally female virtues such as "moral suasion" and nonviolence and passive tactics such as the petition to carry their message to the people. But by the late 1840s, abolitionists were questioning whether their strategies were effective *by themselves* as a method for ending the system of slavery. Thus Josephine would come of age when abolitionism switched from a purely "moral" form to a morally based "political" form.[16]

This is a particularly important point to make: the Shaws were by no means abandoning the moral dimension of their critique of slavery; they were simply infusing it into the political realm. George William Curtis hammered this idea home again and again in his antislavery speeches. The responsibility of the educated citizen, he claimed, was to bring morality into politics and fearlessly reform the affairs of the country. The belief that political action *could* promote moral causes, such as antislavery, and that the state *should* take a moral stand, as when the abolitionists demanded that the federal government refuse to capture runaway slaves, would deeply impress Josephine Shaw and influence her later career in Gilded Age reform.

Indeed, Curtis was (along with many others) articulating a new basis for American nationalism and citizenship. In one of his most popular speeches, "Patriotism," he advised Americans that they must reject the idea, put forward so eloquently by Whig statesmen Daniel Webster and Henry Clay, that citizens must be loyal to the *whole* nation, whether it be right or wrong. The true basis for American citizenship, Curtis admonished his listeners, was not in an unthinking worship of their land but in an intelligent and passionate defense of the ideals of liberty and freedom as embodied in the Declaration of Independence and the Constitution. He reminded his audiences that Americans should be dedicated to upholding these ideals, in theory and in practice, for all people, black or white. Slavery, an abomination to freedom-loving citizens, was an evil that could no longer be countenanced or compromised. Now was the time, Curtis declared, for the "moral citizen" to stand up and be counted, to work for the preservation and strengthening of the "love of liberty" in this country. "Americans cannot be fulfilled," he stated, "without a sensitive national conscience."

Curtis vividly linked America's destiny and progress with the higher development of morality, character, and good citizenship. There was, he said, a battle going on for the true destiny of the United States—a battle in which "the victory is to those who fight with faith and unsparing devotion."[17] Curtis rejected the more popular linkage of national greatness with the acquisition of a continental empire, or manifest destiny, which in part was based on the enslavement of human beings. He became less concerned with the consequences of sectional strife than with establishing a moral stewardship that would uphold the birthright of all Americans to live in freedom and dignity. In fact, Curtis was becoming increasingly hostile to any northern accommodation with slavery and the South. His growing support of the Republican party underscored his belief in the efficacy of uniting political action with moral zeal to preserve America's republican virtue and democratic ideals.

Complementing the new emphasis on political action for many abolitionists (as well as a sizable number of nonabolitionist northerners) was the increased willingness to consider using force to end slavery.

Theodore Parker, Thomas Wentworth Higginson, Wendell Phillips, and William Lloyd Garrison all concluded at some point in the 1850s that blood would have to be shed in order to cleanse the nation of its moral stain. The bitter violence attending the protests against the Fugitive Slave Act, the intrastate warfare in Kansas, and the powerful imagery of an avenging Christian abolitionist warrior called forth by John Brown's extraordinary 1859 raid on Harpers Ferry all elicited a sanction of violence from these formerly pacifistic men. Frank and Sarah Shaw's close friends all supported the Harpers Ferry raid, which became a rallying point for Christian militance against slavery. As Sarah wrote to a British correspondent in the early years of the war,

> That dreadful curse of slavery has so permeated the people, and . . . has caused such a rot in society, that it still holds many in its horrid grasp. You must not think me superstitious, if I say that I still see the hand of Divine Providence even in that. Every defeat opens hundreds of blind eyes to the fact that slavery is at the bottom of all. . . . Would God have inspired now again thousands of noble, brave young men to take up this cross, and thousands of mothers and young wives to look upon it with resignation, but for some great end?[18]

Sarah Shaw's dramatic portrayal of a pitched battle between the forces of good and evil was rooted firmly in the Christian abolitionist's belief in and fear of a terrible punishment for the sin of slavery. "Before other nations we must all suffer, as indeed we always have done, for the sins of a wicked pro-slavery democracy," she mourned to her friend.[19] It was in this highly charged atmosphere that Effie spent her adolescence.

ᴄᴏ *"The Best of Times and the Worst of Times"* ᴏᴠ

Despite the growing political turbulence of the 1850s, Josephine and her sisters, like the majority of the people in the United States, engaged in the normal, day-to-day business of living. For them, this meant being educated in genteel institutions such as Miss Gibson's School in New York City, where Effie was sent until she was seventeen; then her parents sent her to Anna Lowell's school in Boston, where she stayed until the winter of her eighteenth year. A college education was evidently never considered for the Shaw girls. Daughters of the elite did not start attending college in significant numbers until the twentieth century, although, on the other hand, many middle-class women took advantage of the state universities and women's colleges beginning in the 1860s and 1870s.[20] Effie, however, like her own mother and many other nineteenth-century women who became prominent in public affairs, took her education from many places. She was listening and learning from George Curtis's speeches and writings on the importance of citizenship, but at a time when "citizen" was defined as male, what message did he have for an intelligent, well-informed young woman? Like Frank Shaw, George William Curtis was an ardent supporter of women's rights, both in the educational and political arenas. "The sphere of the family," he said, "is not the sole sphere either of men or women. They are not only parents, they are human beings, with genius, talents, aspirations, ambition. They are also members of the State, and . . . they are equally interested in its welfare."[21] In Curtis's view, citizenship and gender were not separated, as they so often were during the nineteenth century. Effie's strongly developed political nature and confident bearing owed much to a father and brother-in-law who respected women's achievements.

Josephine Shaw was very fortunate to grow up in a household where women's intellectual aspirations were taken seriously. Sarah Shaw had eagerly attended classes at Brook Farm and participated in Margaret Fuller's "conversations," and she was full of love for literature and learning. Frank Shaw was well known as a translator of European novels, and his intellectual interests ranged far and wide, drawing out his younger daughter's natural curiosity about political economy and the way things worked in their world. Effie was the most enthusiastic student among the Shaw children, easily outdistancing her sisters in vigor and breadth and giving her much better educated brother a run for his money. "Ask Effie to excuse me," Rob once complained to Sarah, "if I don't fully understand everything she writes me. I will try to read up on 'Plato' and 'Socrates,' when I have time, and can get the books; her last fairly floored me."[22] Frank took great pleasure in reading aloud to his four daughters and introducing them to the great works of literature.[23] Making good use of her European education and her parents' and Curtis's well-stocked libraries, Effie familiarized herself with the classics in political economy, history, and literature, and nobody in her family thought it at all odd. "She spoke French, German and Italian and, when I first knew her, was studying Latin and Greek, and reading philosophical books," remembered a neighbor from Staten Island, Louisa Schuyler.[24] Effie Shaw consciously sought out and cultivated relationships with older and wiser heads than her own, beginning, quite naturally, with her parents and family members but always expanding outward to friends, acquaintances, and colleagues. Later, she joyously assumed the role of mentor, influencing and guiding many younger men and women with whom she came into contact.

Between school sessions and during summer vacations, Josephine and her family enjoyed the diversions of the New England upper class. There were summer trips to Newport; many weekends on Naushon Island, at a summer retreat owned by the Shaws' cousins the John Murray Forbeses; and longer excursions to Nassau and Havana. Alice Forbes, John's daughter, was Effie Shaw's closest friend and companion in many of the delightful activities that occupied the young people's time on Naushon. By day, there was riding, driving, sailing, fishing, and picnics; by night, games and singing. The elder Forbeses, their children, and numerous visitors engaged in an exuberant athleticism. "We left Newport yesterday at 11 o'clock A.M.," breathlessly recorded Effie, "and arrived here (Naushon) at 6 P.M. . . . This morning we had a bath and after dinner took a splendid ride. . . . Lilly Ward and I swam across Mary's Lake. . . . Tried shooting at a mark for the first time in my life. Hit the target five times out of six at 100 yards. Took a long walk and ended the day by a row in the harbor. Two boats raced. We beat."[25] The pleasantries also included much singing around the piano, although the after-dinner walks across the lush green lawns were perhaps more popular with the romantically inclined, after which the young men would settle themselves comfortably on the piazza puffing their cigars, watching the girls in their pretty white summer outfits, heads covered with straw hats.[26] These luxuries, available to the Shaws as they were not to most Americans in the best of times, did not stop even in the worst days of the Panic of 1857, during which Frank Shaw was rumored to have lost half of his investment income and some of the family's closest relations faced ruin.[27] But these types of diversions became a thing of the past for the young men of the family as the election of 1860 signaled the end of one era and the beginning of another.

The frenzy of the 1860 northern election, attended by huge rallies and torchlight parades, pitted Republican Abraham Lincoln against Democrat Stephen Douglas. George William Curtis attended the Republican convention in Chicago, where he first supported William H. Seward of New York, whose more radical antislavery views coincided with his own. After Lincoln was chosen, however, Curtis threw his support behind the ticket, and was given the task of writing the letter informing the candidate of his nomination. Curtis assumed the chairmanship of the Staten Island Republican party and actively campaigned for the ticket. He would not fight in the Civil War because of his age and the fact that his talent as an orator for the northern cause was more prized than his fighting potential. Joining Curtis, both Shaw father and son supported Lincoln. It was the twenty-three-year-old Robert Gould Shaw's first voting experience, and from his home in New York City he relished the excitement of the campaign. His biographer wrote that "Shaw, the young man in the street, his straw hat worn at a slight angle, a thin cigar in his teeth, listened to the speeches and in the evenings, with his friends, watched the torchlight parades."[28]

Lincoln's victory ensured the ascendancy of the Republican party in the North and the undying enmity of southerners who, by February of 1861, had formed themselves into the Confederate States of America. War was now expected, but the Shaws, along with millions of Americans, were still stunned when they heard that the Confederate soldiers had attacked Fort Sumter in Charleston, South Carolina, on April 12. Shortly thereafter, the Unionists surrendered as the American flag came down and the Confederate flag rose over the former symbol of national power and unity. The new president declared the South in a state of insurrection, and on April 15, 1861, he issued a proclamation calling 75,000 militiamen to national service for 90 days. The North responded with jubilation: the Civil War had begun. Nothing would ever be the same again for the country and its divided citizenry. One friend of the Shaws best expressed the feelings of many when he wrote his thoughts on entering the Union Army: "The past was annihilated, the future was all."[29]

Like other young northern men, Rob Shaw dropped everything when Lincoln called for volunteers in that spring of 1861 and enlisted as a private in New York's elite Seventh Regiment. As bad luck would have it, the rest of his family (except for Anna) was vacationing in the Bahamas when war broke out, and Rob departed with his regiment for Washington, D.C., without their knowledge. "It is very hard to go off without bidding you goodbye, and the only thing that upset me, in the least, is the thought of how you will feel when you find me so unexpectedly gone," wrote Rob to Sarah. "But I know, dearest Mother, that you wouldn't have me stay, when it is so clearly my duty to go."[30] Later he commented to Effie, "I never liked the house and place so much as the day I went down to pack up my things—My feelings were rather too much for me when I thought of your all being back there in two days and finding my room empty."[31] At least he enjoyed the benefits of the powerful wave of patriotism that swept the North in the early days of the war. Even in pro-South New York City, where only a few months earlier Democratic Mayor Fernando Wood advocated secession from the North, a Union rally gathered hundreds of thousands to its cause. The passage of New York's Seventh Regiment from the city to Washington drew similar sentiments. "The crowd and the enthusiasm were tremendous," declared Rob to sister Susie; "the people would hardly let us pass, actually catching hold of our hands and slapping us on the back, yelling and screaming like wild men."[32] Rob did not stay a private for long. The volunteers of the Seventh were only in for thirty days, and when their time was up, most left the service and went home. Rob stayed a soldier. He requested and was granted a commission in the Second Massachusetts Regiment. Now Lieutenant Shaw, he promptly left Washington for training camp in West Roxbury, Massachusetts, near his childhood home by Brook Farm. There he was greeted by familiar faces—his cousin and best friend, Harry Russell; Henry Lee Higginson; Greeley Curtis; and Charles F. Morse, all of whom would become close wartime comrades.[33]

✑ A *Young Girl's Wartime Diary* ✑

Soon after Rob joined the Second Massachusetts, Effie began a diary in which she would record her thoughts and feelings about the war. "Yesterday was the saddest day this country has ever experienced," she wrote of the Union Army's retreat at Bull Run.[34] Effie eventually filled four crammed cardboard copybooks with her penciled observations. She had much to write about as the daughter of a highly politicized abolitionist family and the sister whose soldier brother exemplified for her the courage, daring, and drama of the war. From the earliest days of the war, the Shaw household was in a state of constant agitation and excitement, and not just because Rob was in uniform. The first flush of northern support for the Union's cause that Rob experienced in his parade was destined to wax and wane over the next four years with battlefield ups and downs, but that support was powerful enough to propel abolitionists into their first position of political respectability.

They would proclaim themselves the conscience of the Republican party throughout the war, and from the beginning they came prepared with an ambitious agenda, which included immediate emancipation, the formation of black regiments, a government-created Freedmen's Bureau, and a legislative program for guaranteeing African-American civil and political rights. Of course their demands were predicated on the assumption that the Civil War was being fought to free the slaves, and not just to preserve the Union, as Lincoln and the rest of the North at first insisted. The abolitionists, however, fitfully bided their time, and eventually most of their proposals were adopted by the Republicans.[35]

The Shaws were galvanized into action to help put forth in word and deed their vision of the war's outcome. Every aspect of the war would be examined and discussed for its moral and political repercussions in daily family gatherings. Effie depicted this in her diary:

> In the morning the papers said that we had gained a great victory at Bull's Run [sic] . . . We found afterwards that the accounts were exaggerated . . . About half past three, Anna and Mother had gone to drive and I was sitting in Mother's room, when Nellie came up crying, and said, "Our whole Army has been cut to pieces and entirely routed." . . . I went down to ask Anna, but she could tell nothing excepting that our men had run from the enemy and lost everything. In a few moments Father, George and Mother . . . came in and we all sat on the piazza in a most unhappy state of mind. . . . George didn't enliven us much by saying, "The next thing they will do will be to march on Washington, take possession of it, and then Jeff Davis [president of the Confederacy] will issue his condition from the Capitol and offer us peace." After talking it over we all felt better and prepared to hear that it wasn't quite so bad as the reports said.[36]

The Shaws, like most Americans, would continue to feel frustrated and anxious over conflicting accounts of the war battles even though their close friend and neighbor, Sidney Howard Gay, was now the managing editor of the *New York Tribune* and thoughtfully provided them with the latest bulletins. The bulletins that really brought them all together, however, were Rob's letters, which arrived with a comforting regularity and were read aloud so that everybody could enjoy them and comment on their contents.

Rob was a faithful and diligent correspondent; he wrote to every member of his family and filled his letters with amusing anecdotes about his experiences. This was particularly true in the early part of the war, when he, along with most of the Northern army, had little to do but languish in camps. "I often think of the house and you all sitting on the porch looking across the lawn and Anna and George and the Children and Tib walking over from their house," wrote Rob wistfully.[37] In another letter to his mother that delighted the family, Rob described a visit he and a friend paid to William H. Seward, the secretary of state, who "gave me the impression of being a pretty sly old fellow, and really didn't look as if he could have written all those great speeches." Nevertheless, the secretary granted their request for an audience with the president, so "off we trotted, to make a call." Rob found the president welcoming and commented that "it is really too bad to call him one of the ugliest men in the country, for I have seldom seen a pleasanter or more kind-hearted-looking one and he has certainly a very striking face." The letter continues to sing Lincoln's praises, even bringing forth the ultimate compliment from this young Brahmin: "He gives you the impression, too, of being a gentleman." All in all, declared Rob proudly, "we did a pretty good afternoon's work in calling on the President and the Secretary of State."[38]

Josephine also enjoyed recording presidential anecdotes she heard from Sidney Gay or her parents. She, like Rob, approved of Lincoln: "It is a year day after tomorrow since Old uncle Abe was elected, and he has not made himself despised by the people yet. If he is a little too good natured, he knows how to hold his tongue,—one of the first and cardinal virtues."[39] This bit of political sagacity reflected the intelligent, self-confident manner in which the affairs of the country were discussed by the teenage diarist.

The practical side of Effie was in constant battle with her intense idealism, as exemplified by her description of Lincoln's treatment of her "first hero," John C. Fremont. Fremont was appointed by Lincoln early in the war to be commander of the Western Department, where he suffered a humiliating string of military defeats that stalled his ambitions. In an effort to revive his political and military reputation, Fremont issued a proclamation freeing the slaves in Missouri on August 30, 1861. The fact that Fremont's deed was done without Lincoln's knowledge (and when he did know, without his approval) did not diminish the abolitionist excitement over this first bold stroke on behalf of ending slavery. "Hurrah! Hurrah! Hurrah!" gushed Effie. "The *Tri-*

bune says today that Fremont has declared Missouri to be under martial law and granted freedom to all the slaves. . . . Oh! If Fremont only has freed the slaves, what a step it will be. Joy! Joy! Joy!"

That joy was somewhat lessened as the controversy generated by Fremont's actions swelled: "Yesterday there was a letter from the President to Fremont saying that he wished him to modify his proclamation in regard to slaves and that he expressed his desire publicly at the request of General Fremont, whom he had privately informed of it before. Today those nasty papers say that Fremont will resign. I wish they might be cut off in the midst of their career and not be allowed to publish a single issue for six months." Finally, a somewhat chastened Josephine confided to her diary that "a subordinate officer should obey the orders of the Commander-in-Chief."[40] Although the Shaws knew and corresponded with General Fremont and his wife, Jessie Benton Fremont, their sympathies and support would ultimately be with Lincoln and the Republican party throughout the war.

Still, Effie could hardly contain her excitement about the war and its lessons for the country: "These are extraordinary times and splendid to live in. This war will purify the country of some of its extravagance and selfishness, even if we are stopped midway. . . . I suppose we need something every few years to teach us that riches, luxury and comfort are not the great end in life, and this will surely teach us that at least." This sentiment would be much modified as the casualties mounted and the horror of the war became increasingly apparent. Yet one thread running throughout Effie's diary is her admiration of soldiers and what she believed to be their cause: "All the account of brave deeds, bayonet charges, calmly receiving the fire of the enemy and withholding their own, and all the stirring accounts of courageous men, make one so long to be with them." Effie mused that she herself would make a good soldier, "for I'm not an atom afraid of death and the enthusiasm of the moment would be sublime." And while acknowledging that "Mother says she hates to hear me talk so," she later wrote, "Dear boys! How noble they are, and yet how can they help being noble? I have longed so to go myself that it seemed unbearable."[41]

Effie's comments regarding soldierly virtues showed the enthusiastic level of her patriotism, but they also mirrored her adolescence. When the war began in 1861, she was seventeen and still in her most impressionable and sensitive stage of development. And the war's twin messages, as mediated by her radical abolitionist family, were those of the value of self-sacrifice and a dedication to the public good. As the war progressed, these ideals became even more meaningful by the sacrifices of Rob and Charley in particular and her generation and class in general. The Civil War's intense idealism combined with Effie's youthful receptivity made her lavish in her admiration of the unselfish courage of soldiers. Always, for Josephine as for so many others of that era, American citizenship was defined by the willingness of a large number of virtuous people to assume public responsibility no matter what the cost. The "Union" was being saved at a dear price, but it was a price worth paying because it cleansed the nation, as Sarah phrased it, of the "sins of a pro-slavery democracy." The survivors of the Shaw family would emerge from the Civil War years with a firm belief that the American nation had redefined itself by producing a second birth of freedom for black people, and that that moral achievement had to be built upon for the generations to follow.

✑ The Women's Central ✑

The patriotic fervor that accompanied the outbreak of the Civil War stirred women as well as men to action. "We never knew before how much we loved our country," Effie wrote. "To think that we suffer and fear all this for her! The Stars and Stripes will always be infinitely dear to us now after we have sacrificed so much to them, or rather to the right which they represent." What sacrifices could women make? What could they contribute to the war effort that would be worthy of men's sacrifices? Effie provided the answer: "We can work though if we can't enlist, and we do. It is very pleasant to see how well the girls and women do work everywhere, sewing meetings, sanitary hospitals and all."[42]

The women of Effie's family and generation had an important historical precedent for turning private, domestic duties into public, politicized wartime activities without incurring charges of unfeminine behavior. During the Revolutionary period, thousands of women considered themselves "The Daughters of Liberty" and labored mightily for the war effort through petitions, boycotts, and the creation of supportive organizations. For their efforts, women were showered with praise and recognition, but not voting rights; rather, they received a separate and unequal place alongside their menfolk in the new republic.[43] Subsequent generations of American women built upon their ancestors' Revolutionary experience, and by the time the Civil War erupted, they had successfully carved out a niche for themselves in the public sphere through their strong presence in religious, reform, and benevolent organizations. Now, women's well-honed organizational skills would be put to the test, and they would not be found wanting.

To assist the war effort, Effie, her mother, and her sisters all joined the New York City Woman's Central Association of Relief for the Army and Navy of the United States in 1861. The Woman's Central began as one of many grassroots organizations of women who wanted to support their brothers, husbands, and sons. The U.S. government had mobilized a huge number of men to engage in war but was clearly unprepared to feed and clothe them and bind their wounds in a timely and humane manner. Into this breach stepped American women, who formed approximately 20,000 local aid societies (North and South) to assist in this giant enterprise. And no aid society was more powerful or resourceful than the Woman's Central, which very early on established itself as a national clearinghouse for all other societies. The Woman's Central was founded in late April 1861, when 3,000 women attended a meeting at Cooper Union to consider more efficient provisioning methods for the Union soldiers.

From this meeting came the appointment of a twenty-five-member board (twelve of them women) that included many prominent New York residents. The leaders of the Woman's Central (which included Dr. Elizabeth Blackwell, the first woman to receive a medical degree in the United States) soon collected thousands of letters from all over the country. These letters were powerful testimony to the fact that the urgent needs of the soldiers were going unmet. A delegation of "gentlemen" was sent to Washington to meet with Lincoln and persuaded him to establish a civilian advisory board to the Army Medical Bureau. On June 13, 1861, the president signed the order bringing the U.S. Sanitary Commission into existence. Armed with only advisory and investigative powers, the Sanitary Commission made its great contribution to the war effort by, among other things, raising $25 million in cash, goods, and services. Working side by side with military medical personnel (and not always amicably), the commission demonstrated that cooperation among the military, business, professional, and volunteer sectors could visibly improve the health and morale of the Union army.[44]

The Woman's Central was considered throughout the country to be "the main branch" of the Sanitary Commission. And it was no accident that Effie, Nan, Susie, and Nellie went to work for the Woman's Central. One of their closest friends, twenty-three-year-old Louisa Lee Schuyler, was the organization's manager. "Today I went up to the Cooper Union instead of Susie," wrote Effie. "Lou Schuyler and Miss Collins were there and I copied lists of donations for the papers, while they unpacked, arranged and repacked articles for soldiers."[45] Effie's diary is filled with accounts of her work for the Woman's Central. She collected money, rolled bandages, gave out work for women, and knitted a slew of mittens: "December 16th: Today is my birthday,—18 years. Sent today 42 pairs of mittens to Rob."[46] Those mittens were very much appreciated, as Rob indicated in a letter to Sarah: "Tell the girls that Harry would be very much obliged if they would send him seventy or eighty pairs of mittens. I heard him say he would like to have some. The men were all glad to get them, though, as usual, they didn't express their thanks."[47] Effie occasionally sprang into action at a moment's notice: "Today Mother received a note from Dr. Walser, the physician of the Hospital at Quarantine, saying that 250 wounded and sick are expected tomorrow and that his provisions were most insufficient, so we have been very busy trying to get some new things to help him. The letter came at 5 P.M., and now at 10:30 A.M., we have already got $100. to pay sewing women, seven pieces of cotton, 12 made shirts, 22 cut out, slippers, etc. This is doing pretty well, I think."[48]

Despite doing plentiful good deeds, Effie at times longed to be closer to the action: "Oh, I wish I were old enough to go on a hospital ship or offer my services as a nurse."[49] She thrilled to the exploits of Clara Barton, the "angel of the battlefield" whose single-minded dedication to the injured and sick soldiers of the Army of the Potomac was already making her a legend of the war.[50] But Effie's work, however mundane, kept her busy, was important, and mostly satisfied her patriotic impulse. The Sanitary Fairs, which were held in every major northern city and raised money for the commission's work, were emblematic of northern women's efforts to aid the war through a blending of charity, patriotism, symbol, and spectacle. Josephine Shaw undoubtedly attended the New York City fair and must have been impressed with women's power and the visible expression of their duty. Moreover, Effie's war work introduced her to a small network of like-minded women who would later be her colleagues in the New York

City charity movements. Effie Shaw, Lou Schuyler, and their friend and co-worker in the Woman's Central, Gertrude Stevens (later Mrs. William B. Rice), forged a lasting friendship during these years. Later, at the height of their careers, these women were known as the "Big Three" of New York charity.[51] A fourth friend, Ellen Collins, was a thirty-two-year-old single woman of genteel background whose duties for the Woman's Central enabled her later to achieve a distinguished although discreet career in social work. Effie, Lou, Gertrude, and Ellen worked jointly for the soldiers in the Civil War and together would work for New York's poor and underprivileged in the postwar era.

One of the ties that first bound these young women (and many other future charity leaders as well) was their firm belief in the new kind of disciplined and efficient benevolence represented by the U.S. Sanitary Commission. Josephine and other young women willingly embraced this philosophy, which offered them a chance to serve as charitable "soldiers," fighting for a great cause. Moreover, the new ideology was entirely appropriate to the exigencies of the moment: the Civil War demanded and received an unprecedented level of effort and resources from philanthropic agencies. A more practical, efficient, and nationally based organization was a rational response to the immediate and critical material demands of war. Thus with its educated, elite leadership, its army of paid agents who emphasized professionalism over unpaid enthusiasm, its frank embrace of a large, organized response to need, and its rejection of individualized charity, the U.S. Sanitary Commission would provide a model for the postwar benevolent world. The Sanitary Commission and the Woman's Central represented more than the volunteer organization par excellence; they carried within their programs the seeds of an ideological revolution in the field of charity and philanthropy.[52] There is no doubt that the Sanitary Commission and the Woman's Central paved the way for the introduction of scientific charity in America. And Josephine Shaw Lowell would be its leading philosopher and the founder of its flagship organization.

To be sure, Josephine Shaw and the women in her family worked hard and knew that their contributions, and all women's contributions to the military effort, were critical, but a nation at war necessarily focused its admiration and hopes on the soldiers whose collective bravery and fighting spirit became the object of the North's (and South's) veneration. Women had a part to play here as well. They had to keep the morale of their fighting men high through letters expressing their love and support. Indeed, when women, North or South, withdrew their support of the war, when they wrote sad and frightened and angry letters to their men, letters of protest against the sacrifice and the violence of the war, the desertion rates rose notably. In the gendered world of mid-Victorian America, men were expected to be courageous on the battlefield, and women were expected to be brave on the homefront. And the homefront—lovingly portrayed in sentimental songs, books, and magazine and newspaper articles widely sung and read by soldiers—was symbolized by that bastion of domesticity and security presided over by women: the home. The warmth and safety of home and family were what men missed most when they were mustered into service. Mothers, daughters, sweethearts, and sisters embodied this home for which the soldier was fighting: "For, finally," wrote Reid Mitchell, "wasn't the Civil War a war over the meaning of the home?"[53] So it was that women, along with politicians, generals, and ministers, were critical in providing ideological as well as logistical support of the war. And Josephine Shaw volunteered her services in both areas.

⇜ *Rob's Story* ⇝

"I know a great many men in the army," Effie proudly recorded in her diary. And first on her list was "my brother," but it also included many cousins, an uncle, friends, and one "Capt. Lowell of the U.S.A."[54] Even though Effie admired the soldiers' bravery, she still fretted about the possibility of Rob getting hurt, and when she expressed in a letter to her brother the wish that he could sustain a minor injury and thus be able to come home, Rob replied humorously, "I am much obliged to you, for wishing me a wound—Is there any other little favor, I could do you?"[55]

Before Effie's romance with Charles Russell Lowell began, her most tender feelings were reserved for her brother. She wrote weekly to him while he was in camp, and judging by his replies, her letters were very much appreciated: "My dear Effie, I have received your last two letters and I owe you thanks for writing so regularly—you have managed to find something interesting to write about always."[56] Their correspondence was full of family gossip, humorous anecdotes, and much discussion of the war and its political ramifications. The letters clearly show that Rob respected Effie's intelligence and valued her opinions on public affairs. Effie in turn adored her only brother, whom she most resembled in the family. Referring lovingly to their relationship in a letter, Rob wrote of Effie, "She and I have always been together, more than any other two of the family."[57]

Rob's position as the general favorite of the family was powerfully cemented by his wartime role. Sarah's recollection that Rob "had been the pride, joy and happiness of his parents and sisters, all through his short and perfect life" had the ring of truth, for he always seemed to be first in the hearts of his family.[58] Whether this owed to his being the only son among four daughters or to his unusually attractive and pleasant disposition (or a combination of both) is hard to say. A friend remembered Rob as "a beautiful, sunny-haired, blue-eyed boy, gay and droll, and winning in his ways."[59] Slight in stature (his mature height was only five feet five) and very handsome, Robert Gould Shaw possessed a natural charm that attracted many feminine admirers from his teenage stay in Europe to his more mature years in Boston and New York.

Although never a brilliant soldier, Rob Shaw did nonetheless compile a record of solid achievements during the war—something he failed to do as a civilian. After completing his education, he returned to America to enroll at Harvard, where he was accepted in August of 1856, joining the famous "fighting class" of 1860. An indifferent student, he dropped out after two years and accepted a position in his Uncle Henry P. Sturgis's mercantile firm in New York City. Rob Shaw did not shine as a businessman either. Restless and unhappy in a boring position, he angrily wrote that he would "rather be a chimney sweep" than continue on with his business career.[60] Shaw's discontent was a source of worry to his parents, particularly his strong, intelligent, and demanding mother, who expected great things of him. Sarah and Rob were very close, and she later described him as "the most intimate friend from his earliest boyhood, he loved me with a devotion of which I was unworthy. . . . Our whole intercourse is without a shadow."[61] Sarah's comments, which were written after her son's death, must be taken with a grain of salt. Their correspondence revealed repeated clashes over Rob's tendency to spend too much money and waste too much time on frivolities, and she constantly encouraged him to find a direction in life. As the object of his mother's fierce devotions and expectations, Shaw felt depressed from time to time. He dealt with these feelings, however, and generally enjoyed his year in New York, using the time he was not devoting to business to attend his beloved opera and theater.

What did interest Rob Shaw was politics. Like the rest of his family, he was an abolitionist, although, as he wrote in protest to his ever more stalwart mother, he couldn't possibly "talk and think of slavery all the time."[62] At this point, in fact, Shaw's abolitionism was lukewarm, and like most northerners, he thought of African Americans in terms of racial stereotypes, as being inferior to whites.[63] He was much more fascinated by the political spectacle of a divided nation and closely followed the news of the disintegrating union in the months before the war. As he wrote to his sister Susanna after Fort Sumter had been attacked, "There seems to be no way of making a peaceable separation without giving up everything."[64] He considered war inevitable, and gave himself over to the fray. Rob's brief stay in Washington convinced him of the importance of good, reliable officers to the Union cause, and when his training with the Second Massachusetts Regiment ended in June 1861, he was ready to fight. This time the whole Shaw family got to say good-bye to Rob from the Staten Island Ferry, which crossed the path of the ship carrying his regiment: "Shaw stood on the paddle box and waved to his family—his father in sober black, his mother and sisters in their summer finery of delicate pink and white and powder blue as they waved their handkerchiefs in the breeze."[65]

The Second Massachusetts joined the Army of the Potomac and settled down in Virginia to languish in the inactivity and confusion that marked the eastern theater's early contribution to the Civil War effort. Despite the boredom, Shaw performed his duties well and was promoted to first lieutenant in the summer of 1861. The fighting experience for which he longed came the next year, when his regiment engaged the enemy in two battles of note: Cedar Mountain in Virginia's Shenandoah Valley and Antietam Creek near Sharpsburg, Maryland. Shaw's good performance under fire gained him a promotion to captain, but it also brought him face to face with the grim consequences of war, as his unit participated in the ill-fated second Bull Run campaign led by General John Pope. At Cedar Mountain on August 9, 1862, Shaw took part in the fighting against the fabled Confederate General Stonewall Jackson. After Jackson and his Confederates defeated the Union forces, Rob surveyed the battlefield to assess the losses. What he found was shocking: his cousin Harry Russell was taken prisoner of war, and five of his friends lay dead on the battlefield.

Autumn brought a new terror. In early September, General Robert E. Lee's Army of Northern Virginia crossed the Potomac River into Maryland to invade the North. The Second Massachusetts, assigned to the Twelfth Corps under General Mansfield, moved into position with the rest of the Army of the Potomac under the command of General George B. McClellan to face off the Rebels near Sharpsburg by a tiny creek called Antietam. Early in the morning of September 17, these two great armies began a battle that would go down in history as the single bloodiest day of the Civil War. Rob, much to the relief of his family, escaped unharmed, and his company's losses were minor. This was not so with thousands of the combatants, as the record showed 6,000 dead and 17,000 wounded. Rob's own anguished recollections testify to the effect of the carnage: "It was a terrible sight, and our men had to be very careful to avoid treading on them [injured and dead soldiers]; many were mangled and torn to pieces by artillery, but most of them had been wounded by musketry fire. . . . There are so many young boys and old men among the Rebels, that it hardly seems possible that they have come out on their own accord to fight us, and it makes you pity them all the more, as they lie moaning on the field."[66] Despite the terrible losses, Antietam (Sharpsburg in the South) was considered a northern victory and provided the war with one of its major turning points. And this particular turning point provided Rob Shaw a golden opportunity to advance the abolitionist cause and his military career simultaneously.

The Union effort at Antietam did not destroy the Confederate forces, as Lincoln had hoped, but it did provide just enough of a victory to stop Lee's invasion of Maryland, and thus dashed southern hopes for recognition of the Confederate government by England. Most important, Antietam gave Lincoln the opportunity to issue the preliminary Proclamation of Emancipation. "God bless Abraham Lincoln," a rejoicing Effie wrote in her diary. "He has issued a proclamation emancipating all slaves on the 1st of January 1863, in any State then in rebellion against the Government. . . . Old Abe is wise and I guess this will work."[67] With this step, Lincoln openly acknowledged what was already a fact in Union-held southern territory where slaves had been coming by the thousands behind northern army lines: that the war was being fought not only to preserve the Union but to free the slaves as well.

Abolitionists generally hailed Lincoln's action (some of them felt he should have declared unconditional emancipation), and plans to help the slaves, or ex-slaves, were set in motion. One plan, hitherto thwarted, was the brainchild of John A. Andrew, the wartime abolitionist governor of Massachusetts, whose dream it was to see African-American regiments in battle, fighting for their rights as citizens and their dignity as men. His dream could now be realized, because in early January of 1863, the war department authorized Governor Andrew to form the first Northern African-American regiments (the Massachusetts Fifty-fourth and Fifty-fifth). Black and white abolitionists rose to the challenge. Andrew set in motion his well-laid plans for the recruitment of officers and men for the Fifty-fourth. For the latter, he formed a committee of concerned citizens, led by the manufacturer George L. Stearns and including Francis George Shaw, who helped to raise money and recruit from a New York office. The committee raised funds to defray the costs of recruiting the thousand privates needed for the Fifty-fourth. It also hired recruiting agents (among them black abolitionists Frederick Douglass, Henry Highland Garnet, and Martin R. Delany) to travel throughout the northern states and Canada to persuade free African Americans to become Union soldiers.

For the officers, Andrew was required to search for whites only. President Lincoln and Secretary of War Stanton refused his request to commission black officers in fear that northern public opinion would not support that advancement. Andrew was disappointed but did what he thought was the next best thing: recruit the officers from the cream of abolitionist society. He wrote a letter to Frank Shaw on January 30, 1863, crisply outlining the high moral standards he wished to see in the leadership of the Fifty-fourth: "Such officers must be necessarily gentlemen of the highest tone and honor; and I shall look for them in those circles of educated Anti-Slavery Society, which next to the colored race itself have the greatest interest in the success of this experiment."[68] Andrew then offered the colonelcy of the regiment to Captain Shaw, with the lieutenant colonelcy going to the captain of the Twentieth Massachusetts, Ned Hallowell, the son of prominent Philadelphia abolitionists. The governor asked Frank Shaw to deliver to Rob in person at camp in Stafford Courthouse, Virginia, an enclosed, shorter letter asking him to accept the commission. Frank and Sarah were thrilled. They knew that this was an undertaking of unique importance, one whose "success or . . . failure" would, in Andrew's words, "go far to elevate or depress the estimation in which the character of the colored Americans will be held throughout the world."[69] Indeed, by the time Frank left that night with Rob's letter in hand, the governor was assured that the Shaws had given their heartfelt "consent and sympathy and support" to the planned project.[70]

But one Shaw had not given his "consent and sympathy and support" as yet. As he traveled to Washington by train, Frank felt misgivings about their assumption that Rob would automatically accept the colonelcy, fearing that his son's modesty might hold him back. Frank proved partially correct, but Rob had other reasons for hesitating. He was doing well in his regiment, was popular with both officers and men, and had acquitted himself in battle. Further advancement seemed guaranteed. Then, too, the position of white commanding officer of the first free black regiment was, Andrew's and the Shaws' feelings to the contrary, hardly desirable in the eyes of most officers. Years later, William James succinctly described Shaw's dilemma: "In this new negro-soldier venture, loneliness was certain, ridicule inevitable, failure possible; and Shaw was only twenty-five, and, although he had stood among bullets at Cedar Mountain and Antietam, he had till then been walking socially on the sunny side of life."[71] Father and son had a long talk about the commission, after which Rob declined, saying that he was not worthy of its honor. Frank spent the night in camp, hoping his son would change his mind, but in the morning Rob handed him a letter to Governor Andrew refusing the honor, and the case seemed to be closed. Frank Shaw left the camp in Virginia and, back at his Washington hotel, immediately wired the news of Rob's refusal to Sarah, prompting her to lament it as "the bitterest disappointment I have ever experienced."[72]

Frank and Sarah Shaw's despair at Rob's evident lack of courage to seize this historical moment for the abolitionist cause was bitterly felt but short-lived. Rob had changed his mind shortly after Frank's departure, and sent this telegraph message to his father on February 5, 1863: "Please Destroy My Letter and Telegraph to the Governor that I Accept."[73] Rob, after reflection, found it impossible to turn his back on a lifetime steeped in abolitionist character training, even if his enthusiasm was, at this point, only a pale reflection of his parents'. Emerson said it best in his commemorative poem of the Fifty-fourth, "Voluntaries," with the lines

> So nigh is grandeur to our dust,
> So near is God to man,
> When duty whispers low, *Thou must,*
> The youth replies, *I can.*

Shaw's family was jubilant, and when Rob arrived in Boston on February 15, 1863, to commence the planning and training of the Fifty-fourth Massachusetts Regiment, they were waiting to welcome him. Rob would spend the next few months at the Fifty-fourth's training grounds in Readville, near the city, and most of his free time was taken up in the company of his friends and family. He especially favored a New York woman, Anna Kneeland Haggerty, to whom he had become engaged just after Christmas of 1862. Romance was in the air for the Shaw children. Susanna (Susie) Shaw had married Robert Minturn, a civilian, the previous fall. Susie's new husband was the son of the wealthy shipping magnate Robert Bowne Minturn (Grinnell, Minturn & Co.). In 1843 Minturn and other philanthropists founded the Association for Improving the Condition of the Poor, one of the most influential reform charitable societies in prewar New York City and a forerunner to Josephine Lowell's Charity Organization Society.

Susie's wedding—relatively free from the ominous undertones of the war—was celebrated joyously and lavishly by the entire Shaw family, including Rob, who was able to get leave for the event.[74] Rob and Annie's courtship, however, was not looked on as favorably. Sarah and Frank frowned on marriage for Rob at this point, fearing it would be a distraction to his greater duties.[75] During the war, all parents had good reasons to be concerned about hasty marriages. Wartime romances were conducted in an impassioned environment—one in which meetings between young women and their soldier beaux during furloughs or other short periods of time away from the war could ignite smoldering feelings into permanent commitments. Parents often urged their children to put off their marriages until the war was over. Children just as often ignored their parents' advice, preferring to take their happiness while they could.[76] Certainly this was the case with Rob and Annie, and it was the case with Effie and her new beau, Charles Russell Lowell. For their story, we turn to Chapter 3.

3

Lights and Shadows

Josephine Shaw and Captain Charles Russell Lowell began their romance just as she put away her diary in late 1862. Perhaps her life had become too interesting to faithfully record. Indeed, the next two years would bring "lights and shadows, in swift succession," as Effie was romanced and married, as she gloried in the successes and fulfilled wartime ambitions of her brother and husband, as she grieved at their deaths, and, finally, as she gave birth to a daughter in late 1864, thus bringing to an end an emotionally tumultuous period.[1] But all that lay ahead as the now nearly nineteen-year-old woman met her first and only lover. Although 1862 marked the year when Effie and Charley's relationship became intimate, within the boundaries of the peculiar Boston kinship system they had always known of each other. Effie's parents were longtime friends of Charley's uncle, the poet James Russell Lowell, who in turn was Effie's godfather.[2] In the 1840s, Charley often accompanied his uncle on visits to Brook Farm, where the two stopped off to pay their respects to the Shaw family. John Murray Forbes, Sarah's cousin, was Charley's mentor and was responsible for getting him appointed as colonel of the Second Massachusetts Cavalry. Effie was a student at Anna Lowell's school until December of 1861, and her brother, Rob, had the highest respect and liking for Charley as a soldier and fellow Harvard man.

Effie and Charley may have known of each other forever, but they became romantically involved in the closing months of 1862. It must have seemed to them that fate brought them together, for Charley, the very picture of a young Brahmin officer, was in Boston recruiting for his new regiment—the Second Massachusetts Cavalry—at the same time that Effie was in town for a prolonged visit. Lowell's training camp was at Readville, near Boston, the same place where Rob Shaw would be training the Fifty-fourth. This coincidence delighted members of several families: the Shaws, the Lowells, the Haggertys, and the Forbeses, who cherished Charley like a son. Indeed, it was probably at the Forbes family's Boston home at Milton Hill, overlooking the harbor, that Effie and Charley fell in love. Like all members of her immediate family, Effie moved easily and often between Staten Island and Boston. This visiting did not stop because of the war. Although she stayed with several relations, Effie favored the home of Cousin John and Sarah, perhaps because that was where she could visit with her best friend, Alice H. Forbes, to her heart's content. References to Effie and Charley's courtship begin appearing in family letters in November 1862, during one of Effie's extended stays at Milton Hill. She wrote to Rob telling him all about the progress of the Second Massachusetts Cavalry and urged him to think about joining that unit. By January, Effie's romance with Charley was well enough known in the family for Rob to tease her in a letter, "*Did* you go to tea at Col. Lowell's at last?"[3]

Their courtship moved at whirlwind speed, and Shaw family history records Charley asking for Effie's hand in marriage in early March, after only nine meetings. "March 5th is *my* day . . . the day my husband and I were engaged," wrote Josephine Lowell to a friend many years later. "We had one anniversary of it—but none of our wedding day."[4] Elizabeth Putnam recalled meeting Effie for the first time: "She was sitting on a packing box at the Camp at Readville, the afternoon sun striking across the feather on her hat, and lighting up her delicate complexion, her fine hair and fair brow. She was staying with Mrs. John Forbes at Milton, and Lowell had asked her to be his wife."[5] At nineteen, Effie radiated a youthful attractiveness and intelligent good humor that had already impressed many would-be suitors. Lou Schuyler described Effie as having "a slight figure, with the typical Shaw coloring, of light hair, blue eyes and fair complexion."[6]

Charley, nine years her senior at twenty-eight, possessed the fine features and sensitive mien of the upper-class Bostonian that he was. He had blue eyes, brown hair, and stood about five feet ten. There was a steely quality to his stare that belied his gentle mustached countenance and slender physiognomy but made his reputation for battle heroics believable. One relative remembered him as having a "flashing glance and his face full of fire, emotion, power and fun."[7] A portrait, taken just after the couple's engagement, reveals a tender moment. Effie, hair severely parted and swept back behind her ears, is intently reading a letter. Her face, composed and unsmiling, reflects Richard Watson Gilder's later poetic description of her as having a "thinking, inward-lighted countenance."[8] Dressed fashionably but simply, Effie is the perfect embodiment of the young Victorian lady. Charley, in uniform, is seated slightly behind Effie with his hand on the top of her chair, glancing over her shoulder at the letter. The effect is restrained yet surprisingly intimate. The portrait calls to mind the motto that Charley selected for their betrothal: "In essentials, unity;—in non-essentials, freedom; in all things, love."[9]

Effie and Charley were a good match, and they knew it; their friends and family were delighted with the engagement as well. "My dear Charley," a happy Uncle James wrote, "you could not have done anything better for yourself or your friends, and as for me, the name of her and hers is associated with my dearest recollections. . . . To be the betrothed of such a woman as Effie . . . is the most honorable brevet a man can receive."[10] An equally approving friend reported that "Charles appears perfectly happy, as well he may be for Effie is a very fine girl, true and full of character."[11] From Effie's side, Rob affectionately remembered to Charley that "just after you were engaged you said to me: 'Am I not a lucky fellow?' and I must say I think you are. There are not many girls like Effie; though she is my sister, I may say it."[12] Even Sarah, who had reservations about war marriages, expressed her delight "when we found this new son (who I will say in passing, *suits* us exactly)."[13] Despite the nine-year gap in their ages, Charley and Effie had much in common: a love of art, literature, and music; a devotion to sporting activities, especially horseback riding; and most of all an earnest approach to life. Years later, Josephine wrote a description of her husband in which she enumerated his outstanding qualities: "energy, public spirit, courage, intellect . . . [and] idealism."[14]

By the time Effie met the battle-weary Charley, however, some of his idealism and much of his earnestness had been rubbed thin; perhaps her enthusiasms reminded him of his own youthful inclinations for pure intellectual pursuits. In the fall of 1862 Lowell had already established a reputation as a brave and intelligent soldier, but unlike Rob, who had no earlier career to speak of, Charley brought to his army post a wealth of experience and talents. In fact, he was considered by peers to be the best and brightest of his generation of Boston Brahmins. Chosen at nineteen to give the valedictorian speech at the 1854 Harvard Commencement, Charley delivered "The Reverence Due from Old Men to Young" with a natural élan that was his characteristic style. An ardent admirer of Emerson's idea of "self-culture," Charley blended his intellectual bent with a life of action. To this end, he was successively a mechanic in an iron mill, a treasurer for a western railroad, a manager for an ironworks manufacturing company, and now, as Effie became engaged to him, a newly minted cavalry commander. Despite his successes, however, and despite the many things that he and Effie had in common, there was one outstanding, and for Charley, painful, difference: the Shaws were a family of wealth, power, and distinction, whereas Charley's branch of the Lowell family was relatively poor, struggling, and, because of his father, disgraced. It had not always been so.

✑ *"Where the Lowells Talk Only to Cabots"* ✑

Charles Russell Lowell was born on January 2, 1835, into a family whose bloodlines typify the old comic adage: "And this is good old Boston / The home of the bean and the cod / Where the Lowells talk only to Cabots / And the Cabots talk only to God." His mother, Anna Cabot Lowell Jackson, was the daughter of Patrick Tracy Jackson, who with his brother-in-law Francis Cabot Lowell founded the Boston Manufacturing Company, pioneering the cotton manufacturing industry that would thrive on New England soil. Charley's father, also named Charles Russell, was the first born of six to the Reverend Charles Lowell and Harriet Spence of Elmwood, Massachusetts. The Reverend Lowell was senior minister of Boston's elite West Church for fifty years and a staunch supporter of abolitionism in the 1840s and 1850s.[15] Francis Cabot Lowell, the business partner of Charley's maternal grandfather, was the older brother of Reverend Lowell. The youngest of that family was James Russell Lowell, who would become nineteenth-century America's most famous poet and critic.

Charles Russell Senior graduated from Harvard in 1826 and went to work in the family business. His marriage to his cousin Anna, followed by the birth of their son Charley in 1835, solidified his standing as a young prosperous merchant with an assured future. A change of fortune, however, soon dimmed the prospects of this attractive family, which would grow to include three more children (Anna, Harriet, and James). Charles Lowell lost all of his assets in the financial panic of 1837, and worse yet, as custodian of his parents' estate while they were traveling in Europe, he lost theirs as well. This catastrophe meant that the entire family fortune (estimated at $400,000) was wiped out for Lowell's brothers and sisters and that his aging father would have to rely solely on his small ministerial income. There were also rumors of financial mismanagement and moral turpitude on the part of Charles Lowell that ended once and for all his business career in Boston. For the rest of his life he occupied a series of menial jobs that were beneath his education, his dignity, and his expectations of material comfort. It was a bitter pill for his family to swallow.[16]

Fortunately, Anna Lowell possessed pluck and intelligence. She began a finishing school for young ladies out of the family home in Winter Place, a few yards away from the Boston Common. She became a successful teacher, published several books on education, and was known for her no-nonsense approach to the intellectual training of the fashionable girls who attended her school. Effie Shaw was just one of the students who benefited from her plain, down-to-earth way of teaching. Anna Lowell's school helped to preserve her family's social position and was just successful enough to provide a marginal income. Effie later wrote that Charley and his siblings "were brought up in *poverty* though surrounded by people of refinement and education, having, in fact, all the advantages of both poverty and riches, and none of the disadvantages of either."[17] Anna's burdens were considerably lightened by her enjoyment of her children, particularly Charley, who was a bright, energetic boy who excelled in both school and sports. He was first scholar at both the English and Latin high schools in Boston and, at age fifteen, the youngest of his class at Harvard. Charley, his brother, Jim, and their cousin William Lowell Putnam (Willie) were the beloved young companions of their doting Uncle James. He took his three nephews on long summer vacations to the Adirondacks and engaged in vigorous snow battles with them during the Boston winters. Later, after all three of his nephews had died in the Civil War, their grieving uncle commemorated them in his poem "Memoriae Positum": "I speak of one while with sad eyes I think of three."

Charley Lowell shone brilliantly at Harvard, and his future seemed limitless in that spring of 1854. Yet the one path his family expected him to embark on—a business career to recoup the family fortunes—was the one least attractive to him. He had cut his scholarly teeth on the philosophy of Ralph Waldo Emerson, the sage of Concord: "If young men bring nothing but their strength and their spirit, the world may well spare them," Lowell wrote for his valedictory address. "But they do bring it something better: they bring it their fresher and purer ideals."[18] Charley felt himself most suited for writing or teaching, but, alas, a life devoted to learning was never to be his good fortune to possess. "For our family, work is absolutely necessary," he wrote his mother from the Ames Company Iron Mill in Chicopee, Massachusetts, where he was already employed as a laborer to learn the ropes of the business.[19] For the next year, Charley would strive to lessen his parents' financial burdens. His work at the Chicopee mill was rewarded with an offer of a position in management at the iron-rolling mills in Trenton, New Jersey. There he briefly excelled until his health failed him. Always possessed of a somewhat frail constitution, Charley suffered increasingly from bouts of "listlessness" at Trenton. One day a friend found him in his rooms bleeding from the lungs. Upon hearing the diagnosis of tuberculosis, Lowell resigned from his job and came home to recover.

His recovery was accelerated by the news that his grandmother Jackson was going to supply the funds that would enable him to enjoy a two-year European sojourn, where months of horseback riding, walking and hiking trips, rest and relaxation would make him, for the first time in his life, completely hardy and healthy. Lowell's stay encompassed trips to Spain, Switzerland, Austria, Germany, and Algiers and included an attendance at the maneuvers of the French and Austrian armies. He became an expert horseman and took swordsmanship lessons in Algiers. He became proficient in French, German, and Italian, and by the time he arrived back in America in July 1858, he was not only fit in body but had notably expanded his mental horizons as well. Charley's trip had allowed him to contemplate in leisure his ambivalent feelings about his career in business. He speculated in letters to his best friends from Harvard—Henry Lee Higginson, James Savage, Stephen Perkins, William James Potter, John C. Bancroft, and Franklin B. Sanborn—about different life options: farming, opening a school, emigration to Kansas as an antislavery man.[20] All of these plans foundered, however, in the painful reality of the Lowell family finances.

Fortunately for Charley, a very powerful man, John Murray Forbes, the Boston magnate and the Shaws' cousin, developed a fatherly interest in him (dating from Charley's Harvard years) and advanced a plan for his future. Forbes invited Charley to Naushon in August 1858 to persuade him to accept the position of assistant treasurer of the Burlington and Missouri River Railroad. Very soon, Charley found himself installed in Burlington, Iowa, far away from the capitals of Europe.

Charley could have done worse than accept the wealthy and cultivated John Murray Forbes as his mentor. Forbes was one of the most powerful men in Boston. He was currently in the process of divesting himself of his interests in shipping and merchandising and switching his investments to railroads when he bought and renamed the Chicago, Burlington, and Quincy Railroad in 1856. Forbes had big plans for railroad investment and big plans for Charley as a man whom he could train to assume an important position in his business. Forbes's impressions of Charley were recorded in a letter to a friend who also knew him: "One of the strange things has been how he magnetized you and me at first sight. We are both practical, unsentimental, and perhaps hard . . . Yet he captivated me, just as he did you, and I came home and told my wife I had fallen in love; and from that day I never saw anything too good or too high for him."[21] Forbes would be instrumental in securing for Charley his next two positions in industry as well as his most important post in the Civil War. A nice aspect of this relationship for Lowell was that Forbes shared many of his intellectual interests, as well as a commitment to antislavery sentiments. At Burlington, where the "pin feathers [were] still very apparent," Charley worked long and hard, not only putting the railroad's financial house in order but bearing the responsibility for the development of 300,000 acres of a government land grant. His salary for the year was $800.[22] Forbes thought his work brilliant and wanted to send him to Calcutta to work for Russell & Co. to gain international business experience.

Lowell regretfully declined this tempting offer, fearing that his newly gained health would be endangered by a long stay in India. He was also concerned about the effect of another prolonged absence on his family, who depended on him not only for financial support but for emotional sustenance as well. Anna Lowell shared with him the burden of Charles Senior's failure. Charley wrote, "A sound man feels that he has a right, himself, to dispose of himself, but a fellow who has been ill feels that his kindred have a new claim on him. My mother's hold upon me has increased tenfold within four years,—and she *must* be included in my plans for the next ten years."[23] Lowell's responsibilities were heavy, and while other young men of his age were having fun courting young ladies and getting married, he pledged his loyalty to his mother. "At present," he reassured her, "I am not against marriage, but certainly not for it—if ever I meet *the* wife, the matter may have some interest for me."[24]

By then, in the spring of 1860, his fancy was turned by other prospects. Like Rob Shaw, he followed the political breakdown of the country with keen interest: "Deliberately I prefer Lincoln to Seward," he wrote a friend.[25] With the politics of secession in the air, Lowell once again switched jobs. Through the good auspices of John Murray Forbes, he secured a position as iron master at the Mount Savage, Maryland, ironworks, where he presided over a small army of laborers. From the vantage point of a border state, Lowell watched the unfolding drama of the dissolution of the union. When war broke out, he for the last time quit a job in industry and went to Washington on foot to offer his services as a citizen-soldier for the Union Army. On July 1, 1861, Charley was commissioned as a captain in the regular army. A new career had begun.

By the time Effie met Charley in the fall of 1862, he had advanced quickly through the regular army's ranks and had earned a reputation as a fine soldier. After his appointment as captain in the Third (later Sixth) U.S. Cavalry, Lowell was put in charge of a squadron. The Third participated in General McClellan's Peninsular campaign, where Charley distinguished himself in the battles of Williamsburg and Slaterville. For his services, Charley was not only promoted to major but placed on General McClellan's staff. Again under McClellan, Charley fought in the battle of Antietam, where he escaped serious injury but where he did not emerge unscathed: "His horse was shot twice, his scabbard cut in two, and the overcoat on the saddle spoiled by a piercing bullet."[26] For a spectacular act of bravery during the battle, the young major was selected by McClellan to present the captured Confederate battle flags to President Lincoln, which was, as Rob approvingly wrote his mother, "considered a good deal of an honour."[27] Around this time, Effie recorded in her diary the death of a friend, Wilder Dwight, who was killed at Antietam. "One after the other," she wrote, "we hear of our friends falling off and still our dearest aren't touched. I wonder why?"[28] Charley did not share in her good fortune. On July 4, 1862, his only brother, James Jackson Lowell, died of wounds received in the battle of Glendale. Jim, a first lieutenant in the Twentieth Massachusetts Infantry, was, like Charley, a superb scholar at Harvard, and a lawyer.

✍ Departures ✍

After Antietam, Lowell was offered the command of a new cavalry unit, which would be called the Second Massachusetts Cavalry. Among the backers of the battalion was none other than John Murray Forbes, who was as impressed with Charley's military prowess as he had been with his business skills. Charley eagerly accepted this challenge, was promoted to colonel, and came home to Boston in late 1862 to begin recruiting the men for his own regiment. His pleasure and pride in doing this were doubled when he became engaged to Effie. Charley also took pride in viewing the progress of Rob's unit, which trained near his own on the Readville grounds. "You will be very glad to hear that Bob Shaw is to be Colonel, . . . of the Governor's Negro Regiment," he wrote to his mother. "It is very important that it should be started soberly and not spoilt by too much fanaticism. Bob Shaw is not a fanatic."[29]

The early months of 1863 were an exciting time for the two young engaged couples, Charley and Effie and Rob and Annie. Charley and Rob were staying at a Mrs. Crehore's boardinghouse while training their soldiers at Camp Meigs, less than half a mile away. These pleasant accommodations were also used by the Shaws, the Haggertys, and the Lowells while visiting their sons at camp and viewing the training of their respective regiments. Effie and Annie stayed at Mrs. Crehore's with their families, and without them as well, in separate rooms from their fiancés, of course. Maintaining propriety was important, especially in wartime. Sarah kept a watchful eye on her children both when she was in Boston and from her Staten Island home. Perhaps it was receiving a series of breezy lines ("Effie and Charley are well and enjoying each other," Rob had written her) that prompted Sarah to issue a stern warning to her son and daughter to behave themselves. "I have received 2 notes from you, one about our course of conduct at Aunt Mary's," a chastened Rob replied to Sarah. He burned her letter and promised to be more careful about their behavior.[30] Nonetheless, romance and war combined to create a festive atmosphere for the young couples. Henry Lee Higginson reported to Effie that "all the girls in Boston are wild about your engagement."[31] Numerous Boston relatives feted the couple with tea parties, dinners, and dances. "Charley and Effie arrived safely night before last," Rob reassured his mother. "The latter found some beautiful bouquets awaiting her, and yesterday received a swarm of visitors."[32]

Robert Gould Shaw and Annie Kneeland Haggerty were married on May 2, 1863, in New York City. They had a brief honeymoon in the Lenox, Massachusetts, farmhouse of Annie's father and the next week returned to Mrs. Crehore's (presumably to share one room), where Effie was currently residing.[33] Their married life together, even more so than Effie and Charley's, was destined to be brief, for on May 18, Secretary of War Stanton sent a telegram to Colonel Shaw ordering him to report to General David Hunter, commander of the South, with headquarters at Hilton Head Island, off the coast of South Carolina. The historic regiment was ready to fight. The Fifty-fourth Massachusetts, under the command of Rob Shaw, had already become a powerful symbol of hope for all abolitionists and African Americans. "I stand or fall as a man and a magistrate, with the rise and fall in history of the Fifty-Fourth Massachusetts Regiment," declared Governor Andrew at the ceremony for the presentation of regimental colors the day before the unit departed Boston. Present in the audience was the Shaw family, including Effie and Charley, and how their hearts must have swelled with pride to hear the governor address these remarks directly to Rob: "I know not, Sir, when in all human history, to any given thousands of men in arms, there has been committed a work at once so proud, so precious, so full of hope and glory, as the work committed to you."[34]

The sun shone brilliantly in a cloudless blue sky the next day, May 28, 1863, as the handsome and ramrod-straight twenty-six-year-old Colonel Robert Gould Shaw led his Negro troops down Boston's Beacon Street to the accompaniment of cheers and huzzahs from the 20,000 spectators who lined the route. Finally, after months of training at Readville, near the site of the old Brook Farm, Rob's Fifty-fourth Massachusetts Regiment, the first authorized northern all-black fighting unit, was leaving with fanfare and bound for South Carolina in a new transport ship, the *De Molay*. As Rob neared the family house (from his mother's side) at 44 Beacon Street where his bride, his parents, and his sisters were watching from the second-floor balcony, he stopped his horse briefly to raise and kiss his sword. He may have recalled his mother's warm words of praise to him on hearing of his acceptance, after hesitation, of the command: "God rewards a hundred fold every good aspiration of his children, and this is my reward for asking [for] my children not earthly honors, but souls to see the right and courage to follow it. Now I feel ready to die, for I see you willing to give your support to the cause of truth that is lying crushed and bleeding."[35] At this grand moment, soon enough to be followed by a lifetime of grief, Frank and Sarah had every reason to glory in their son's dedication to duty. The arming and training of black soldiers to fight for their own freedom had long been an abolitionist goal. Rob was a major instrument in fulfilling that goal, not only because he was battle-tested but because of who his parents were and what they stood for.

Among the scores of dignitaries, great and small, attending the festivities was a very young William James, whose brother Wilkinson (Wilkie) was an officer with the Fifty-fourth. The future philosopher, who along with his brother Henry would watch the war from the sidelines, caught sight of his friend Effie and her fiancé, Charley, watching the parade. Josephine Shaw Lowell, he later wrote, was "surely one of our noblest and freest." Together Effie and Charley "came whirling up on horseback, and drew up close behind to where I was standing among the crowd of spectators. I looked back and saw their faces and figures against the evening sky, and they looked so young and victorious, that I, much gnawed by questions as to my own duty of enlisting or not, shrank back—they had not seen me—from being recognized."[36]

As they watched the *De Molay* sail off to the Carolinas, Effie and Charley were keenly aware of their own now limited time. Charley also had orders to move. Army headquarters requested that the Second Massachusetts Cavalry report for action immediately in Maryland. There Colonel Lowell and the Second would soon be occupied with guarding the Potomac against Confederate attacks while the great campaign of Gettysburg was in its early stages. Later, the Second protected Washington's lines of communications against Colonel John S. Mosby's raiders, the notorious Confederate guerrilla unit that plagued the Union Army in northern Virginia. It was late May when

Charley's orders were received, and the advent of summer meant the resumption of hard fighting. Before he left, Charley and Effie fixed their wedding date for the upcoming fall. During the next few months, with Effie back in Staten Island, letters would have to suffice until they could be together again. ("I picked a morning-glory (a white one) for you," wrote Charley.)[37] Meanwhile, in June, Effie resumed her work for the Sanitary Commission, hoping against hope that September would find both her betrothed and her brother alive and well.

✑ The Staten Island Draft Riots ✑

Events were moving swiftly well before the summer. When President Lincoln issued the final Emancipation Proclamation on New Year's Day, 1863, he released the joyous emotions of African Americans, abolitionists, and their sympathizers within the Republican party. The early months of 1863 also witnessed the rise to power of the Peace Democrats, so called because they desired an end to the war on terms favorable to the South. Tired of the war's seemingly endless killing and destruction, unencumbered by any idealistic desire to end slavery, and fearful that the consequences of the Emancipation Proclamation would bring forth hordes of ex-slaves to inhabit the North, large numbers of voters, particularly in the Northwest, strongly supported the nearly treasonous proposals of the Peace Democrats.

As Lincoln and the Republicans wrestled with the troublesome issues of wartime civil liberties now raised by these Democrats, they were also burdened by the defeats of the Army of the Potomac at Fredericksburg and Chancellorsville, and the apparently fruitless maneuvers by General Ulysses S. Grant's western Army of the Tennessee to capture Vicksburg, the Confederate citadel guarding the Mississippi River. "If there is a worse place than Hell, than I am in it," declared Lincoln during this low point for the Union cause.[38] The war's nadir was made grimmer for the Republican party, which had already suffered setbacks in the fall elections of 1862, when in March 1863 Congress passed a Conscription Act, calling for the first inductions that July. Deeply resented by many working-class people was the provision that allowed for the hiring of a substitute for $300, thus in their eyes making it a "rich man's war." Even though subsequent research has shown that the draft did not penalize the working poor unduly, and that, in fact, they were far less likely to serve than other social groups, the draft and the substitution clause became rallying points for those dissatisfied with the war and its perceived injustices.[39]

The Peace Democrats and their supporters reserved a special animus for abolitionist New Englanders, who were allegedly urging the president to prolong the war. In the East, New York City's Democratic politicians and party newspapers fanned the flames of working-class resentment created by the Emancipation Proclamation, the draft, the specter of growing job competition with blacks, and the unpopular Yankee-Protestant leadership of the Republican party to create a volatile atmosphere. Thus, when the federal draft officers entered the city on July 11, 1863, to begin the drawing of names, angry men and women commenced their four-day rampage on the streets of New York, which left 105 people dead. The New York City Draft Riots, which actually began early on July 13, involved mobs of mostly Irish Americans, whose violence terrorized New Yorkers until the police, with help from Union Army troops called away from Gettysburg, restored peace to the city on July 17. Those particularly at risk were African Americans, well-known abolitionists, Republicans, and any man who looked as if he could pay the $300 exemption fee. In addition, the rioters' actions starkly illuminated a city deeply divided along racial and class lines.[40] The shock waves and the violence also extended to nearby Staten Island, where the African-American population was tiny, but where a visible and distinguished enclave of abolitionists and Republicans, including the Shaws, the Gays, and the Curtises, had established itself.

The Staten Island draft riots were hardly of the same magnitude as the one in New York City, but they elicited similar fearful responses from the black and white citizenry. From July 14 to July 20, small bands of Irish youth terrified the island's inhabitants. At first they attacked all the African Americans they could locate and burned their homes and businesses. One black woman was beaten to death, and a Mr. Green, a former butler for the Shaw family who had established a thriving catering business, suffered the total destruction of his shop. Most African-American Staten Islanders found refuge in the woods until the rioters had run their course. When the mob ran out of black targets, it turned its rage on the people known to be friends of African Americans, the abolitionists, and the Republicans. "The little colony of Abolitionists," according to one local history, "who lived in the neighborhood of Sailors Snug Harbor were in imminent danger. Many threats of violence were reported to them, and many families left their own homes at night and sought safety with neighbors who had arms, or who were not so obnoxious to the mobocrats."[41]

The Shaws and the Curtises were among those who lived in Sailors Snug Harbor. George Curtis spirited Anna and their two children away to Boston and then returned to New York City to collect Horace Greeley and Wendell Phillips, two men who attracted the mob's anger, and hid them safely in his Staten Island house. John Murray Forbes recollected how the Shaws comported themselves during the disturbance. Forbes had arrived in New York City just as the riots began, and so "for safety we dispatched Alice early Monday morning to Staten Island to our cousin, Frank Shaw, where, as he was a well-known abolitionist, she found herself out of the frying pan and into the fire; but good George Ward took her and all the Shaws into his house, and no harm came to them."[42] George Ward was a neighbor of the Shaws and the Gays who sheltered both families during the worst of the rioting.

Effie must have been greatly comforted to have Alice Forbes by her side as they spent several nights together hiding at the Wards' home. Martin Gay, a son of Sidney and Elizabeth Gay, later wrote about one of those nights:

> As the reports grew worse and the mob was said to be only waiting for a leader to start up the street, we gathered in the kitchen, which was at the end of the house nearest the back gate, ready to make our run the moment the word came that the mob had started. That July night of '63 was hot, close and threatening rain, and the fire which had cooked dinner had not yet gone out in the range, and we women and children were packed close in the hot, dark kitchen, waiting for the order to run . . . and then presently a scout . . . came in and said the mob was dispersing.[43]

Finally, order was restored to Staten Island as it had been in New York City, but any relief the Shaws may have felt was obliterated by the news that on July 18 Rob was killed leading his regiment into battle at Fort Wagner, South Carolina.

✑ *"One Gallant Rush"* ✐

The fate of Rob and Charley and their respective regiments was being watched anxiously by the Shaws of Staten Island that June and

July of 1863. While Charley was chasing after Mosby's raiders, the Fifty-fourth Massachusetts had proven itself a viable fighting force on James Island along the South Carolina coast. Rob was eager to build on his regiment's successes and asked to be included in a planned assault on Fort Wagner, located on Morris Island, which had so far defended Charleston from the constant bombardments of the Union Army. Northern guns had already begun to shell the fort, but to no avail. It was not an auspicious beginning, and several officers expressed misgivings about the strategic wisdom of the operation. Shaw's commanding officer, General George C. Strong, a thirty-three-year-old West Pointer, announced that they would attempt a direct assault on the previously impregnable Confederate earthwork: "He looked straight at Shaw. 'You may lead the column if you say yes. Your men, I know, are worn out, but do as you choose.'"[44] The Fifty-fourth was indeed tired out from their recent fighting on James Island, and suffered as well from shortages of food and water, but Shaw and his men gladly accepted Strong's challenge.

The inclusion of the Fifty-fourth Massachusetts Regiment in this assault testified to Rob's persistence in bringing the bright potential of his unit to the attention of his superiors. In both conversations and letters, Rob insisted that the black soldier, contrary to the low expectations expressed by northern white doubters within and without the military, would prove himself if given a chance. The Fifty-fourth had shown its fighting ability on James Island, but it was a relatively minor battle compared with the imminent attack on Fort Wagner, which, if successful, could have led to the fall of Charleston, a major goal of Union forces in the South. With such an outcome, it was believed that the Fifty-fourth would vindicate its founders and well-wishers.[45]

Others have written at length and in great detail about the Fifty-fourth Massachusetts Regiment's dramatic failure at Fort Wagner, which remained impervious to Union attacks. Suffice it to say that Colonel Shaw and his men, both officers and enlisted, acquitted themselves with an almost inhuman display of courage and daring. Rob's death came as he scaled the battery's defenses:

> Right in the van on the red rampart's slippery swell
> With heart that beat a charge he fell
> Forward as fits a man

> But the high soul burns on to light men's feet
> Where death for noble ends makes dying sweet.[46]

James Russell Lowell's poetic depiction stands in stark contrast to the reality of the battle's aftermath. Rob's body was thrown into a trench with those of his privates, in contrast to the "decent" burials given the other Union officers who died. The Confederate officer responsible for this decision, General Johnson Hagood, explained: "I shall bury him in the common trench with the Negroes that fell with him." In the North, a shortened and more potent version of his quote circulated: "He is buried with his niggers."[47] Later, when efforts were made to retrieve Shaw's remains from the mass grave, Frank protested. The poet Robert Lowell later immortalized that protest: "Shaw's father wanted no monument / except the ditch, where his son's body was thrown / and lost with his 'niggers.'"[48]

The northern press and public celebrated the sacrifice of the Fifty-fourth, and overnight the regiment became a powerful symbol for African-American manliness. Now the path was cleared for the full-scale recruitment of African-American regiments, which added significantly to the Union's manpower. And the young Colonel Shaw was already being memorialized as an abolitionist hero. This offered some cold comfort in the Shaw homestead, where many tears were being shed. The strength of their convictions and the fact that they had urged and expected Rob to accept the command could not cushion his family from the sorrow they felt upon his death. A grieving Sarah tried to explain her feelings to a friend: "He and I . . . had often talked over this possible end, and we thought we were ready, if it should come. It found him ready, but not so, his Mother."[49]

Among the letters of condolence flooding the Shaw household were those of Charley to Effie. Just a month earlier Lowell had received a letter from his prospective brother-in-law affectionately reminding him of their new family connection and expressing hope that "this war will not finish one or both of us, and that we shall live to know each other well."[50] Charley's letters to Effie were full of warm praise for Rob: "When I think how Rob's usefulness had latterly been increasing, how the beauty of his character had been becoming a power, widely felt, how his life had become something more than a promise, I feel as if his father's loss were the heaviest: sometime perhaps we can make him feel that he has other sons, but now remember that in a man's grief for a son whose manhood had just opened . . . there is something different from what any woman's grief can be." In another letter he consoled Sarah: "Give my love to your mother;—it is a very great comfort to know that his life had such a perfect ending. I see now that the best Colonel of the best black regiment had to die, it was a sacrifice we owed,—and how could it have been paid more gloriously?"[51]

✎ Marriage ✎

The tragedy of Rob's death did not deter—indeed, it seemed to make more urgent—Effie and Charley's wedding plans. And as the summer faded into fall, their excitement increased as the date drew close. Charley expected to receive a twenty-day leave of absence sometime in the fall, get married in a "quiet, simple and sacred" ceremony, and then live with his bride at winter headquarters in Vienna, Virginia. He wrote to a friend describing Effie as his "Commander-in-Chief." Laughingly, Charley went on to say, "She is not such a veteran as Halleck, but I think she can manage men better, in the field or anywhere else." These were good days for Charley, although a persistent worry for him (besides being killed in the war) was his chronic lack of funds. The young and penniless colonel wrote on the eve of their marriage, "I have nothing as you know; I am going to marry upon nothing; I am going to make my wife as happy upon nothing as if I could give her a fortune." Charley often wrote to Effie about the necessity of their living frugally until his position in life was secured: "I don't mean to worry about money, and I don't mean to have you worry; *ergo,* you must expect to see me keep an account-book, and occasionally pull it out and warn you how much water we are drawing, and how much there is under our keel."

Charley's insistence to Effie and others on the scarcity of their resources and the merits of frugality may have arisen out of a proud desire to not accept any money from Frank and Sarah, at least in the immediate future, but it did not reflect the reality of the Shaws' great wealth. Effie and her sisters were all provided with comfortable incomes during their parents' lifetimes with the knowledge that their inheritance would be considerable. Had he lived, Charley would have been a rich man, both through his marriage and perhaps through a continuation of his business career. Charley's concern about finances was part of his sensitivity to the imbalance of power in their relation-ship, one that his greater age, his worldly experiences, and his man-hood could not assuage. This feeling would be entirely in keeping with Charley's sense of pride and honor, which gave rise to his belief, as stated to Effie, that "we can live suitably and worthily . . . and be very happy . . . only we must start right."[52]

They did "start right," and their wedding ceremony was as under-stated as they both wished. Josephine Shaw and Charles Russell Low-ell were married on October 31, 1863, in Staten Island's Unitarian Chapel, where "the light comes softened and glorified through win-dows of richly colored glass."[53] Soon afterward Josephine went to live in the small farmhouse that also served as her husband's headquarters in Vienna. Officers' wives in camp were hardly an uncommon sight during the Civil War, especially in the winter months when fighting was at a minimum. This was especially true with the Army of the Potomac, where wives (and sometimes the whole family) were joined by many other women working as cooks, laundresses, nurses, and of course the inevitable contingent of prostitutes. Thus the dreary winter months were enlivened by balls, parties, feasts, and various celebra-tory occasions that boosted the men's morale. Many ordinary married soldiers, however, resented the officers' privilege of having their wives in camp, while they had to content themselves with letters and occa-sional furloughs home. Sarah Shaw was very much opposed to this class-based injustice and feared that Rob would take advantage of his officer rank to live with Annie in camp. Rob never did ask his wife to come, as he said "it is the last thing I should desire, as I have seen the evil consequences of it very often."[54] Apparently Sarah's advice went unheeded (if ever offered) in the case of her daughter and Charley, and they began their married life in the relatively peaceful environment of the winter army camp.

As might be expected, the young couple spent as much time as possible together, despite Charley's frequent absences in pursuit of Mosby's raiders, who did not take the winter off. "We have a good canter every day," Charley wrote to his best friend, and "have enough books, and only have not enough time to read them."[55] Their first and only home together boasted just a few of the necessary amenities, but what it lacked in civilization it made up for in happiness and content-ment. The Lowells soon became known for their simple hospitality, and their home offered a lively gathering place for other officers and their families. Effie characteristically chafed at idle days, and with Charley's approval, she volunteered her services to the camp's hospital. "I remember you quite well as a young wife at Vienna," wrote one of Charley's soldiers, "during the winter of 1863–64 when you would tramp through the Virginia mud from the house on the hill where Brigade Headquarters were down to the tavern used as a hospital near the railroad track."[56]

Once there, Effie wrote letters for disabled patients, attended the last rites of the dying, and brought cheer and good news to the injured soldiers. Her uncommon language skills were also put to good use. The camp's chaplain recalled that "she delighted the Frenchmen, Italians, and Germans, by conversing with them in their own languages, that so vividly recalled their early homes."[57] When not in attendance at the hospital, Effie tutored a few ex-slaves in the rudiments of reading and writing. Finally, in whatever spare time she had left over—when not with Charley or entertaining or volunteering at the hospital or teaching—she read serious books, bringing forth this amazed response from friend Henry Higginson: "Do you know that I found Effie had read Mill's 'Political Economy,' three times this winter?"[58] Effie was not always so serious. She dreamed of a time when Charley would be removed from the constant danger of war and they could travel abroad together for a delayed honeymoon.[59]

In the nine months they lived together as husband and wife, Effie and Charley showed themselves to be an exemplary couple both in terms of private happiness and public spirit. Effie's extracurricular activities elicited much favorable comment from all quarters in Vienna, and she was even said to have brought a "kindly and refining influence" to the camp. But Effie's wifely role came to its inevitable end in July 1864, when the guns of war once again thundered, and Charley was called away. Before Effie left the camp, Charley presented her with his favorite horse, Berold, who was then stabled at her parents' home, and who outlived his master by many years. Effie returned to Staten Island to await the birth of their first child, due that November. She was also left to suffer the intense anxiety of the Civil War soldier's wife, as one relative vividly described: "Ah, my Effie! well I remember the white and firm set lips with which more than once last summer, you went to the Post office before driving round the island— the eager clutch—with which you seized your letter and gave one glance at it, to see if it bore tidings of life or death, then sank back with a sigh of half relief."[60]

Effie's departure from Virginia roughly coincided with a new and concerted effort on the part of President Lincoln to reinvigorate the Army of the Potomac with new leadership and a grand strategy to win the war. To this end, Lincoln brought east the hero of Vicksburg and Chattanooga, General Ulysses S. Grant, who came with his own plan to activate all Union armies simultaneously to destroy the Army of Virginia, capture Richmond and Atlanta, and clear out the Shenandoah Valley. The latter campaign involved Colonel Charles Russell Lowell, who since July of 1863 commanded a brigade consisting of the Second Massachusetts and two small regiments from New York. Lowell was placed under the command of another newly arrived western hero, General Philip H. Sheridan, head of all units of the U.S. Cavalry. In early August 1864, against the background of the siege of Petersburg and General William T. Sherman's battle for Atlanta, Grant ordered Sheridan to remove from the Shenandoah Valley the Confederates and their general, Jubal Early, and to destroy the abundant resources of the valley, which were being used to succor the enemy. Charley's excellent battle record was rewarded in early September when General Sheridan appointed him to lead the Reserve Brigade, which was comprised of the First, Second, and Fifth U.S. Cavalry regiments, Battery D of the Second U.S. Artillery, and of course Charley's own Second Massachusetts. After training, Charley and his brigade were ready for the tough fighting that lay ahead, as Sheridan pushed forward with the fall campaign. Charley's by-now polished soldiering skills never shone brighter than in the battles that raged throughout the Shenandoah Valley in the autumn of 1864. "Colonel Lowell is a brave man," declared General Sheridan after observing Charley "leaping rail fences to get at the foe . . . and . . . when a stone wall proved too high for leaping, actually riding along it whacking their rifles with his sabre."[61]

Indeed, Charley had gained such a formidable reputation for tireless and ferocious fighting that his friends and comrades wondered aloud when his lucky star would fade. The surgeon of the Second Massachusetts recalled that Charley exposed himself to Confederate bullets so fearlessly that he "dared not look at him for *I knew he would fall,* and yet he came back steadily and all right, his horse always wounded or killed, and himself never, until I began to feel that he was safe—but how, God alone knew."[62] Even Charley half-believed himself to be invincible, and it did seem as if his death-defying actions were somehow miraculously ordained. During the Shenandoah campaign alone, for example, thirteen horses were shot from underneath him. Lowell was considered by his peers to embody the ideals of the officer-gentleman: honorable, modest, brave, and fair. Those ideals were much aspired to but seldom achieved in the heat of battle, to say nothing of the boredom of camp life. Charley seemed to possess them naturally, in a manner that did not arouse jealousy or suspicion but instead inspired loyalty and emulation. Sheridan summed up Lowell's battlefield qualities in this way: "There was no better soldier or brighter man. . . . [H]e united the rare judgment and good eye of a leader to the unflinching courage which marked so many others."[63] Charley enjoyed exercising his role as an officer, which gave him a chance to demonstrate the leadership qualities that he felt were lacking in his business career.

Despite his busy days at the front, Charley found the time to write to Effie often, and their letters reflected tentative hopes for a united future. There was some discussion about whether Charley should remain with the army after the war or seek a position in industry. Effie preferred that he leave the army, and he was coming around to her point of view. In that fall of 1864, Charley was ready to fulfill the brilliant promise of his youth, if he survived the war. In one of his last letters to Effie, he wrote, "I don't want to be shot till I've had a chance to come home. I have no idea that I shall be hit, but I *want* so much not to now, that it sometimes frightens me."[64]

∽ "A Lonely, Lovely Widow" ∾

Several days after that letter was written, Charley finally became unlucky in the battle of Cedar Creek. The background for Cedar Creek was this: the previous two months' campaign by the Union Army had extracted a terrible toll on the Confederates and their resources. Grant's two-part plan to destroy the enemy forces and their breadbasket had worked: Sheridan's attack at Winchester, Virginia, on September 19 had decimated Early's regiments, and when not engaging their foes in action, the Union soldiers were busy burning crops and destroying buildings and livestock.

Although the battle at Winchester proved a devastating blow to the Confederates' position in the Shenandoah Valley, General Robert E.

Lee made one last stand and sent Early reinforcements from Petersburg. In the predawn hours of September 19, 1864, the Union Army was camped near Cedar Creek, awaiting Sheridan's return from a Washington conference, when they were subjected to a surprise attack by Early and his soldiers. The attack focused on the infantry divisions, leaving Colonel Lowell and the cavalry free to engage in some bitter fighting. By 10 A.M., however, the Confederates had decisively routed the Union Army and believed themselves to be the victors in a major battle. But they did not count on Sheridan's swift return by noon, and with his return a brilliant display of generalship by regrouping his frightened men into a fighting unit.

Charley played a large part that day in helping to snatch victory from the jaws of defeat in this important battle, and he was busy fighting at 1 P.M. when he caught a bullet from a sniper's rifle. The force of the bullet collapsed his bad lung, precipitating bleeding, faintness, and hoarseness. His arm had also been broken. Despite this shattering injury, Charley was determined to continue fighting. During a lull in the battle, he reserved his strength by lying on the ground with his coat placed over him for warmth. At 2:30 Sheridan gave orders for Charley's brigade to capture a troublesome battery. Charley had himself lifted back onto his horse, whispered the appropriate commands to his subordinates, and led the charge on the battery. This time Charley's luck truly deserted him, for he was shot immediately, and the bullet severed his spinal cord, leaving him paralyzed below the waist.

While his brigade was winning the fight for the battery, Charley was transported to nearby Middletown, Virginia, where he was placed in a small hospital to await his death. Dr. Oscar DeWolf, the assistant surgeon attached to the Second Massachusetts, was with Charley in his dying hours and remembered that while he seemed to accept his death calmly, he was afraid for Effie. Visibly agitated, Charley grasped the doctor's hand and said, "My poor wife—I am afraid it will kill her." After some discussion on this point, during which Dr. DeWolf pointed out to Charley that Effie had probably considered the possibility of his death and would accept it bravely, Lowell replied that although *he* had thought about his death a lot, he and Effie *together* had never spoken of it much. Finally, Charley seemed reassured about Effie's acceptance of his death, and turned to his friend and said, "She will bear it, Doctor, better than you I think."[65] Later that night Charley, with the assistance of Dr. DeWolf, wrote a few words of farewell to Effie. Colonel Charles Russell Lowell lingered until dawn on October 20, 1864, and then died peacefully in his twenty-ninth year. While Lowell was fighting at Cedar Creek, a commission was signed promoting him to brigadier general. The eight-months-pregnant Effie received the news of Charley's death while embroidering him a pair of shoulder straps for his uniform. According to family legend, she stoically finished them.

Effie was too far advanced in her pregnancy to attend Charley's funeral, held on October 28 at the Harvard College Chapel, three days before their first wedding anniversary. That Friday morning dawned cold and rainy, matching the mood of the grief-stricken relatives and friends who gathered to pay their last respects. The first group of mourners to arrive and take their places was the family—the parents, Anna and Charles, who had lost both their sons in the war, and two of Effie's sisters, whose faces were described as "shining white as marble through their black veils."[66] Charley's body, brought from his parents' house, was placed in a flag-wrapped coffin and set by soldiers on the chapel altar, which was decorated with leaves, evergreens, and flowers. As the college choir chanted, the congregation looked upon his remains for the last time. "I never saw so much grief, on so large a number of faces," wrote one mourner afterwards. The attending minister, Dr. Walker, read lines from a poem composed to honor the Union dead:

> Wrap round his breast the flag that breast defended
> His Country's flag, in battle's front enrolled
> For it he died,—on earth forever ended
> His brave young life lives in each sacred fold.[67]

After the service, the congregation rose as the body was taken out of the chapel to its final resting place at Mount Auburn Cemetery in Cambridge.

On November 30, 1864, five weeks after Charley's death, Effie gave birth to a daughter, Carlotta Russell Lowell, in her parents' Staten Island home. Effie must have been desperately hoping for a boy to replace her dead husband, for when informed that her baby was a girl she "turned her face to the wall and wanted to die."[68] Charles Senior and Anna Lowell, Charley's parents, were also bitterly disappointed by the news of a granddaughter instead of a grandson to carry on the family name and to ease their grief at the loss of their son. It was definitely not an auspicious entrance into the world for the infant Carlotta, but, as one relative remarked kindly, "Isn't it a mercy babies are unconscious when they first come?" But, she continued, at least she "is a splendid looking child, large and strong-looking."[69]

At first Effie was "going about the house with her little girl in her arms, not sad but with a quiet look, as if she were living in another world."[70] Effie's cousin, Fanny Hooper, repeated Sarah Shaw's words describing her daughter as "growing sadder every day. She hardly ever goes downstairs and sees almost no one."[71] Effie was often to be found in her sitting room, where she spent many hours surrounded by the mementos of her brief marriage. In this room she contemplated her lonely future and began the painful process of reassembling her life. It would not be easy for her.

Effie's experiences in the Civil War defined both her private and public identities. Seventeen years old when the war began, the adolescent Effie witnessed the most turbulent, devastating, and bloody period in American history. At the war's end, she was a twenty-one-year-old widow with a baby girl to raise. During these few years, Effie endured terrible tragedy within an exceedingly dramatic and exciting context. With her widowhood, however, came a realization of a heavy burden being placed on her youthful shoulders. After the war, Effie no longer thought of herself as an individual, free to do this or that as she pleased. She believed that the war and her family's sacrifices in that war obligated her to make the world a better place, as her brother and husband would have done had they lived.

As she sat in her little study, reading and rereading Charley's letters, Effie must have been impressed by the thread that ran through all of his writing: the importance of public service. "I hope," Charley wrote in a letter to Henry Lee Higginson, which Henry shared with Effie, ". . . that you are going to live like a plain Republican, mindful of the beauty and the duty of simplicity. . . . I hope you have outgrown all foolish ambitions and are now content to become a 'useful citizen.' Don't grow rich; if you once begin, you will find it much more difficult to be a useful citizen. The useful citizen is a mighty unpretending hero. But we are not going to have any Country very long unless such heroism is developed."[72] Doubtless these words were etched into Effie's heart, for the idea of the "useful citizen" provided her with the vehicle for reconstructing her life in a way that would bring honor to her husband's and her brother's memories.

That Josephine Shaw Lowell felt this so deeply can be seen in the fact that she never remarried and dressed in black every day for the rest of her life. It can also be seen in the importance she attached to preserving and extending the meaning of the Civil War in her life. One example among many will suffice. During a trip to Europe in 1870, Lowell made the acquaintance of the eminent essayist and historian Thomas Carlyle, who was closely read and admired by both herself and her husband. Carlyle shocked his Northern American admirers by casting his sympathies with the Confederacy during the war. Lowell and Carlyle engaged in several animated discussions on his pro-South views, and she used all of her eloquence to persuade him of the correctness of the Union cause. Shortly after her return to the States, Lowell sent him a marked set of the *Harvard Memorial Biographies*, which commemorated the sacrifices made by Harvard men during the war. Carlyle's emotional reply must have been gratifying to her, to say the least:

> I received your gentle, kind and beautiful message and in obedience to so touching a command, soft to me as sunlight, or moonlight, but imperative as few could be, I have read those lives you marked for me; . . . It would need a heart much harder than mine not to recognize the high and noble spirit that dwelt in those young men, their heroic readiness, complete devotedness, their patience, diligence, shining valor and virtue in the cause they saw to be the highest, while alas! any difference I may feel on that latter point, only deepens to me the sorrowful and noble tragedy each of their lives is. You may believe me . . . I would strew flowers on their graves along with you, and piously bid them rest in Hope! It is not doubtful to me that they also have added this mite to what is the eternal cause of God and man; or that, in circuitous but sure ways, all men Black and White, will infallibly get their profit of the same.[73]

Carlyle's letter shows the power of the recently published (1867) *Biographies* to evoke a visceral response to the collective tragedies of so many young men dead in the prime of their lives. For Lowell, they were more than just a poignant reminder of her late friends and relations, to be dusted off less frequently as the years passed. Indeed, the *Biographies* signified the deepest meaning of her life; they described the crucible in which her character was formed and her destiny clarified through tragic but glorious deaths for an idealistic cause. "Her face was a sad one," remembered a colleague. "She was never able to forget the crushing sorrow of her young womanhood. But we who could not enter into that sorrow, only wonder at its intensity and its duration, recognized that it had sanctified her life."[74]

And so whenever Lowell wished to communicate an intimacy that she could not bring herself to speak of directly—to make someone new and special in her life understand exactly why she was the way she was—she sent them a set of the *Harvard Memorial Biographies*, marked, as usual, by her husband's and her brother's names. They were the key that unlocked the secrets of her heart. Lowell emerged from the Civil War already a symbol of her generation, just because of the fate of her male relations. She set out for herself the task of making her husband's and her brother's sacrifices mean something for her personally and for the larger society. "I do not see that this war has done us as a nation any good," Charles Lowell lamented to his wife, "except on the slave question,—in one sense that is enough; but how is it that it has not taught us a great many other things which we hoped it would?"[75] Josephine Lowell's future would be devoted to ensuring that the country would, in fact, confront and solve the problems it faced in the postwar world.

In 1869 Josephine Shaw Lowell sat for a crayon portrait, elegantly dressed in a black gown with a small ruffle encircling the neckline. She conveys a pensive sadness, entirely suitable for a still-grieving war widow. Yet the portrait also brings out a mature beauty, accentuating her large eyes and generous mouth. The twenty-six-year-old Lowell is noticeably plumper than in her engagement picture of seven years earlier, but her half-turned features are similarly endowed with modesty and reserve. The picture commemorates a special passage in her life—one that straddled the end of the Civil War and the beginning of a new era for herself and her country. Her early widowhood was a time of adjustment—to the demands and the responsibilities of motherhood and to a future without a husband. She was searching for the appropriate work that would do justice to the memories of her loved ones.

✧ *Motherhood and Freedmen's Work* ✧

Lowell quickly forgot her early disappointment in Carlotta's gender and soon became an adoring, attentive parent to her baby, also called "Lotta" and "Bonny." Mother and child remained in Sarah and Frank's home, and their lives were made much brighter by the constant attendance of cousins, aunts, uncles, and grandparents. At this time all three of Lowell's sisters resided in close proximity on Staten Island, and visits between houses were frequent. Josephine's youngest sister, Nellie (Ellen), was married in 1867 to the widower Francis Channing Barlow, dubbed "The Boy General" by journalists during the war. Barlow knew the Shaws from Brook Farm, and Francis, an excellent student who in 1855 graduated first in his Harvard class, tutored Rob for his 1856 entrance examinations. Trained in law, Francis Barlow launched a long and successful career in public service, when in November 1865 he was elected as New York's secretary of state. Shortly after their marriage, Francis and Ellen Shaw Barlow came to live on Staten Island, joining Frank and Sarah, George and Anna Shaw Curtis, and Robert and Susanna Shaw Minturn.

Lowell and her daughter also made frequent visits to Massachusetts to visit Charley's parents and sisters. And, of course, there were many other relatives to visit as well. One year, when Carlotta was three, Lowell came to Boston to visit her cousin Clover Hooper, who would shortly marry Henry Adams. That occasion was recorded for posterity by Clover's sister-in-law, Fanny Hooper. Lowell's stay, wrote Fanny, "has been a great spice for the family," for although she "looks tired and worn all the time," she is "lovely with Bonny, who is very much interested in everything going on." Hooper offered to give Lotta a children's party featuring the traditional food of "bread and milk and sponge cake, but Mrs. Lowell assured her that [Bonny] would be contented with nothing short of ice cream and flowers on the table."[76]

During that same visit, Lowell and Hooper sallied forth one evening to a women's suffrage meeting where they signed a petition in favor of the suffrage movement. In 1867 suffragists were reeling from the Fourteenth Amendment's insertion of the word "male" in the Constitution and thus making women's nonvoting status the law of the land. They fought against the Fourteenth (and the Fifteenth) Amendments, most notably in a referendum campaign in Kansas. Sarah and Frank Shaw supported their efforts with financial donations, and their daughter echoed their feelings. Lowell would be a firm but quiet supporter of the suffragists, writing that "I . . . desire very strongly to vote myself, and it seems to me that sex is an absurd qualification."[77] But women's suffrage was not closest to Lowell's heart at this or at any other time in her life. In the mid- to late 1860s, all of the Shaws were involved in another worthy enterprise—freedmen's education—and it was this activity that would mark Lowell's emergence from her mourning and her entrance into public service.

Frank and Sarah's old friend William Lloyd Garrison declared at the end of 1864 that the ex-slaves' new freedom would find them "in need of everything that pertains to their physical, intellectual and moral condition."[78] Indeed, many abolitionists had been involved since the early months of the war in founding organizations whose main goals were to bring relief and provide education for the millions of African Americans expected to be liberated by the end of the war. Frank Shaw was active in the Freedmen's Aid movement and served as president of the New England Freedmen's Aid Society, which, along with numerous other local societies, both secular and religious, sought to provide contrabands and ex-slaves with food, medicine, clothes, and other necessities. The limited resources of the voluntary sector proved inadequate to the task at hand and for the future, and abolitionists were among those who pressed the government to create a special agency to address the social, legal, and political challenges posed by the freed slaves. In their most sanguine moments, abolitionists hoped that an array of private and public support services would enable the ex-slaves to achieve within a reasonable amount of time a dignified and stable existence as (Republican-voting) citizens within a flourishing, capitalistic, democratic, and integrated South. As a first step, Frank Shaw (along with J. Miller McKim and Levi Coffin) spent two weeks in Washington, D.C., during the winter of 1863–64, lobbying for the passage of a bill authorizing a Freedmen's Bureau. The bill did not pass until the 1865 congressional session.[79]

Lee's surrender to Grant on April 9, 1865, brought an end to the great war. At incredible cost, the North had established the political and legal primacy of the Union and, in northerners' eyes, the superiority of its social and cultural institutions. Now the South had to be reconstructed in the northern image. As part of the reconstruction process, abolitionists planned to bring education to the black masses not only to enlighten the ex-slaves but to change fundamentally the white southerner's racist mind-set by demonstrating the power of progressive policy. In 1866 this became a major goal of the secular Freedmen's Aid societies as they joined together under an umbrella organization called the American Freedmen's Union Commission (AFUC), of which Frank Shaw was a vice president and executive committee member. Their purpose was to raise money; to build, fund, and furnish schools; and to hire and support teachers for those schools. After these schools were established entities, the southern states would then take them over as part of their public school systems.

The foot soldiers in the (now former) abolitionists' new campaign effort were the teachers. During the war, hundreds of northern teachers went south to help in the contraband camps, and after the war thousands of them, including many women, traveled to teach in the freedmen's schools. Despite tiny salaries and uncomfortable living and working conditions, these idealistic men and women instructed the liberated African Americans on the basic rudiments of reading and writing—something that more than 95 percent of them had been denied under slavery. Lowell had participated in this movement in a small way when she tutored ex-slaves at Charley's camp in Vienna, Virginia. Her interest was already strong, and her family supportive, when she decided to accept the post of a supervisor of freedmen's schoolteachers in 1866. The New York branch of the AFUC, the National Freedmen's Relief Association of New York, had its offices on lower Fourth Avenue in Manhattan, and Lowell joined one of its committees to oversee the school system that the society had set up in Virginia. Later that year, leaving her toddler Carlotta in the care of nannies and grandparents, Lowell and her co-worker from the Sanitary Commission, Ellen Collins, were sent to Virginia to visit and report on the "colored schools," in Petersburg, Richmond, and other destinations.

Josephine Lowell became the secretary of the New York society and served in that capacity until 1871. By this time the AFUC had been disbanded because of declining contributions and a destructive rivalry with their religious counterpart, the American Missionary Association. Thus only the strongest member societies, such as New York and New England, were left to carry on the work. As early as 1869, even the New York society was being shut down, and as part of this process, Lowell negotiated with representatives of the New England society (which would continue until 1874) to take over the New York society's Virginia freedmen's schools. Basically, her work for the Freedmen's Aid societies was administrative and included recommendations for appointments, terminations, and transfers of teachers within the Virginia district and in a few other areas. From her office in New York, for example, Lowell interviewed applicants for teaching positions and made the necessary arrangements for their hiring and placement.

Lowell traveled on a regular basis to Virginia to evaluate the quality of the teaching and the viability of the schools, and she wrote reports suggesting appropriate changes. Another important part of her job involved keeping the schools financially afloat by raising money from reluctant contributors. Even though the New York society was turning over the management of its schools to the New England branch, it was still going to offer financial support by paying the salaries and the traveling expenses of the teachers. Lowell frequently solicited money from her friends and relatives to help defray the costs of the schools, and she also dipped into her own pocketbook.[80]

In 1871 the New York society closed its offices for good, and although sad at the society's failure, Lowell looked back with pride on her accomplishments. She had demonstrated to herself and others that she could function in a capable and adult manner. The nature of the work itself conflated her reform heritage with the immediate wartime ideals for which her husband and brother had died. In these bittersweet years after the war, Lowell was just beginning to answer the question she had posed to herself: How could she possibly do justice to their legacy? Significantly, Lowell's service for the Freedmen's Aid society uncovered a genius on her part for organizational work, which would flourish in the years to come. Personnel management, devising sensible bureaucratic rules and regulations, enforcement of same, fundraising, and much tedious work constitute the nuts and bolts of any associative enterprise, and Lowell's experience in the late 1860s and early 1870s inspired her to continue in other philanthropic endeavors.

"What Is Man [or Woman] Born For . . . ?"

Now in her late twenties, with her first real work behind her, Lowell had some important decisions to make regarding her future. Realistically, she could not expect to duplicate *exactly* the lives of her husband and brother in terms of carrying on their legacy as she perceived it. *Her* life decisions were severely constrained by gender considerations. A major option for widows—remarriage—was closed to her by both personal inclination and the cruel demographics of the Civil War in which so many of the males of her generation and class were killed. On the other hand, Lowell was not educated for, nor would she consider, the almost exclusively male-dominated fields of law, medicine, or business. The political world, always of great interest to her, was similarly closed to women. The Civil War years had brought a great explosion in women's employment. As teachers, government clerks, nurses, and workers in retail establishments and factories, women entered into the labor force as never before. But these jobs would not do for Josephine Shaw Lowell: women of her social position and class never worked for wages but bestowed their talents free of charge. In this sense, Lowell, although increasingly professional in her standards and demeanor, never had a "career" in the way that later generations of college-educated women would. She was a leader of that generation of women who were poised between the "amateur" philanthropists of the antebellum age and the new "professional" social workers of the early twentieth century.

In the end, only one field beckoned, and that was charity. In 1871 Josephine Lowell began to work full time, as a volunteer, for the State Charities Aid Association, a creation of Louisa Lee Schuyler. Why? Long a traditional bailiwick for socially prominent activist women, charity work was, in the postwar era, undergoing an exciting transformation. At the dawn of the Gilded Age, charity encompassed a wealth of different concerns: poverty, crime, welfare, children's rights, and the care of the mentally ill and indigent. It was concerned with both the causes and effects of dependence and poverty, and thus frequently intersected with the male world of political economy. Charity was the one public arena where nineteenth-century women could and did claim legitimate rights for exercising power for the good of the community; it offered intellectual stimulation and a chance to reform some of society's major problems, and it did not threaten gender boundaries. Charity work drew Lowell like a moth to a flame. Her entrance into this work would be a logical progression from her earlier service with the U.S. Sanitary Commission and the Freedmen's Aid activities. This is an important point to make. The commission and the freedmen's societies both sought close ties with the government in attaining their goals for reform. Lowell's experiences with these two organizations would predispose her to accept an enlarged but carefully proscribed role for the state in welfare activities.

Moreover, there was a bridge between Lowell's sanitary service, her freedmen's work, and her imminent charitable activities for New York's poor population. Lowell believed that education was necessary to inculcate the moral values in order to "uplift" African Americans from their former state of degradation to citizenship status. The Shaw family offered their firm support for the Republican party's efforts to impose a political reconstruction, but they stopped short of advocating a major redistribution of economic resources. First, they believed, the ex-slaves must be educated in the ways of middle-class values and exposed, through the mediating force of Freedmen's Bureau labor contracts, to the discipline of free labor.[81] Rewards would then come to black citizens as they came to most white citizens: through their own hard work and achievement. In the ensuing decades, this rosy assessment would be compromised by the harsh reality of racism in the South. For now, Lowell turned her attention to her own New York City. It occurred to her that the northern people most in need of lessons were the urban underprivileged, like the poor Irish immigrants, whose dangerous and disloyal actions during the war alerted Lowell and others to the potentially dire political and social consequences of doing nothing.

Historians have made the connection between the motives of Gilded Age reformers, like Lowell, and their Civil War experiences very explicit.[82] This has been especially true in regard to the origins of the scientific or organized charity movement, the major philanthropic reform of the 1870s and 1880s. This movement, of which Josephine Shaw Lowell was a national leader, has been portrayed as elitist and mean-spirited in its attempt to control the behavior of the poor through a combination of vagrancy laws and reduced benefits and to systematize and make efficient the means and ends of administering welfare programs, public or private. Scientific charity, with its emphasis on the head rather than the heart, seemed to be the perfect complement to the harsh ideology of social Darwinism, in which "the survival of the fittest" offered cold comfort to the victims of the rapidly industrializing urban areas. Scholars searching for explanations for this prevalent type of charity in the postbellum era have, not surprisingly, identified Gilded Age reformers who participated in the Civil War as being particularly impressed by the need to impose order on what they saw as an unruly and fractious northern population. Their work in the Sanitary Commission, which strongly advocated many of the values later embodied in the scientific charity movement, was one of the major bonds among prominent reformers. This kind of analysis is made manifest when considering the career of Josephine Shaw Lowell.

Paul Boyer has argued that Lowell's later charitable endeavors allowed her "not only to sublimate her bitterness and perhaps even hatred toward the urban poor who had behaved so ignobly during her own and the nation's great ordeal, but to instill into them something of the moral strength and sense of purpose that her martyred brother and husband displayed on the battlefield."[83] In other words, one could easily imagine how the youthful Lowell's abolitionist sensibilities were outraged at the knowledge that immigrant Irish mobs were roving the streets of New York with the intention of seeking out, terrorizing, beating, and killing African Americans. One can also assume that she contrasted the behavior of her brother's regiment, filled with patriotic African Americans who were fighting for the North even as the looting, burning, and rioting raged in the city, with the angry, racist working-class men and women, much to the latter's detriment. Boyer offers a compelling explanation for Lowell's youthful motives, especially if one is convinced that scientific charity and the reforms Lowell sought to implement were indeed as oppressive as they are often portrayed.

Yet a more balanced and dispassionate study of scientific charity would surely shed light on the many positive as well as negative aspects of that reform movement. A close examination of Lowell's career will help in this endeavor. So, too, a more even-handed analysis of Lowell's motives will shed more light on what Boyer very perceptively describes as her didactic impulse—that is, her desire "to instill" in the urban poor worthy values. We can begin this analysis with an examination of her family's class attitudes during the war.

As the Staten Island riots ended, a realization came over the small community that between the Irish working class and their "betters" there had developed a chasm that seemed unbridgeable. This realization elicited temporary feelings of betrayal on the part of the abolitionist community, who felt deeply "the ingratitude of the people who had come to our shores and accepted our hospitality, who had been nursed when they were sick and fed . . . but who at the first opportunity had turned against us; who had not only turned against us in political disloyalty, but had made war on us at night by pillage and arson and murder."[84] Perhaps more than one of those Irish youths had partaken of Lowell's genteel ice cream and cake tea parties for the local poor families in the late 1850s. The Shaws' own observations of the riots were not recorded, but the juxtaposition of the antidraft disturbances with Rob's death must have deeply affected the family. On the other hand, it is highly unlikely that the behavior exhibited by the Irish rioters could have induced Lowell or the rest of the Shaws to despise or even "hate" them for their disloyalty. Indeed, like many of the native-born upper and middle class, they had had a long history with, and intimate knowledge of, the Irish, and had developed strong opinions on their presence in America well before the Civil War.

The Shaws' position vis-à-vis the Irish was somewhat ambivalent. They were at once employers of the Irish, dispensers of alms to them, and political opponents. As Lowell later wrote, "With all their weaknesses, I care very much for them—they are an unselfish and refined race. You know, they are almost our only servants and we know them through and through . . . and upon the whole, they have been a valuable addition to our population." She added, "They have many virtues, and if they had a little more ballast and common sense, it would be better for them and for us."[85] This type of paternalism was commonly expressed in the family. For example, Robert Shaw was highly critical of the Irish-American soldiers, whom he thought in dire need of the kind of discipline the military should provide.[86] The Shaws were particularly affronted when wartime elections in New York City showed the popular disaffection with the war, as expressed in this letter written by Sarah: "I think you will be much grieved at the result of our elections. New England as usual (being the most enlightened part of the country) stands firm, and the absence of thousands of Republican voters in the field explains the defeat in New York, where assisted by our Irish fellow-citizens, the Democratic Party has again lifted its hideous head."[87] Thus the same people who served the Shaws in their homes (in 1860 they employed two servants named Bridget) and were often the objects of their charity were empowered by the state to take an opposite political stance.

It didn't help that during these years the New York City Democratic political machine (known as Tammany Hall) flourished with the votes of the immigrants. In the 1860s and 1870s, "machine politics" gave rise to a new level of corruption, neatly symbolized by William Marcy ("Boss") Tweed's famous $13 million courthouse. In Lowell's adult years, political corruption would replace slavery as the national evil for many former abolitionists, and her brother-in-law George William Curtis would become their national leader. She, too, would become a stalwart in the campaign for civil service reform, or "good government," and explicitly connected that reform to improving a machine-corrupted public welfare system. Along with other civil service reformers, Lowell expressed concern that the immigrants came by their rights of citizenship too easily, and thus were manipulated by ward bosses for their own selfish ends. The antidraft riots were just one sign among many that attention would need to be paid to the problems engendered by immigration and urbanization after the war.

The Shaws were also discomfited by their distance from the working-class Irish. For many years they had been involved with various democratizing political and social movements. Yet they were abolitionists, and because they were abolitionists, the Irish were their enemies. Of course, they also believed themselves to be democrats with a small *d*, and this belief underscores the complexities and contradictions inherent in the Shaws' background, which would be carried on in Lowell's life as well. On the one hand, they were Brahmins, one of the most self-conscious, distinctive, and long-lasting group of elites ever to flourish in the United States. And as Brahmins, they had inherited a culturally and historically rooted concept of "the public good," which, based in the tenets of Protestant Christianity and virtuous republicanism, was used to spread the New England influence far and wide.

On the other hand, however, Frank and Sarah Shaw and their children were dedicated to an inclusive vision of American society—a vision at odds with the paternalistic exclusivity of many of their peers. Moreover, their Brook Farm days and later social commitments revealed a genuine concern for the injustices wrought by capitalism for all working people, white and black, native-born and immigrant. These broadly conflicting family traditions—elitism versus democracy, exclusiveness versus inclusiveness, paternalism versus liberalism—produced oppositions in Josephine Shaw Lowell's work and reform aims that only become understandable when grounded in a knowledge of her personal history.

The Brahmin and the reformer shared one powerful desire, however: to influence, to teach, to sway, and to change. "What is man born for," asked the family hero Emerson, "but to be a Reformer, a Remaker of what man had made; a renouncer of lies; a restorer of truth and good?"[88] In turning to a life of public service, Lowell was doing what came to her by right of her twin inheritance of class and reform, each laden with the burden of stewardship. And so she turned to the field of philanthropy, which she now thought had been terribly neglected owing to her country's preoccupation with slavery. She admitted to an English correspondent that Americans tended to lag far behind their overseas cousins when it came to many reforms, but "there is one excuse for us, however, and that is that during the thirty years when you were . . . making such immense advances, the men and women in this country who would naturally have turned their thoughts in the same direction, were devoting heart and soul to fighting slavery—then came the war, which took all our lives."[89] Now for the young widow, one war was over and another would begin. But before she took up arms in the battle against crime, poverty, and corruption, she would need to be trained in the latest methods of combat. These new methods would transform the battlefields of charity just as surely as the innovations in warfare developed in the Civil War transformed the way military campaigns were conducted. Charley and Rob were soldiers in the military for the greater glory of America, and now Josephine, too, would be a soldier—and perhaps a hero—trained in the new field of social science to fight a different kind of battle on an unfamiliar terrain.

4

Charity Is Our Science

✎ The Great Debate ✎

Consider the case of poor Julia Deems, who in the Christmas season of 1876 sat on a freezing New York City street nursing her tiny baby while asking for alms from the bustling crowds. A common enough sight in that depression-plagued city, some might have said, yet Deems's story became widely known when the infant died at her breast from exposure. The press reported this shocking incident and drew from it the poignant lesson that prosperous Christians ignored the plight of their less fortunate brethren at the risk of losing their spiritual well-being. Deems's predicament was also held up as an example of the inadequate response of New York's charities to the increased number of needy people. Further controversy was sparked by the publication of three letters to the *New York Tribune,* each representing a different view of charity.[1]

The first letter came from a J. G. Holland and called attention to the abuse of alcohol. These "begging women and their drugged babies" who were clogging the city's sidewalks were the unfortunate victims of alcoholic husbands. The remedy was as simple as the imposition of strict controls on the liquor industry and the closing down of the saloon trade. Josephine Shaw Lowell wrote the second letter, which contained a more thoughtful critique of the *Tribune's* article from the position of scientific or organized charity, whose presence was just beginning to be felt in American cities. Lowell began by asking why the *Tribune* blamed "society" for Mrs. Deems's tragedy when it was clearly the fault of the errant Mr. Deems. The structural problem, she commented, was instead to be found in the lax enforcement of the beggary laws by the police department. If the police would do their duty, then "the really poor would be relieved and the impostors punished." Furthermore, it was misguided to condemn people for not giving alms, when the true un-Christian act was in neglecting to find Deems and her baby shelter for the night. Lowell summed up her argument thus: "So long as indiscriminate almsgiving continues, so long will the streets be full of beggars, and so long will such cases as this occur to shock and distress the hearts of all humane persons."[2]

The third letter, published in reaction to those of Holland and Lowell, came from Rebecca Harding Davis of Philadelphia. Davis, a writer and a contributing editor to the *Tribune*, congratulated the newspaper on its enlightened Christian position and went on to condemn organized charity: "But the objections urged to this course by those who probably represent the morality and philanthropy of society seemed to me more comfortless than the story of the poor dead baby. If their arguments are right . . . the wind blows due east in the world to-day and cold."[3] The *Tribune* concurred with Davis, and in an editorial reviewing the merits of the debate, commented that Lowell's words seemed "cold and cruel." However more efficient and sound organized charity claimed to be, it could and should never replace the instinctive generosity of the Christian heart.[4]

These approaches to charity, represented by Holland, Lowell, Davis, and the *Tribune*, exemplify the existing alternatives around which interested citizens rallied themselves in response to the problems of the "dead weight of pauperism" afflicting America's cities.[5] Most, if not all, Gilded Age philanthropists would have agreed with Samuel Johnson's remark that "a decent provision for the poor is the true test of civilization," yet the precise nature of "decent provision" was hotly debated, just as it is today. A particularly dramatic shift in the American ideology of poverty, charity, and political reform occurred in the decades following the Civil War. The waxing industrial revolution created the profound social problems of overcrowded, unhealthy, and dangerous urban areas and prompted spirited public debate about the nature and causes of poverty. Newspapers played an important role in this discussion. Their often sensationalistic and sentimental coverage of the victims of poverty, such as Julia Deems, sparked strong reactions like those from Josephine Shaw Lowell and Rebecca Harding Davis.[6]

Women, individually and in groups, helped to direct both public and private relief policies to meet the new circumstances. Josephine Lowell was a beneficiary of a well-established role for charitable women, in which philanthropy was considered an area suitable for genteel female public activity. Yet as a volunteer worker for the State Charities Aid Association of New York and as commissioner of the Board of State Commissioners of Public Charities, she was also a pioneer in expanding and changing that role in four significant ways: she confronted a corrupt political system; she was instrumental in the rise of a new kind of charity; she emerged as a social scientist; and she was an effective public policy-maker. Lowell, of course, did not work alone but was part of a larger cohort of male and female elite and middle-class reformers who developed a special blend of Christian, liberal, and quasi-Darwinian views of poverty and poor relief. The members of this group were assuming a distinctive identity as professional "experts," and they often took an independent and critical stance toward government. Josephine Shaw Lowell's identity as a social scientist and charity reformer did not spring full blown into existence when she began to toil in the charitable fields in 1871. Rather, it developed slowly over the years and took its nourishment from many sources, including an important trip abroad that exposed her to a number of new and exciting ideas flourishing in England.

ᴄᴏ *The English Experience* ᴏᴗ

In late May of 1871, Lowell, together with a cousin, a friend, and seven-year-old Lotta, visited Europe, where they had "a very pleasant time, wandering round in England and Wales for several months."[7] This was the trip in which her meeting with Carlyle elicited his warm response to her family's tragedy. But Carlyle was just one of the English personages to whom Lowell carried letters of introduction. Others included Charles and Fanny Kingsley of Eversley, old friends of her parents, as well as Dean Howson at Chester and Canon Benson, who later became archbishop of Canterbury.[8] Besides touring the great cathedrals accompanied by these learned English churchmen, Lowell was engaging in serious discussions about the social problems of the day with some of the brightest stars of English reform. Indeed, this trip may have given Lowell what Jane Addams's more famous European travels provided her sixteen years later: both inspiration and practical direction for a life of philanthropic leadership. Three movements stirring in England—Christian socialism, liberal philanthropy, and scientific charity—were particularly important in shaping Lowell's ideas about charity and charity reform.

Charles Kingsley was in the forefront of an effort to bring laboring people into the folds of the Anglican Church through a program of benign socialism.[9] The tenets of Christian socialism as elucidated by Kingsley and others emphasized the inevitability of human progress under a benevolent divine presence. Yes, they agreed, it was undeniably true that the emergent industrial system fostered unjust inequalities of wealth and power that led to the degradation of the working classes. Christians were exhorted to reverse this situation by pouring their energies into improving the lot of the masses through education, association, and political and social reform. Lowell, who had grown up reading and discussing Kingsley's novels and tracts on the subject of Christian socialism, found that his doctrine meshed nicely with her own heritage of Unitarianism and social activism. Indeed, the Christian socialist philosophy echoed some of the principles of Fourierism, earlier embraced by Frank and Sarah at Brook Farm. From a very early age, Josephine had been exposed to powerful objections to the excesses of capitalism, and she always evinced a great concern with working-class issues, although most of her activism in that area would occur after 1885.

More important for Josephine Shaw Lowell's immediate future was the inspirational role for philanthropists envisioned by the Christian socialists. This role embraced volunteerism and offered socially conscious men and women an opportunity to do God's work on earth by helping to erase the effects of poverty. "We must believe in, we must feel, the 'Brotherhood of Man,'" Lowell explained. "We cannot be just, we cannot be charitable, we cannot be anything without this. If we talk of 'the poor,' if we say what 'they do,' if we judge ourselves by one standard and our brothers by another, we cannot help them."[10] Religious sentiments and a belief in a just and humane God permeated Lowell's work and imbued it with a gravity that would have been lacking had she only viewed her career as a professional social worker, as did later generations. This spiritual foundation was complemented by other ideas about poverty and the role of philanthropy that were grounded firmly in the secular and scientific advancements of the nineteenth century.

For example, the supposition that the Christian socialists advanced—that poverty could be eradicated if enough right-thinking people applied themselves to the problem—was very much a reflection of the power of that part of nineteenth-century liberal ideology that emphasized the responsibilities individuals owed their society. John Stuart Mill is best known for developing this side of liberalism, and it may be remembered that Lowell read his *Principles of Political Economy* three times on her honeymoon. Liberal philanthropy was concerned not only with the *giving* of alms but also with the *consequences* of the act. That is the major distinction between liberal and nonliberal philanthropy. A nonliberal philanthropist gives alms freely and often, out of a reflexive religious impulse and without due consideration as to the good or bad effects that could ensue. A liberal philanthropist, such as Lowell would become, intellectualizes the process and asks how her or his action will help or harm both the character of the recipient and the general welfare of the community. Most of all, "liberal moral virtue" demands an activism on the part of the philanthropist in both the formulation and the implementation of charitable practices in order to ensure the proper results.[11]

The liberal philanthropists' emphasis on community did not clash with the individualism that buttressed nineteenth-century liberalism's free-market system and restrained constitutional government. Instead, it was envisioned as the moral glue that bound together society, economy, and government. Liberal philanthropy was very much a part of the new forward thinking that prided itself on using scientific reasoning to solve social problems. To many, the notion of a "scientific charity" might have seemed a contradiction in terms. Yet to Josephine Shaw Lowell and many other liberal philanthropists studying society in England and America in the early 1870s, scientific charity represented a modern approach to poverty that combined the new concepts and techniques of science with older Christian traditions.

Scientific charity or philanthropy, which swept across America after the depression of 1873, had its origins in the English industrial experience. In mid-Victorian England, a number of issues combined to elevate poverty and its eradication into a major focus of social and political attention from the 1850s to the early 1900s. These concerns were addressed in 1869 by the founding of the first Charity Organization Society (COS) in London, which became the mouthpiece for publicizing the principles of scientific charity. Significantly, during her trip,

Lowell met and was deeply impressed by one of the founders of the London COS, Octavia Hill.[12]

Scientific charity was predicated on the belief that the principles of science could be applied to solve social problems. The distillation of these principles came to be known as "social science," which was developed over the course of the nineteenth century by such thinkers as John Stuart Mill, Auguste Comte, and Herbert Spencer. Called social scientists, the practitioners represented a new breed of educated experts whose goal would be to identify, investigate, and solve the thorniest problems of the day. And it was firmly believed by this self-identified group that these problems were too complex for ordinary citizens to solve in an increasingly interdependent industrial world.

Of course, reformers still held able-bodied individuals to account for their moral failings and expected a change (for the better) in character to accompany aid and the hoped-for ascension out of degradation. The emphasis on individual moral defects as a major cause of poverty had its roots deep in eighteenth- and nineteenth-century English and American social thought and continues to influence the shaping of welfare programs today. Scientific reformers thought that individualism and community responsibility were inextricably entwined and that one balanced off the other. In other words, reformers were confident that intelligent, capable individuals could come together and scientifically study social problems, ameliorate those problems, and then together (with the support of the larger community) produce a progressive, stable society. Three key concepts of social science—organization, cooperation, and rationalization—guided charity reformers to embrace a different understanding of poverty from that of their forebears: one that was informed by knowledge and experience, not just humanitarian impulses. This first generation of social scientists, unlike the succeeding, did not, for the most part, repudiate their Christian roots but cultivated and nourished them alongside the other thriving plants in the nineteenth-century intellectual garden.[13]

⌘ The Challenge of American Poverty ⌘

The conceptualization of poverty as an area for scientific study and applied methods would have profound consequences for private and public charity in the postbellum era. In America, the growing interest in the field of social science was institutionalized by the establishment of the American Social Science Association in 1865 and applied to related fields such as economics, history, political science, and of course philanthropy. Later, offshoot organizations such as the National Conference of Charities and Corrections would provide the meeting grounds for young philanthropists such as Josephine to discuss the latest methods and practices of their field. Josephine Shaw Lowell was among the earliest of these social scientists of charity in the United States, and with the excitement typical of a convert she proclaimed that "the task of dealing with the poor and degraded has become a science."[14]

Yet the task of "dealing with the poor" faced two monumental challenges in the early 1870s, when Lowell made her entrance into the philanthropic field. The first was the sheer scale of urban poverty. The reasons for the rise in the number of "paupers" or "tramps," as they were interchangeably known, were manifold, complex, and structural.[15] The tramp problem was actually just the tip of the iceberg of a growing (and unmet) demand on the nation's charitable resources, both public and private. The strain was particularly noticeable in the Northeast, where urbanization and population growth were proceeding the fastest. This growth was accompanied by the tremendous economic development that was transforming the social landscape at a heretofore unimaginable rate for millions of Americans, making possible both the excesses and the accomplishments of the Gilded Age.

New York State statistics alone can demonstrate the swift pace of change. In the twenty-five years after the Civil War, the state's population increased from 3,831,777 to nearly 6 million. During the same period, the state became predominantly urban, symbolized by the unquestioned dominance of New York City as the nation's premier business, industrial, and cultural capital. The country's internal human migration was supplanted and then overwhelmed by the flow of immigrants. And because the majority of immigrants entered through the Port of New York, it is notable that 40 percent listed the state as their destination. Moreover, of the approximately 20 million people who streamed into America during the nineteenth century, four out of five came after 1860.[16]

Given the level of changes, it is not surprising that social dislocation followed both the rural-urban movement and the immigrants' arrival.

There was no "conspiracy" to dump pauper immigrants on the United States, as some people feared, but there was a noticeable rise on the poor-relief rolls and a concomitant rise in taxes that could be attributed to the rise in the population of the very poor. The permanent social disruptions caused by the Civil War added to the problems. Besides the widows and orphans left by the deaths of more than 600,000 soldiers, the North alone found itself with more than 1 million permanently unemployable men.[17] Finally, the nation found itself absorbing these disruptions in the midst of a major depression that began in 1873 and lasted until 1877. Certainly not the first, nor the last, financial panic experienced by the American capitalistic system, it was nonetheless notable for the severity of its effects. Beginning with the collapse of the New York City financial markets in September 1873, the depression quickly spread to the business and industrial sectors, causing widespread unemployment and much social and political discontent among the working class.[18]

Tramps were the most disturbing sign of the 1873 depression and the new industrial order in which people by the hundreds of thousands clogged the roads and rails of the country looking for work. Unemployment as well as underemployment swelled the ranks of the tramp population as never before, spreading alarm among the populace as the able-bodied paupers flocked to urban areas looking for work, begging for food, seeking out scarce charitable resources, and swelling the cities' cheap flophouses and free police lodgings. Tramps were almost always unfavorably portrayed in the press as affronting ordinary (and employed) citizens with their unwelcome presence in both urban and rural life. They especially challenged the bedrock values of hard work, discipline, and family morality that guided middle-class Victorian life in the nineteenth century.

The second obstacle facing those who would try to ameliorate these conditions and change the values of the poor was the deeply ingrained corruption that characterized urban and national politics. The political machines of every large American city generously dispensed welfare benefits to immigrants, whose gratefulness would presumably translate into votes and support for the machine. Boss Tweed, of New York, for instance, distributed large sums of city and state money to schools, hospitals, and charities, particularly Catholic institutions. An often-cited statistic reveals the level of change: in the seventeen years between 1852 and 1869, New York State gave private charities only $2 million, but in the three years between 1869 and 1871, when the Tweed ring was at the height of its power in the legislature, the budget appropriations were increased to $2.2 million. Charity reformers were angry that Tweed was widely known as a friend of the poor through his generosity with public funds. They objected on three counts: first, that the amount of money spent on the poor was negligible compared with the amount of money the ring stole from the citizenry; second, there was no attempt to account for the money given to all the charities in any intelligent or enlightened way; and third, the underlying problems of poverty, crime, and public health were not being addressed in any serious manner.[19]

In the 1870s, therefore, charity and political reform became inextricably linked, profoundly affecting Lowell's attitudes and career. She in turn deeply influenced political culture in New York, as the work of social scientists and charity reformers merged with the efforts of political reformers to make the Gilded Age the seedbed of the modern American state.[20] It is important to take a moment to see how this was so.

Briefly, reformers mounted a campaign to professionalize government. The leaders of this reform movement were upper- and middle-class disaffected Republican "liberals" and included Lowell's brother-in-law George William Curtis. They argued that in the industrial age, the functions of government were too important to be left in the hands of party hacks and ring politicians whose corrupt practices tainted the country. The shocking scandals of the Grant administration on the national level and the Tweed ring on the municipal level testified to the need for governmental reform. Reformers claimed that government employees and appointees should be hired and promoted according to a merit system and implemented through an honest and fair examination process. Civil service reformers wanted an educated meritocracy to replace patronage and to bring order and efficiency to government as quickly as possible.

At the local and state level, where Lowell was working, New York civil service reformers fought tooth and nail with ring politicians who "pandered" to their clients' basest vices by sustaining a network of firehouse gangs, clubhouses, and saloons as part of their political network. George William Curtis, Josephine Shaw Lowell, and others argued that the stifling grip of the political machine on the nation's cities choked the lifeblood of democracy through its cynical bargain of favors (jobs, cash, influence) for political support or, more precisely, votes. Machine corruption in New York City, the reformers claimed, not only compromised the ideals on which the nation was founded but seriously impeded the solving of the structural problems—health, sanitation, education, transportation—created during the Gilded Age.[21]

The downfall of Boss Tweed of Democratic Tammany Hall demonstrated how mutually supportive civil service reform and charity reform were and how they enlarged the possibilities for philanthropic women's political action. The grip of William Marcy Tweed on New York City and New York State politics began to loosen in 1871, when sensational details of the corruption of his $13 million still-unfinished courthouse (the original appropriation was $250,000) were leaked to the *New York Times*. In a series of stinging editorials in *Harper's Weekly*, the most widely read magazine in America, George William Curtis exploited these revelations to help bring down the House of Tweed. When Tweed jeered, "What are you going to do about it?," Curtis and his brilliant cartoonist Thomas Nast responded with perhaps the most famous series of editorial cartoons in American history, prominently featuring Tweed as a huge vulture feasting on the honest citizens of New York. The cartoons hit home, for as Tweed himself admitted, while most of his supporters could not read, "they can't help seeing them damned pictures."[22] Lowell was extraordinarily well informed about these events. Not only was brother-in-law George Curtis in the thick of it and soon to be a major force in the Mugwump political reform movement, but another brother-in-law, Francis Barlow, was the New York State attorney general who had brought the original charges against the Tweed ring.[23]

This is where the women reformers came in, after a typically all-male political melee involving the press, lawyers, politicians, and reformers and after which Tweed and members of his ring were stripped of their positions. As a result of Tweed's fall, city expenditures plummeted. The Department of Charities and Corrections, responsible for distributing funds to needy New Yorkers and a major dispenser of machine patronage, was denied a large part of its funding. Thus the department, temporarily denuded of power, provided an inviting target for charity reformers such as Josephine Shaw Lowell and Louisa Lee

Schuyler. In the late 1870s, Lowell and Schuyler led a successful, and nationally influential, campaign to end *all* outdoor relief ordinarily provided by the New York City Department of Charities and Corrections. In their eyes, this campaign struck down two evils for the price of one: it eliminated a source of political patronage for the machine *and* a corrupting influence for the poor.[24] The genteel reformer learned an important lesson from the Tweed scandal: improvements in the honest and efficient delivery of charity could not occur until the political system was also made honest and efficient. Moral aims and political change could and should be conflated to achieve desirable social goals. And to participate in this process, Josephine Shaw Lowell would require a larger sphere of political action than was then enjoyed by women.[25]

Civil service reform offered women a safe public space in which to insinuate themselves into the political realm. Because the male reformers self-consciously placed themselves above "politics as usual," they created an innovative style of political discourse that relied on a blend of old-fashioned morality and new ideas of progressive, efficient management. This appealing blend would convince voters to throw out the bosses, *and* it would also make certain public issues a concern for both men and women. A good example is the concept of nonpartisanship, developed by liberal reformers in the 1870s and 1880s and put into practice in full force in the 1890s.

Nonpartisanship changed the American political landscape by undermining the popular style of politics that characterized most of the nineteenth century. The gradual expansion of white male voting rights in the early 1800s produced by the 1840s a colorful and expressive political life that revolved around rituals, entertainments, and the traditional male preserve of the saloon. This political culture united men of all classes and ethnic groups and helped to define "maleness" in American society. But according to many, the staggering problems created by postwar industrialism defied traditional political solutions. Nonpartisan civil service reformers and their allies urged citizens not to vote unthinkingly but to educate themselves about the issues and vote with their heads instead of their hearts or pocketbooks. Reformers thus actively promoted such antiparty values as independent voting and merit-based government jobs. And, most important, they declared whole new territories—public health and sanitation, control of the municipal fire and police departments, and welfare institutions—to be nonpolitical and thus open to the purview and control of concerned women as well as men.

When women such as Josephine Shaw Lowell and Louisa Lee Schuyler seized this new opportunity to reform the social welfare system of New York State, they were doing more than simply forcing the state to accept or at least debate the notion of a different, and expanded, public responsibility for its dependents: they were also becoming an integral part of the political process. By exposing the inadequacies and corruption of the prevailing order, they opposed, and hoped to destroy, the ring politicians who used the welfare system as a dumping ground for patronage. Here Lowell, Schuyler, and many other women were using their investigations as social scientists to achieve political ends. For Lowell, scientific philanthropy provided a beacon for enhanced political understanding and achievement.

New York State Charities Aid Association

Lowell's career as a charity reformer was thus closely bound up with the political and economic currents of her time. When she returned to America from her European trip in 1871, she confronted a city teeming with poverty and corruption and was eager to put the new ideas she had formed about scientific charity to work. On arrival, she not only heard about political scandal but also learned that her friend and mentor from the Sanitary Commission, Louisa Lee Schuyler, had formed a new charitable organization dedicated to putting into practice many of the reform principles she had been hearing about in England. Born to a distinguished, wealthy, and socially conscious New York family, Schuyler was in her early twenties when the Civil War began and a neighbor of the Shaws on Staten Island. Schuyler's mother was one of the founders of the Woman's Central, and when Schuyler herself went to work for the Sanitary Commission, her talent and hard work quickly established her as the most successful manager in the organization. After the war, Schuyler, depressed and in ill health, headed for Europe, where she spent the next six years recuperating. Nonetheless, like many of the young women who worked in the Civil War, she could not forget the experience, because it "was a great educator to the women of that day. I regard it as one of the greatest blessings of my life to have been privileged to take part in it. Among other things, it opened my eyes to the great value and the great power of organization."[26] And when Schuyler recovered her health, she discovered there was much work to be done in organizing social welfare in New York State.

While Lowell was finishing off her freedmen's work and traveling in Europe, Schuyler was immersing herself in the annual reports of New York's Board of State Commissioners of Public Charities, which revealed sordid conditions in the state's poorhouses, almshouses, and county jails. The Board of State Commissioners, founded in 1867, was an outstanding example of early social science at work. This board, which was established to systematize and reform the bewildering tangle of local private and public relief systems that crisscrossed New York (and most states) in the nineteenth century, was charged with inspecting charities and institutions, drawing up reports, and making recommendations for legislative changes. The Boards of State Commissioners of Public Charities were part of a larger system of state investigatory commissions that attempted to regulate labor, health, and industrial conditions beginning in the late 1860s. The "boards" of these commissions usually consisted of private citizens, who, unpaid, performed a public service for the community good.[27]

Schuyler knew several of the members of the New York board, and, interested in the results of their work, she was horrified to read of the terrible conditions in New York's welfare system. Poor health cast aside, Schuyler in January of 1872 began to organize and staff volunteer visiting committees for each county of New York State with the purpose of inspecting poorhouses and reporting violations to the proper authorities. She created a parent body to these committees called the State Charities Aid Association (SCAA), whose purpose was to oversee and coordinate the work of the committees, prepare special reports to the state board, recommend needed reforms to the state legislature, and develop campaigns to drum up public support for social welfare issues.[28]

One of the SCAA's earliest recruits, Josephine Shaw Lowell was an outstanding volunteer for that organization from 1873 to 1877. She joined the Richmond County Visiting Committee (Staten Island) and then became a member, secretary, and chairwoman of the SCAA's standing committee on adult able-bodied paupers, one of several standing committees at the heart of the organization's centrally located headquarters in New York City. Lowell quickly turned her experience as a visitor into a project that demonstrated both her ambition and initiative. Noticing that the Richmond County pauper case histories were characterized by an extraordinarily high rate of recidivism among the inmates of both the poorhouse and local jail, she launched an investigation to determine why the Richmond County jail had such a dismal record. She found the answer in the corruption of the system that appointed the officials: "The Sheriff," she wrote in her report, "who is also the Keeper of the Jail, has no salary, his sole emoluments being his fees, and what he can make on the board of prisoners; in fact, he keeps a cheap boarding-house, and depends on the good will of his customers. When he has a good many boarders, he makes money; therefore it is not for his interest either to attempt to reform prisoners, or to keep them under such strict discipline as to render the Jail an unpleasant place of residence."[29]

Lowell went on to record that the present arrangements for prisoners were wasteful of both money and human capital and recommended more discipline and, better yet, an opportunity for the inmates to learn a trade. She persuaded the Board of Supervisors for Richmond County that, for prisoners sentenced to sixty days or more, the King's County Penitentiary, which featured a vocational training program, would be a more appropriate destination than the county jail. The responsible officials signed an agreement to this effect on June 18, 1873, causing Lowell to note approvingly that now the reformed situation "would tend to deter from crime those to whom a temporary residence in a well-warmed Jail, with good food and congenial associates, might be more attractive than a resort to honest labor."[30]

Lowell's simultaneous examination of the Richmond County almshouse brought much less satisfaction. Her recommendations to provide the able-bodied (but noncriminal) pauper with the same kind of vocation or "work-house" atmosphere fell on deaf ears. She was also alarmed at the promiscuous intermingling of human beings in the poorhouse, particularly by the presence of so many mentally ill people and children. Lowell's influential reports on both the almshouse and the jail illuminated some major themes of reform that the SCAA had set out for itself: making the administrators of these types of institutions more professional and less beholden to local politicians; devising a medically and scientifically progressive way of identifying, separating, and placing different categories of dependents within a network of state-run institutions that would care for them in a low-cost, efficient, and humane manner; and, finally, implementing a rigorous work program for those people who were not mentally ill or otherwise disabled with the goal of making them self-supporting and thus not a drain on taxpaying citizens.

The goal of creating the progressive, scientific management of welfare institutions placed Lowell, Schuyler, and the SCAA at odds with the prevailing political system in which patronage came first: reward your friends and punish your enemies. Every time Lowell, as a visitor for the SCAA and shortly as a commissioner for the Board of State Commissioners of Public Charities, condemned the corrupt officials who, she claimed, were running (and ruining) the New York State system of poorhouses, she was helping to mold a new ideal of governance—one that emphasized responsibility over democracy. The poorhouse was the first target for reform and a battleground between politicians and reformers. Nourished by corrupt politics, the poorhouse by the early 1870s had become a symbol for the deterioration of New York's (and, indeed, the nation's) welfare system. Originally built early in the nineteenth century, poorhouses, or almshouses, and other institutions for the dependent offered a humane and purposeful corrective to the then-prevalent and combined system of outdoor relief, auctioning the poor to the highest bidder or "shunting" hapless groups from one place to another in order to avoid the costs of support. In 1824 the New York legislature passed a law mandating each county to erect a poorhouse, which would be maintained through local taxation and administered by a new group of elected officials, the county superintendents of the poor. The new law underscored a growing interest by reformers to limit outdoor relief (funds or goods given to the poor in their homes) in favor of indoor relief, which stressed inculcating work habits for able-bodied adults and education for dependent children in an institutional and thus controlled setting.[31]

Yet the hope for the moral and physical rehabilitation initially envisioned for the poorhouse inhabitants was overwhelmed by the realities of immigration, industrialization, and economic dislocation, which led to overcrowding and tightfisted budgets, as government sought to spend less while packing in more inmates. SCAA volunteer visitors to poorhouses such as Lowell found "insane men and women, chained naked in outhouses; children born, growing up and bringing forth more children in the poorhouses; the sick, the insane, the idiots, the babies, men, women and children, all together, with no care and no

control, the whole thing was frightful."[32] By the late 1860s, poorhouse
conditions had reached such scandalous levels that the state legislature created the aforementioned supervisory board with the responsibility of visiting annually all institutions for dependents in receipt of
state aid and presenting to the legislature a biennial report on those
institutions. The contents of these reports energized Schuyler to form
the visiting committees that would comprise the SCAA.

From the beginning, private organizations such as the SCAA would
play an important part in making the Board of State Commissioners of
Public Charities (soon changed to, and hereafter referred to, as the
New York State Board of Charities, or SBC) a success or failure. The
board consisted of eight commissioners, drawn from the state's judi-
cial districts, who were to be "men of high character, imbued with the
spirit of public service."[33] These commissioners were all unpaid, except
for the secretary, who drew a small salary. The powers of the board
commissioners were severely circumscribed: they could investigate,
inquire, examine, and report, but their recommendations carried no
legislative imperative or executive force. In order for the board's suggestions to carry weight, they would have to rely on both the power of
public opinion and the sympathetic support of private organizations,
such as the SCAA. And the commissioners generally welcomed the
SCAA's assistance, specifically in the form of appointing visitors recommended by them and accepting their annual reports to the state
board. Moreover, this arrangement was codified in the *Laws of 1873*
(and amended in the *Laws of 1881*), which gave the association's visitors the legal right to enter any county, city, or state almshouse they
wished to inspect.[34]

The special relationship between the SCAA and the SBC meant
something to Lowell. She was one of the earliest visitors and an influential report maker for the SCAA. It was to her benefit that the
SCAA visiting privileges be officially recognized by New York State law.
She would also soon be appointed as the first woman commissioner on
the board, where she would find an important source of continued
support and information from her former colleagues in the SCAA.
Thus an important aspect of Lowell's early career was facilitating a
constant and creative interplay between private and public institutions. Indeed, this interplay would be a major feature of her work in
philanthropy. The historical precedents for close relations between the

state and private sectors in welfare were many, but for Lowell's generation, the immediate precedent was established by the U.S. Sanitary Commission's service to the government in the Civil War.

Significantly, the same people who were active in the Sanitary Commission (and the Woman's Central) were foremost in the new engagement with social problems. Josephine Shaw Lowell and her cohort were united by more than their war experiences. They comprised the leaders of the charitable field. Overwhelmingly white Anglo-Saxon Protestants, they adhered to the standard of volunteerism exemplified by their service in the Sanitary Commission and fortified by the socially conscious background they all shared. The aims of the SCAA were clear: "We are men and women working together . . . with the one object of helping and elevating our poorer classes."[35] While this statement was firmly grounded in paternalism, it also expressed an awareness of need and a responsibility to address that need. The SCAA's first annual report thus listed among its supporters and workers familiar names from the worlds of reform and society: A. L. Delano, Howard Potter, Alexander Hamilton, Philip L. Van Rensselaer, Charles L. Brace, Jane S. Woolsey, Dr. Emily Blackwell, Frederick Law Olmsted, and J. Miller McKim.[36]

The same names would also appear in the records of the New York State Board of Charities and the COS (Lowell's own reform organization), giving rise to a kind of "charity trust" not unlike the "oil trust" or the "steel trust" of Gilded Age businesses. For example, Theodore W. Dwight, vice president of the SBC, was the first president of the SCAA, with Schuyler assuming presidency for life the next year. Joseph Choate, Elihu Root, J. P. Morgan, Robert W. de Forest, and Charles S. Fairchild would all have close ties with both Schuyler's SCAA and Lowell's COS. And of course Lowell herself provided the perfect example of this intermingling of charitable enterprises—first as worker for the SCAA, then as a commissioner for the SBC with close ties to her former organization, and finally as both commissioner and founder of the COS in the 1880s.[37]

✧ The 1876 Report on Paupers ✧

In these years Lowell immersed herself in the details of poorhouse administration and became ever more convinced that it was best "to exclude from the almshouses all but the sick and aged poor."[38] Accordingly, Lowell and other leaders of the SCAA worked closely with the SBC to pass in 1875 a piece of groundbreaking legislation to remove all children from poorhouses. She also worked hard on the SCAA campaign to eliminate all mentally ill people from poorhouses and to place them in a unified system of state care.[39] Schuyler, impressed with her friend's dedication and talents, decided to appoint Lowell to the committee on able-bodied paupers, where in three years she rose to be its chair. Simultaneously, she also served on the committee for outdoor relief, from 1875 to 1876. Lowell's recommendations from her investigations of paupers and the practices of outdoor relief helped to lay the groundwork for the SCAA reform program in the 1870s and beyond. The interest of the SCAA not surprisingly coincided with the unprecedented rise in "habitual pauperism" in the post–Civil War era—a condition that, in many people's eyes, represented one of the gravest threats yet to American society, not least because the "shiftless" poor appeared to undermine the Victorian values that upheld society. It was this moral imperative that most attracted the attention of Lowell and the SCAA as they set out to scientifically investigate pauperism and make recommendations for reform. The subject was one Josephine now knew well, and in 1876 her published work on pauperism brought her the attention and acclaim that so warmly recommended her to the governor of New York and led to her appointment as state commissioner.

In the clear, forceful prose that made her reports both controversial and eminently readable, Lowell put forth her reform agenda. Central to the solving of the tramp or pauper problem, she argued, was a vigorous reexamination and redirection of public relief measures. In the town, elected officials called "overseers of the poor" were responsible for dispensing outdoor relief and, in some cases, feeding and lodging the transient poor. As in the case with the county superintendents of the poor (who ran the poorhouses), their tenure was short and their wages minimal or nonexistent. And because property taxes were the only legal source of funding for the local welfare measures, money was always in short supply. Then as now, politicians were reluctant to raise taxes for social services. In addition, however, these financially hard-pressed, short-term officials often turned the situation to their own advantage by profiting from their labors for the poor.

Lowell's 1876 committee report on able-bodied paupers zeroed in on this unfortunate situation in no uncertain terms. It was bad enough, she wrote, that there was such a huge increase in tramps, but the situation was made much worse when "these communities say to the vicious and idle: 'We will board you free of cost, if you will only come and stay among us.' The money wasted in this way is the least of the evils of the present system; the corrupting influence of these worthless men and women, as they pass from town to town, lodging among the people, must be incalculable."[40] Her language here and in other writings on the tramps and the underclass often portrays them as carriers of a moral contagion, which, unless controlled swiftly and firmly, could easily be "caught" by the weaker and more susceptible members of the community. Many early charity professionals were captivated by the nomenclature of social Darwinism, and used biological metaphors that inevitably cast, at least for modern sensibilities, a somewhat sinister aura over the problem. Lowell's immersion in social science gave her a predisposition to accept Darwinian ideas in social context. These ideas were seen as part of a whole new way of trying to analyze and to solve the often confusing and frightening problems thrown up by the industrial age.

The publication of the English naturalist Charles Darwin's *Origin of Species* (1859) produced a stunning new scientific paradigm that challenged all previous theories of human development.[41] Darwin's theory of evolution by natural selection offered a powerful and convincing explanation for the advancement of all life and concomitantly an accounting for the failure of those less strong. His steps in the progression of evolution—accidental variation, overpopulation, struggle for survival, and the survival of the fittest—suggested a parallel to human society. Herbert Spencer, the English philosopher, and his American disciple, William Graham Sumner, the Yale sociologist, adduced from Darwin's principles that people were not born equal, that individuals fought over limited resources, and that, in the process, the strongest and most capable triumphed. This application of evolutionary theory to human achievement came to be called social Darwinism and captivated some of the best minds of the nineteenth century.

"Better leave people to the hard working of natural laws than to run the risk of interfering with those laws in a mischievous manner," warned Lowell in one of many statements that seem to confirm her agreement with the social Darwinists. Indeed, it is perhaps fitting that this explanation for human society found such a receptive audience among Northern American intellectuals in the immediate post–Civil

War era, when the lingering triumph of the North's victory began to lend it an aura of inevitability.[42] The general acceptance of Darwin's theory of evolution also signaled a trend to revise, but not replace, religious explanations of reality with scientific or "natural" ones. Even such a redoubtable Christian as Lydia Maria Child exclaimed to Sarah Shaw that "I bow respectfully to Science as I think she is the safest guide we have."[43] Letters from Child to Shaw reveal an intense interest on the part of both women in the revelations of the new science and a familiarity with the writings of Darwin and Spencer. Frank Shaw was an accomplished amateur biologist, an avocation that must have brought Darwin into family discussions on a regular basis. There was an uneasiness, however, among many American intellectuals and reformers about accepting a theory that espoused biological determinism and that clearly conflicted with religious beliefs. This uneasiness led to attempts to search for an integration of more traditional, moralistic, and religious explanations of reality with the new science. One of the major ways American reformers tried to integrate their old and new beliefs was through their approach to identifying and solving the problems of pauperism.

Josephine Shaw Lowell was just one of many eager philanthropists attending the Conference of Charities held at Saratoga, New York, in the mid-1870s. Here she met with other charity professionals to discuss innovative ideas and reforms that were promising to change forever the way states dealt with their dependent populations. On the subject of pauperism, the most influential paper Lowell heard at Saratoga was one presented by Richard L. Dugdale, a New York State prison reformer and an acquaintance with whom she carried on a lively exchange of ideas. Dugdale's paper, "Hereditary Pauperism as Illustrated in the Juke Family," reported on a study of five generations of an upstate New York family whose penchant for crime and degenerate behavior had gained them notoriety. He was deeply influenced by the new science of eugenics, developed by Francis Galton, a cousin of Darwin and an admirer of his theory of evolution. Following Galton's ideas, Dugdale's research demonstrated the possibility of links between heredity and negative behavioral characteristics that could lead to a generational perpetuation of pauperism and crime. Dugdale's work, in turn, was applied by the secretary of the SBC, Dr. Charles S. Hoyt, in his influential report to the state legislature on the causes of pauperism, in which he claimed that pauperism was due to inherited moral depravity. Lowell, like many other social scientists working in philanthropy in the 1870s, read both men's work closely and was impressed with their arguments.[44]

Indeed, Dugdale's and Hoyt's conclusions were pretty much accepted uncritically by most reformers, Lowell included, who not only used them to demonstrate the necessity of harsh measures to wipe out chronic pauperism but applied them to another poorhouse group—"feeble-minded" women. Lowell would be a leader in the New York State movement to identify these women, remove them from the poorhouse, and place them in a special asylum where they would be prevented from reproducing.[45] Although the term "eugenics" was not used until the twentieth century, when its applications were much more enthusiastically endorsed and applied than during Lowell's career, the idea of separating the "fit" from the "unfit" gained wide currency among both reformers and the general population. In other words, the fit should be encouraged to have children, while the unfit should be prevented, through coercive means if necessary, from reproduction. How was this to be done? One obvious way was to identify, separate, and care for the "unfit" in designated institutions, as Lowell and many others would work to achieve. The reformers' attitude toward tramps allowed little room for sentiment. In their view, the consequences of not acting would only perpetuate indefinitely the "link" so firmly established between a chronic state of pauperism and the crime, poverty, and high expense engendered by allowing these people to flourish without any type of control.

Thus throughout her report on pauperism, Lowell displayed little sympathy for the rights of tramps. They had, she argued, given up their rights when they took up living off public largesse. Her recommendation and subsequent campaign for a state antivagrancy law (which she wrote and which finally passed in 1880) underscored her firm belief that unemployed men and women should be forced to labor for their aid. It was Lowell's contention that "vagrancy and homelessness need not be permanent evils, . . . that they can be cured, and that they ought to be cured."[46] And if there were those who wouldn't be "cured," she warned, steps should be taken "to provide permanently for the incorrigibly idle and vicious, who should . . . be withdrawn from the jails and poor-houses of the State, and committed, until reformed, to district work-houses, there to be kept at hard-labor, and educated morally and mentally."[47] While Lowell's harsh words for tramps showed the unforgiving side of Gilded Age charity so well illuminated in Dugdale's and Hoyt's reports, so, too, her forceful statement imagining a "cure" for pauperism brought forth the possibility of a new and vigorous philanthropic movement. These two dynamics—one negative and one positive—would play off each other throughout her career to produce a flexible and creative philosophy of philanthropy.

Eugenics was just one strand in an evolving ideological tapestry that was being woven out of Darwin's scientific theories. Another strand was the concept of "degeneration," which argued that negative environmental factors such as alcoholism or poverty might cause "retrograde evolution" or a decline in otherwise healthy genetic stock. The degeneracy theory proved popular among reformers because it corresponded with their understanding of the wellsprings of human nature—that is, that one can prevent deterioration through improving environmental conditions. One historian of this period wrote that the strength of the reformers' religious heritage and the weakness of their devotion to liberal economic theory "counteract the notion that *laissez faire* and social Darwinism dominated American thought during the late nineteenth century. If this had been true much that happened would have been inexplicable."[48] This is why a more activist approach to the problem of poverty by both government and private organizations first blossomed in the decades after the Civil War. Lowell and other charity professionals did not agree entirely with social Darwinists that human intervention in the natural processes of society should always be discouraged as futile and dangerous.[49] The truth is that many Gilded Age charity professionals acknowledged the complexity and interconnectedness of poverty, pauperism, and societal conditions.

"What are the remedies?" Lowell asked. "How can we really help those of whom it has well been said that it is impossible to determine whether they are miserable because they are vicious, or vicious because they are miserable! The vice and the misery reproduce each other, and the two must be attacked together or little impression will be made."[50] She posed a hard question for herself, and it took a lot of learning about both the limitations and possibilities of reform before she could answer it to her satisfaction. Lowell's early questions about the causes of poverty and her subsequent attempts to answer them placed her securely in that generation of Americans who created the modern conceptualization of the dynamics of poverty. Over one hundred years later the ways in which Gilded Age reformers defined poverty, and the solutions they advanced, are still very much a part of the discourse of social welfare in this country.

Sarah Blake Sturgis Shaw, with grandson, 1863

Susanna Shaw

Ellen Shaw

Anna Shaw Curtis

George William Curtis

Francis George Shaw, 1863

Josephine Shaw and Colonel Charles Russell Lowell, 1863

Colonel Robert Gould Shaw

Josephine Shaw Lowell, 1869

Josephine Shaw Lowell, 1880

United Charities Building

IN MEMORY OF JOSEPHINE SHAW LOWELL
MDCCCXLIII~MCMV
FOUNDER OF THE CHARITY ORGANIZATION SOCIETY
MDCCCLXXXII
SHE GAVE TO IT SO LONG AS HER LIFE LASTED
HER QUICKENING SPIRIT~HER CALM WISDOM
AND HER ALL EMBRACING SYMPATHY

Josephine Shaw Lowell, bas-relief by Saint-Gaudens, 1899

5

The Commissioner

⊷ *A Groundbreaking Appointment* ⊶

Josephine Shaw Lowell's 1876 SCAA report on pauperism was considered a model of the new social-scientific approach to presenting material: it collected, classified, and interpreted both statistics and other evidence with the purpose of discovering the "truth" about poverty and hence society. Once the truth was made manifest, its scientific aura of "neutrality" would impress both legislatures and the public to approve the needed reforms. Even though Lowell's report made moral judgments of the poor, its conclusions also pointed to a more activist approach to the problem of poverty by both government and private organizations working together. The pessimism about human nature was balanced by an optimistic assumption that human beings should acknowledge their social obligations to one another and rely on an articulated body of moral, ethical, and religious principles to demonstrate the joint capability of solving a serious problem. It would not be an exaggeration to say that Lowell became the talk of the charitable town and that she was fast becoming an acknowledged star. Indeed, her work had brought her to the attention of some very powerful people, including the governor of New York, Samuel Tilden.

Lowell was not present but was much remarked on at the fourth annual meeting of the SCAA, which, gushed a New York newspaper, "was a very brilliant affair."[1] The evening gathering, held at the Masonic Temple on February 24, 1876, boasted some of the most prominent citizens in New York. Among those sharing a place of honor on the speaker's platform were such luminaries as Governor Tilden,

James Roosevelt, Theodore Roosevelt, Sr., Frederick Law Olmsted, and Charles L. Brace. The audience was similarly sprinkled with distinguished members of the city's social and political elite, and they all leaned forward eagerly to hear Charles O'Conor and Joseph H. Choate, distinguished lawyers and two of the best speakers in New York, describe the accomplishments of the SCAA. In between the speeches of O'Conor and Choate, the audience was treated to extracts of Lowell's work, commended by Choate as a "masterly report."[2]

Governor Tilden was also impressed by the crisp and authoritative assertions of the young charity volunteer. He wondered aloud to his friend Louisa Lee Schuyler, president of the SCAA, if Mrs. Lowell would consider filling a current vacancy on the SBC. He had already been turned down by one worthy citizen, and it occurred to him that a person with Lowell's impressive credentials might be just right for the SBC.[3] Tilden later waffled a bit when it was pointed out to him that no woman in New York had ever been appointed to an official state position. Nevertheless, Schuyler's enthusiasm and the empty commissioner's seat kept Tilden's interest piqued, and in the end, he offered Lowell the appointment.

With the governor's offer firmly secured, Schuyler went to the Shaws' house on Staten Island to inform her friend:

> I remember so well my interview with Mrs. Lowell; the arguments I turned over in my mind on the Staten Island ferryboat to induce her to look favorably upon the proposition, the sweet smile and friendly greeting of the young widow in her simple black dress. I stated the object of my visit, and was proceeding to argue why it was so important that she should consider it, when she said very quietly: "If the Governor and the Senate wish to appoint me, I will gladly serve." "Do you wish to think it over?" I asked. "No," she said, "I know what the work of the Board is. I shall try to do it."[4]

Evidently Schuyler was very much surprised at Lowell's eager acceptance of what was clearly a groundbreaking appointment for women in public service. This move would distinguish her not only from her friends in private charity but from her mother and sisters and other female relatives in the reform-minded Shaw family. Now Lowell would self-consciously embrace a career that gave her a unique public visibility. When viewed in the light of family tradition and personal ambition, however, Lowell's acceptance of Governor Tilden's offer was less out of character than Schuyler assumed. To begin with, the mise-en-scène described by Schuyler very much followed the Shaw family's dedication to the public good. When duty called for Lowell, then, could she do any less than her husband and brother? "I will gladly serve" was in keeping with her family tradition.

Second, while Lowell, at thirty-two, maintained the shyness and simplicity of manner that had charmed so many in her youth (and would continue to enchant the friends and colleagues of her adult years), the fact is that she had developed an aggressive and vigorous approach to her work for the SCAA. She never overtly challenged gender boundaries, preferring to use tact and discretion to preempt male co-workers who might otherwise be offended by her intellectual and practical accomplishments. Lowell's ambition was real, but it served a higher purpose. Thus, even while Lowell was enlarging the realms in which women might act, she was always aware that as one of the first women in a high-profile public position, she could advance her policy goals more effectively by being "every inch a woman" than she could by insisting on equality of the sexes in all areas.[5]

✎ The Family Circle ✎

There is also no doubt that Josephine Shaw Lowell's early career was nurtured by a network of friends and family who approved of her ambitions. "*Of course* Effie made a good impression," wrote Lydia Maria Child in reply to Sarah's proud letter announcing Josephine's appointment as state commissioner. "How could it be otherwise, with her dignity, and gracefulness, and good sense, and thorough knowledge of what she was talking about?"[6] And earlier, when Lowell took up her duties with the Richmond County visiting committee, she had not only the comradeship of her close friends from the Sanitary Commission (Lou Schuyler, Gertrude Stevens Rice, and Ellen Collins) but also the visible support of her family. Two of her brothers-in-law, George Curtis and Francis Barlow, were on the SCAA's advisory board, and her sister Anna and father, Frank, served on the visiting committee with her. The affirming atmosphere she enjoyed within her family circle remained a constant throughout her life, and must be considered a major factor in explaining her success in public work. Lowell cherished her family, and they, in turn, returned her devotion in full.[7]

In 1869, Francis and Sarah sold their large homestead on Bard Avenue to their daughter and son-in-law, Susanna and Robert Minturn. The elder Shaws then purchased a more modest residence on the shores of the Kill Van Kull, where they lived with Josephine and Carlotta. Although small by their previous standards, the Shaws' new three-story house was still generously proportioned with an attractive verandah looking out over a beautiful lawn with trees and with a view of a "broad expanse of water, shimmering in the sunlight, with vessels and steamboats constantly passing their bright flags fluttering in the breeze."[8]

An intimate portrait of the Shaw family life was provided by their lifelong friend Lydia Maria Child. An inveterate letter writer and acute observer of social customs, Child stayed as a guest in Frank and Sarah's home after the death of her husband, David Lee Child, in late 1874, just a few months before Josephine and Carlotta's move to a house in New York City. Child's visit coincided with one of the most bitter winters on record, and thus provided her with ample opportunity to comment on her fellow shut-ins at close range. The Shaws installed their friend in a large bedroom that contained all of Rob's old furniture. Child relished sitting in Rob's favorite chair and using his table to write letters from where she could look out the window and enjoy a lovely panorama of Staten Island scenery. The exterior pleasantries were more than matched by the graceful elegance of the interior, which was "adorned with every form of artistic beauty," including valuable books and works of art.[9]

The running of the four-member household was facilitated by the labor of seven servants, including a coachman, who was always available to take Child anywhere she wished to go in the gleaming Shaw carriage. This unaccustomed luxury alternately irritated and amused Child, whose self-imposed exile and penurious existence in Wayland, Massachusetts, had ill prepared her for the Shaws' "luxurious" lifestyle. Nevertheless, she obviously relished her inclusion in their activities and recorded them with warmth and in detail. Every morning, Child recalled, the Shaws would gather in the pretty breakfast room, where the food was accompanied by much lively banter, which included heated discussions of current issues. Particularly memorable was Josephine, fair and comely, with "the becoming little cow-lick on each side of the forehead, laying down the law, moral and scientific to her father." And if Frank dared to disagree with his daughter, he would humorously be declared "an infidel, to be excommunicated from the Progressive Scientific Church, and consigned to the dark, moss-covered chapel of holy St. Fogg."[10]

The invigorating morning discussions undoubtedly fueled the Shaws' busy days, which were filled with the running of the homestead, paying social calls, and "innumerable charitable missions, (to which they devote a vast deal of personal attention, as well as money)."[11] Weather permitting, Frank and Sarah would go into New York two or three times a week, to take care of business affairs or to enjoy the many social and cultural attractions that the city had to offer. Josephine, of course, was constantly coming and going, attending to her duties for the SCAA. And ten-year-old Lotta, dressed in her "wide-stiff skirts and broad-sash," would be picked up in her cousin's carriage in the afternoons to attend dancing school. Every Sunday the whole family would walk a mile to the Gothic-style Unitarian church where they would enjoy a simple service. As there was at that time no minister, son-in-law and neighbor George Curtis would read "so finely" from the best of recent American and English sermons. The small congregation also enjoyed listening to excellent organ music while they prayed together in the church where Josephine and Charley were married.

After the service, there was a gathering of the four Shaw daughters and their families at Sarah and Frank's for dinner. The Curtises, the Minturns, the Barlows, and the Lowells all mingled happily and boisterously on that special day. The Shaws' numerous grandchildren were especially dear to them, and much of the socializing done was devoted to children's activities. Even so, Child found the adult company more to her liking, and she particularly enjoyed the "pleasing and profitable" conversation of Curtis, whose "highly cultured presence" added to the cosmopolitan atmosphere exuded by the family. One occasion was fondly remembered by Child in a letter to Sarah:

> I see dear Frank's pleasant smile, his soft, silky ringlets, his snow-white collar and kerchief, his prismatic diamond, and his golden cross. I see your smiling face, looking anything like a grandmother. I see Anna's great innocent, honest eyes, through which the sincere soul looks so earnestly. I see Susie Minturn's handsome face, radiant and smiling. I see Effie's noble fair countenance, and graceful figure,

float by, like some Lady-Abbess, of a royal line; and I see Lotta flitting about, with her cavalier-cap and feather, ready to plunge into the midst of whatever is going on, and keenly desirous to have everything in the universe explained to her.[12]

Carlotta, described by her proud mother as "a very pretty girl," flourished in the center of an affectionate circle of grandparents, aunts, uncles, and cousins. From a very early age, she was aware of her father's sacrifice in the Civil War. Every year mother and daughter would journey to Massachusetts to visit Charley's parents and sisters. But there was another tangible reminder of Charley at her Staten Island home. This was Berold, her father's now aged war horse. Tenderly cared for by Josephine, observed Child, "the horse knows Effie's voice, and step, and always expects a caress from her. When he stands harnessed at the door, I often see her kiss him before she enters the carriage."[13] The burden of this history may have rested rather heavily on Carlotta's shoulders as the years wore on. As her cousins grew up, and one by one married and raised their own families, she chose to remain with her mother and grandmother, often working and traveling alongside Josephine, which had its own excitements and rewards. During the last few years of Josephine's life, when she was periodically debilitated by illness, Carlotta served loyally as her amanuensis.

Their pleasant life in Staten Island existed until early 1875, when Josephine decided that Carlotta should attend Miss Brackett's School in New York City. Frank then bought her an attractive brownstone at 120 East 30th Street between Park Avenue and Lexington. Josephine's new home was much more convenient for her work as well as beneficial to her daughter's education. They continued to spend most weekends and holidays at Frank and Sarah's. At this time, there were no bridges connecting Staten Island with the city, and so Josephine and Carlotta would take the Staten Island Ferry to New Brighton, and from there a brisk five-minute walk (weather permitting) would bring them to the corner of Davis Avenue and Richmond Terrace, their home near the river. This time-consuming commute was frequently interrupted or made impossible during the winter storms, and weather, along with a better education for Carlotta, was a determining factor in Josephine's permanent move into the city. From her brownstone on 30th Street, she would begin a new phase of her career, that of a commissioner on the New York State Board of Charities.

✑ *The New York State Board of Charities* ✑

On April 30, 1876, Josephine Shaw Lowell's appointment to the SBC was printed on the front page of the *New York Times*. Announcement of her appointment also appeared in the *New York Tribune*, which offered a lengthy and flattering portrayal of Lowell as a young and idealistic philanthropist who had already achieved an enviable and impressive service record with the SCAA. The press placed great emphasis on the fact that Lowell would occupy an unusually public position for a woman and would presumably bring to her board duties a distinctly feminine sensibility. The *Tribune* described her as "the first woman . . . who has ever received an office from the state of New York."[14] Lowell herself was very much aware of this kind of attention. Her appointment underscored the catalytic role Gilded Age women were beginning to play in moving philanthropy toward its more modern outlines. As the issue of poverty moved to center stage in the 1870s and 1880s, female charity workers were especially well placed to redefine and reorient the private and public relief systems. This power that women were starting to exercise in 1870s New York State was demonstrated by their prominence in the SCAA and the ties that were being forged between that organization and the SBC, now visibly symbolized by Lowell's appointment. Any discussion of Lowell's thirteen-year service as commissioner on the SBC must begin with a consideration of her pioneering role for women in this arena.

It might be helpful to provide a job description for a commissioner, which was then a new position for both men and women. First and foremost, Lowell and her fellow appointees were required to "visit and inspect" each social welfare institution receiving public money in the state of New York every two years. This included prisons, reformatories, county poorhouses, orphanages, and asylums for the mentally incapacitated. This was a tall order, and not unexpectedly many institutions went unreported on by the overburdened commissioners and their staff. As one of the two commissioners representing New York County, Lowell was also expected to (and did) produce reports on the institutions under the aegis of the New York Department of Charities and Corrections, the public agency responsible for the city's dependent populations.

Commissioner Lowell was also required to attend the board's public meetings, held at various times during the year in different locations.

For example, in 1880, the SBC annual report records three meetings in Albany, one in Binghamton, one in Saratoga, and one in New York City. Lowell attended all of them, and throughout her career on the board she was extremely conscientious about her duties, even when other, more pressing activities began to pull her away from the SBC. (She resigned in 1889.) Additionally, she served on board committees responsible for the whole state, such as the Standing Committee on Outdoor Relief, the Standing Committee on the Deaf, Dumb, and Idiots, and the Committee on Reformatories.[15] A letter to her sister-in-law, Annie Shaw, confirms a hectic schedule:

> I am all in a whirl of business, present and to come. Last week I finished off our report on New York City Charities, which, although it does not look like it, has kept me busy for six months, and it went to the Legislature on Thursday. Then I had to take up a case of abuse of a patient at the Lunatic Asylum, and on Wednesday . . . I and a lady stenographer went over to Blackwell's Island, where I examined four attendants who were a good deal frightened. . . . Of course I did not learn much, but it will have a salutary effect and make them see that such things will not be overlooked. I am also busy about the Women's Reformatory Bill and petitions in favor of it; and altogether, as usual, I should like to be fifty people, and could lead fifty very pleasant lives.[16]

Investigations, reports, recommendations to the state legislature, meetings, and a commitment to reform drew Lowell and her male colleagues together in their work. The majority of the commissioners were from the upper class, illuminating the fact that during these last decades of the nineteenth century the elite's participation on state boards, in private charities, and in political reform movements such as civil service and municipal reform represented an apogee of public service for them. Brief biographies of two of her early colleagues on the board are instructive.

The work of the board's president, William P. Letchworth, is an excellent example of a life dedicated to the public good. An upstate New York native, Letchworth was born in comfortable circumstances to a family active in educational and abolitionist reform movements. A lifelong bachelor, he devoted himself to building up his business, from which he retired at fifty in the early 1870s to work in social reform. In 1873 Letchworth declined a safe congressional nomination in favor of an appointment to the SBC, where he could pursue his interests in bettering poorhouses, providing education for delinquents, and improving the mental health system. In all of these fields, Letchworth made significant contributions during his long tenure on the state board, of which he was made president in 1878.[17]

Lowell's most admired co-worker of her early years on the SBC, however, was not Letchworth, whom she criticized in private as weak and ineffective, but her fellow New York City commissioner, Theodore Roosevelt, Sr.[18] Even more than Letchworth, Roosevelt was an exemplar of noblesse oblige and the scion of a wealthy Knickerbocker family. Roosevelt, like his friend Louisa Schuyler, was deeply committed to living up to the ideals of the Knickerbocker elite, who were at one with their Boston Brahmin counterparts in promoting community service as a necessary corollary to class position. Lowell had very strong opinions on the necessity of the wealthier class involving themselves in the life of the country. "All our men are so busy," she once complained to a correspondent, "that they cannot spend their lives on public work and so, gradually, the women are coming to take part in them, which is not to be regretted, but we need the men too, and I hope that in time, we shall have a 'leisure class' composed of both men and women who will join together in taking care of public matters."[19] Although Lowell's public-spirited "leisure class" never massed in the numbers that she hoped, few men of her class could be more congenial or seem more worthy than Roosevelt, who retired from the family business at an early age to plunge into the world of cultural patronage and social reform.

By the time Lowell met Roosevelt he had already helped to found both the Metropolitan Museum of Art and the American Museum of Natural History as well as to establish two of the city's premier charities, the Children's Aid Society and the Newsboys Lodging House. Roosevelt's philanthropic service was further burnished with his appointment to the SBC, where he distinguished himself with able reports and a growing opposition to the intrusion of corrupt politics into charity. Lowell and Roosevelt worked extremely well together on the board until his death from stomach cancer at the age of forty-six in 1878. With the other commissioners—Edward O. Donnelly (Roosevelt's replacement), Riley Ropes, and John C. Devereux—Lowell established amiable working relations. But it was not until the arrival of William Rhinelander Stewart in 1882 that she again enjoyed the warm friendship and close professional ties that she had so cherished with Roosevelt.

"The Sole and Solitary Woman"

As one woman working among many men, it might be expected that Lowell would be self-conscious and even hesitant to put forward her views in meetings or other arenas with her colleagues and other state and county officials.[20] Yet this was not the case. She was gracious and diplomatic but very strong-minded and quietly aggressive in leaving her imprint upon the SBC. She did this through sheer determination and hard work. In fact, Lowell contributed greatly to the prestige and the reform successes of the SBC both before and after her founding of the Charity Organization Society in 1882. An exact comparison of Lowell's board work with that of her colleagues is impossible to ascertain, yet a glimmer of light on her substantial contributions can be found in the twelfth annual report of the SBC, which provided a detailed schedule of each commissioner's work for the previous year. Commissioner Lowell came in first with fifty-six visits, President Letchworth made a decent showing at thirty-five visits, and Commissioners Devereux, Donnelly, Foster, and Miller trailed badly with nine, fourteen, nine, and one visits, respectively. Unfortunately, this was the last time such a schedule was to appear in the report, making further exact comparisons impossible. But the next annual report records that Lowell kept up the pace, making forty-seven visits to twelve institutions, and additionally writing two major reports for the board. Over the next decade, Lowell would produce forty-three SBC reports, both major and minor, by herself and with colleagues.[21]

A typical week for Commissioner Lowell went something like this:

Last Monday I left here [New York City] at eight and went, by train, to Binghamton, arriving at 5 P.M. I at once procured a buggy and went off two miles to visit an Inebriate Asylum and stayed till eight, when the Superintendent drove me back to my boarding house. Tuesday at nine I called on a lady on business (about poorhouse work), and then went off to a Convention of the Superintendents of the Poor; there were about a hundred, I should think, and I was the sole and solitary woman! They talked away until twelve, when we scattered for dinner and returned at two and stayed till five. . . . At five I drove out to an Orphan Asylum, with one of the Managers, and then to his house to tea and back again to the convention, where again there were no other ladies, and where I addressed the meeting on the subject of tramps. A little after ten the session came to an end, but the next morning at nine, they were at it again and sat until twelve.[22]

In this rare accounting of her time, Lowell goes on to describe other late-night visits to poorhouses, a trip to Rochester to attend a thirteen-hour meeting of the SBC, then on to Syracuse to visit children's asylums and schools before finally taking the train back to the city, arriving late in the evening at her home on 30th Street.

Sandwiched in between Lowell's description of her schedule are two pointed remarks about her "solitary" womanly presence among many men. This arrangement may have contributed to feelings of loneliness for her, and it certainly shows how few women were included in the ranks of state welfare in the 1870s. She was a role model for the many women who would come later to work in official capacities in New York State welfare. On the other hand, she also demonstrated an ability to work effectively under such trying circumstances. Lowell cultivated a solid network of male support from relations, friends, colleagues, and prominent figures from the world of reform, politics, government, and business. From this network she drew sustenance in her work for the board, as well as later endeavors. Lowell's well-developed web of male friendships appeared in stark contrast to the perceived lack of similar support from a female network. "Why was this noble worker for good allowed to so toil but with few women to stand with her and to be by her side?" asked an admiring female reformer of a later generation, Kate Bond.[23]

Lowell's situation might be viewed as unusual to a twentieth-century feminist accustomed to locating nineteenth-century women *only* within a network of female friends and relations. This network, moreover, has been declared as indispensable support for women who engaged in the public realm, where cultural approval was noticeably lacking. Thus some might surmise that Lowell aligned herself with the male power elite at the expense of other women. Yet a more sensible approach would be to locate her in a complex network of gender, class, religious, and educational concerns in which men and women were not necessarily at odds with each other but shared similar interests and acted together to carry out common goals.[24]

Additionally, Lowell was not as alone as Kate Bond claimed. Lowell cultivated good working and personal relations with a group of similarly minded women—Schuyler, Rice, and Collins—who were representative of the hundreds of thousands of women, past and present, toiling in the private charitable fields. Ellen Collins, for example, proved herself to be an exemplary visitor for the SBC throughout the years. As chief investigator for New York County, she helped to gather the raw material Lowell needed to make her comprehensive reports for the board. Collins was Lowell's trusted colleague in the SCAA, the SBC, and the COS.[25] Unsalaried and modest, Collins did not work in a high-profile official capacity and was more typical of the female charity worker of the 1870s. But in the next few decades, the number of women professionally trained and employed by the state would grow, a phenomenon Lowell herself would help to create. Many of these younger women looked to Josephine Shaw Lowell as an example of how they could learn to gain and use power to effect public policy. They considered her a master of the political skills necessary to translate ideas into action.

✎ The Female Reformatory Movement ✎

An early and outstanding example of Josephine Shaw Lowell's ability to control the reform agenda was in her successful effort, beginning in the late 1870s, to establish the first reformatory for women in New York State. This campaign also reveals the way in which she perfected her skills as a social scientist and advocate for reform on the SBC. First, a problem was identified and investigated. The knowledge gained from such an examination was both statistical and anecdotal. Second, a series of reports was issued based on the research but, significantly, drawing as well on a growing pool of knowledge from national and international social scientists. Lowell's active membership in organizations such as the National Conference of Charities and Correction (NCCC) was one way in which she both received and proffered information. The sharing of knowledge from a wide variety of sources dressed the material with sophisticated analysis. And third, the information was delivered to the legislature as part of the board's annual report.

An important aspect of the presentation to the legislature included a well-coordinated effort to gain support from sympathetic friends in the reform and political community. In this particular case, and in subsequent campaigns, Lowell benefited from the wisdom and experience of former abolitionist and Quaker Abigail Hopper Gibbons, a longtime advocate for prison reform and a leader of the Women's Prison Association, as well as the SCAA and other notable reformers and reform organizations.[26] Finally, appropriate legislation was drawn up (and in this case and many others, Lowell wrote the bill herself) in an attempt to expedite the process of reform. Usually the bill would not pass first muster and would die in committee, so Lowell would have to begin again when she judged the timing auspicious.

While making her first rounds as commissioner in 1876, Lowell was outraged by the terrible conditions that women convicted of crimes continued to endure in county jails, almshouses, and houses of refuge. And there were more female prisoners than ever before: during and after the Civil War, women's presence in Massachusetts and New York prisons increased by one-half. The explanation for the rise was the war's unsettling legacy, the rise in poor immigrants, and the flood of rural residents into urban areas. The majority of the women were arrested for prostitution, public drunkenness, and petty crimes. The female inmates were often mistreated; their welfare was ignored, and they were subject to abuse by both the male jailers and the male inmates.

The traditional system of caring for women was custodial and run very much along the same lines as male prisons. These regular prisons, usually attached to the men's, accommodated the majority of female inmates. And even though these inmates were mostly very young (at least one-third under the age of twenty-one), Lowell declared that "they have entered on the downward course." The reason for this, she went on, was that these institutions were unconcerned with reforming their denizens: "In neither jail, poorhouse nor penitentiary, will they find anything to help them turn back; on the contrary, all the surroundings will force them lower." Lowell presented her findings in a conference paper given at the annual meeting of the NCCC in Chicago. Her paper painted a vivid portrait of "fallen women" and their illegitimate offspring (often born and raised in the poorhouses), who were made permanently "bad" because of their environment, "where every avenue to vice and crime is open." Drawing a parallel between the justifiable lifetime commitment of the incurably insane to prevent generative transmission, Lowell asked in regard to long-term incarceration for female criminals, "Why should we not also prevent the transmission of moral insanity, as fatal as that of the mind?" And the worst crime of all, she declared, was that against the larger community and that cost the "hardworking inhabitants" of the state too much money just to keep the women in terrible places with no hope of improving their lives.[27]

The solution? Lowell had one ready at her fingertips. We as a society, she claimed, must take responsibility for our degraded fellow human beings, and she advocated that the state build a system of reformatories designed especially to house and educate "all women under thirty, when arrested for misdemeanors, or upon the birth of a second illegitimate child."[28] The reformatories, which would be staffed exclusively by women, would consist of a group of "homelike" buildings in a rural environment far away from the distractions of cities and provide the type of training, both moral and practical, that would allow the graduates to earn an honest and upright living. Lowell argued very strongly for the educational benefits to be gained from such a system, not only for the women but also for the society at large. Of course, she admitted that in the short term the reformatories would be more expensive to build and maintain than the current system. However, an intelligent commitment of public resources, she claimed, would be more cost-effective and humanitarian in the long term and benefit future generations as well. Lowell not only relied on her reputation as an expert in putting forth her reform plan but also borrowed heavily from a wider base of evidence from Europe, especially the work of Thomas Barwick Lloyd Baker, whose findings on youthful offenders in England deeply influenced the building of American reformatories.[29]

Lowell was well prepared when the legislative campaign commenced in 1881. "I believe it to be the duty of the Board to guide the Legislature," she told her colleagues.[30] And she placed a bill for the funding and building of a female reformatory onto the 1881 legislative agenda, with the formal backing of the SBC and with the support of other reform groups, the press, and the public. It also helped her cause that by this time she knew many of the legislators both in the Senate and the Assembly from her earlier work to establish an Asylum for Feeble-Minded Women, which was more easily accomplished than the work for women prisoners. The reformatory bill failed to pass in that session. It was put on the back burner for two years. Disappointed but not daunted, Lowell geared up in 1884 for another go: "I have become quite enthusiastic for our poor House of Refuge," she wrote to the board's assistant secretary, James O. Fanning, "and want to start a new crusade for it! I shall write a note to each member of the Legislature and send to you to be delivered at the Capitol, together with copies of the enclosed papers and my paper on Reformatories for Women."[31]

This time it worked, and the House of Refuge Bill passed on May 21, 1884, with the reform becoming a reality when the Women's House of Refuge accepted its first inmate on April 15, 1887, at Hudson. Lowell continued to be involved in every aspect of the Hudson reformatory's progress, which included appointing its personnel and fighting to maintain its institutional integrity (as well as the ones established later at Bedford and Albion).[32] Other states followed in New York's footsteps and established similar reformatories for women. Indeed, Lowell's success in this and other areas of her SBC work established her nationwide reputation as a no-nonsense reformer who got things done. She set out the problem and the solution in a clear, forceful, and persuasive way, always completely sure of her evidence. She was willing to do the tedious work not only of writing the legislation but also of guiding it through the legislature, meeting with politicians, and testifying in front of committees for as many times and as many years as it took. Lowell was also adept at using pressure groups such as the SCAA, interested government officials, or citizens to force the legislature to act. And after a bill she supported passed, she followed it through the often bumpy process of making reform into reality. Along the way, she became an astute observer of the way the American political system really worked. In short, Commissioner Lowell established her credibility both as a woman reformer among men and as an expert on issues related particularly to women.

The assumptions that underlie Lowell's desire to "save" young women from a life of degradation are well worth examining for what they reveal about her ideas about gender and class. Three guiding principles were articulated during the reformatory campaign: first, the wholesome benefits to be gained from separating male and female prisoners; second, the necessity for "female-centered" care revolving around the creation of a nurturing, homelike environment and job training appropriate for young offenders; and third, the involvement of women at every level of maintenance and management of the institution—from guard to nurse to doctor to member of the board of directors.

The principles of the reformatory campaign were embedded in the nineteenth-century ideology of "separate spheres," in which the sexes were assigned to increasingly distinct and separate social and economic roles. Women, who were primarily defined by their relations to men, were the keepers of the traditional values that protected the home and the community from the harsher aspects of commercial and business life. It was by forcefully expanding this ideology to encompass public concerns that middle-class and elite women, working individually and in groups, were able to flex their muscles as moral guardians of late-nineteenth- and early-twentieth-century American society. This was not only seen in charity and prison reform movements but in the related movements of temperance, moral purity, the women's club, and the settlement house.[33]

The women who led their sisters in the battles for moral and social reform have been labeled "social feminists" or, more aptly, "civic maternalists" by historians because of their belief in the efficacy of applying women's superior moral power (which arose out of the separate-sphere ideology) to society's problems in the Gilded Age and the Progressive era.[34] That Lowell shared these assumptions is shown in her oft-stated belief that women, historically deprived of a public presence, could nonetheless effect change through their collective morality. "Whatever other advantages or disadvantages may have come to the human race, and to women themselves from their being shut off in the main from the struggle for existence," she wrote, "it seems to me that there has been one great gain, their more acute moral sense." Women had a duty to use this "acute moral sense," Lowell explained, because "as a class they have a more sensitive moral instinct than men as a class, and I therefore hold them to a stricter moral responsibility."[35] Lowell knew well that the very idea of women in prison was shocking to the majority of middle-class women because it perverted the ideals of feminine moral virtue so cherished in Victorian America. She used the widespread public acceptance of these ideals when developing a program to care for these "fallen angels."

The reformatory concept was especially appealing because it was assumed that the very young character could still be molded in a socially acceptable direction. Older women offenders would not be welcome inside the gates because it was feared that they would "taint" the younger and more vulnerable women. Lowell's reports on women in prison drove home the point that the primary goal of the new female reformatory was to "rescue and reform" female criminals whose morality had been stunted due to circumstances beyond their control. The victims needed to be saved and placed in an environment conducive to restoring the dignity of their womanhood.

A crucial part of the reform process Lowell described as "educative" involved shaping the inmate into a productive member of society. She was especially concerned that the girls be trained in appropriate skills that would enable them to earn a living until marriage. She did not want them to sit around doing "fancy-work, talking and leading a life . . . which would quite unfit them for hard work after leaving."[36] At Hudson, Lowell was influential in making sure a strong vocational training program was put in place. The emphasis on vocational training reflected both the status and sex of Hudson's clients: working-class (mainly Irish immigrant) girls who were being funneled into the traditional fields of women's work—domestic service and sewing. Modern critics of the women's reformatory movement have stressed its negative impact much more strongly than its positive effects. Why, they ask, were the most vulnerable members of society—poor, immigrant, sexually disgraced women—singled out in a way that young male criminals were not, and given a long-term punishment for what was really a minor offense? The answer, they argue, is that these young women were victims of a sexual double standard imposed on them by elite women reformers, who, by founding and running reformatories such as Hudson, *institutionalized* unjust Victorian standards of sexual conduct.[37]

Scholars' attacks on the reformatory movement are embedded in a much larger critique of nineteenth-century American society in which institution-building—prisons, poorhouses, reformatories, hospitals, asylums for the mentally incapacitated, public schools—is portrayed as an attempt by the upper and middle classes to limit the more dangerous and unstable tendencies of a vast, democratic, and potentially anarchic country. Welfare institutions, so the argument goes, were used as vehicles of repression in which the dominant ideological values central to maintaining a capitalist hegemony—Christianity, domesticity, order, self-restraint—could be inculcated into even the youngest or most excluded members of society.[38]

These are serious charges. Although there can be little doubt as to the good intentions of Lowell and her colleagues, this by itself is insufficient to justify their reform program. What is meaningful is that the abuse suffered by women confined in county jails and workhouses, observed firsthand by Lowell and many others, was painfully real. For Lowell, this state of affairs demanded action. What options did she entertain? Lowell was not a radical sex reformer; nor did she ever advocate the destruction of the capitalist order, only its adjustment. She thus fashioned a reform program that reflected the best and most scientific information available and within the limitation of the time. This kind of reform had a progressive message: that environment could and should be used to remold and refashion the human spirit, no matter how downtrodden. That is why it was so important to reformers that the reformatories be placed in a pleasant rural atmosphere and that the architecture be simple and homelike. In turn, the domestic, nurturing, pastoral environment would be powerfully reinforced by an educative program that fused religion, proper etiquette training, and work discipline.

Lowell used the ideology of Victorian sisterhood to build a bridge between middle-class and working-class women. If just one young woman suffered unduly for her crimes, she asserted, then all women were implicated and responsible for that suffering. Moreover, the double standard was not created (although it was sustained) by reformers. Rather, the double standard was upheld firmly by a society that proclaimed the greater moral virtue of women over men: indeed, this moral superiority was a source of power for middle-class women of the nineteenth century. Women who "disgraced" themselves by committing crimes of prostitution, drunkenness, or other public misbehavior were at much greater risk than men for harsh and repeated punishments. The new women's reformatories gave thousands of poor women over the years an opportunity to change their lives by staying away from the "bad influences" they might encounter at home or in the county jail.

The reformatories' emphasis on work as a character-building experience—with the concomitant program of vocational training—was part and parcel of the nineteenth-century ideology that glorified work as a good moral end in itself. Few people could express this idea more eloquently and with such fervor as Josephine Shaw Lowell. She held that life was hard for all working people, who were the majority. Yet it was essential that they keep working, that they imbibe the virtues of thrift, honesty, and above all patience, so that they could go on with their lives and strive for better ones. Lowell was afraid that if society made it too easy for poor people not to work, for example, through overly generous relief programs, that the weaker, more susceptible members of the "honest" working class would be tempted to give up their upright but difficult lives, with little immediate reward, for the pleasure of living off of taxpayers.

To this end, Lowell was especially concerned that Hudson women should be trained in a program that realistically reflected their expectations. The majority of working-class immigrant women would in fact earn wages in domestic service and related work. Furthermore, she personally saw to it that their domestic training would be accompanied by lessons in morality and deportment, which would give them the strength of character to accept their lot and to refuse the temptations of easy money that prostitution or petty larceny held out to them. Lowell's ultimate goal at Hudson was to make these young women economically functional, and to give them a degree of independence and self-esteem.[39]

Did it work? Sometimes. Many problems that Lowell and the reformatories' leaders had to face were typical (and still are) of all social welfare reform: chronic underfunding and overcrowding dimmed the movement's initial bright ideals. Yet despite these setbacks, many inmates in the 1880s and 1890s did indeed become the "dutiful daughters" envisioned by the reformers. Undoubtedly, the young women, perhaps a majority of whom were from severely disorganized homes, benefited from a strict regimen of discipline, domesticity, and moral uplift. Thus any evaluation of the reformatory movement must take into account the gains from a clearly defined program that included not only punishments but realistic rewards.[40]

✎ *Female Institution-Building* ✑

Another fascinating aspect of the reformatory movement needs to be considered: its contribution to the growth of female institution-building. Lowell and the thousands of volunteer women who worked alongside their state or national government during the Civil War were comfortable with and impressed by the results achieved by big organizations and expanded state power. After the war, women who had been trained as nurses, administrators, and charity workers by their local aid societies were ready and willing to continue their contributions. Moreover, many of them needed to work to support themselves and their families. The reforms initiated by the women and men serving on the new state boards in New York, Massachusetts, Ohio, and Indiana opened up job opportunities for many women when the new institutions had to be staffed and managed. Lowell informed her male colleagues on the board that women were proving quite capable as managers and employees of these enterprises.[41] From this point on, she was a leader in advocating and then securing positions for women, not only in reformatories but also as charity agents and police matrons as well as in government. In short, gender inevitably shaped Lowell's career. She could and did advance the opportunities for wage-earning women as well as attempt to improve conditions for the countless dependents in her charity work.

Lowell's service on the SBC always demonstrated a strong concern for poor women. Unlike some other leaders within the scientific charity movement, she supported generous relief measures to poor mothers who were not "morally deficient," which, as she freely admitted, were most of them. "This sort of help is not demoralizing nor pauperizing," she insisted, "because it only places the family in a natural position. Women and children ought to be supported, and there is no sense of degradation in receiving support."[42] Any mother, she went on, had an immense amount of work to do just raising her children properly, and if disaster befalls her, society should help her get back on her feet. Lowell's concern for women and children reflected her larger view of the family, in which the father provided for, and protected, his wife and children. Violations of this natural order, either by individuals or by the failure of the economy or the state, brought forth from Lowell some of her more radical proposals for social change. Those same positions on women and children, however, also revealed her belief in traditional gender roles. For example, she did not favor equal *roles* for men and women, although she did favor equal *rights*, as her support for the suffrage movement demonstrated. All of Lowell's prescriptions for women's activism depended on using their distinctive moral qualities to advantage. In this she was no different from the majority of her contemporaries.

There was a paradox embedded in Lowell's life and her thinking, however—one that was shared by generations of female reformers and activists. The more she expanded the scope of her own power, the more she made it possible for other women to consider alternative career choices. From the 1870s on, she promoted female professionalism, albeit one that did not conflict with family duties, and tied the benefits of civil service reform to increased employment opportunities for women. On a personal level, clearly she considered herself a professional woman.

Her career also demonstrated the very real limits on women's advancement in the Gilded Age. While every bit as ambitious and intelligent (and in many cases much more so) as any of her male co-workers, Lowell strictly confined her career to charity—and even within charity to certain areas. One painful example occurred in 1885, when Lowell was nominated as one of the three commissioners in charge of New York City's "paupers, insane and criminals." At first Lowell was elated: now her vast knowledge of reformatories, prisons, and poorhouses accumulated through years of visiting, report-making, policy-making, and research could be put to use in a position that she considered a very powerful one. Mayor William R. Grace, however, turned her appointment down "because he thinks a woman could not know anything about the prisons." Lowell was bitterly disappointed at the loss of this opportunity to put her ideas into effect, just because of her gender. "It does seem hard," she wrote regretfully, "to be prevented from undertaking it because the Mayor thinks a *woman* would not know how to deal with prisoners."[43] That she was ready to consider accepting such a high-profile, *paid* position spoke volumes about the depth and seriousness of her ambition. The mayor's denial drove home to her a reminder of the precariousness of her position in a man's world.

Lowell kept silent on the other reason that the mayor of New York City might have turned her down: by this time she was an eloquent and influential advocate for reforms that constantly placed her at odds with most of the politicians in charge of city government. Next to establishing women's reformatories, Commissioner Lowell was most concerned with the charitable state of affairs in New York City. Lowell's analysis of pauperism had led her to voice frequent criticisms of the lax administration, costly inefficiencies, and cruelly indifferent care-giving that she believed characterized the city's public institutional structure. She added to her ongoing critique a complaint about the frequently unexamined public outlays of money to the city's vast network of private charities that further compromised the welfare system.

ᥱᥩ Charity Organization ᥰᥩ

Josephine Shaw Lowell's increasingly vocal, public criticisms of New York City's welfare system were grounded in her extensive investigations of its charitable institutions and its methods of dispensing public relief. As early as 1877, she informed the SBC of her intention to study public relief policy when she asked for its approval of a blank form to be sent out to all county relief officials in New York State. Lowell's own investigations as commissioner for the city would provide much of the raw data for the study. The results of her work appeared in two separate reports published simultaneously in the SBC's 1882 annual report.[44]

The first of these, "Report of the Charities of New York City," was nothing less than a manifesto for change. Clearly written and forcefully argued, Lowell proposed sweeping changes in welfare administration but warned that its success had to be tied to an attack on the corrupt political system. "Tammany Hall," she wrote indignantly, "is a corporation which wants to hold the control of New York City Government, not to serve the people of the city, not to give the city clean streets, pure water, efficient protection for life and property, smooth pavements, beautiful parks, or any other thing that it is necessary for the people to have, but because the yearly expenditure of the city for these and other purposes is more than forty million dollars."[45] Her biting critique of municipal government was interwoven with evidence gained from her repeated examination of New York City's dense web of welfare institutions: hospitals, mental asylums, poorhouses, workhouses, reformatories, and prisons. Always, however, she returned to her persistent theme of using civil service reform as a bludgeon to force the political system to become more honest, efficient, and humanitarian: "The government of the Department of Public Charities and Correction appears to be that of a personal despotism; everything seemingly depends upon the will of the Commissioners; little power is delegated to the heads of institutions." She went on to portray a department in which sensible and thoughtful recommendations for improvement by educated "gentlemen" within the institutions were steadfastly ignored by politicians whose interests were not served by reforming from within but rather maintaining the status quo. "We can hope for no really radical improvement in the department, until the people demand that men shall be appointed to whom the public welfare, apart from personal or political advantage, is the one object."[46] Lowell's linkage of political reform to welfare reform brought her even more into the open as a sworn enemy of machine government.

The two issues of city mismanagement and misuse of money were wedded in a short but powerful indictment of New York's relief-giving societies in the second of Lowell's reports for the SBC in 1882. Dismayed by the careless methods and waste of money that characterized relief policy among the city's many private charities and public agencies, she argued for organized charity. "So important a business as the administration of charity has become in New York City," Lowell claimed, "requires to be carried on business principles. . . . Some system is required to enable these various societies and organizations to work in harmony, to attain the end they all aim at—some plan by which each may be helped by the knowledge and experience of all."[47] At Lowell's urging, a short resolution was passed by the SBC on July 15, 1881, to the effect that a committee be appointed (with herself as chair) whose objective was "to take such steps as they may deem wise to inaugurate a system of mutual help and cooperation" between relief agencies in the city. In a stunning move, Lowell engineered state authority to establish a charity organization society in New York.

The blossoming of social science, the creation of state boards of charities, and the proliferation of private charities in the 1870s all occurred within an explosive and unstable environment that seemed to cry out for a new and concerted effort to restore harmony and ensure order. Lowell believed that charity organization offered one solution to social chaos. Not only would charity organization provide the balm to soothe class conflict, but it would also provide the young, motivated elite with an opportunity to declare "a ruling class's war on poverty."[48] She thus enthusiastically embraced the charity organization movement that was beginning to spring up in large and small cities across America.

The impetus and rationale for beginning a new organization developed out of Lowell's board work, of course. She now knew almost everything there was to know about institutions and what it would take to make them better. But Lowell was also very much aware, as she wrote to her friend and fellow reformer Thomas Baker, that "to educate and elevate the mass of the poor and ignorant so that they shall not get into prisons and the poorhouses is the main thing." Lowell now believed that her time could be more productively spent in "educating and elevating" the poor *outside* of institutions, and at the same time engaging in a higher profile battle with machine politicians in order to reform corrupt charitable practices. This could be done by leading the charity organization movement in New York City, where, Lowell contended, she had spent "great sums to encourage pauperism but so far ha[d] not done much to stop its growth." In the past five years Lowell had done much reading on the subject of organized charity, and by 1882 she was thoroughly familiar with its bright promise of increased cooperation and efficiency among charities, which so happily conflated with the ideals of civil service reform. "If no one else steps forward to do it," declared Lowell, "I shall soon try what I can do to bring the present chaos of charity into shape. . . . Somebody must do it, so why not I?"[49]

Lowell had progressed from SCAA volunteer to the state's first female SBC commissioner to the brink of becoming the founder and force behind her own organization, the Charity Organization Society of the City of New York. After serving on the SBC, Lowell's reputation as an expert in the areas of pauperism and dependency was never more respected. The experience she gained from the constant rounds of visiting, inspecting, and reporting on the many institutions for the dependent added immeasurably to her knowledge and her public status as an expert on welfare issues. On May 25, 1881, Governor Alonzo B. Cornell reappointed her for a full term of eight years. Lowell was now assured of continuing her work on the board throughout the 1880s. She was determined to fulfill her duties for the SBC while at the same time bringing charity organization to New York City, to balance official public duties against her private initiative. Lowell was clearly manipulating the system to accommodate her ambition to make changes in the way charity and politics were operating in the city and state. Josephine Shaw Lowell was ready to found the Charity Organization Society of New York City.

ᔆ *Public Relief and Private Charity* ᔆ

Lowell's first book, *Public Relief and Private Charity*, was published in 1884 but was the fruit of several years of hard thinking and writing. Before turning to the next chapter's examination of the *details* of building a successful institution, it is important to elucidate the broad deductive principles on which Lowell expected the COS to bring about a stable social order at whose heart lay the productive individual. This latter ideological perspective is clearly described in *Public Relief and Private Charity* and provides an excellent starting point for understanding the message of charity organization. Lowell's book, it should be noted, was immediately influential within the charitable field and remained the standard work on charity organization for a generation.[50]

As its title suggests, *Public Relief and Private Charity* is divided into two parts: the first addressing the role of the state in providing welfare and the second defining the duties of the private charitable sector. The first step in implementing a new charity policy for the industrial age, Lowell asserted, was the immediate abolition of government-provided outdoor public relief: "It is not right to tax one part of the community for the benefit of another part; it is not right to take money by law from one man and give it to another, unless for the benefit of both." This abolition, however, was not unconditional, because "there are in every community, persons who cannot maintain themselves, and who have no friends upon whom they have a claim, and that it would not be well . . . that these should be driven to desperation by the absolute pressure of want. . . . [P]ublic relief is a benefit to the whole people, acting as a preventive to violence." Thus individual relief was justified by the benefits and social order it brought to those who paid for it.[51]

The key, Lowell argued, was to make all public relief *indoor* rather than to run the risk "that the need supplied by public out-door relief is in fact created by it." Here, according to Lowell, the evidence was overwhelming, and she frequently cited from both the English and American experience. Society's task, then, was to define strictly, and thus limit, the categories of dependents who could truly be said to have a moral and legal claim on the state. These would include anyone in danger of immediate starvation, the impoverished elderly, and various groups of the mentally ill and disabled. She proposed a clearly defined system of public agencies and institutions to be established "in every city and county." Critically, this system must be free of all baneful political influences and be run on civil service principles that would ensure its efficient and honest administration. Implementing those policies would lessen or remove the unfair transfer of wealth within a community as well as the unnecessary and harmful dependence of individuals on state aid.[52]

Lowell used her own career experiences to buttress her ideological argument for abolishing outdoor relief. She had honed this argument in the 1870s, when she and SCAA President Louisa Lee Schuyler had been leaders in the successful effort to end outdoor relief in New York City. Then, too, the bulk of her SBC work was in large part directed toward defining and separating the worthy dependent from the unworthy dependent in asylums, poorhouses, jails, and other institutions. She was constantly pushing for more humane and professional (in her mind they were inextricably linked) conditions in those same institutions. By the end of the first section of her book, Lowell clarified the proper role of public relief and, in theory at least, diminished the role of worthy supplicants on state relief.

Readers of *Public Relief and Private Charity* turned to the second part to envision, along with Lowell, a new and expanded role for private charity. But first, a definition of the word itself was in order. Charity, Lowell wrote, was "a voluntary, free, beneficent action performed toward those who are in more destitute circumstances and inferior in worldly position." She added, "By this definition, of course, all official and public relief is outside the pale of charity, since it lacks the voluntary element." Furthermore, she asserted confidently, "Private charity can and will provide for every case that should be kept from resorting to public sources of relief."[53] This, of course, enlarged the role and the importance of the leadership of private charities, dominated in New York by men and women of Lowell's class. In turn, this brought up the question of what benefits accrued to those who gave of their time and money. The answer: moral improvement for both the rich and the poor.

Here Lowell underlined the major tenet of the charity organization movement: that the point of charity was not primarily to assuage suffering but rather to uplift and reform the recipient into a productive and independent member of society. The wealthy would benefit as well because they would be forced out of their own selfish preoccupations with material and social pleasures. Service to the less fortunate would also make them aware of the severe conditions under which the majority of the human race lived. Both the rich and the poor would improve the moral climate of their communities through the benevolent actions exercised by the philanthropically minded toward the underprivileged.

Lowell labored mightily to keep her charity organization society a "service" organization and not a "relief-giving" one. Her beliefs, crisply outlined in *Public Relief and Private Charity*, were repeated many times in her subsequent writing and speeches. "What is a little ease or comfort or pleasure worth," she would ask, "compared to nobility of character?" In this way, she hammered home the point that material relief must always be accompanied by moral uplift. "If we help the body only," she admonished, "our help is worth nothing; like the body itself, it perishes daily and has to be daily renewed. If we help the soul, if we teach something, our help is eternal, like the soul, and there is no end to the good we have done." She seized on this idea and emphasized it repeatedly: "The fundamental principle is that all charity must tend to raise the character and elevate the moral nature, and so improve the condition of those toward whom it is exercised, and must not tend to injure the character or condition of others."[54] How could she put it more plainly? Lowell believed that the charitable impulse should not be "selfish." Rather, it should be directed to the improvement of the individuals, and this improvement would then lead directly to the betterment of society.

Despite separating and clarifying the functions of public relief and private charity, Lowell admitted that together they performed equally important functions. In the public sphere, she argued, outdoor relief should be abolished (with certain exceptions) and designated categories of dependents should be institutionalized according to their needs. And these needs should be attended to in nurturing, educative environments, which would be regularly and carefully inspected by a combination of volunteer and professional charity workers. Private charity, transformed by the principles of charity organization, would provide for the majority of the poor: elderly widows, deserted wives, unemployed men, children, and the pauperized population. These people would benefit from the wise council of trained private relief officials immersed in the ideology of the new kind of philanthropy. Relief would be given, but only after all other sources of help were found to be lacking. The state not only would be saved money but also would benefit from the growth of untold numbers of hardworking, responsible citizens. Charity must be administered not as an end in itself but as a moral instructive that benefited the total community by combining the objectivity of the new social science, the principles of charity organization, and the subjectivity of personal contact of the fortunate with the less fortunate.

Public Relief and Private Charity united policies designed to further implement social control with the goal of promoting individualism and economic independence. These conflicting means and ends have characterized the operation of social-welfare policy from its beginnings in the industrial age and continue to complicate policy to this day. Hidden in Lowell's optimistic blueprint for a better society were troublesome contradictions that only became apparent after years of trying to inculcate the principles and practices of charity organization into the lives of New Yorkers. Her sensitivity to these contradictions explains why, when all was said and done, she found the charity organization movement inadequate to solving the problems of poverty in the United States. But that revelation would come later. For now, Lowell, with the approval of the SBC, could look forward to implementing her vision of charitable reform on a grand scale in the most important city in the nation. The eyes of the country's philanthropic community would be on her new organization, and it was with a sense of understandable excitement and anticipation that she sent out a letter to a selected group of gentlemen asking the question, "Have you any time to spare for a very important public work?"[55]

6

Charity Organization

Imagine, if you will, Josephine Shaw Lowell in her vigorous middle age, walking briskly down the crowded streets of New York City. She is on her way to a meeting at one of the Charity Organization Society's nine district offices. This particular district office, known as Corlears, is bounded by Canal and Houston streets, just east of the Bowery. If one of Mrs. Lowell's fellow pedestrians happened to glance her way, he would notice a pleasant-looking woman of medium height and weight, blessed with a glowing complexion and fine, penetrating eyes, her abundant, shining light brown hair covered neatly in a small black bonnet to protect it from the city's notorious dirt and grime. He might well conclude the woman had been widowed, for she was dressed in black from head to toe. And he would be correct, although more than a quarter of a century had passed since her bereavement.

If this hypothetical New Yorker possessed a fine sense of social distinction, he would be able to identify Mrs. Lowell as a member of the upper class by her genteel bearing and gracious demeanor. Yet he might scratch his head in puzzlement, for here was a lady displaying a street manner that did not quite conform with proper Victorian etiquette.[1] Instead, she was stopping to chat with a street cleaner and complimenting him, in her beautiful, clear voice, on a job well done. She then pulled a small black notebook from her purse to jot down his employee number and promised to write a good recommendation to his supervisor.

Sufficiently intrigued, Mrs. Lowell's observer might have followed her down a few more streets, now teeming with the Italian and Jewish immigrants who, with other nationalities, had recently joined the Irish and Germans to help to make the city at once the most prosperous, populous, and turbulent place in America. Suddenly, she stopped to murmur a few encouraging words to a schoolchild. Straightening up, she frowned, watching yet another street cleaner lounging in a desultory manner at his post. This time, her conversation with a cleaner bore the unmistakable tone of reproof, and the unlucky city employee had his number taken as well, so that his poor performance could be reported to the authorities.

Finally, the curious New Yorker would see Josephine Shaw Lowell no more, for she had arrived at her destination at 297 Broome Street and had disappeared into the Corlears district office. Once inside, she went straight to the business at hand—the disposition of welfare cases that had come to the attention of the district committee during the previous week. One family needed to find a place for a sick mother. Another needed medical attention for an injured father. Still another needed emergency funds with which to bury a stillborn baby. Here Lowell's attention to detail paralleled her behavior on the street. In fact, her executive talents simultaneously guaranteed the swift treatment of family emergencies, the kind but businesslike oversight of the agents who handled the cases, and the well-ordered office atmosphere that complemented efficient charity work. It was largely due to these abilities of hers that the Corlears office gained a reputation as the smoothest and best run district office of the COS. When her work was done at the district office, she donned her bonnet, wrapped an old-fashioned black shawl around her shoulders, and was off, either to attend other meetings, meet with city or state officials, write reports, visit institutions, or arrange protest gatherings—all of which could easily be on her schedule any day in the late 1880s and early 1890s.[2]

Josephine Shaw Lowell belonged to a generation of philanthropists poised between the "amateur" reformers of the nineteenth century and the "professional" reformers who, by the early twentieth century, dominated the ranks of social scientists and charity workers. Lowell and many of her colleagues in Gilded Age charity were a self-identified group of upper-class leaders whose family traditions encouraged social activism. Lowell, who cherished her family's history of civic participation, was also an important transitional figure who embodied *both* the old and the new ways. That delicate balance between eras was illustrated in her bold actions on the city's sidewalks. Lowell's comments to working-class citizens were redolent with noblesse oblige, yet her intentions were modern: to instill professional pride into a group of workers employed by political bosses who were unconcerned whether the streets were cleaned, and whose work—good, bad, or indifferent— went unrecorded.

And so it was on such walks as Lowell took to Corlears, as well as in committee meetings in which she considered individual cases, that she developed a broad understanding of the needs of the underprivileged. This knowledge affected her COS work and moved her into other organizations to attack poverty from different angles. Lowell's contributions to the New York City labor movement and to municipal reform marked a later phase of her career but sprang from her involvement with the COS.

৩ৎ *Starting Up* ৩ৎ

At this point in her career, Lowell was going to put her previous experience to work by painstakingly building an organization that would become, by 1893, a major player not only in the city's philanthropic community but also in its governance. This was, of course, exactly its founder's intention. Lowell's career trajectory paralleled the establishment and growth of the COS from 1882 to 1893, the flowering of the charity organization movement. As earlier, she continued to mix charity with political reform, igniting controversy over issues central to the shaping of social-welfare polity in New York. During these years, Lowell emerged as a key national leader of the charity organization movement. Her book, *Public Relief and Private Charity,* was extremely well received, and its message widely publicized by her frequent and eloquent speeches, articles, and conference appearances on behalf of scientific charity and charity organization. Lowell's public and private comments alike reflected her exuberant optimism about the ability of scientifically applied charity to solve the apparently intractable problems of poverty.

Lowell's optimism was grounded in her belief that pauperism could be cured through individual correction and discipline. In her view, poverty was largely the result of behavioral failures, so that the moral adjustment of the individual was the key to uplifting the "degraded" population and bringing them into mainstream American life. She had another reason for feeling optimistic about the future of scientific charity in New York City: for the first time, she could flex her managerial muscles, and she immediately demonstrated a brilliant flair for organizational work that boded well for the fledgling COS. Lowell's skillful leadership drew attention to the small but growing charity organization movement in the United States.[3]

Indeed, three leaders arose in the early years—the 1870s and first part of the 1880s—to guide and define the American movement. They were Stephen Humphreys Gurteen of Buffalo, Robert Treat Paine of Boston, and Josephine Shaw Lowell of New York.[4] Lowell willingly became the instrument through which the charity organization movement would flourish in the biggest city in the nation. As a member of the SBC as well as the NCCC, she had witnessed the earliest efforts to bring English charity reform principles to the United States. The first society had been established in 1877 in Buffalo by the English-born and Cambridge-educated Reverend Stephen Humphreys Gurteen, whose *Handbook of Charity Organization* quickly became the sine qua non of every beginning society. Gurteen made an extensive tour to establish charity organization societies in American cities and provided valuable assistance to Lowell as she struggled to establish her own organization.[5]

Lowell also looked to the successful charity organization societies led by Paine and Annie Adams Fields in Boston and those in such other cities as Philadelphia, Baltimore, and Indianapolis for advice. She was keenly aware of the fact that the New York organization would be started on her initiative or not at all. Before her efforts, she wrote to a friend, "No one . . . had the courage to take hold of it."[6] Lowell's letters to Annie Fields, who along with Paine founded the Associated Charities of Boston and served as a director and vice president of that organization until 1906, attest to her eagerness to start off the New York COS on the right foot. "I hope to see you this summer," she wrote in early 1882, "to consult and get advice." Lowell later attempted to recruit (unsuccessfully) Zilpha Smith, Boston's gifted registration bureau chief and soon-to-be general secretary, away from Fields, pleading, "Remember what a missionary field this is and how disastrous it will be if we fail, or even if we do not do our work in the best and wisest way; disastrous not only here in this great City, but for all Charity Organization."[7] Clearly Lowell considered New York above all other cities in America to be the key place to test whether the charity organization idea could in fact work. Thus infused with enthusiasm and purpose, she literally set out to create something out of nothing.

"Have you any time to spare for a very important public work?" asked the thirty-eight-year-old Josephine Shaw Lowell of Charles Stebbins Fairchild, a prominent New York Reform Democrat with whom she was to establish a productive working and personal relationship within charitable and political reform.[8] The same request was mailed out to a number of carefully selected gentlemen, requiring their assistance with the formation of the COS. Nearly a month later, armed with positive responses from at least eight "earnest men," including Fairchild, Alfred and James R. Roosevelt, Arthur M. Dodge, and J. Kennedy Tod, Lowell was able to announce that the first committee meeting to establish a charity organization society in New York City would take place at the office of the State Board of Charities, 67 Madison Avenue.[9] On February 8, 1882, the election of officers took place, with Dr. S. O. Vanderpoel as the first president, shortly to be replaced by Robert Weeks de Forest. Although not herself an elected officer, Lowell assumed a position of power and influence within the COS, and her contributions to its creation and viability as an organization were widely known from its inception.

The dominance of men in the public face of the society represented a conscious strategy on Lowell's part, and it deserves explication.[10] This strategy reflected her long-held belief that the majority of men, representing the wealth and power of society, would not respect or support a cause or an organization in which women were perceived as the leaders. "However just the cause she may defend," warned Lowell, "a scolding woman is a terror to all men; no one will listen to her, no one will sympathize with her; she only injures her own cause."[11] It is extremely significant, for example, that she used her married name, Mrs. Charles Russell Lowell, on all COS printed material—a departure from her SBC position as well as from every one of her later reform activities. Indeed, as she knew well, scientific charity exalted the business and professional approach and denigrated the soft-hearted. In other words, it would not be prudent to start out with the COS known for being "a sentimental woman's affair."[12] This trend, given powerful impetus by Civil War philanthropy, as exemplified in the U.S. Sanitary Commission, was one in which Lowell, Louisa Lee Schuyler, Gertrude Rice, and many other women heartily concurred. Yes, they argued, women, just like men, *could* believe in business principles and efficient management of resources without abandoning their humanitarian sensibilities. And, of course, the female presence within the organized charity movement increased exponentially until, in the 1890s, Lowell felt she could be less circumspect about her leadership position in the COS.

In the early 1880s, however, Lowell could not take for granted that the COS would be the well-funded and respected institution it became in the 1890s and into the twentieth century. Rather, she assumed that its success or failure would in part hinge on the financial and moral support garnered from the city's business and philanthropic community. "I see many pleasant people," she wrote, "especially men, upon whom we are trying to throw the responsibility of this work, so as to bring the business faculty to bear on the charity problem."[13] This putative support, which was crucial because the COS depended on private sources only, would be imperiled from the start if it were too obvious that women ran the organization. Thus it was that the society's official publications, press releases, and especially its annual reports showed a preponderance of distinguished men as officers on the Central Council and in the standing committees.

✍ The Gentlemen Reformers of the COS ✍

Now is the appropriate time to introduce some of the men with whom Josephine Shaw Lowell worked closely in establishing the COS. First is Robert Weeks de Forest, who was appointed president in 1887 and who served forty years in that position. More than anyone else, he was the public face of the COS. For Lowell, de Forest embodied all the elements necessary to make the fledgling organization a success: he was a wealthy lawyer from an old New York family and consequently felt at ease with the business community from which he was expected to solicit funds and bequests on behalf of the COS. And in this de Forest succeeded brilliantly, by all accounts. It was, for example, largely due to his efforts that the New York philanthropist John S. Kennedy built the United Charities Building, which, when opened in 1893, provided spacious quarters for the COS and ensured its institutional solidity. Robert de Forest also persuaded Kennedy to endow the COS's New York School of Philanthropy (later the School for Social Work) in the early 1900s.[14]

Lowell and de Forest became close friends and spent many hours together in the COS's early years, planning how best to place the organization on a sound financial footing. De Forest's son recalled that every Sunday afternoon his father "invariably left us for a while during the afternoon and went for little talks with Mrs. Lowell."[15] It cannot be stressed enough that starting a charitable society in the highly competitive and contentious environment of New York City was a risky undertaking, and no one knew that better than Lowell. Much like small businesses, city charitable enterprises came and went with the seasons, and even the best, most idealistic intentions were not guarantees of longevity. An additional handicap was that scientific charity was seen as being too "cold" to warm the hearts of wealthy contributors. "Charity Organization has not awakened any enthusiasm here," warned a prominent city minister to a prospective COS employee.[16] That Lowell set out to recruit men like de Forest speaks of the depth of her commitment to making the COS a permanent and prominent part of New York City's philanthropic community.

Thus from the beginning Lowell was thinking of the long-term capabilities of her organization as well as its short-term necessities. This is why she surrounded herself with professional/businessmen philanthropists—men who balanced her lack of experience in the area of finance. The following anecdote is telling. De Forest recalled that he and Lowell had only one major difference in their long association, and that was over the COS's first major bequest of $10,000. She characteristically wanted to spend it all, but de Forest demurred, and persuaded her to use it as the beginning of an endowment. That early, modest endowment would grow to $7 million by the 1930s and to $82 million by the late 1980s.[17]

Josephine Shaw Lowell and Robert de Forest worked together to recruit for the COS the kind of men who not only would attract funds via their impeccable business and social credentials but also would contribute creatively to the organization's programs and its day-to-day administration. One such man was Otto T. Bannard, a banker and president of the New York Trust Company, who volunteered his services to the COS for many years.[18] Bannard, a Republican who ran for mayor of New York City in 1907, was one of the more conservative members of the society. He and Lowell often clashed over the costs of running the society, with her priorities firmly on the side of promoting human services over fiscal soundness. They came out about even. Lowell had differences with other members as well. "About the

C.O.S.," wrote her great friend Charles C. Burlingham, a prominent New York lawyer, "one time she almost broke it up. I remember Mr. James Jackson Higginson was a member and threatened to resign, and several others did, because she declared in her calm and beautiful voice that a deficit was an excellent thing for a society of that nature. That was too much for them."[19]

Bannard, however, did put his banking experience to good use for the COS when he served as treasurer and trustee of the "Penny Provident Fund," an innovative program (first put into practice by the Baltimore COS) that encouraged savings among poor children. Bannard's example shows that Lowell was comfortable working with people who did not always agree with her agenda. She was never, nor did she desire to be, the sole controlling power behind the COS. A good executive, she early on realized that the sharing and delegating of powers, responsibilities, and honors would be the key to the organization's success.

Other bankers and lawyers dominated the ranks of COS officers. Constant A. Andrews, the treasurer, was president of the U.S. Savings Bank. Later that post would fall to J. P. Morgan. Henry B. Anderson, who worked closely with Lowell in restructuring the COS's district committee system, was a lawyer, as were George Rowell and Charles Stebbins Fairchild. Lowell especially wanted Fairchild, the recipient of her first letter of recruitment, within the charity organization fold. New York–born but of New England origin, Fairchild was working for the railroads when Governor Tilden lured him into politics as part of his reform team to combat the corrupt Democratic machine in 1875. Lowell had met and immediately liked Fairchild when, as the attorney general, he served as an ex officio member of the SBC in the 1870s. Their shared interest in charity reform extended into the national political arena after he was appointed secretary of the treasury under President Grover Cleveland in 1885.[20] It was especially pleasing to Lowell that Fairchild, like Tilden, and the president he served, supported the goals of civil service reform and thus represented the reform wing of the Democratic party. In New York, Fairchild was a leader of the "Swallowtail" Democratic faction opposing machine politicians in city and state elections.

A year after Fairchild assumed leadership of the Treasury Department, Lowell teased him "to come out of your disreputable party, as we have come out of our disreputable party, and let us all join to make a decent one of our own! It is a strain on the feelings of a mugwump to remember that you . . . for party reasons, helped to saddle New York with [David B.] Hill for governor for three years!"[21] Lowell's correspondence with the Fairchilds (both husband and wife) remains a testament to her vital interest in politics and reminds us of her deeply held belief in the interconnectedness among charity, reform, and the healthy political life of the state. Through Fairchild, she established a friendly relationship with President Cleveland and considered herself to be one of his greatest supporters.

George William Curtis, Lowell's brother-in-law, was now the national leader of the Mugwumps, the disaffected Republicans who "bolted" their party in 1884 to support Cleveland and civil service reform. Curtis was also active in the New York effort to reform its own political machines.[22] Lowell's earnest attempts to improve civil service in the state and city in the charitable arena complemented Curtis's on the national level. Her desire to make the COS a fiscally sound entity did not mean she wanted it to be a conservative organization in its policy objectives as well. In fact, Lowell guided the COS to progressive reform advocacy, in both the charitable and political arenas, especially in its advocating of civil service reform, which placed it in the forefront of the groups agitating for municipal reform in the 1890s.

Lowell also wished to preserve the strong ties between the SBC and the COS, which was, in a sense, the SBC's step-child. These ties were personified in her close relationship with her colleague on the board, William Rhinelander Stewart. Stewart, another descendant of a venerable New York family, gave up his law career when a young man to serve the public interest.[23] He was appointed by Governor Cornell in 1882 to the SBC, where he remained for the next forty-seven years, serving as its president for twenty-four of those years. Lowell cultivated Stewart as an ally and a friend from the beginning of their work together as commissioners for New York City. He regarded her as his mentor and, in a touching gesture of respect and affection for her memory, carefully collected her letters, papers, and reports into a memorial volume after her death in 1905. Stewart served, alongside Lowell, as an ex officio member of the SBC for the COS. Lowell's continuing experience as commissioner sharpened her perceptions on which welfare functions should be under the control of the state and which should be taken over or preserved by private charities.

✑ "The Femality" ✑

The fact that so many of Lowell's colleagues were men cannot conceal that much of the society's work was done by women, and they, too, were present from the beginning of the organization. Lowell playfully described one of the earliest meetings as being attended by "the clergy," "the laity," and "the femality."[24] The "femality" on this occasion included Gertrude Stevens Rice, Ellen Collins, and a Mrs. Lockwood. Rice, already an officer with Louisa Lee Schuyler's SCAA, would be especially important as a liaison between that organization and the COS, just as Lowell served in that role between the COS and the SBC. In 1892 Rice became the first woman to serve as a COS vice president.[25] Her intelligent and perceptive advice must have lightened Lowell's executive load considerably. Collins served all three of the above organizations simultaneously in her role as a volunteer visitor for the SCAA to the SBC, and as a member of the COS District Board. Organizational interaction was facilitated by their proximity: after 1886 the SCAA and the COS shared office space when they rented a large house at 21 University Place.[26]

Homer Folks of the SCAA later dramatized the complex relationships between these women and the organizations they founded and served:

> One day I was there and Mrs. Lowell said (it was always Gertrude, Louisa and Effie; it was of great interest to me to see their intimacy and friendship); "Oh about that matter of taking care of the mother and babies. It worked well in Boston and it was useful in Philadelphia and I think we ought to try it in New York and, if so, why don't we get ready and start." The other agreed and she said "I don't think it could be done by the COS. We have all we can undertake at the moment. Why doesn't the State Charities Aid do it?" They nodded. "It will cost some amount. I'll be glad to contribute so much." And the others enrolled some more and it was all settled there on the spot.[27]

Especially interesting in Folks's observation is the way in which Lowell and her colleagues drew on their practical experience to devise solutions to problems that confronted them in new settings. This pragmatism was an outstanding feature of Lowell's thinking about reform and charity.

In the 1880s Josephine Shaw Lowell operated within the still small world of nineteenth-century upper-class philanthropy. The men and women who comprised the leadership of the COS, however, should not be confused with the new generation of fabulously wealthy New Yorkers, such as the Astors, whose excesses have helped to give the Gilded Age its bad name. As David Hammack has conclusively shown, elites in the city were divided into competing groups whose disparate economic, cultural, and political goals belied their shared class position. Lowell was born into an upper class with long-standing commitments to public service and whose family ties with Protestant churches and reform organizations stretched back across the decades to the very settlement of America. So it was with de Forest, Stewart, Schuyler, Seth Low, Theodore Roosevelt, Sr., and the many others who constituted the bulk of the supporters of the city's charitable and reform establishment. "Among the 43 male officers and directors of the COS," Hammack observed, "only one had been invited to Mrs. Astor's 1892 ball for the '400,' and only one was among the 'patriarchs' of New York society."[28]

This undoubtedly was a point of pride for Lowell, who despised the well-publicized frivolity of the new wealth. Her family tradition dictated that benefits that accrued from money and privilege were to be used discreetly. This philosophy suited her personally as well. Always plainly dressed (in black, of course), she preferred walking or using a streetcar in favor of the more ostentatious carriage. Her brownstone at 120 East 30th Street was comfortably, but not richly, furnished. The first floor of her home contained two spacious rooms from where she conducted her business and social life. One was a pleasant sitting room where she entertained her many guests and visitors and from where she often set off to attend the opera or other musical concerts, which were her favorite form of entertainment. A letter written to Annie Shaw in 1888 records the more social side of her days: "I am going to give you a list of the friends we had here yesterday. Friday, Howard White [a cousin raised by Frank and Sarah] slept here so he was at breakfast. At 10—young lady from Iowa on business; at 11—Amy White and Lucy Russell [cousins]; at 1—Rose Howard . . . she and Amy to lunch; at 4 Nannie Codman; at 4:30—Mrs. Wister and two young cousins of hers, McAllisters; at 5—May Minturn and at 6— G.W.C. (Nannie, May and George to dinner); at 8—Rob Minturn; at 8:30—Mrs. and Mrs. Burlingham."[29]

The second room was her dining area, but Lowell had installed her desk there to take advantage of the room's superior lighting. When she was not out attending meetings, visiting institutions, or interviewing society applicants, she could be found in this room writing the letters and reports that seemed to flow endlessly from her pen. "I have just counted the record of my letters since January 1, 1893," she declared. "I find this is the 1899th!"[30] Hundreds of local, state, and national officials were the beneficiaries of her letters, written in a large, bold, and clear hand. One good friend recalled her sitting at her "flat-top" desk after dinner and composing twelve letters on the spot. "There wasn't a city official that did not fear to get her letters," Charles Burlingham wrote. "If she saw anything wrong anywhere, she would write at once and it meant something."[31]

City officials might well have feared Lowell's letters because they knew they could expect a follow-up visit from her in the near future. She was a frequent visitor to city hall, in both her role as an SBC commissioner and her COS work. In one instance, she went to see Mayor Hugh J. Grant with her friend and fellow reformer Jacob Riis. He recalled that they "nagged and nagged" the mayor about building municipal lodging houses for the homeless. Lowell urged Grant to consider the stellar example of Boston, whose success with city lodging houses she much admired. "Boston, Boston, I am sick of the name of Boston," cried the beleaguered mayor. Riis, worried that Lowell would be offended, stole a glance at her, but to his relief "she was leaning back in her chair and laughing heartily."[32]

Lowell also needed her sense of humor in Albany, to where she quite often traveled via train to lobby for or against bills that would affect charity and social welfare in New York City and New York State. On one such trip she and Jacob Riis were working together again, this time in an effort to convince an Assembly committee to pass an important bill. After listening impatiently to their testimony, an assemblyman interrupted rudely, directing his remarks to Riis but clearly including both of them. "Professor," he sneered, "you people come here year after year arguing for these things; let me ask you, what do you get for it?" Riis, shaken by the hostile nature of his remarks, replied, "What do you mean?" The politician answered by holding out his open palm, the well-known gesture for receiving graft. Riis went on to record that this legislator "was the only one I ever knew to distrust or question Mrs. Lowell's motives." But when he turned to her to express his shock he saw that she had assumed "a patient, far-away look in her face. Those things meant nothing to her. She was there in a cause. It was God's cause, and it was bound to prevail."[33]

Lowell was well respected but not necessarily well liked among the state legislators, who were not always hospitable to the relentless campaigns by reformers. They also could have been put off by her deserved reputation for plain speaking. The SCAA's Edward T. Devine, a perceptive observer of Lowell, remarked: "Mrs. Lowell would not like to be called tactful, however much she valued that trait in others."[34] Her blunt manner turned many genteel COS meetings into spirited and contentious gatherings. She would regularly denounce the corrupt political situation in city hall or take the COS to task for not living up to its reputation or ideals. She often spoke eloquently at large and small public meetings, although she proclaimed her discomfort at this activity. William Rhinelander Stewart praised her for being "content to sit with folded hands, and depart without opening her lips," a trait he doubtless found attractive in women. Yet time and time again in the many meetings they attended together he marveled at her ability to stand up and to speak eloquently if she felt that the subject had not been presented to her satisfaction. Indeed, Lowell could be quite bold in presenting her views. In one meeting she had given a speech in favor of labor and, afterwards, had left the platform to sit in the audience only to hear a Mr. Lewis denounce her position. He had barely finished when an angry Lowell climbed the platform stairs requesting from the chair a chance to reply and defend herself.[35] All in all, her class position, her public prominence, and her growing importance in the philanthropic community helped to make the COS into a formidable institution.

Besides recruiting the socially minded wealth and power of the city, Lowell was directly involved in the more mundane aspects of setting up the COS. These included everything from renting offices, engaging clerical workers, doing mailings, and going around to the city's numerous charities to introduce the society. She also was busy helping to write the organization's constitution, along with Charles Fairchild, Arthur Dodge, and R. Duncan Harris, members of a subcommittee charged with that task.[36] The COS officially came into existence when the state legislature approved its incorporation in an act passed on May 10, 1882. By that time Lowell and others had finished the organizational structure of the society, as laid out in the constitution. The Central Council, whose members were drawn from the officers, ex officio members, and the district offices, was responsible for the society's overall management and was endowed with the power to add, change, or delete its bylaws. Members of the council were elected annually and were expected to attend the monthly meetings or be dismissed from their duties. Lowell was one of the ex officio members, representing the SBC along with her colleague, William Rhinelander Stewart, until her resignation in 1889 allowed her to become a full-fledged member. She was also one of a three-member committee whose duties were to nominate the officers of the society and of its Central Council.[37]

Lowell positioned herself securely within the center of power of the COS, which was cemented by her membership on two of the most important standing committees of the Central Council, the Executive and the District Work committees. The Executive Committee was chaired by President Robert de Forest and usually included the most powerful and active people in the organization. Lowell was virtually the only woman to serve on this committee, which functioned as a troubleshooter for the various controversies and problems encountered by the society. It also served as a mini–Central Council, which usually rubber-stamped its reports and recommendations. Lowell assisted in the initial and critical task of dividing the city up into fourteen districts, each of which would eventually be endowed with its own office, a committee to run it, and a hired district agent, of whom the majority were women.

Lowell was aware that a big part of the future success for the COS would lie in hiring committed, idealistic, *and* capable people to help run it. To this end, she hired Charles Kellogg as general secretary away from the Philadelphia COS, where he had been employed for four years and where he had acquired an excellent reputation. His responsibilities would include the hiring, training, and supervising of the district agents and other employees who would become the COS representatives to the poor clients they were serving. "I am very glad indeed," wrote Lowell to Kellogg, "that you have decided to come to New York. It is a great relief to know that we are to have your help, for we have as hard a piece of work before us as is to be found in this country."[38] Kellogg later recalled that on his arrival in New York he was pleasantly surprised to find that so many of the troublesome details of starting a new COS were efficiently and quickly accomplished—a feat he attributed to Lowell.[39]

✌ *Organization for the Prevention of Charity?* ✍

In the early years, it was the repressive principles and programs of the New York COS that made it stand out in the crowded field of city charities and captured the attention of the press and the public. Indeed, the harsh ideology that lay beneath the society's unyielding opposition to "pauperism" prompted more than one critic to remark that the COS was more of an "Organization for the Prevention of Charity" than anything else.[40] And Josephine Shaw Lowell was the guiding spirit behind repression just as she was in the more positive parts of the COS's program. As in her SCAA days, she continued to advocate harsh measures to cure pauperism: "Mrs. Lowell was by far the most outspoken, persistent and logical advocate of strong repressive measures among the leaders of the C.O. movement," wrote one historian of her efforts.[41] Moreover, throughout her career, even when she articulated a sophisticated analysis of the shortcomings of the capitalist economy, Lowell was still preaching against the dangers of unattended pauperism. For example, she led various campaigns in the late 1880s and the 1890s to abolish cheap or free city lodging houses (often in police stations), arguing that what was needed was "a home which takes entire charge of its inmates, which teaches them and raises their standard and makes them hate the life they are leading; which keeps them only so long as is necessary to train them for self-support; which pushes them on and up continually."[42] This was the subject of her and Riis's meeting with Mayor Grant, and her views were widely reported in New York newspapers. In newspaper articles, papers, and speeches, Lowell defined three categories of tramps—from the vagrants to the honest if befuddled workers to the very youngest and most salvageable—and advocated different forms of treatment for each group.[43]

Her position was firmly rooted in the belief that the underclass must not be allowed to "enjoy" their idleness but rather must pay the consequences in strict but humane reform facilities. She feared that their shiftless example might be followed by the working poor, who would compare their life of hard work unfavorably with the "easy" lot of the homeless who lived off of public relief and charity. Lowell was

aware that economic downturns would increase the number of paupers but warned that "every additional provision, good, bad, or indifferent, made to shelter homeless men, will serve to draw men, who have
homes, but who for any reason do not like them, from their homes into
a homeless state."[44] Lowell's thinking on pauperism—steady on from
the 1870s to the end of her life—demonstrated a strong commitment to
moral individualism for poor and rich alike. While she did seem to
assign a disproportionate importance to the effect of the homeless
and pauperized part of the population, this was because she believed that their bad influence far outweighed the smallness of their
numbers.

Yet Lowell's pessimistic—or, some would say, realistic—view of human nature as shown in her concern over moral "backsliding" must
ultimately be weighed against her romantic, optimistic view of the
working class. This view assumed great importance later, when she
became prominent in labor relations. Lowell's views on pauperism are
cited disapprovingly as evidence of the mean spirit of Gilded Age charity, shortly to be rectified by the more enlightened Progressive era
reformers, righteously ensconced in their settlement houses. Yet there
is abundant evidence that many Progressive reformers agreed with
harsh measures for paupers, reserving their praise, support, and programs for the working, "deserving" poor, just as Lowell did.[45]

Not surprisingly, political considerations were also behind Lowell's
opposition to cheap lodging for the homeless. New York City's police
force was neither honest nor efficient, and its ties with Tammany Hall
were well documented.[46] Accordingly, homeless men in city lodging
houses often benefited around election time when Tammany politicians would pay for their votes—a practice that outraged civil service
reformers such as Lowell. The connection between crime, vice, poverty, and the police department would erupt in scandals in the 1890s
and become a political advantage for reformers in the anti-Tammany
campaigns in which Lowell would play an important role.

The COS's early tough image was reinforced by its Committee on
Mendicancy, which maintained a special department for the control
of vagrancy and beggary on the city's streets. Ideally, Lowell and the
COS wished to develop institutional structures—a farm school for the
youngest homeless and model lodging houses run on reform principles
for the majority, coupled with a vigorous, graft-free police department
and police court system—to ensure properly that the homeless popula-

tion would be taken off the streets once and for all. Because these were all long-term goals at best, the COS undertook the immediately doable task of seeing that the laws on beggary were enforced to the fullest extent possible. The society hired a "special agent" endowed by the city government with the power to arrest beggars off the streets and to make sure they were punished accordingly. A monthly "cautionary bulletin" listing all charity impostors by name was sent as a warning to members to avoid indiscriminate charity. Within a few years, the COS developed a tenuous working relationship with the police, the police justice courts, and the Department of Charities and Correction with the goal of reducing pauperism on city streets. By these means, the society was establishing itself as a part of city government, so that, by 1890, the COS could proclaim that "with the Department of Public Charities and Correction we have an excellent understanding, and we receive all the assistance from them that we can properly ask."[47]

The COS was very proud of its program of stopping beggary, which placed it in the forefront of the fight against "vice."[48] Lowell herself was a member of the Committee for the Advancement of Public Morality and was a close reform colleague of the Reverend Charles H. Parkhurst, head of the Society for the Suppression of Crime and a prominent figure in 1890s political campaigns.[49] Vice control was part of the social purity movement of the late nineteenth century and was closely linked to other reform movements in New York City. It was also a potent weapon in the arsenal used by reformers to defeat Tammany Hall. Lowell's and the COS's successful drive to establish police matrons in the city's police stations and prisons is a good example of the link between vice control and reform. A gross corruption of morals occurred, Lowell charged, when women prisoners were not segregated from male prisoners and when male officers abused their charges. Vice was tied to existing police corruption when the department resisted the reformers' entreaties for change. Lowell and her fellow reformers wished to show that the politicians who protected this "evil system" were symptomatic of the larger problems of machine government. Reform, which would include but not be limited to vice control, came with the introduction of a corps of female matrons, vetted by civil service examiners, who would ensure the proper and dignified handling of female prisoners. Lowell believed vice to be one part of the seamless web of corruption, dishonesty, and immorality that enfolded the governance of city institutions, and to attack one problem was to attack them all.[50]

✌ The District Committees ✌

Lowell did much more than just formulate COS policy behind closed doors. She was not afraid to get her hands dirty with the real work of building an organization from the ground up. The best way to really appreciate Lowell's contribution to the COS is to examine her leadership of and immersion in the district committee work in the 1880s and 1890s. A brief background on the importance of the district committees to the COS is necessary. Investigation, cooperation, and registration provided the methodology behind the bureaucratic apparatus of the society and its district committees as well. The gathering and recording of information on people who applied for any sort of assistance was undertaken by the society's district agents, or other officials at the main office or one of the district offices, and then transmitted into personal histories of the clients and their families. This information, however, was only as valuable as its availability. The next two stages ensured that the information would be widely shared and benefit the reputation of both the COS and the city's charities.

Again and again, SBC Commissioner Lowell had pilloried the lamentable mess of the city's numerous charities that engendered duplication, waste, and inefficient use of scarce charitable resources. One of the first things she did as leader of the COS was to get out the word to philanthropically minded individuals, churches, and private societies that the best way for them to improve their service was to cooperate through the auspices of the COS. In the society's fifth annual report, Lowell was pleased to announce that the COS had enlisted "nearly every important and influential relief-giving agency and nearly every self-supporting church in the city" to share information and tactics. This part of the program was greatly successful. And one of the key factors in the society's success was its reliance on a nonsectarian philosophy clearly enunciated in its constitution. This way the Protestant-dominated society could be inclusive of, and influential with, the powerful Jewish and Catholic charities that catered to immigrant populations, who, after all, would form the majority of the society's clients, especially after 1890.[51]

Cooperation worked through the mechanics of the registry bureau, which by 1887 contained information and histories on an estimated 88,338 families. The bureau additionally kept records of "27,400 houses occupied by the dependent and disreputable classes."[52] The registry provided a clearinghouse through which the cooperating members of the society could obtain information on clients that would supposedly prevent duplication, waste, inefficiency, and so forth. Investigation, cooperation, and registration, as developed and practiced by the COS, represented an advance in social-work methods and marked the elevation of casework as the primary tool of social welfare. "Co-operation is a mark of advancing civilization, and lack of it a sign of barbarism," announced the COS.[53] And it certainly helped to fulfill one of the society's main tasks—to educate the wealthy and the philanthropic sector on the correct way to give. Still, the society's lofty and sometimes arrogant assumptions about the superiority of scientific charity as compared with every other kind engendered conflict when the organization tried to practice what it preached.

This conflict occurred primarily within the society's district committees, each of which was composed of approximately fourteen "gentlemen of clear minds and kind hearts," who were charged with recruiting friendly visitors, doing some visiting themselves, and reviewing agents' and visitors' reports and making recommendations involving the relief and rehabilitation of the clients.[54] At least five of the members would ideally live in the district they served, as a big part of the work would involve educating community institutions as to the proper ways of dispensing charity.

The district committee members—the corps of friendly visitors and the district agents (and their assistants)—were the linchpins of the COS ideology. This triad comprised the much vaunted "personal service" ideal of charity organization that lay at the heart of the COS's motto, "Not alms but a friend." The system worked this way: a notification would be made to a COS representative of a family or an individual in distress. Often this would be in the form of a letter written by a landlord, friend, minister, boss, newspaper, or patron. An interesting and little-known fact about the COS is the large number of upper-class people who used the society to investigate charity cases. Of course, this is what the society encouraged, in order to inculcate an informed responsibility in the well-born.[55] The notification began the investigation process, and a district agent would be assigned to the case. The agent would write letters to anyone and everyone (parents, children, employers, ministers) who could give information regarding the "worthiness" of the supplicants. The agent was required to keep an ongoing record of the case, and these records were reviewed regularly by the district committee—and in some cases a special standing committee—until the case was closed. This could happen in a week, as was usually the case, but some cases remained, on and off, in the files for five years, ten years, or even twenty years. The opening of a case file by an agent was accompanied by the assignment to the family of a friendly visitor whose interest in the problems would provide the human dimension that would counteract the more businesslike demeanor of the agent.

The disposition of the cases was decided in weekly meetings by the district committee, in which four represented a quorum. Service to the poor came in varied forms and could be speedy or slow, depending on the particular urgency of the case. Because it was the official policy of the COS not to give immediate cash relief but to study the long-term needs of the family involved, the relief package could include access to food or heating supplies, legal advice, arranging a long-term welfare stipend through a church or patron, or simply providing information on the many medical, educational, or charitable services that the city had to offer. Indeed, agents and friendly visitors were trained to direct their clients to the appropriate agency for assistance. Often this involved any number of agencies and institutions with which the COS had close working relations: the Association for the Improvement of the Condition of the Poor or the SCAA, for example. Creating a dependable charity network gave the COS its special élan among the city's welfare agencies. The results of each district committee's efforts among the poor were printed in the annual reports and often provided the most interesting and provocative reading in those publications.[56]

Lowell's involvement with the society's district committees' work was intense and long-lasting. She helped to set overall policy for the district committees through her chairwomanship of the Committee on District Work. The work of this committee, described as an "appellate body," was subject only to review by the Central Council and its Executive Committee, both of which Lowell served on as well. The committee was also a sounding board for many of the sticky issues encountered by district committee members and agents throughout their service. These issues included agents' training and salaries and the establishment of proper rules, regulations, and guidelines for the relief of the poor. In 1892 Lowell joined the third district (later known as Corlears) as a committee member and also volunteered there as a friendly visitor.

The minutes of the committee meetings not only demonstrate Lowell's capacity to deal effortlessly with the bureaucratic minutiae but also draw attention to her larger management style, which elicited admiration from her colleagues. "What a worker she was!" remembered one friend. "I said to her once, 'why do you go to those awful meetings with those women, and men who are no better than the women, who talk and talk and talk.' She said, 'Oh, you don't understand at all. My work is to create and develop opinion and that can't be developed by efficiency and running through the meeting and having agendas and doing matters quickly and having done with them. It's talk that does the trick.'"[57]

Lowell did much more than talk, of course. She had the ability to cut through to the heart of any matter and suggest practical and workable solutions. Her idealism was always tempered with a hard-edged practical side, and she was described as "a harmonizer of the ideal and the realistic." When the principles of scientific charity clashed with the factual evidence, Lowell possessed the "intellectual honesty" to admit her errors.[58] Homer Folks recalled her success as an administrator and commented that Lowell possessed an abundance of certain traits that were "common to men and women alike." He thus acknowledged her brilliant mind, her executive capabilities, and her sound judgment. But her most powerful quality, Folks claimed, was that of a true motivator: she made people want to do things for her. "She never missed the distinction between conversation and action," Folks wrote. "So many of us do. We have thought about a thing, we have said it and reached a conclusion and adopted a program and then were ready to go home and call it a day. Mrs. Lowell would do that too, but the next morning she would ask, 'What have you done about this business?' She never failed to check on herself."[59]

Lowell was especially remembered in the district committee meetings for the constancy of her patience and diligence in tending to difficult cases. She was a commanding, sometimes intimidating presence. Her efforts to shape the district committee work were directed toward avoiding the fate that had befallen so many previous organizations, such as the Association for the Improvement of the Condition of the Poor, which had become purely a relief-giving society. "I believe that among the many causes of poverty," Lowell asserted in a speech to COS trainees, "one of the most potent is careless relief-giving, whether by what are called charitable societies, by private individuals, or from public funds."[60]

⊷ No Lady Bountiful ⊶

Ironically, Lowell could not keep her own purse strings closed—a fact that bemused her colleagues. If there were needy people waiting at the Corlears district office, she immediately introduced herself, listened to their stories in a sympathetic manner, "and always wished to give immediate relief." She was described as a "lavish" almoner and could be counted on to fund programs for the organizations she believed in as well as for individual families in need.[61] Devoted to a more professional philanthropy, she engaged in personal charity as well. Proof of this abounds in testimonials, letters, and COS records. She was particularly interested that the work of women's reformatories be advanced. William Rhinelander Stewart thanked her for her "generous action in providing the salary for a teacher of amusements."[62] This was just one of the times when Lowell complemented her private charitable contributions with the funding of several salaried positions in the public sphere, which she provided for the women's reformatories in New York State. Here she was using old-style benevolence to support new-style professionals.

Lowell's actual relations with the working class, the poor, and the dependent men and women whom she sought to control, teach, serve, and understand are obscured by the fog of official reports, filtered accounts, and pious remembrances. "It would have been a privilege for some of us to have placed ourselves among the poor and lowly," wrote Robert de Forest, "so that we might go to her as they could do, and thus gain for ourselves a brighter ray." Louise F. Ford, a society agent, personally knew many of the "beneficiaries" of Lowell's charitable attention and claimed, "It is remarkable what an impression she made upon them. They have come to me and talked about her, and how much she has been a part of their lives, what an inspiration she was, and how strongly she impressed upon them the real meaning of true friendship for those in a different class in life, but whose strong good characters she seemed to understand and appreciate." These kinds of tributes lend credence to the sanctified portrait of Lowell that permeated institutional and historical accounts of her work shortly after her death and for many years later. Josephine Shaw Lowell as a "secular saint" tended to emphasize the more conservative elements of her career. Perhaps a little more realistic portrait was penned by a friend of hers in the labor movement, Father James O. S. Huntington. "She did not offer patronage: that word is inconsistent with our memory of her," he remarked. "She did not come playing the part of Lady Bountiful, that half-pathetic, half-romantic figure. She came in her own natural way. She did not attempt to lay aside the advantages of the position that belonged to her; she did not try to transport herself into their conditions; there was nothing unreal or unnatural in her or her work." This last characterization of Lowell's behavior strikes the right note in assessing her cross-class relationships.[63]

Yet Lowell was most decidedly not a proto-multiculturalist but rather very much a product of the late-Victorian era, which celebrated patriotism and traditional American virtues. She was intimately familiar with her family history, which linked her ancestors with the greatest events in the American past. Lowell often proudly referred to the character of "Uncle Sam" Shaw, a minor Revolutionary War hero and a pioneer of the China trade, as being a perfect blend of idealism and action. The very best ideals of Christianity, republicanism, and democracy were something she wanted to see the immigrant and poor populations embrace as enthusiastically as she did.

Lowell's vision of a prosperous, middle-class America was predicated on uplifting the poor and transforming their more troublesome behavioral traits into solid Victorian mores. "The Society's laundry and work rooms for unskilled women . . . were results of her earnest endeavors to aid the poor by educating them up to higher earning powers, rather than to weaken their moral fiber by unearned alms," recalled Charles Kellogg. Lowell's belief in moral individualism and spiritual uplift is nicely illustrated in the following story. Lowell was a great fan of Leo Tolstoy and was deeply moved when she read an essay of his proclaiming his love and sympathy for the poor. Yet she was horrified by his conclusion: "Culture and cleanliness keep us from our brothers—we cannot make them clean—let us be dirty." What a difference between the Russian reformers and ourselves, she exclaimed to a friend: "It is pathetic and shows the immensity of the evils in Russia. With us we feel and say: 'Let Us Make Them Clean.'"[64]

✑ Controversies and Hard Choices ✑

Lowell's involvement with the Corlears District Committee largely ensured its smooth running according to charity organization principles, but the same could not be said for the rest of the districts. Three developments in the first ten years of the COS determined the subsequent character of the organization: the district committees experienced turnover and disarray at a high rate, there was a dismal lack of interest on the part of the affluent in friendly visiting, and this lack of interest in turn fostered the importance of an increasingly professionalized corps of district agents, anticipating the rise of the professional social worker.[65]

The tensions of running a charity organization dedicated to scientific principles with a largely amateur and volunteer workforce manifested themselves within the first few years of the COS, much to Lowell's dismay. By 1887 it had come to her attention that a number of district committees had been shockingly neglectful of their duties. In her capacity as chair of the Committee on District Work, Lowell sent a circular letter to all the district committee chairmen asking them to report on the work habits of their members. On receiving the largely negative reports, Lowell then fired off to offending members a short but cogent letter asking them to resume "active personal service" or resign.[66] In Lowell's ideology, individual discipline applied to the wealthy as well as the poor, although, of course, the consequences for the former were less serious and the circumstances less humiliating.

Lowell and other members of the Committee on District Work appointed George Rowell, who was in the publishing business and a member of the COS's Finance Committee, to evaluate the poor performance of the district committees. His report noted that the independence of the district committees from the main governing body of the COS, the Central Council, made the close oversight of these committees nearly impossible. "The plans upon which this Society conducts its work," Rowell wrote, "are complex, cumbersome and difficult to understand. They ought to be simplified."[67] One solution, offered by yet another inside critic, was to dismantle the district committees altogether and run the entire operation out of the central office. Lowell rejected this out of hand but acknowledged the difficulties: "I wish I could make the Executive Committee take up this subject—We talk sometimes about the COS 'principles,' but a good many of us do not know very clearly what they are."[68] All around, it was a delicate situation, for the district committee operation, although expensive and complicated to run, represented the practical working out of COS ideology, and its perceived successes were crucial to maintaining the COS's public image as well as keeping its fund-raising machinery well oiled.

Another problem highlighted in the internal reports was the appearance of "slush funds" in some of the district committees, out of which cash relief was dispensed by members, friendly visitors, and agents. It was true that occasionally COS officials were allowed to give small amounts of cash, but only in the direst of emergencies. Doing so on a regular basis, however, not only contradicted the COS constitution but seemingly placed the society in direct competition with other relief organizations. Policing this situation proved to be difficult for COS officials and demoralizing to district committee members, who were described as "discontented and dissatisfied" with their duties.[69]

While many district chairmen complained of being overburdened with work, one of the internal critics saw the whole system as not only expensive and cumbersome to maintain but one that was every day departing from the ideal of personal service held so dear by scientific charity advocates. This was because, in Lowell's words, the COS had "miserably failed" to recruit even the barest minimum of friendly visitors.[70] As a result, the workload was increasingly falling on the shoulders of the hired agents, who were underpaid and ill-trained, at least in the early years, for the heavy caseloads they were encountering. There is, scholars of the COS agree, "abundant evidence that most of the c.o. [charity organization] functions were carried out by paid agents."[71] The dimensions of the failure can be put into perspective by considering the number of cases the COS tallied. By its tenth year, 300,000 reports had been filed covering an estimated 160,000 families, but only 35,000 cases had been treated.[72] The declining number of friendly visitors contrasted with the slowly ascending number of agents and cases: the COS's fifth annual report listed 130 visitors (compared with 870 in Boston); the eighth annual report listed 109. By 1888, the ninth annual report recorded a drop to 71, and by the eleventh annual report in 1892 the number was 58.

Lowell struggled valiantly to make the friendly visitor program work in New York City as it was working in Boston but in no other American city. Friendly visiting, of course, was not new to charity organization societies. It had deep roots in nineteenth- and even eighteenth-century philanthropy, where it grew out of Christian and democratic strains of volunteerism. This religious base was leavened by the 1880s with the principles of social science, so that, by the time Lowell was fashioning the New York programs, friendly visitors were closer to the modern social worker than to their earlier models. Lowell, however, believed that they were essential to the moral success of the society: "It is they who come into personal contact with those we seek to aid, and it is they whose influence will raise or degrade them."[73] The latter statement is from a pamphlet Lowell prepared to instruct upper-class visitors in the ways of scientific charity—first by a discussion of general principles and then by giving explicit examples. It is clear that she hoped to give the volunteers the professional knowledge that would enable them to be social scientists as well as humanitarians.

Lowell could often be found giving speeches to local churches and charitable groups explaining the aims of the COS and the necessity for friendly visitors who were immersed in the new rules of charity. She seemed to have a great success in recruiting her family and friends to serve on district committees and as friendly visitors. The annual reports are sprinkled with familiar family names such as Curtis, Barlow, and Minturn. In the 1890s Lowell's daughter and her nieces and nephews represented the new generation of socially conscious Shaws, as they, too, did their stint in the COS. The twenty-year-old Carlotta Lowell first appeared in the 1893 annual report doing service as a friendly visitor and a committee member. Joining Lotta on the committee was a cousin, Sarah Sturgis. Josephine's sister Ellen served on the Committee on District Work, of which Lowell was the chair, and her nephew and niece, Frank L. Curtis and Elizabeth Burrill Curtis, were also active in the COS. Often whole families were represented on one district committee.[74]

In 1888 the writer William Dean Howells gave service, perhaps in part to gather evidence for his "realistic" novels. In fact, the report issued from Howells's committee that year carried a distinctly literary tone: "The workings of the Ladies' Auxiliary Committee and Board of Visitors have been of great service to the Committee. These ladies are constant attendants at the meetings of our Relief Committee, and, fearlessly penetrating into the dark abodes of poverty and distress, have not only cheered affliction by their presence, but also been the medium of information to this Committee which has been of essential aid to its operations."[75]

Howells's report focused on one major change Lowell fashioned to save the friendly visiting program—the creation of "Ladies' Auxiliary Committees." These were attached to most of the male-dominated district committees. The ladies' committees, which were eventually subsumed into the regular district committees, took up much of the workload as well as the responsibilities for the recruitment and training of friendly visitors. Lowell's reform did not solve the problem but pointed to the gender-based short-term solution: there were simply more women available and willing to serve as committee members and volunteers than there were men of a comparable class position. Lowell continued the COS appeal for more, not less, friendly visiting, even while she was involved in upgrading and enlarging the COS group of paid agents. "It has always been a matter of great regret to me," she wrote to a friend, "that you have not felt that we were right in clinging to our ideal of 'Friendly Visitors.'"[76]

As can be imagined, there was much soul-searching within the COS committees over the failure of the friendly-visitor program. Various reasons were advanced and discussed, but the most compelling explanation lay in the increased demands of time and knowledge that scientific charity placed on its workers. Part-time volunteers simply could not and would not put the time or effort into learning the technical aspects of the job. This exposed a contradiction within the COS ideology: personal service versus professional methods. As it turned out, the latter prevailed. Inevitably, paid agents dominated the casework of the COS, just as highly educated and trained professionals would shortly replace the upper-class philanthropists who currently ran the organization.

For all the talk of failure, there should be a nod of appreciation for the efforts of Lowell and the COS to compel the well-born to perform their charitable duties. After all, the COS *did* function reasonably well throughout the 1880s and 1890s with its all-volunteer district committees, leadership structure, and small group of friendly visitors. Moreover, the problems of providing quality service to the needy did not disappear with the advent of the educated professional and the trained agent but were merely transmuted. As the first decade in the life of the COS passed, Lowell could point with pride to its many accomplishments, including moving from rented quarters to a new and handsome building from which to expand its operations and programs.

↶ *The United Charities Building* ↷

"Charity's Fine Temple," proclaimed the headline in the March 7, 1893, edition of the *New York Daily Tribune*'s account of the opening of the United Charities Building at the corner of Fourth Avenue and Twenty-second Street. Formerly St. Paul's Methodist Episcopal Church, the newly rebuilt structure provided offices for four of the city's premier charities: the Charity Organization Society of the City of New York, the Association for the Improvement of the Condition of the Poor, the Children's Aid Society, and the New York City Mission and Tract Society. This "secular temple" was endowed by the wealthy philanthropist John S. Kennedy, who was inspired to do it by an 1886 COS proposal outlining the need for such a building.[77] The United Charities Building, an imposing Victorian structure, was more than just a central place from which the most modern and efficient charities could conduct their work. As one admiring newspaper reporter wrote, "It will be a place to which any applicant for relief can apply with the assurance that, if deserving, he can find all the resources which the charities of New York have provided."[78]

After the excitement of the opening, at which 3,000 invited guests were treated to tours and speeches, Lowell and the rest of the COS leadership settled down not only to enjoy their brand-new third-floor offices but also to relish the fact that they now were a firmly established presence within the city's charity community. The COS was acknowledged by the press, the public, and other charities as an innovator and leader of the philanthropic field. "In Anglo-American cities in the latter half of the [nineteenth] century," Peter Mandler argued, "the relief of families was almost totally handed over to the 'scientific charities,' such as the various Charity Organization Societies." Another scholar wrote that "the New York Charity Organization Society served as a model for similar organizations throughout the country and was deeply involved in shaping private philanthropic and public policies toward the dependent individual."[79] The 1890s had arrived, and with it the promise of a golden age for scientific charity.

A particular point of pride for Lowell was the fact that throughout the 1880s applications for private charity did not rise when public relief had been abolished, thus confirming her belief that much public relief was superfluous. The needs of the city's poor, she argued, were being met without having to resort to outdoor relief and with the proper investigative tools that only the COS had to offer. Both contemporary critics and recent historians of the charity organization movement have pointed out that the COS so effectively stigmatized public relief (as well as private charity) that thousands of poor people were too ashamed to ask for aid.[80] Requests for charity relief were down, however, and no doubt the privatization of relief in New York City was somewhat mitigated by a surging economy, which, except for a mild depression in the mid-1880s, prevailed until 1893. Thus the COS could "specialize" in helping certain parts of the dependent population, such as homeless men, while the SCAA directed most of its efforts toward children, with the Association for the Improvement of the Condition of the Poor used by both organizations as a dispenser of cash relief.

Of course, COS agents were trained to evaluate the "worthiness" of a case, and in doing so they gathered data that revealed contradictory information on the causes of poverty. How these data were interpreted changed during the first twenty-five years of the COS, moving from a highly individualistic focus in the first years to an increasing emphasis on environment and structural causes as well. The society was nudged in this direction by much criticism in the press as to its so-called heartlessness.[81] In response to such criticism and as a logical growth of its own philosophy, the COS by the late 1880s began to downplay its repressive programs in favor of a shift toward a more positive and proactive slant. "Prominence is given in the minds even of its best friends to the Society's repressive and disciplinary work," complained one COS worker.[82] New programs were developed and publicized with great zeal. The "Penny Provident Fund" was established in 1888 to create a banking institution that would accept savings under one dollar. Run by the banker Otto T. Bannard, the fund successfully encouraged poor children to begin developing habits of thrift and independence. Between 1891 and 1897 the COS opened a workroom for unskilled women laborers and a "Wayfarer's Lodge" for the homeless. It began a "Provident Loan Society" to complement its Penny Provident Fund. Other programs, such as "The Laundry" (a particular favorite of Lowell), provided unemployed women with job training and wages. This more positive approach underscored the COS's commit-ment to providing opportunities to working-class people, not just to punishing the charitable impostor.

Such programs as the Penny Provident Fund and The Laundry can be described as "preventive" philanthropy. They not only encouraged individuals to engage in self-help but also promoted the establishment of community-developed social services that would provide the envi-ronmental incentive for people to exercise independence. The COS programs thus advocated a dual emphasis on self-help measures as embodied in their case-method approach and the prevention of pau-perism through improving social conditions. The greatest triumph of the preventive-style programs came in 1900, when the COS opened its famous "Tenement House Exhibition," which not only exposed the shocking conditions in the slums for the edification of the prosperous classes but provided a detailed guide for reform. Through COS-led efforts, the New York Tenement Act of 1901 was passed. Just as the disciplinary approach aimed at cleansing the environment of baleful examples of individual misbehavior, so the preventive approach aimed at creating modes of proper behavior.

Finally, the centralized location of the United Charities Building offered the opportunity to streamline and improve service to appli-cants. New employees, both in the central office and the district offices, were hired to expedite paperwork, and nighttime hours were established to accommodate the sudden emergencies for poor people. It was in the 1890s that the final expansion of the district committees took place, as the whole island of Manhattan was now covered by the COS.[83]

The COS's high profile in New York City's charitable community was cemented by its role in the Park Place disaster in the summer of 1891, when the collapse of a tenement building resulted in the loss of more than sixty lives and the tragic disruption of livelihood for many families. Then, as in earlier disasters, a mayor's relief committee raised funds to aid the victims, and newspapers such as the *New York Herald* appealed to their readers for contributions. Unlike the followed procedures of earlier disasters, however, both these sources turned to the COS as the medium to distribute the donations using its by-now acknowledged efficient and scientific methods. This acknowl-edgment by city agencies and newspapers was especially satisfying to Lowell, who felt that the COS's active response to earlier and continuing newspaper attacks was paying off in dividends of goodwill and respect.[84]

✎ *Lowell, the COS, and the Settlement House Movement* ✎

If Josephine Shaw Lowell was well known for her support of the COS's repressive programs, did she also direct and inspire the COS in its drive to establish a more positive image using preventive philanthropy? The answer is yes. Lowell was a power behind this side of the society as well. She was instrumental in suggesting and planning many new programs such as The Laundry and also in forging organizational ties to other similarly minded organizations. An excellent example of this can be found in her relationship with a new and exciting addition to the country's reform scene, the settlement house movement.

Lowell found the settlement house movement congenial because of its strong and passionate agenda for social welfare reform. Much has been made of the early competition and antagonism between members of the COS and the settlement houses, but when the dust settled down, it quickly became apparent that the two had more in common than not. For example, both movements originated in England, where Americans found the inspiration and the organizational models to bring back home. And both sought to ease class tensions by emphasizing the essential communitarian basis of society: charity organization through friendly visiting and the settlement houses through neighborhood contact.[85]

New York City was the site of the first settlement house in 1886. Founded by Stanton Coit, the Neighborhood Settlement (later reorganized and renamed University Settlement) attracted talented and dedicated young reformers to its premises. Two of these, Charles B. Stover and Edward King, would work with Lowell in various reform efforts throughout the 1890s. Women founded their own settlement in 1889. Vida Scudder of Wellesley College started the College Settlement, which boasted such stellar residents as Lillian Wald (who would shortly thereafter found the Henry Street Settlement), Dr. Jane E. Robbins, and Leonora O'Reilly, who was also a good friend of King. If not the first, by far the most famous settlement house, Hull House, was founded in 1889 by Jane Addams and Ellen Gates Starr. This Chicago house would soon become widely known for its brilliant circle of women social activists, who, led by Florence Kelley, would make the midwestern city an exciting center for innovative reform and advocacy of protective legislation.

Far from looking askance at the new kids on the block, Lowell welcomed their presence in the city neighborhoods: "What we ought to have are settlements in every street, to help civilize and lift the people." Her enthusiastic response to the settlement house movement was apparent immediately in the inclusion of settlement workers in the COS district committees. She also began projects in the district committees, such as the study of tenement conditions, which relied on the aid and resources of the local settlement house. Lowell viewed the settlement house workers as potent allies in the fight to eradicate poverty. "Experts are required in every field," she observed. More than ever, Lowell claimed, we all need to determine what we as a society have to do to help improve conditions for the poor, and that means obtaining the knowledge on which to build a program of reform. How can we do this? "The first step," according to Lowell, "is to know exactly what they need, and this knowledge the 'residents' . . . in college settlements must get for us. They must report the neglect of the city government to do its duty, whether as street-cleaners, as police, or as educator. They must report the oppression of employers, whether the oppression be the result of individual carelessness or, as is often the case, the result of trade conditions. They must cry aloud for more air, more space, for a larger and better life in every way for the great masses of men and women in our cities."[86]

✒ Toward the Emancipation of Labor ✒

Lowell's receptiveness to settlement house workers and their movement also underscored her growing interest in labor problems. Her position as commissioner in the SBC and leader in the COS broadened her knowledge about the needs of the dependent and the underprivileged. Now, in the late 1880s and early 1890s, she became ever more aware of the plight of the working poor. And that knowledge did not just come from working for the society's clients or forging contacts with other city reform groups. It was right under her nose: it came from the needs of the COS's own workforce, which she helped to supervise. Thinking about these people's needs helped to move Lowell into a more critical stance of industrial capitalism and made her a stalwart in the fledgling labor reform movement in New York City.

Here was the situation as she knew it: women comprised the bulk of the paid agents from the start of the COS. The fourth annual report (1886) showed eight women (four married, four unmarried) as agents, compared with one man, and by the sixth annual report (1888) the number rose to sixteen paid agents, the majority remaining women. Great care was taken by Lowell to improve the quality of paid-agent casework, as problems manifested themselves.

The majority of "problems" arose from the agents' lack of experience and education in the charity field. To put it bluntly, Lowell was very dissatisfied with the class of agents the COS was hiring. As early as 1887 she was demanding "that a higher grade of agents should be employed, persons of very superior intelligence and cultivation being required in that position."[87] Lowell naturally saw this as an opportunity to apply her civil service principles to the COS employee pool. But alas, budget constraints, as well as a dearth of qualified people, hampered her recruitment efforts. Lowell glumly accepted the situation, writing that "circumstances have arisen that have made it necessary for the Society to engage, as Agents and Assistants, persons totally unacquainted with its work."[88]

Characteristically, Lowell attacked the problem in a practical way. Necessity is the mother of invention, and out of such necessity came the COS training programs. Largely drawn from the lower middle class, the mostly female COS workforce presented Lowell with two challenges. The first was devising a training program for agents *after* they were hired, and the second centered on creating an esprit de corps through higher wages, better hours, and improved working conditions. Lowell, Charles Kellogg, and the society's secretary, Robert Hebbard, comprised a subcommittee responsible for the selection and training of the district agents as well as the central office staff. They also defined and enforced the standards to which the COS agents were expected to adhere.[89] To this end, Lowell's subcommittee regularly produced such handbooks as *Rules and Guidance of Agents*. These handbooks were discussed in special training classes recommended by Lowell for newly hired agents.

From the beginning, Lowell realized that the agents' work would have to be closely supervised, not only by the district committees but by the Central Council as well.[90] Regular staff conferences were established, as were regularly scheduled meetings by the district agents, assistant district agents, and friendly visitors. By the early 1890s, some of the more obvious and painful irregularities had been ironed out. The early training classes for the assistant agents instituted by Lowell, as well as the classes for the friendly visitors, easily merged into the more career-oriented milieu of that era. A good example of the impulse toward professional social work came when the COS opened a "Summer School of Philanthropy" in 1896 and soon thereafter established close ties with Columbia University. Indeed, by the early twentieth century, a more sleek annual report offered the information that a high number of its employees were now graduates of major universities with degrees in social work, and many had taken classes at the School of Philanthropy. Led by the New York COS, the charity organization movement could take credit for creating and sustaining a new profession of social work.

Salaries, however, remained low in the 1880s and 1890s. This adversely affected morale and made for a high turnover rate among young agents. The records are studded with Lowell's efforts to increase the salaries of the lowest-paid workers. "I do not remember a single instance in which the salary of any woman employee of the Charitable Organization Society, which was proposed to be raised, or hours of work which were proposed to be shortened, which Mrs. Lowell did not favor," stated Robert de Forest.[91] Lowell wrote angry memos denouncing low wages. She began one of them by noting, once again, the "meagre remuneration" given by the COS to its employees in training. "These assistants," she continued, "are required to be respectable, educated, energetic, patient and sympathetic; able to collect statistics, to estimate character, to give good advice, and to endure hard work." She reminded her colleagues that these young people represented the society's future and its potential and "are certainly deserving of living wages." She then brought some sarcasm to bear on the issue: "Yet our Society, one of whose objects is to prevent pauperism, pays these Assistants the inadequate salary of $30 per month at first; and when they are experienced and found satisfactory, they receive only $40 per month, without any promise of future increase, even after many years' service." Lowell unfavorably compared the COS's salary scale with similar organizations and made the recommendation "both on humane and business principles" that the wage scale be restructured so that it reflected, at the very least, those of other institutions.[92] Perhaps it was at moments like these that she felt some regret over her strategy to incorporate so many businessmen and bankers into the leadership structure of the COS, who consistently opposed her efforts to raise salaries.

Lowell's frustration about the injustices of the working and living conditions of low-paid workers (in the COS case female workers) burst out of the boundaries of the COS meeting rooms and into the public sphere, where she became a force for labor reform. "I feel myself . . . almost obliged to apologize for belonging to the charity organization society," she declared in response to an attack on labor at an 1895 charities conference. "If the charity organization societies of the country are going to take the position of defenders of the rich against the poor which I do think is the danger which stands before us, then I shall be very sorry that I ever had anything to do with the work."[93] At least by the mid-1880s, Lowell's quest for solutions to the labor question brought her out of charity and into the Working Women's Society; it prompted her to cheer on and forge alliances with the new settlement house movement, and it compelled her to begin writing on the need for reconciliation and fairness between capitalists and workers, to advocate the right to strike and organize, and to champion the virtues of the laboring class.

Josephine Shaw Lowell's influence and stature in the philanthropic and reform communities reached its peak when she headed the East Side Relief Committee, formed in response to the terrible depression of 1893 and composed of the city's most prominent reformers, businessmen, labor leaders, and clergy. Her work on the East Side Relief Committee was extremely significant, for it combined, in her view, the best of charity organization principles with a vigorous commitment to working-class concerns. It represented both the high mark for Gilded Age scientific charity and the beginning of its decline. Lowell's involvement in labor, the Consumers' League, and the East Side Relief Committee opened a new and exhilarating chapter in her life.

7

The Labor Question

On March 16, 1885, Josephine Shaw Lowell gave a speech in front of the Congregational Club of New York in which she pleaded for a new understanding of the causes of poverty. Heed the call of "The Bitter Cry of the Poor in New York," she said, and know that the causes are *both* individual and societal. The remedies are not going to come easily, and they call for a massive infusion of moral, monetary, and institutional reform as never before imagined. "Where is fresh air to be found?" asked Lowell, referring to the reeking tenements that confined thousands of the poor. "Where is there any refuge from crowds and filth and vileness? There is scarcely an open place to be found in the crowded parts of the city; the children can only play in the gutters. . . . The dead monotony of a life of poverty must have some break, something to change the horror of incessant squalid misery. The mere physical exhaustion consequent on bad air, bad food, insufficient clothing, calls for a stimulant."[1]

While Lowell in 1885 still allowed for equal importance to be given to the personal transformation that must necessarily accompany any rise out of pauperism, her ideas changed from earlier, published writings and speeches. This change would be carried on and elaborated in her work on labor relations. "If the working people had all they ought to have," Lowell wrote, "we should not have the paupers and criminals."[2] During these years she was grappling with the consequences of not just unemployment but underemployment, which led her to an openly critical position on capitalism. And this shift in focus from pauperism to justice for the working class was reflected in a more broadly based philanthropy as well.

By the late 1880s, Lowell questioned whether charity organization *alone* had the power to help the majority of poor people or to cure poverty. She instead stressed society's obligation to assist the under-privileged and downplayed the individual's responsibility for self-reform. Lowell expressed her convictions in terms of the respective rights and duties of individuals and communities. She believed, and would always insist, that it was the duty of everyone to be a thrifty, industrious, and virtuous member of society. The poor, she thought, needed help from philanthropic organizations such as the COS in achieving these goals, as their temptations to fail were so much greater than most. These temptations, such as easy relief, economic hard-ships, and exposure to vice and immorality, were countered in the COS's programs directed toward helping the poor to help themselves. But Lowell argued that the poor had rights as well. They, like the more affluent citizenry, had the right to certain essential services that would enhance their lives and enable them to be independent and worthy citizens.

Similarly, Lowell argued, communities had rights and duties. The larger community had the right to be protected from impostors and charity frauds, the right to make sure that its charity dollars were being spent wisely and efficiently. The COS performed *this* service well, per-haps too well for some sensibilities. Yet the community also had the moral obligation to ensure that all its citizens were well housed, well educated, and healthy. To this end, Lowell and the COS initiated programs that reflected an environmental approach to poverty, grounded in the larger concept of "interdependence." Emphasizing that society was the sum of its individual parts held together by a common glue, interdependence was an idea familiar to Lowell through the Shaw family intellectual tradition and the discipline of social science as it developed in the 1870s. In short, she developed the critical perspective to confront what she perceived as a growing crisis of social inequality and injustice. "Almost alone among her col-leagues," noted one historian, "she grasped the economic complicity as well as the philanthropic and cultural responsibilities of the elite."[3] Lowell's embrace of the concept of interdependence, so critical to interpreting the change in social thought at the end of the nineteenth century, and her efforts to bring it to full realization are what make her life a narrative of dynamism rather than one of stasis.

Lowell's labor reform work by no means diminishes her achievement in the founding and the establishment of the COS, which would continue to occupy much of her time. Nor did it, in her eyes, do away with the necessity for organized charity. Rather, as was the case in the 1870s, the 1880s and 1890s would see her intellectual and reform interests continue to expand, eventually embracing a plethora of methods and strategies to achieve social justice in the economic, social, and political arena. As one of her colleagues remarked, "She was well aware that no single institution, old or new, was enough."[4] Lowell was imbued with the spirit to seek social justice; it was with this spirit that she set out to learn everything she could about the labor movement; it was with this spirit that she participated in and founded new organizations dedicated to ending unfair labor practices; and it was with this spirit that she created the Eastside Work Relief Committee to combat the depression of 1893. Her father, Francis George Shaw, set her sights on "The Labor Question" when he introduced her to *Progress and Poverty*.

✎ *Progress and Poverty* ✐

The year 1882 was one of significant beginnings and endings for Lowell. On February 8, 1882, she observed the formal birth of the COS. That fall, on November 7, 1882, her father died of pneumonia in his home on Staten Island at the age of seventy-three. "My dear father . . . has died . . . and left us very lonely," she informed a friend.[5] But before he died, Frank Shaw bequeathed his daughter an intellectual gift that helped to nudge her from the more narrow streams of Gilded Age reform into the wider currents of early Progressive reform in the 1890s. His death, the first to occur in that close-knit family since Rob's and Charley's, is an appropriate time to review Frank Shaw's interests during the postwar years and to delineate his continuing influence on his daughter's life.

Frank and Sarah Shaw pursued their traditional avocations in reform, philanthropy, and cultural activities throughout the 1870s. Although they never again crossed the Atlantic, the Shaws frequently traveled to Boston and its environs to visit with relatives and friends.

After the turmoil of the Civil War and its aftermath subsided, Shaw withdrew from his active public life to one of troubled contemplation on his Staten Island estate. Although he still maintained his interest in outside affairs through monetary contributions and participation in local governance, friends described him as once again preoccupied with the problems of capital and labor, recalling his youthful Brook Farm days. As he knew well from Josephine's earnest instruction, poverty in this new age was a dangerous menace to the country's welfare and had to be attacked vigorously. Yet for Shaw, who possessed a deeply spiritual, almost saintly, demeanor, scientific charity was not going to resolve the larger question of economic justice for the masses; he yearned for "a great remedy" to accomplish this feat. Frank Shaw never lost his romanticized vision of a classless society that first gripped him in the 1830s and 1840s. His dormant utopian socialist vision was powerfully revitalized by the appearance of Henry George, a self-taught political economist whose theories appeared to quench his thirst for an all-encompassing solution for a troubled America.[6]

Henry George, a California journalist by way of Philadelphia, established a national reputation in 1880 with the publication of his book *Progress and Poverty,* which was embraced by the working class of America but had a powerful appeal to the middle class as well.[7] "Poverty in the midst of plenty," George declared, "is the great enigma of our times. It is the central fact from which spring industrial, social, and political difficulties that perplex the world, and with which statesmanship and philanthropy and education grapple in vain. From it come the clouds that overhang the future of the most progressive and self-reliant nations."[8] *Progress and Poverty* analyzed the paradox contained in its title by fusing the fervor of Christian perfectionism, the labor theory of value, and utopian solutions into a powerful moral vision of hope and regeneration. What made George's work so appealing to both the middle class and the working class was this moral vision, not the complicated array of solutions he offered—solutions that later were fused into "The Single Tax" national movement beginning in the late 1880s.

In the summer of 1881, George embarked on a tour of New York State to spread the message of *Progress and Poverty.* George's tours generated the excitement and the commitment of a Protestant revival meeting, in which the epiphany was called "seeing the cat." While in New York he met an ardent admirer, Francis George Shaw, who told him that until he read *Progress and Poverty* he had "despaired of true moral progress," which was a decidedly genteel way of having "seen the cat."[9] At this meeting Shaw indicated his desire to help the movement in a concrete way. George, in turn, suggested that Shaw fund the printing of a thousand copies of *Progress and Poverty* for distribution to libraries across the country. Shaw agreed, and his gesture touched off the sales phenomenon of the book, second only to the Bible in the nineteenth century. This marked the beginning of a short but deeply felt relationship between the two men, who kept in constant correspondence with each other until Shaw's death. Shaw also became George's financial angel when he dispensed several cash gifts to the always impecunious younger man, declaring, "I know of no better way to help the cause than by enabling you to devote yourself to it without being distracted by worry."[10] After Shaw's death, George dedicated his next book, *Social Problems*, to his memory, and appended a small essay on land monopoly written by Shaw, "A Piece of Land," as a tribute.

Henry George was warmly encouraged by the Shaw family to retain his relationship with them. And as if ensuring this bond, Henry wrote to Josephine that he was the sum of her father's hopes for the future: "I was in some respects, his younger man, whom he sent into the struggle he would have made himself."[11] Sarah and Josephine embraced Henry as a family member in those sad November days. Henry George seemed to have a particular affinity for women, although they were conspicuously absent from his own movement. He enthused to Lowell over the prospect of "how bright women are everywhere coming to the front. This to me seems one of the most hopeful signs of the times."[12] When George's daughter, Anna De Mille, recalled her father's close circle of friends, she was struck by the large number of women. And prominent among them, she noted, were "Mrs. Francis George Shaw and her brilliant daughter, Josephine Shaw Lowell."[13] Lowell continued the lively relationship with George begun by her father, which was further cemented by their mutual fascination with the great events unfolding in the decades that comprised the nation's Gilded Age.

Lowell and George were living in the midst of an era of unparalleled economic expansion that profoundly altered political and social arrangements. The oft-told triumphal story of how, in the postwar era, America completed a transportation and communication network, which in turn facilitated the tremendous growth of the industrial sector, must be tempered alongside the uneasiness that many thoughtful observers felt. Lowell and George were two of many who expressed disquiet at the dominance of the industrial order in American life, and they did not believe that the brilliant entrepreneurial capitalist class could or would ensure social peace. Indeed, they joined a growing chorus of dissent: farmers, workers, women, and churches were all voicing their discontent with the *consequences* of industrial development in the 1870s and 1880s. Organizations such as the Grange, the Knights of Labor, and the Women's Christian Temperance Union, as well as Lowell's COS, the settlement house movement, and the social gospel movement, sprang up to accommodate various anxieties and grievances. Running along a spectrum from radical to conservative, these organizations and their memberships were focused on the downside of the capitalist revolution, where the possibility of unassimilated immigrants, a dysfunctional and corrupt political system, and a growing gap between rich and poor threatened to shake the United States off its republican and democratic foundation.

Many critics boiled down the nation's ills into what was called the labor question. A cluster of injustices engendered by the industrial system, combined with the severe economic depression of 1873–77, compelled workers to express their dissatisfaction through a growing number of strikes and other labor disturbances. When, in 1877, a nationwide strike of railway workers resulted in bitter clashes between the strikers, the police, and the military, Americans realized that they were no longer immune from the dangers of class conflict familiar to European societies. Socialism added an extra "foreign" element to the labor disturbances and served to alienate further the middle class from the demands of the workers in the 1880s and 1890s.

New York, the nation's most populous and industrialized state, was also a center of strike activity. From 1885 to 1891, there were more than 20,000 strikes involving almost 500,000 workers.[14] National labor movements, such as the Knights of Labor in the 1870s and 1880s and the American Federation of Labor led by Samuel Gompers in the 1890s, made significant progress in establishing an economic and social agenda for the working class. And New York City, wrote a labor historian, "had a well-developed tradition of working-class organization long before . . . the Progressive Era."[15] In fact, trade unionism flourished in New York City, and its triumphs, discontents, and failures were familiar to both Lowell and George as they pursued their respective careers in the 1880s. George became the candidate of the Independent Labor party in the New York mayoral election of 1886, one of the few times in American history when labor formed a distinct political entity.

Lowell and George formulated their responses to Gilded Age social upheaval in different ways, and they often disagreed sharply over the means to cure poverty.[16] Nevertheless, George's work did make explicit the connection between poverty and unemployment, and he was one of the first major figures in American social reform thought to do so. Society, George argued, not the individual, was responsible for the poor and the homeless. Lowell needed to have that point made intellectually, as it would be made experientially in her work. She was just one of many New York reformers who were deeply influenced by George's message and who sought to give his work practical meaning—something he could never do. And Lowell, to her credit, displayed an eagerness to become engaged by Henry George's programs, even if she did not embrace them as fully and as uncritically as did her father. "Whether Henry George and Father are right," she wrote in 1883, "and that plan will help to make things straight I can't say, but that they need putting straight I am very sure of."[17]

◦๑ Industrial Arbitration and Conciliation ๑◦

Confirmed in the belief that something needed to be done to address the labor question, Lowell began an intensive study of it, following the by now familiar pattern of obtaining knowledge and information. First she read widely on the subject, seeking to master the sources from the capitalist, the worker, the state, and the international point of view. Second, from the early 1880s onward, she corresponded with leaders in business, labor, and politics, such as the "New York City Commissioner of Street Cleaning." In this way she supplemented her experiences and knowledge with an even wider base of information, and within a few years she was ready to express herself on the issues relevant to labor. She began to publish a stream of articles and a short book that articulated her point of view.[18]

Lowell's overall philosophy on the labor question combined her newly acquired knowledge with her republican heritage, democratic principles, and experience in the charity field into a straightforward platform advocating social justice for the working class. "The Labor Question is, after all," she announced, "only another phase of the

Liberty Question." Working people themselves, Lowell pointed out, have had a long tradition of placing their demands not within a context of self-interest but rather "as contending for liberty against tyrannical power."[19] She explicitly and repeatedly drew an analogy between to-day's strikers and Revolutionary lawbreakers such as Sam Adams, now a hero but considered a dangerous criminal by the ruling classes of the 1770s. In this way she presented the working class as the legitimate heirs to a proud *American* political tradition and not beholden to a foreign ideology such as anarchism or Marxist socialism. Labor, she argued, deserved to be intimately linked with freedom and liberty.

Lowell vigorously defended strike actions as legitimate exercises of power, as long as all other avenues of negotiation had been cut off. Here she asked middle-class citizens to stand back and admire the courage and selflessness of the workers, who risked their families' health and welfare for the sake of principle. These traits, of course, were immensely appealing to Lowell, and of course she grew up hearing similar praises of slaves, ex-slaves, and abolitionists. She explained her position in detail in a published letter responding to the public's negative reaction to the Homestead Strike of 1892: "The underlying conception of their own rights and wrongs which inspired the recent action of the men at Homestead, and which is also the animating principle of members of labor organizations who strike but yet refuse to allow others to do the work which they will not do . . . is certainly not understood by the generality of thinking persons."[20]

Declaring the strikers "legally wrong but morally right," Lowell argued that the rise of a new industrial order had brought with it an incipient economic revolution in property rights whose outlines were only dimly perceived by the public but were crystal clear to workers: "The theory to which I refer, and which, whether put into words or not, is firmly fixed in the minds of all trade unionists, is that the man who by his labor for a series of years helps to build up a great business, be it factory, mine or railroad, thereby acquires a distinct right of property in that business, while the general view is that it is only the man who helps to build up the business by his money who has a property right in it."[21] This argument led to her main point, which was that workingmen considered that they had the right to retain their jobs, even while partaking in a strike action, and that, conversely, owners did not have the right to take it away because of that strike, or because a man decided to join a union against his employer's wishes.

Lowell ended her article by admitting that many of her relatively affluent readers might find this idea absurd at first hearing but reminded them that property rights are not fixed notions but fluctuate with different and expanding definitions of justice and equity. In this case, she was urging affluent Americans to consider the rights of working men and women—which was probably a new idea to many of them. She was well aware that the workers themselves, and workers' advocates such as the socialists, drew upon a long tradition of theory and rhetoric to defend their rights.

Lowell defined two goals for American capitalists: first, to accept the right for unions to exist, and second, to treat workers as equals in determining the conditions under which they labored. "There will never be justice between employers and employees," she stated, "and consequently there will never be a lasting peace, until the public and the employers recognize the claim of the employees to a vote in the settlements of questions relating to wages and conditions of labor."[22] Lowell was determined to do everything she could to bring this situation about, and she believed that the instrument, or institutional expression, best suited for American conditions was the board of arbitration, which had worked well in England and Belgium but rarely in America. A board of arbitration was based on the principle of cooperation and respect between management and labor. Many boards were set up within the workplace; some were government-controlled, and still others originated from independent, public-spirited citizens who wished to help initiate "industrial peace." Cooperation was, of course, a familiar and congenial concept to Lowell through her work as a social scientist with charity organizations. Cooperation was indispensable in the modern age, and, in her view, it was high time it was applied to labor in America, where the overwhelming power of capitalists was exercised in an "arbitrary and tyrannical way toward the workers."[23]

Lowell was hardly alone in embracing arbitration as a way of bringing about peaceful solutions to industrial problems or other conflicts. Indeed, arbitration as a method of resolving international disputes was an important element in revitalizing the moribund American Peace Society in the late nineteenth century. Because Lowell was a member of that society, she may well have become acquainted with the ideals and practices of arbitration through its councils as well as through labor sources. It was also the favored method of the early social gospel movement and advocated, for example, by New York's Henry Potter, the Episcopal bishop and leader of the city's social gospel and social reform movements.[24] Boards of arbitration also appealed to Lowell because they promoted the idea that both sides had rights and duties to be exercised toward each other. The employers had the right to expect a fair day's work, but they also had the duty to provide a living wage. The workers, conversely, had the right to demand decent working conditions but had the obligation to limit their demands within the bounds of a reasonable framework. Lowell also expected boards of arbitration to be the kind of educational vehicle for the prosperous classes in labor relations that the COS was for scientific charity. Most important, she believed that the cooperative ideology of the boards would appeal to Americans' sense of fair play, especially once they realized how skewed relations were in favor of capital.

➣ *Lowell and CAIL* ➢

In 1893 Lowell published *Industrial Arbitration and Conciliation*, essentially a narrative of the successes of conciliation in England, Belgium, and America, with an introductory essay written by her. It was the fruit of several years' thinking on the issue and proved to be an influential tract. In the late 1880s and early 1890s, however, Lowell was aware that the outlook for boards of arbitration in New York was gloomy. The majority of strikes in the city and state before 1890 had been settled privately, usually to the employer's benefit, and business saw no reason to change this pleasant situation. Labor was also cool to the idea: "I have never looked hopefully upon arbitration as a method for achieving satisfactory industrial results," wrote Samuel Gompers of the American Federation of Labor.[25] Lowell was delighted, nonetheless, when in response to Bishop Potter's call for clergy involvement in labor issues, Father James Otis Sargent Huntington organized the Church Association for the Advancement of the Interests of Labor (CAIL) in 1887. In its initial stages, CAIL provided a platform for public education on labor issues through lectures, public meetings, and other forums; it also advocated arbitration for the settling of disputes. In addition, CAIL undertook an advocacy role for progressive labor legislation as revelations of sweatshops and other inhumane working conditions became widely publicized.[26]

Huntington and CAIL provided a concrete link between the philosophy of Henry George and the formation of groups dedicated to bringing economic and social justice to the American labor scene. Huntington was a dedicated follower of George and often gave speeches expounding the benefits of "The Single Tax" to society. Another founder of CAIL, and a close friend of Huntington, was the Reverend B. F. De Costa, an Episcopal minister at the Church of St. John the Evangelist and a bitter critic of the COS, accusing it of "making pumice stone of [the poor] to polish up the values of their patrons."[27] How De Costa and Lowell, who was active in CAIL from its start, got along is anybody's guess, but it is documented that Huntington, who was also a sharp critic of organized charity, regarded Lowell very highly and vice versa. This is another example of her unusual ability to absorb, consider, and accept different views, however harsh and contrary to her own, and then change accordingly. Her very presence in CAIL's counsels attests to this ability.

Father Huntington resigned from CAIL in 1892 in order to devote himself to the religious order he founded earlier. His departure paved the way for a less idealistic and more practical focus for CAIL, exemplified by the organization's embrace of Samuel Gompers's conservative brand of trade-unionism that stressed extracting tangible economic benefits from capitalists in as nonthreatening a way as possible. The ascendance of Gompers's philosophy of trade-unionism was accompanied by an intense interest in arbitration. Harriette Keyser, the organizing secretary of CAIL, credited Lowell with bringing this about. "The subject," Keyser wrote, "had been discussed by individuals, and in this country much is due to the writings and efforts of Josephine Shaw Lowell, whose book upon the subject puts in concise form valuable information."[28] In 1893 a New York State Board of Arbitration was formed (a year later it was reorganized as the New York Council of Mediation and Conciliation), headed by Henry Potter and containing representatives of business, labor, and the public. Lowell joined the newly formed board along with Felix Adler and Seth Low, two prominent reformers. The board advertised its services among business and unions in New York City, receiving harsh criticism from "newspapers and individuals who thought the church had no business intervening in labor disputes."[29] Despite this initial controversy, the board could count among its early successes the resolution of the electrical workers' strike in 1895, the marble cutters' dispute in that same year, and the cloakmakers' strike in 1899, in all of which Lowell played an important role as an arbitrator.

Lowell took her work as a conciliator between labor and capital very seriously, as shown in her role in the tailors' dispute of 1894, in which she acted as an "individual arbitrator" under the auspices of CAIL.[30] Having determined that the tailors' cause was just and their demands reasonable, Lowell felt that it was "now the duty of all public spirited men and women . . . to support them in their demands and to render a strike unnecessary, or, at least make it as short as possible."[31] The first step she took was to announce a meeting among herself, Dr. Jane E. Robbins of the College Settlement, and a selected group of prominent citizens to decide how best to conciliate the dispute. Here we see the reason that arbitration was not particularly well liked by either labor or capital: prominent ladies and gentlemen defining the problems, setting out the terms of reconciliation, then electing representatives (in this case, Lowell and Robbins) to scuttle between the various groups to work out an agreement. It seemed an unwarranted intrusion into working-class and business affairs by meddlesome reformers. Yet to Lowell it seemed a fine way to publicize favorably the demands of labor, whose side was not fairly reported by a largely hostile press. To this end, she made sure "reporters of all the influential papers" were at the meeting and were apprised of the subsequent negotiations. Her efforts were rewarded with supportive coverage and even a few enthusiastic editorials praising the courage of the tailors.[32]

Lowell and Robbins, not unexpectedly, encountered some hostility when they met with representatives of the retail clothing manufacturers. Robbins recalled that "the presiding officer was markedly discourteous, but Mrs. Lowell entirely ignored his rudeness and quietly presented the cause of the poor tailor. . . . What she said was so convincing that before we left the meeting the executive committee had given us a message to take back to the strikers."[33] Lowell wrote to her sister-in-law,

> The poor sweated tailors struck last Monday, asking for ten hours' work a day and weekly pay, instead of fifteen hours' and piece work, and everything went beautifully for the sweaters and the wholesale manufacturers and the newspapers were all agreed that the men were quite right and that the change must be made. Now, however,

the men seem to have got puffed up by too much success, and they are asking unreasonable things and there is to be hard work in showing them that it was the righteousness of their cause and not their strength that won approval.[34]

The message contained in this letter to Annie Shaw underlined Lowell's conception of her labor efforts as being rooted in fairness to both sides, even when the manufacturers were at fault. It also betrayed her moral sensibilities—"righteousness," not brute power, won the victory, and reasonableness, not "pride," paved the way. As in earlier arenas, she was guided by a strong sense of "character" and reason. If people followed rational paths, avoided the pitfalls of emotion, and performed their work properly, there was no excuse for not solving even the thorniest of problems confronting them. In this case, Lowell had her work cut out for her, and she began the process of "running around, seeing various people connected with the trade and having a very good time."[35] Armed with little more than moral persuasion, she helped the tailors win their demands. "I learned to depend upon Mrs. Lowell's judgment in all labor questions," wrote Robbins at the conclusion of the strike.[36]

The tailors' strike was one of the few settled successfully by arbitration methods. Both workers and employers found it hard to place their trust in the hands of conciliators, and their efforts more often floundered than not. But the very existence of the board, its membership, and the actions it inspired brought labor grievances out into the light of day and into mainstream reform, which was a major accomplishment in itself. Lowell also became involved with other labor reform organizations. Similar to CAIL in methods and aims was the Social Reform Club of New York City. Another outgrowth of the Henry George movement, it was begun in 1894 by a self-described group of disinterested citizens who wanted to help Americans understand the necessity of trade-unionism and labor activism.[37] Lowell was on the advisory board of the club along with Felix Adler, William Dean Howells, and Samuel Gompers. Gompers remembered that Lowell was one of the more active members, who, working with Charles Stover, Jacob Riis, Albert Shaw, Edward King, E. W. Ordway, and E. R. A. Seligmen, helped to publicize labor issues, develop and support labor legislation, and educate the public to do its duty and above all to realize that "the laboring classes are the people—all the people. The few people that don't belong to the laboring classes don't amount to anything."[38]

✑ *The Consumers' League of the City of New York* ✑

The ideals of cooperation, social justice, and social responsibility that lay at the heart of arbitration and conciliation also animated Lowell's work in the Consumers' League of the City of New York. Several of the founding members of CAIL, including Father Huntington and his sister Arria Huntington, were involved in the activities that led to the establishment of the Consumers' League. The league was formed in response to the oppression of city "salesgirls" who worked in the department stores that now dotted the commercial landscape of New York City and that created the material basis for the consumer society of the twentieth century.[39] Lowell first became aware of the female workers' problems when in 1886 she was invited to attend a series of meetings chaired by Leonora O'Reilly, a working-class activist formerly of the Boston branch of the Knights of Labor. O'Reilly would later achieve a brilliant career in reform, including serving as vice president of the Social Reform Club and in the same capacity for the New York branch of the National Women's Trade Union League. O'Reilly's upper-class friend and mentor from Boston, Louise S. W. Perkins, was also invited, and together Lowell and Perkins heard the testimony of many working women who described terrible exploitation by employers in the form of sexual harassment, low pay, long hours, dangerous physical conditions, and uncompensated overtime. Perkins later recalled Lowell's presence at those meetings: "The very sight of her benignant, loving face, as she sat on the platform, in a dimly lighted room, up flights of stairs, among the handful of women who consulted about the necessities of working women, stirred us all to a better way of doing things, to a finer devotion and determination to keep out the note of injustice or bitterness."[40]

The result of this series of meetings was the establishment of the Working Women's Society of the City of New York (WWS), to which Lowell was appointed the principal advisor. The society's immediate task was to investigate the conditions under which women department store employees labored and then prepare and publicize a report. The society's secretary, Alice Woodbridge, had worked in department stores herself and became an expert at eliciting testimony from frightened salesgirls.[41] Lowell helped to compile the evidence, and she received many letters detailing the sordid environment with which the young women had to contend. She also made the first of many on-site investigations of department stores.

Lowell described how she conducted her investigations in the testimony she gave to a New York State legislative committee looking into shop conditions—in this case, to see if the salesgirls were being allowed to sit down during slow periods, as prescribed by law. "I have investigated the retail dry goods establishments known as Macy's, at Sixth Avenue and Fourteenth Street, and Adam's at Sixth Avenue, for the purpose of ascertaining how they complied with the law," she began. "I have been to Macy's four times within the last few days. I went at different hours, but although the firm has placed seats for the saleswomen behind the counters, I rarely saw them being used." Lowell then told of her return visit to Macy's that included a morning and an evening check. "There were very few customers in the shop on either of these occasions, but, nevertheless, only a few of the saleswomen were seated. During my morning visit, I saw only 5 out of 83 girls sitting down. At 5:30 P.M. I found out of 68 girls, 2 sitting."[42] Lowell and the leaders of the WWS used this type of information in 1888 in a successful effort to force the state legislature to pass a law hiring female factory inspectors, as well as in later attempts to strengthen existing protective legislation.[43]

When the larger investigation was completed by the WWS, the society held a public meeting on May 6, 1890, at Chickering Hall (located at the corner of Fifth Avenue and Eighteenth Street), at which philanthropists and clergymen (including representatives from CAIL) were invited to listen to the report and to consider various options for action. A committee was appointed at the meeting to consider the most viable and practical method to achieve the desired reforms. It was decided by Lowell and other advisors to the WWS to form an organization along the same lines of the English Consumers' Society that had been started earlier in the year. To distinguish between the two, the American one would be called the Consumers' League of the City of New York. (WWS would remain dedicated to bettering the working conditions among salesgirls by promoting unionization.) The league was officially declared in existence on January 21, 1891, and Josephine Shaw Lowell served as its first president, with many prominent women on its membership roster. Lowell's home served as the meeting place of the Governing Board until 1896, when she resigned the presidency. The offices of the Consumers' League were in the United Charities Building, which also housed the COS.[44]

And like the COS, the league depended on "society ladies" for its first task force. On the early lists of the league's volunteers can be found the names of many COS workers, including Mrs. Seth Low, Mrs. H. M. Dewees, and Mrs. D. M. Stimson. In addition, Lowell's sister Ellen Barlow and her niece Edith Minturn served as a vice president and member of the Governing Board, respectively.[45] These volunteer inspectors sent out circulars to businesses requesting permission to visit their premises to determine whether they lived up to the "Standard of a Fair House." When the initial response proved lukewarm, Lowell and Maude Nathan, a fellow volunteer and the next president of the league, set out to visit the leading firms of the city to explain in person the objectives of the league and to urge their participation and cooperation. From these early investigations, they drew up a "white list" of department stores whose labor practices were considered fair and humane. The lists were then published in leading newspapers, and at first much to the dismay of the chosen department stores, which did not want the disapproval of the less enlightened businesses to fall upon them. When apprised of this situation, Lowell remarked, "We can't help that, we are sorry they don't approve of the League. But we will get information from the working girls themselves, and if the firms have good conditions and are just, they must go on the white list." That being on the white list was considered by many businesses as a punishment, not a reward, for good labor practices is an indication of how far the league had to go before it commanded respect.[46] Yet the women persevered, and in a relatively short time they were pleased to announce that thirty-one establishments had made the "White List," including B. Altman & Co., Bloomingdale Brothers, Lord & Taylor, F. A. O. Schwarz, and John Wanamaker. This, of course, represented only a small number of the establishments that the league hoped to improve, but the businesses named were among the most prominent, and it was hoped that they would set a shining example for the others.

The Consumers' League persisted throughout the 1890s in its efforts to improve conditions for the city's salesgirls. In 1895 Lowell and others went to Albany to lobby for a bill that would strengthen and expand the existing legislation. This bill, applying to towns of more than three thousand, would set ten hours a day or sixty hours a week as the legal standard. It would also give more muscle to the factory inspectors and ban children from mercantile establishments. Lowell's testimony before the legislative committee helped to pave the way for the bill's passage. It was a triumphant day for the league when the Mercantile Inspection Act of 1896 passed, for it had survived not only the attacks of businesses but a hostile newspaper editorial calling the whole plan "socialistic." Consumers' leagues mushroomed throughout New York State after the attendant publicity, and in 1898 they were consolidated into one organization called the New York State Consumers' League. In 1899 the National Consumers' League was founded, and with the formidable Florence Kelley as its executive secretary, it contributed mightily to the growing movement for protective legislation, particularly for women and children.[47]

It is worth taking a moment here to summarize the tactics Lowell employed in this campaign and their influential role in shaping politics. Consistent with her paternalistic background and philanthropic enterprises, she undertook to mobilize women of her class to correct a problem—in this case, labor relations. She then wielded two weapons that broke from this elitist tradition. The first was the collection of information, testimony from the workers themselves. The second was publicizing her findings. Lowell used popular opinion, through newspapers, as a weapon against entrenched interests. Armed with this weapon, she could more effectively lobby the legislature for change. The process clearly highlighted her position at the fulcrum of political change—straddling the worlds of paternalistic and popular politics in the realm of social reform. Paradoxically, therefore, while the object of so much of her political and charitable work can be summed up as character-building—inculcating the moral and personal traits necessary, as she saw it, for a responsible, independent life—she did not hesitate to use the power of group cohesion or mass media to achieve her ends. Finally, the goal Lowell sought to achieve was to make the state accept responsibility for its citizens' welfare, within limits and under certain conditions. The Consumers' League, wrote Lowell, believed in placing vulnerable "young women and children under the protection of the Government, in order that their health may not suffer by excessive hours of labor and other unfavorable conditions."[48]

Lowell's labor activity in CAIL and the Consumers' League led her to articulate the concept of a living wage for workers. Here she acknowledged her debt to the English political economist Thorold Rogers, whose *The History of Work and Wages* (1885) influenced her thinking in this area. The great principle of the Consumers' League, she declared, is that consumers "have the power to secure just and humane conditions of labor if they would only use it."[49] The consumer, Lowell argued, bore a great responsibility to not demand that products be so cheap that workers not be able to sustain themselves on the salaries they earned:

> The great objects to be striven for, both for a nation as a whole, and for the individual working men and women, is that this standard of living should be constantly rising, in order that the condition of the people may rise constantly. It will be a good thing for the American nation when a piano and a bicycle are regarded as necessaries of life by everybody, provided that the truth is also recognized that the necessaries of life are to be earned by honest hard work, and not by gambling and cheating, whether on a large scale on Wall Street, or on a small scale on Hester Street.[50]

Lowell considered the league, like boards of arbitration, an essential vehicle for educating the employers and the public to do their part in providing a living wage for workers.

Thus it can be seen that Lowell's thinking on labor fleshed out her COS work. Laborers who were underemployed and underpaid relied on charity to supplement their income, which benefited their employers. This, she thought, was a dangerous situation, for it undermined the worker's character and provided an easy out for the boss. The league came into existence with the expressed intent of bringing to an end this inconsistency by supporting a living wage for women workers. This it did in a generally nonthreatening manner, by urging cooperation among employers, employees, and the public. Cooperation, as always, had to be complemented by knowledge, and the investigative and publicity skills of the league would supply that precious commodity as a basis for social change and reform. The white list was the embodiment of this process.

Lowell was struck by the complex nature of the industrial economy that made it imperative to explain to people their moral duties: "The great difficulty which has presented itself to conscientious individuals who desire not to take part in the oppression of their fellow-men by buying goods made and sold under inhuman conditions has always been that of learning what those conditions were." She went on to say how easy it was for the abolitionists to identify the slave-made products of sugar and cotton and to then give them up. Under the free-market system, however, it was much more difficult to know about the conditions under which goods are made and sold, and thus "it is necessary to have concerted action, and from this necessity was developed the idea of the Consumers' League."[51] Lowell's involvement with the labor reform movement—whether through arbitration, support for unions, or the treatment of saleswomen—made her aware of the difficulties of working people's lives in a way she had never been before. This awareness, in turn, deeply affected her charity work in the greatest challenge of her career.

✑ The Depression of 1893 ✑

The COS's premier position among New York City's charities in the 1890s and into the twentieth century, two welfare historians have concluded, was really rooted in its innovative response to the 1893 depression.[52] In this area, as in so many others, the founder of the COS, Josephine Shaw Lowell, assumed a leadership position in which she drew upon her charity experience first and foremost but gathered forces with churches, labor unions, and settlement houses as well to launch an all-out, if only temporary, assault on the extreme suffering caused by the depression. "Of course there were able and devoted men and women working with Mrs. Lowell," remembered Lillian D. Wald, "but she was the animating spirit."[53]

The 1893 depression was by far the worst one in American history. The boom years of the Gilded Age had raised the standard of living for the working class as well as increased the strength, numbers, and influence of a rising, powerful, and dominant middle class. In other words, not just plutocrats but a majority of Americans, native-born and immigrants, benefited from the prosperity that characterized post–Civil War America. Yet as bad financial news from overseas began to trickle in, by 1892 Americans became uneasily aware of their involvement in an international economy that made them dependent on the good health of foreign economies. Then, early in 1893, the stock market crashed, partly in response to overconstruction at home. Confidence in the economy plummeted, financial panic ensued, farmers and factory workers alike suffered heavily, and within the year there were approximately 3 million people out of work, or an estimated 20 percent of the American workforce.

As grim as these statistics were, they paled before the sense of despair felt by the unemployed in the summer of 1893. Few citizens looked to or expected the federal government to come to their assistance. "The lessons of paternalism ought to be unlearned and the better lesson taught that while the people should support their Government its functions do not include the support of the people," declared President Cleveland in his second inaugural address. Most Americans accepted this, but a few thousand did not. Jacob Coxey led an army of unemployed into Washington, D.C., in the summer of 1894 to demand federal work-relief programs, an idea whose time had not come as far as the president and the national leadership were concerned. Welfare was a state and local issue, and it was to their local government and private charities that people turned in hard times. The problem of unemployment loomed large on the nation's horizon, and, as might be expected, it loomed largest and most dangerously in the urban centers, where hungry, restless, angry, and idle workers posed a danger to social peace.[54]

১৯ East Side Relief-Work Committee ৩০

It was in this atmosphere that Lowell took the initiative in the summer of 1893 and formed the East Side Relief-Work Committee (ESRC), which she explicitly designed as a model to be used throughout New York City and in cities throughout the country in economic downturns. The COS leadership felt the rumblings of the coming depression early in the summer of 1893 in the form of greatly increased applications for relief. And as the summer progressed into fall, their worst fears were confirmed: October witnessed an increased application rate of 98 percent over the previous years, with November and December keeping pace with an increase of 46 percent and 86 percent, respectively.[55] Another one of the COS's fears was that relief-giving would slip out of their control. Dire economic times brought out in the open the deep divisions that were always present in the charitable community.

Anticipating this division, seventeen major philanthropic organizations, led by the COS but including a fair representation of Catholic, Jewish, German, and Protestant charities, issued a statement in September 1893, published in all the major dailies, warning against any and all who would promote or support "spasmodic and indiscriminate" methods of relief. Two of Lowell's colleagues in the philanthropic field—Thomas M. Mulry, secretary of the St. Vincent de Paul Society of New York, and Nathaniel S. Rosenau, manager of the United Hebrew Charities of New York—were usually staunch allies with the COS in opposing newspaper charities, as well as in many other areas of social welfare policy. The statement that they supported pointedly asked that no free programs for the poor be instituted by newspapers and other organizations, as that would draw even more supplicants from outside the New York City area. Rather, the plan put forward by the group envisioned the reasoned gathering of resources of the city's best and most experienced benevolent agencies, together with the coalition of public and private support groups, all closely monitored, to meet the exigencies of New York's own poor in the coming winter. In fact, this scenario was largely carried out as resources were marshaled, and large amounts were raised in both goods and cash, making New York City the most generous of all American cities in the harsh depression of 1893.[56]

Lowell was particularly adamant that all direct relief to sufferers be ruled out as injurious to moral character. "We should be willing to suffer ourselves and see our poor friends suffer to save them from this fearful permanent evil," she asserted in a widely quoted speech. "We exaggerate the importance of physical suffering." Lowell was not being deliberately hardhearted in saying this; rather, she was concerned about emphasizing the long-term benefits of tying relief to work: "Benevolent people will not take any trouble to help their fellow-creatures in distress, but they will give money. . . . Energy, independence, industry, and self-reliance are undermined by free giving and the capacity for future self-support taken away."[57] Lowell had long-standing beliefs about the deleterious effects of relief, or ill-conceived work-relief programs, on the moral character of the poor. She also believed in social justice for the working class. Simply, the ESRC was created out of her twin desires to control the conditions of welfare while easing the real deprivation that workers and their families were experiencing in the depression winter and ensuring their ultimate well-being.

This was truly a major departure in policy for Lowell, and she was only able to take it because of her exposure to the labor movement. "For the first time in many years," claimed the COS in its report on the relief work for 1893, "measures were taken to provide relief-by-work for the unemployed."[58] Lowell created two committees to facilitate her program: a fund-raising group, named the Citizens' Relief Committee and headed by Seth Low, president of Columbia University, and the ESRC, whose function would be to create and supervise the work-relief programs.

Lowell's ESRC was formed with these critical factors in mind: it was to be local and temporary, serving the needs of the East Side neighborhoods in which the Third District served, and it was to draw upon the talents and experiences of a whole range of people who were already deeply involved in reform and welfare organizations, especially the COS, University Settlement, and College Settlement. As Lowell reported later, "The members brought to their task not only experience and knowledge of the people whom they wished to help, but also a deep-rooted determination that their moral character, their souls, must not be sacrificed in the effort to save their bodies."[59]

The temporary nature of the committee's work was stressed, as the worst outcome would be to take away or degrade existing employment. "Will you not remind employers," Lowell anxiously wrote to a newspaper on Christmas Day 1893,

> whether individuals, firms, or corporations, that, notwithstanding all the appeals for "relief for the unemployed," which this sad season renders necessary, by far the better way for them is to retain in regular work all their employees whom they possibly can, giving half or quarter time, if full time is out of the question? . . . Will you not also point out to those who have been accustomed to spend extravagantly, that, although the "luxury of the rich" is not a benefit to the community, yet, in this emergency . . . they have no right, suddenly and capriciously, to change the direction of their expenditure, thus throwing into the crowded ranks of the "unemployed" those whom they have trained to depend on them for a living . . . ?[60]

Lowell had always argued and would continue to argue about the dangers of relief, whether given through public or private agencies, whether in the form of coal, food, money, or jobs. The depths of this depression, however, which hit so hard the working people she now knew well, determined her course in setting up a work-relief program that would be closely supervised by experts.

By October 1893, ESRC made plans to offer as many people jobs as possible by paying them a decent salary that would allow them to survive the winter, preserve their pride and independence, and yet not undermine or compete with existing jobs. The programs were to be funded through the Citizens' Relief Committee, as well as through discreet newspaper solicitations. The ESRC established its headquarters not at the new COS offices but at the College Settlement at 95 Rivington Street. The committee determined that the employment on the city streets would not threaten any current jobs and worked out a plan with the street cleaning commissioner to put men to work sweeping one hour a day. "The streets of the East Side had not been so clean in a decade."[61] On November 29, 1893, this was begun. The committee gave work tickets to trade unions, churches, and charities to give to known heads of families. In this way the work-relief funding would be kept on a local basis. The program was so successful that the demands from desperate East Siders for work tickets soon exceeded the supply and the ESRC's ability to provide jobs.

"Give this man work," wrote one man to the committee, "if you would keep his wife and children alive; one child has already died from starvation." Investigations were uncovering the sad details of the misery of unemployment in that hungry winter. "Let us send out work to the women and girls who cannot go to the factory," urged Lowell in an effort to ease the effects of poverty for young, single women. In January 1894, acting on the suggestion of member Edith Kendall and with the hearty agreement of the president of the Health Board, Charles G. Wilson, the committee again combined work-relief with improvements in sanitation when they hired men for the whitewashing of tenements. In less than a month's time, 491 men were hired under the supervision of the subcommittee, which had a weekly payroll of $3,000. Yet another program was initiated to relieve distress in the garment industry when Jewish men and women were put to work making clothes for the "poor Negroes of the Sea Islands."[62]

Lowell threw herself into this work with her usual dedication, working day and night in order to execute successfully the ESRC programs. She attended committee meetings at the College Settlement four times a week and took it upon herself to tend personally to such details as hiring shops, foremen, and the sweeping superintendent. "And now," she wearily wrote her sister-in-law, "I am chairman of the Committee that runs the shop and also a member of the Executive Committee that runs the whole thing."[63] As chair, Lowell brought her administrative skills, honed by many years in the COS, to bear on the committee work, ensuring its smooth running and efficient distribution of resources. In the end, the ESRC proved to be a smashing success *if* judged by the terms its founders set out for it. During the five critical months of the winter of 1893, 4,541 men and 466 women had been aided and almost $180,000 expended to pay their wages. "The Committee is now able to look back at its winter's work," Lowell summed up, "and although never, at any time, has the amount of relief provided through its means been adequate to the demand, it has the satisfaction of feeling that its effort has been made upon the right lines."[64] That is to say, in Lowell's opinion, that no moral damage was done, despite the outlay of relief and jobs, because of the careful oversight in distributing the work tickets to selected churches, unions, settlement houses, and charities.

Josephine Shaw Lowell and the ESRC, which began with a $1,000 contribution and provided more than 5,000 East Siders with work-relief, brought their work to an end with a resolution roundly condemning relief efforts in normal times: "The East Side Relief-Work Committee desires to place on record its conviction that the methods by which it has been able to alleviate the distress prevailing on the East Side during the past winter . . . should be adopted only under abnormal conditions, such as have existed in New York for nine months."[65] Even given the self-imposed limits of the committee, it is worth repeating that Lowell would not have organized it without the benefit of her previous involvement in the labor movement, which illuminated for her the harsh struggle average men and women had to endure to maintain the minimum living standard. Afterward, she wrote a friend, "What I feel now is that we must all try to do something which will be *permanent* and deal with the permanent evils, which will remain after the temporary distress has passed."[66] Her sentiments were analyzed and put into action as she acted to change both the leadership structure and the future aspirations of the COS.

The End of One Era . . .

Lowell's ESRC showed the happy results of the flexibility and innovation that she brought to every one of her previous positions: as volunteer charity worker for the SCAA, as commissioner of the SBC, as leader of the COS, as a COS district committee worker, and as a force behind the Consumers' League. The ESRC was just one part of a huge, privately dominated relief effort that, in only one year, raised approximately $2.5 million for the city's estimated 50,000 unemployed. This particular kind of private mobilization of funds and resources was coming to an end, however, as the ensuing forty years would see increased agitation for social insurance programs that would render the 1893 effort anachronistic. The next great depression, beginning in 1929, would bring fundamental changes in the American welfare system—changes that were just beginning to be dimly perceived in the wake of the 1893 depression.[67]

The ESRC can be seen as a bridge linking the past and the future of social welfare. It was a link to the past because the early history of the charity organization movement in which Josephine Shaw Lowell played so large a part was ending. The Lowells, the Paines, the Fields, and the de Forests—the upper-class leaders of American philanthropy of the late nineteenth century—were no longer needed. Because of forces they themselves set in motion with their support of a "science" of charity, devoted, unpaid volunteers (leaders and workers) were being replaced by professionals. With this change, which occurred with great rapidity after the 1893 depression and into the first decades of the twentieth century, a professional ideal of objectivity replaced the passionate advocacy of the amateurs.[68]

The ESRC was part of the future because its members, led by Lowell, recognized that there was a *need* on the part of the unemployed that had to be addressed. This need was socially and politically justifiable but did not necessarily fit in with the limited role of welfare and relief policy as it developed in Lowell's previous thinking and writing. But her involvement with the labor movement had changed her perception about the role of both private and governmental agencies in an economic crisis. Her labor activism also very much sharpened her previously incomplete awareness of the larger social and economic deficiencies of capitalism. Lowell's concern shifted from a focus on the helpless dependent to, as she noted indignantly, the "500,000 wage earners in this city, 200,000 of them women and 75,000 of those working under dreadful conditions or for starvation wages."[69] The ESRC showed how determined Lowell was to fashion a welfare program that would preserve the integrity of scientific charity yet accommodate an extraordinarily dangerous situation through a humanitarian work-relief program. Lowell emerged from the depression of

1893 with a renewed commitment to helping the working class live dignified and prosperous lives. After all, she wrote, "the interests of the working people are of paramount importance, simply because they are the majority of the whole people."[70]

The ESRC was also forward-looking because it tentatively proposed fundamental changes in the way relief was considered and distributed. The Gilded Age industrial system, with its power to wreak havoc in so many lives, demanded that social welfare activists and intellectuals respond with new approaches that did not hold ordinary workers at fault for sudden and precipitous poverty. Lowell realized this fact, and one of her responses was to identify and encourage a new, college-educated generation of charity professionals to assume progressive leadership in the field.

In the history of the COS, a link to the past was severed and a link to the present was forged when Lowell hired Edward T. Devine as general secretary in 1896. Devine, a brilliant economics Ph.D. from Johns Hopkins, brought a much different sensibility to the COS's leadership and programs, and his name would become synonymous with the development of twentieth-century social work. Devine set a fresh agenda for the COS as it moved toward the millennium. He prodded and pushed the COS to explore the social, rather than just the individual, causes of poverty, and, most important, he helped to research, define, and publicize a normal "standard of living" under which, he argued, working-class Americans should not be allowed to fall. Devine and Lowell worked well together, as they both believed in encouraging the structural and environmental aspects of charitable reform. They also urged even closer ties with settlement houses, churches, and like-minded organizations that would make the city government more responsible to social welfare concerns. Lowell's acceptance of professionally trained charity experts such as Devine once again demonstrated her openness to new methods in philanthropy, while at the same time remaining a powerful symbol for a fading vision. More than that, she gladly turned over the day-to-day running of the COS to Devine, for now she was increasingly active in the political arena and concerned with defining and using the growing political power of women to fight and replace the Tammany-dominated machine government in New York City.

8

The Useful Citizen

✍ "Reawakening the Spirit of Liberty" ✍

As the 1880s gave way to the 1890s, Josephine Shaw Lowell lived up to the ideals of "The Useful Citizen" so beautifully articulated by her husband many years before. What were those ideals? "Live like a plain republican," admonished Charley, be forever "mindful of the beauty and the duty of simplicity," and most of all, be an "unpretending hero," because if America did not produce these "useful citizens" in great numbers, then "we are not going to have any Country." What Charles Russell Lowell meant was that every citizen should make it his or her business to participate in the nation's political life, and that if he or she did not, then, simply put, the United States of America could not survive as a democratic republic.[1]

Josephine Shaw Lowell had always given a lot of thought to what it meant to be a citizen of the United States. For her, and for most of the generation of northerners who had fought and lived through the Civil War, the concept of citizenship was inextricably intertwined with the meaning of that terrible conflict. The deeply religious Shaw family believed that the Civil War was Armageddon—a huge and all-encompassing struggle between good and evil—in which the good triumphed with the vanquishing of slavery and the preservation of the Union—in the name of liberty and freedom. George William Curtis spoke for the family when he said that the war showed that "national greatness is a moral, not a financial fact."[2] After the war the great challenge for the United States was how to perfect and advance its moral agenda in areas that had been neglected by "useful citizens" because of their preoccupation with the fight against slavery. For Lowell, these areas were poverty, crime, and corruption. They all needed the attention of a high-minded partnership between the private and the public sectors.

Alas, it was all too clear in the two and a half decades since Lee's surrender at Appomattox that the nation was not living up to its promise as the political system, on every level, was mired in corruption and scandal and the ideals of liberty and freedom were degraded by machine politics and politicians. Lowell, Curtis, and many other upper-class activists advanced civil service reform—that is, the removal of "politics" from governance—as a major step to first restoring honesty and efficiency in government and consequently morality in the country. Only then could the great problems of the Gilded Age be properly addressed. Reformers thus connected an uncorrupted state with patriotism, nationalism, and good citizenship. At the end of the Civil War, Lowell remembered, America "stood before the world as real believers in liberty for all men, for black men as well as for white men." But now, she lamented, the deathlike grip of corruption (cash for votes) in the great cities threatened the loss of liberty, just as surely as the institution of slavery symbolized an earlier danger: "Men must either be free or they must be slaves. To be free men they must have their own opinions and must follow them. . . . If men vote because they are paid to vote, or because they want an office, or because their employer tells them to vote as he does . . . then they are slaves, and though the government continues to be democratic in name, it is actually a despotic government. If we hope to preserve our nation, it must be by reawakening the spirit of liberty in our people."[3]

And so it is in Lowell's civil service reform work where we find her at her most political. Here she grappled with, and came to terms with, the concept of citizenship in the heat of the industrial age, when immigration, urbanization, and corrupt politics seemed to threaten the capacity of the American people for self-rule. Throughout the 1890s to her death in 1905, Lowell was preoccupied with politics and reform—in her city, in her state, and in her nation. Before examining her major activities in these years—which include participation in the New York mayoral elections and the anti-imperialist protest movement—we must understand how important the connection between honest, efficient, and democratic government and an enlightened, educated, and active citizenry was for Josephine Shaw Lowell. And that connection was made most powerfully with Lowell's leadership among the reform-minded women of New York City.

Lowell the charity professional emphasized the importance of merit-based jobs for all state, county, and local institutions serving the dependent. Her lifelong efforts in this area were given explicit political direction in 1894, when she formed the Women's Auxiliary to the Civil Service Reform Association of New York State, for which she selected the motto "The Best Shall serve the State."[4] In establishing the auxiliary, Josephine dedicated her efforts to her now-deceased brother-in-law, George William Curtis. Her work for the auxiliary was very much directed toward the inclusion of women in public life, making them think about the duties of citizenship, even though they could not vote, and urging them to work with men for a common goal of good government.

꒰ A Women's Leader ꒱

Lowell's ideas about women's citizenship grew out of her charity and labor work. Her increasing exposure to the plight of so many female workers aroused strong feelings of maternal compassion in her—feelings grounded in class as well as gender. These feelings should be analyzed with some precision. While Lowell was outraged at the large injustices suffered by both men and women of the working class, her long years in the charity field had educated her in the special disabilities that poor women suffered in society. Indeed, a large number of her social welfare programs and reforms advanced in the SCAA, the SBC, and the COS in the past twenty years were directed toward gender-based solutions predicated on, and measured against, women's place in Victorian society.

Lowell believed women should be included in the organized labor movement, declaring them to "belong to the class, who by head work and hand work, by intelligence or strength or skill, are keeping the world alive, clothing, feeding, housing themselves and everybody else." But, she warned, working women—particularly the youngest who were the most numerous—labored under another handicap. They were "helpless because they are women, and they are helpless also because they are young, and they are moreover exposed to peculiar temptations from the fact that, when wages fall below the living point, the wages of sin are always ready for them." The "moral dangers" faced by working-class women had rallied upper- and middle-class women to their side for at least as long as the nineteenth century and would continue to be a potent factor in many different reform movements encompassing religion, social purity, politics, and temperance well into the twentieth century.[5]

Lowell's maternal feelings were part and parcel of her class background and sensibilities. She felt it her duty to aid this group of young women who "deserve our pity, because of their helplessness," and she assumed her expected place as a protector of the socially vulnerable.[6] From her most successful campaigns to build female reformatories and hire female matrons at those institutions and in police stations, Lowell also knew that public sentiment and ensuing political action was more quickly and surely marshaled at the plight of "helpless" women and children than by working-class men. Why not take advantage of that situation to really do something that she considered valuable? Lowell's relationship with working-class women must thus be analyzed with care in order not to overemphasize her upper-class background at the expense of a gritty determination, based on practical experience, to act judiciously in the political sphere. Her expertise in this area provided one foundation for women's advancement in the public sector.

Connected with Lowell's understanding of how a working woman's agenda could be advanced through enlarging the sphere of female citizenship was her growing interest in tapping the power of upper- and middle-class womanhood to work for reform aims. Two factors can be identified in this process. First, through her conversations with working-class activists such as Leonora O'Reilly and Alice Woolbridge and her on-site investigations of department stores, Lowell became aware of the critical link that drew all women together in a web of responsibility and political action. Second, a new generation of female reformers was springing up, and Lowell was benefiting from their passion and comradeship, and they in turn were benefiting from her leadership and public experience. During these years, Lowell became a mentor to some of these women with both practical and inspirational results.

Lowell worked hard to bring to women an appreciation of the implicit power available to them through their role as consumers. She believed that this power had more to offer than selfish pleasure. During her adult life, Lowell had witnessed the results of a rising income of the typical middle-class American family—high levels of home ownership, an expansion of consumer goods, and an explosion of recreational opportunities. Women had more discretionary income, and they were spending it on clothes, furniture, and accessories in the large department stores that sprang up to cater to their desires. "The Ladies' Mile" shopping area that graced Broadway and that daily attracted droves of women was replicated everywhere throughout the country. One scholar of this phenomenon observed that "the department stores served as quasi clubs for women, with lounges and dining rooms, where women could meet their friends, rest, or read."[7]

Women shoppers thus had the potential to be formed into a strong force for political change. But how to make consumers aware of their responsibilities? Lowell communicated to women that their roles as consumers obligated them—made them *morally* culpable—to care about the ways in which saleswomen were treated. As a leader of the Consumers' League, she urged women again and again to shop during "reasonable hours" and not to accept cheaper goods at the price of the degradation of working women's lives. Be patient, be understanding of the saleswomen who serve you, Lowell counseled in many speeches on behalf of the league, describing in vivid detail the exhaustion that clerks felt after being on their feet fourteen hours a day with no break. She called for a "pathway" to be opened between middle-class and working-class women, and pointed out that the benefits would not all be flowing from the well-off to the less fortunate. She told a group of young working women that they set a shining example for "the women who are pining for want of work and are supported in enforced idleness."[8] Lowell wished to educate women shoppers that the power they possessed as consumers could change the world for the better. Her work with the Consumers' League made her realize, more than ever, that a dedicated group of leaders was needed to motivate and direct the masses of women to do the right thing.

A second factor in Lowell's gendered construction of citizenship came when she consciously began to "mentor" young women whom she identified as having leadership capabilities.[9] One of the most important qualities Lowell looked for in recruiting women leaders was a serious commitment to work. Her words to COS friendly visitors reflected her expectations. "It is hard work which we have undertaken," Lowell said. "Work requiring time, and thought, and patience and judgment."[10] Her attitude applied to her own daughter's life as well. Carlotta, who never married, accompanied her mother to many meetings and lent a sympathetic ear to the inevitable disappointments that Lowell endured in her career as a reformer. Carlotta's nurtured administrative capabilities proved invaluable when Lowell's illness rendered her incapable of communication in the months before her death. Carlotta tended to shun the limelight and preferred to work quietly alongside her mother, aunts, cousins, and friends, both in the COS and in other organizations. After Lowell died in 1905, Carlotta carved out a small niche for herself in educational reform in New York City. Only forty-one in 1905, she adopted three daughters—Emily, Lillian, and Martha, who were sixteen, fifteen, and fourteen, respectively, at the time of Carlotta's own unexpected death from influenza at age sixty on September 19, 1924, in Liverpool, England.[11]

Aside from Carlotta and her numerous nieces, Lowell personally recruited many of the women who would become prominent in the Woman's Municipal League and the Women's Auxiliary to the Civil Service Reform Association—for instance, Lillian Wald and Maude Nathan. Leonora O'Reilly also attracted Lowell's attention for her leadership potential. Indeed, Lowell was always on the lookout for good, smart career women to place at the female reformatories she had worked so hard to establish as an SBC commissioner. To this end, she was active in securing positions for the next generation of college-educated reformers, such as Katharine Bemont Davis and Frances Kellor, both of whom achieved impressive degrees at the University of Chicago. She even asked for the names of promising students to work in the COS: "It is suggested to me that Professors Veblen, Small, Henderson, Zeubline and Vincent would all probably be interested in giving names of graduates from the sociological course," wrote Lowell to Marion Talbot, dean of women at Chicago.[12] Many women in the COS, settlement houses, universities, and female-run institutions had reason to be thankful to Lowell for her example, guidance, and practical assistance.

These relationships impelled Lowell to participate in women-only organizations and movements that she would have shunned earlier. Always a believer in women's suffrage, Lowell became a staunch advocate of it when it became an issue in the 1894 New York Constitutional Convention, where it was defeated. That same year, Lowell and her friend and colleague in the Consumers' League, Mary Putnam Jacobi, were founding members of the League for Political Education, a pro-suffrage advocacy group. Lowell and Putnam were also members of the Sherry Committee, a political action committee comprised of prominent Republican women who were urging legislators to adopt suffrage. Called the Sherry Committee because its members gathered in the rooms of the Sherry Hotel in New York, it included many prominent women, including Lowell's sister Susanna Minturn. Another one of Lowell's nieces, Elizabeth Burrill Curtis, was also very active in the New York State suffrage movement, following in her father's footsteps.[13]

Ellen DuBois examined this group of elite women who worked for New York State suffrage in 1894 and found the majority of them to be desirous of the suffrage for themselves but *not* for their working-class sisters. Lowell differed in that respect. She thought the vote would bring status and strength to working-class women. "I believe," she stated, "that the qualities, needed to help women win good wages for themselves and for each other, courage, self-confidence, public spirit, would be fostered by the suffrage, and that is one reason why I want women to have the suffrage." Lowell admitted privately that while she did "not expect any great general advantage" from suffrage, she thought that the vote might offer some "direct protection to women who are now at the mercy of brutal men," by forcing men to respect the rights of women. This was especially important, Lowell continued, for poor women, because "they are shamefully abused in many ways." The vote would help them, concluded Lowell, "whether they ever voted or not."[14] The fact of the matter was, of course, that no woman in New York State had the right to vote as yet, and the prospects for a national suffrage law looked dim. The challenge for Lowell was to help to fashion an ideological and practical political role for women that communicated the message that public participation was critical even if they did not have the right to vote, that the responsibilities of citizenship were broader than suffrage.

✍ *"Relation of Women to Good Government"* ✍

Lowell's long-held convictions about the linkage between liberty, responsibility, and duty all in the cause of good government came to a boiling point in the 1890s through an explicit call for women to do battle against political corruption. Indeed, an outstanding characteristic of Lowell's career as it took shape in the 1890s was a new gender-based activism that grew out of her involvement with the COS, the Working Women's Society, and the Consumers' League. The league, for example, was founded by and for women and sought to appeal to women as consumers.

Now was the time, Lowell thought, to take the consumer idea a bit further and apply it to shaping, directing, and defining a woman's citizenship. That is, How can women participate in the public sphere and help to direct government policy even if they were based in the private sphere and did not have the vote? What was, she mused in a speech to young women, "The Relation of Women to Good Government"? Lowell would set herself the task of answering this question in the upcoming years by expanding the definition of citizenship. One answer that she came up with was the founding of women's civic organizations. In 1894 she began the Woman's Municipal League (of which more will be said shortly). A year later she began the aforementioned Women's Auxiliary to the New York Civil Service Reform Association, conflating her belief in women's political power with reform. Lowell summed up her philosophy for a reporter: "I consider Civil Service reform the fundamental reform in this country, and, although a very busy woman, I could not refuse when asked to take up this matter for forming an organization of women to use their influence in deepening public interest in its behalf. It is true that women have no apparent voice in public affairs, but it is no less true that they have a real voice if they choose to lift it in private life and can do a great work."[15] Lowell's feminism was contextualized by her observation of, and participation in, an exciting network of women's volunteer organizations that was reaching its peak of power in the 1890s and included the Woman's Christian Temperance Union (WCTU), the General Federation of Women's Clubs, and the settlement house movement.

The contours of women's activism expanded dramatically from the 1870s to the 1890s. The proliferation of women's organizations in such connected movements as temperance, social purity, municipal reform, and clubs was nothing short of astonishing. Surely, the Gilded Age represented the height of women's power and influence within benevolent and reform organizations. Many of these organizations and their members, while conforming to the earlier ideals of Victorian womanhood, were expanding their roles as mothers into public life as "social housekeepers" to the nation. For example, the WCTU's motto, "Do Everything," expressed the organization's desire to involve itself in a plethora of educational, municipal, health, and gender reforms that sprang out of, but were not limited to, temperance.[16] These organizations, comprised largely of white, middle-class Protestant women, promoted "a collective consciousness that took on an explicitly political dimension."[17]

Lowell herself was a member of the New York State Federation of Women's Clubs and used her membership to further the spread of civil service and municipal reform in that organization and similar ones throughout the nation. Indeed, the Women's Auxiliary to the Civil Service Reform Association was actually one of the clubs of the New York State Federation, and under Lowell's chairwomanship it devised innovative contests and educational packages to spread the word on the benefits of civil service reform and women's role in encouraging it.[18] Lowell's career cannot be said to have been built on this network of women's organizations, but certainly she profited from their growing influence in public affairs, particularly in the great campaigns for municipal reform that commenced in New York City.

⚘ Reformers Unite ⚘

The end of the depression winter of 1893–94 brought forth a burst of political energy in which Lowell and the COS joined with other reform groups to challenge—and several times to wrest away—Tammany's grip on city government in the crucial mayoral elections of the 1890s and the early 1900s.[19] Three factors coincided to create a propitious environment for these occurrences. First, the Democrats were being blamed for the 1893 depression. Republicans were already ascending in Albany, and President Cleveland was in deep trouble nationally. Knowledgeable observers were forecasting trouble in the usually safe Democratic precincts of Tammany in the next mayoral election in 1894.

Second, the potential tactical success of "fusion tickets," which allowed reformers of all stripes to coalesce under the broad banner of bringing efficiency and honesty to government, was providing a shot in the arm for reform hopes. Connected with the second factor is the third: the growth of a large number of reform organizations whose membership was made up of the professional middle class: doctors, lawyers, engineers, businessmen, and the like. They joined with social workers, philanthropists, the clergy, and women to present to the voters a plan of civic betterment and reform in municipal government.[20] Included in this network were such groups as the City Club, the Civil Service Reform Association, the East Side Civic Club (which was an outgrowth of Lowell's ESRC), the Woman's Municipal League, and, of course, the COS. These groups ranged from conservative to liberal, and the reforms they sought would place the governance of New York City into the hands of competent professionals whose loyalty would be to the "whole" of the people rather than to one political party.

Thus the municipal reformers were occupying the moral high ground—familiar territory to the many New York reformers who, like Lowell, were aligned with Mugwump efforts and civil service reform. Historians have noted the undemocratic nature of many reforms and reform groups who presumed to speak for a "people" they could hardly relate to on a personal basis, unlike, say, Tammany's politicians, many of whom came from immigrant and working-class backgrounds. To their credit, however, some reform groups realized that their elitism was a barrier not only to winning elections in New York City but to ever realizing the full scope of their planned structural changes, which they believed would make the city livable and manageable in the industrial age. Led by Lowell, de Forest, and Devine, the COS was in the forefront of bringing a more democratic and humanitarian cast to municipal reform. The society sought to offer positive inducements—such as tenement house reform, tuberculosis prevention programs, playgrounds and parks, and street-cleaning programs—to both working-class and immigrant voters to throw the machine out of office.

Lowell was prominent in these political campaigns and wore three hats: the first as a spokesperson for charity, the second as a voice for civil service reform, and the third as a leader of women's right to participate in city elections. Her work with the COS can be seen as an explicit attempt to provide decent and honest welfare service, in contrast to Tammany's "tainted" service. Edward T. Devine remarked that the COS leadership had been "in a position to act at times as pioneers, again as unofficial allies, again as municipal consciences . . . remaining to take a continuous interest in all matters . . . while city officials come and go."[21] Lowell's ESRC illustrated Devine's point beautifully: through its distribution of work tickets (which had been a feature of its regular programs for the homeless for years), its carefully controlled relief programs, and its well-publicized proclamations of sympathy, the reformers had attempted to bypass Tammany and build an alternative system of welfare.

This "alternative" welfare system offered by the COS is a point that cannot be made too strongly. The "churches and the charities," along with the settlement houses, were the only members of the reform coalition that had any contact with the poor and dispossessed.[22] They developed programs to foster rapprochement between the classes; their publicity skills were invaluable as well. Over the years, the COS had cultivated reasonably good relations with the city's major newspapers—the *New York Times,* the *New York Daily Tribune,* the *World,* and the *Evening Post.* And Lowell used the press wisely: it was, after all, the only way she could get her reform message to the masses while circumventing the vast personal communications network that the political machines had established. In doing so, Lowell and the COS had built an appreciative constituency, not only among the elite but among the middle class and working class as well. They brought invaluable experience and skills to the fight with Tammany.[23]

At the beginning of the 1890s, however, Lowell could look back on roughly twenty years of defeat and discouragement in the "good government" battle with the machine.[24] Despite the downfall of Boss Tweed, the New York City machine grew stronger in the 1870s and 1880s; indeed, by 1890, similar organizations dominated "half of the nation's largest cities."[25] Tammany's tight political control of city government continued to be cemented by a combination of graft, vice, corruption, loyalty, and freewheeling and individualistic distribution of social services. Yet Tammany's style of personalized welfare and laissez-faire government by party could not accommodate the more structural problems in health, sanitation, and education brought about by the influx of roughly 300,000 immigrants in the 1880s, and the promise of many more to come in the 1890s.

Tammany's lack of interest in solving the major urban problems proved to be a weak point in these politicians' defense as reformers hammered away at the machine's inattention to efficient government. Lowell's work in charity had from the very beginning promoted the idea of a nonpartisan, professionalized corps of government workers and leaders who would streamline and modernize what she believed to be a hopelessly corrupt and unwieldy system. She had also succeeded in reforming that system on a modest level, as with her introduction of police matrons into stations within the city. But the cold facts were that control of the higher realms of municipal government, and the power that went with it, had eluded the reformers' grasp.

There were always cracks in the Tammany fortress, however, and a big one occurred in the mayoral election of 1886, which demonstrated to alert and sensitive reformers a way to take advantage of those weaknesses. This was the election that pitted Henry George, the candidate of the Independent Labor party ticket, against Democrat Abraham Hewitt and a young Republican named Theodore Roosevelt. George was the embodiment of Tammany's nightmare: a candidate whose appeal was broad-based enough to accommodate working-class immigrants, Irish, Jewish, and German; middle-class native-born New Yorkers; and a significant section of the reform or independent vote. George's call for economic and political justice for workers was accompanied by equally fervent pleas for clean government, good citizenship, and efficiency.[26] The candidacy of Henry George, as we have seen, had reverberations for Lowell in her work for the WWS and CAIL.

But Lowell, who personally knew all three men, did not actively participate in, or comment on, the election, although one suspects that her loyalties were divided between George and Roosevelt. The young Theodore held a special place in her heart as the son of her late and respected colleague on the SBC. She followed his career eagerly and would work side by side with him and Jacob Riis in many a city and state reform campaign in the 1890s. In any event, the 1886 mayoral race proved to be a hotly contested election, which Hewitt won narrowly and, some have argued, only by a massive voter fraud in which "uncounted ballots, nearly all for George, were seen floating down the Hudson for days after the election."[27] Indeed, this election rubbed salt in reformers' wounds as it clearly demonstrated that as long as Tammany controlled the police department, and the police regulated the balloting, there was bound to be unseemly voting practices in every election in which a close vote was assumed. As one Democratic worker sagely remarked, "How can George win? He has no inspectors of election!"[28]

Yet the fact that George's candidacy, which garnered 31 percent of the vote, attracted second-generation Irish, as well as large portions of German and Jewish voters, gave hope to New York's relatively small group of good-government reformers that one day maybe they, too, could develop a platform commodious enough to attract a more diverse base of support for their cause. These hopes prompted a number of reform-minded Republicans, Democrats, and independents to form the nonpartisan City Club, whose goal was to work outside the party system to promote the virtues of civil service reform but with the idea of coalescing behind the candidate who would put the city's house in order. The City Club sponsored a network of "good-government clubs" at the local level, which contributed successfully to the campaigns of the Fusion tickets in 1894, 1897, and 1901. The good-government club example was soon followed in the German community, which strongly supported civil service reform.

∾ Women Fight Tammany Hall ∾

Lowell contributed to this groundswell movement by actively promoting the advantages of civil service reform through speeches, articles, and educational forums. Another strand of the good government impulse is exemplified by the City Reform Club, founded in 1882 by Theodore Roosevelt, Jr., and made up entirely of upper-class gentlemen. They were ineffective until their 1886 reorganization, when they began a series of investigations that attempted to document the charges the club had been making against Tammany rule. Specifically, they hired agents to collect evidence linking Tammany and the police department with the hugely profitable underworld of prostitution and gambling. The evidence of massive corruption was overwhelming, and historians have estimated that Tammany was taking in approximately $7 million a year from this graft.[29] In documenting this, the club had found a powder keg, and the man who ignited it was the Reverend Charles H. Parkhurst of the Madison Square Presbyterian Church.

Parkhurst, a dedicated opponent of all forms of vice currently flourishing in New York City, got his hands on the material gathered by the City Reform Club, and together with information gathered during his own on-site investigations, or "raids," of brothels and gambling dens, he publicized it all. He then urged the Republican-dominated state legislature to investigate more thoroughly, and this they did, forming the Lexow Commission, which published a report confirming the ties among organized vice, the police department, and Tammany Hall. The resultant publicity combined with Parkhurst's sensationalist antivice campaign and the creation of his Society for the Prevention of

Crime (SPC) made the Democrats extremely vulnerable in the upcoming mayoral election. Lowell and Jacob Riis were appointed to the Committee on Vagrancy, a subcommittee of the Lexow Commission, and watched the proceedings with a keen appreciation of the negative ramifications for Tammany.[30]

Lowell's delight in the damage done to Tammany was tempered with the misgivings she felt regarding Parkhurst and his famous raids. She told a friend, "You know . . . I don't think that's the function of a clergyman. I think his function is to hold up an impossible ideal."[31] Parkhurst's antivice agenda, which included closing down beer halls and saloons on Sunday, was too broad for her taste, and it was tainted with a strident moralism that she correctly perceived would be harmful to attracting immigrant voters. Yet it was Parkhurst, who, by objecting to the immorality of protected vice, provided an opportunity for Lowell to enter the political realm, and she eagerly took it.

Even before Parkhurst's campaign, however, Lowell paved the way for her political activism of the 1890s. In the first year of the decade, she had joined with the People's Municipal League, an assortment of reform groups, to urge the overthrow of Tammany in the upcoming election. More than one thousand women—among whom Lowell, her mother, and her sister figured prominently—signed a petition claiming that a *moral* imperative had forced them to oppose the corruption of the machine. In this early petition was formulated the rationale for women's involvement that Lowell developed in her work with the Woman's Municipal League: things had gotten so bad in the city that it was not merely politics that was involved; the very moral fiber of society was at stake. Whereas women's moral superiority had formerly been cited as a reason *not* to indulge in the political arts, now it was seen as a positive reason to do so. This change of attitude had its roots in the civil service reform movement and the Mugwump faction of the Republican party, with its stress on nonpartisanship and independence from party loyalty. Now this same ideology could profitably be applied to women, who, like the male reformers, could portray themselves as "above politics" even while they sought entry into the political processes.

Charles Parkhurst's antivice campaign was the immediate impetus for the inclusion of women in the 1894 campaign. Now that he had documented, decried, and condemned the machine's ties with prostitution, Parkhurst and the SPC turned to an alliance with women, who, as he pointed out, were the moral guardians of the home and family.[32] He announced in the press an effort to enlist women in his cause to rid the city of the "Tiger." A day after Parkhurst's call for women was announced, a leader of the New York WCTU was interviewed in the *Tribune* and declared that "the work of leading women in Dr. Parkhurst's campaign needs, I think, a woman with social or educational prestige or with a reputation in philanthropic work. I think Mrs. Josephine Shaw Lowell would be just the woman to do it well."[33]

The Woman's Municipal League of the City of New York

Evidently Lowell was thinking along similar lines. She quickly wrote the Reverend Parkhurst a letter approving of his efforts, and this led to a meeting between the two leaders. The results of their conferral were announced the next day in the *New York Daily Tribune*: "Mrs. Lowell to Lead the Women." Coming prepared, Lowell had unfolded to Parkhurst a specific plan to educate, organize, and direct women in a campaign to "promote pure government."[34] These activities were to take place within an organizational structure provided by the Woman's Municipal League, with Lowell as president. Significantly, this was to be an independent political organization, not an auxiliary like the other organization Lowell started in 1894, the Women's Auxiliary to the Civil Service Reform Association, although both groups represented similar political responses to the presumed sorry state of New York City government.

The membership of the Woman's Municipal League was small but contained some of the most prominent women in New York, including a number who were active in the suffrage campaign.[35] In many ways, the league resembled exactly its male-dominated reform counterparts, such as the Committee of Seventy, a nonpartisan group of gentlemen pledged to a Fusion victory. As a civic-minded interest group dedicated to improving the moral life of the city, the league's primary goal was to rally public opinion to support reform government through petitions, lobbying, newspaper publicity, and holding "mass meetings." These methods were well known to Lowell, who had used them throughout her career to effect change in social welfare policy. In later elections, most notably the 1901 Seth Low–Edward M. Shepard contest, the league conceived and directed a sensational and effective campaign to expose the ring of police-protected prostitution.[36]

The league's immediate task in the fall of 1894 was to join the coalition of reform groups to help defeat Tammany's Hugh J. Grant and put into office the Fusion candidate, William Strong, a Republican industrialist. This they did effectively, holding small and large meetings, distributing educational material among women's groups, and producing reports on the criminal activities of Tammany.[37] When Strong triumphed, the Woman's Municipal League had earned the gratitude and respect of the New York reform community. The reformers' stunning victory prompted much debate among the women as to their role in supporting the upcoming administration and whether the Woman's Municipal League should remain a viable political entity. Despite misgivings, the league disbanded, with Lowell resigning as president in November 1894.[38] She did not take as active a role in the 1894 election as might have been expected. Several newspaper articles alluded to the disappointment members of the league felt when Mrs. Lowell did not appear at the obligatory mass meeting, which more than eleven hundred attended. And she uncharacteristically gave only one speech, at a private home, during the whole campaign. Evidence of "strained relations" appeared again in the wake of the 1901 Low election, which both sides denied.[39]

It is quite possible that at this stage of her career, and in light of all the other responsibilities she still shouldered, Lowell preferred to be a figurehead who would articulate the program and help recruit the women who would then do the hands-on work. "It was not hers merely to do," observed Robert de Forest, "but to inspire others to do. She was preeminently a quickening spirit. She breathed the breath of life into others."[40] Lowell's disinclination was certainly evident in her reluctance to assume the presidency of the Women's Auxiliary to the Civil Service Reform Association (she served as vice president and chairwoman of the Executive Committee), when she announced that "people were tired of seeing her name in print."[41] There is a kernel of truth in her statement.

Given the fact that Lowell took her work very seriously, and given the fact that she was already spread a bit too thin when she took on the political work, it is not surprising that she made her contribution to the Woman's Municipal League in *publicizing* an argument for a woman's right and duty to participate in electoral politics, not in the nuts-and-bolts organizational work. Although she lamented the fact that women did not have the vote and envisioned a more just society if they did, Lowell insisted that that deficit by no means absolved them of public responsibility. Quite the contrary: "The moment any thought is given to the subject . . . ," Lowell remarked, "it is impossible not to see that good government is really more important to women than it is to men, for the same reason that it is more important to poor men than to rich men, because they have less power to protect themselves from the effects of bad government." Some women may be puzzled, she cautioned, over exactly how they are affected by government. In answer to this, she reminded her listeners that all three levels of government—national, state, and local—had the power to change women's lives: "Each one of these governments has different duties, and takes care of a different part of our lives, but there is not a woman or child in this city who is not influenced, whose life is not made harder or easier, by the things done by these three governments of ours."[42] As examples, Lowell offered the war and tariff powers of the national government, the welfare and regulatory functions of the state government, and especially stressed the functions of the city government, on whose shoulders fell the responsibility of providing for the poor.

Next she expounded on the necessity of civil service reform at all levels to ensure the most efficient and democratic government possible. But, she said, that still leaves us with the question, What can women do if they can't vote? They can, and must, inform, observe, study, think, and act in ways to bring about a change in the way government is run. They must gather together in groups to exert educated pressure on officials as well as to provide personal and steady influence on their male family members and friends. Most of all, she argued, women must cultivate and cherish their "acute moral sense," which, because of their relative isolation from business and political matters, was more fully developed than men's and hence a great asset in "raising the standards of the human race"—particularly those of the country's rulers.

Lowell admitted that women's superior morality had not played the role it should have because females have been shut out of public life: "Now, however, that they are coming forward into the struggle of life, that they are taking part in public work and in movements for the public good, they should prize this power which their sheltered lives have given them and feel to the full the responsibility which its possession imposes upon them. . . . In reform movements, as in other undertakings, the great service which women can render is the maintenance of uncompromising ideals."[43] Certainly Lowell had lived these words and knew it could be done and believed it should be done. In constructing gendered political roles with firm roots in moral superiority, she was also describing how she herself came to terms with public prominence and a female-based activism. The league's insistence on women's moral superiority also protected its members from the hostility of male reform politicians who were uneasy to begin with over women's political participation, and who felt that many ordinary male voters would be alienated by reform if women played too big a part in the campaigns.

Lowell maintained a keen interest in Mayor Strong's policies through her COS work and rejoiced at the hiring of the colorful and effective Colonel George Waring as head of the city's sanitation department, which for the first time in memory provided New Yorkers with clean streets on a regular basis. Improvements in many other areas were also duly noted by the COS, and in general, Strong satisfied many of his supporters as his administration improved services and tried to stop the flow of corruption. He also satisfied his supporters' demands to enforce the Sunday liquor laws, which predictably enraged the very group on which his victory was gained: the Germans. Strong declined to run again, throwing the race wide open. In that election year of 1897, reformers faced the ultimate test of politics: Could they solidify their voting base to preserve their victory?

The year 1897 was a crucial one for New York City for another reason as well: it consolidated with Brooklyn to form the Greater New York Metropolitan area. This merger made who controlled the city's governing machinery even more important. Both reformers and Tammany geared up for another hard-fought election. A new group, called the Citizens' Union, was formed and nominated Seth Low as the Fusion candidate. The major figure behind the Citizens' Union was a COS official, R. Fulton Cutting, who appointed James Reynolds, head of the University Settlement House, as the union's executive director. The Woman's Municipal League aligned itself with the union and declared itself back in business to help defeat Tammany once again. The reformers lost badly, but this time, perhaps spurred by the defeat, the league vowed to be active between campaigns in order to be ready in 1901.[44]

The big role women played in the hard-fought 1901 campaign between Tammany-supported Democrat Edward Morse Shepard and re-peat candidate Low was in their exploitation of the issue of "protected vice," or more specifically, the sale of young immigrant girls to houses of prostitution that paid for and enjoyed the protection of the police department. Tammany had erred badly after its comeback in 1897 and had soared to new heights of corruption and greed, including flaunting its complicity in prostitution and gambling. Renewed investigations brought more scandal, and Tammany was once again vulnerable to attack on moralistic grounds.[45]

Lowell gathered evidence on prostitution from police matrons, which ended up in a pamphlet, *Facts for Fathers and Mothers*.[46] The issue was one that resonated with immigrants, particularly in the Jewish community, where the issue of "white slavery" especially worried parents. While fighting vice was important to Lowell, she was careful to exploit it selectively: "We are taking up the vice question only in its connection to good government in this city," she wrote to Everett P. Wheeler of the Citizens' Union.[47] Lowell was aware that church-sponsored, punitive antivice campaigns, such as the closing of saloons on Sundays during Mayor Strong's tenure, did more to harm the re-formers' cause than to help the immigrants, who enjoyed their Sunday beer outings. For this reason, she preferred to emphasize the connection among vice, the low standard of tenement living, and machine government and to contrast it with the responsive, professional, and health-giving government that reform would engender.

"Tammany killed the children of the poor by hundreds last summer," Lowell dramatically announced in a campaign speech. "One day last summer," she continued, "I had occasion to walk through Clinton Street, and that horrible stench . . . assailed me. On investigating I found that Tammany had taken five hundred men off in the hottest months of the year. In one section garbage was not removed in four of those awful days, and the death rate was twice the normal. Tammany's street department killed the children of the poor."[48] Low's great victory in the campaign of 1901 was credited to the intermingling of moral issues with strident antimachine denunciations, and league women responded with a renewed determination to expand their organizational membership and their activities. Shortly before the next election, however, Lowell had fallen ill with cancer, and had resigned again from active league work. Still, she remained on its governing board and took great interest in its work and subsequent achievements. In

October 1903, she wrote a campaign letter to the *Woman's Municipal League Bulletin* summarizing why it was so important that the great mass of middle-class women make sure that government works for its poorest and most vulnerable citizens: "Let women realize this, and let them appeal to the voters to register and to vote for the sake of these helpless people who live so near to us, but yet whose lives are so cruelly different from ours."[49]

Lowell's words underlined her major achievement in the political realm, which was to provide leadership in pointing out to upper- and middle-class women their public responsibilities, even though they lacked suffrage rights. She was able to bring together complicated issues such as social welfare reform, civil service, antivice, and labor reform and create a foundation from which women could participate in electoral campaigns, not only on the basis of their moral virtue but on the basis of their knowledge and expertise as well.

"Jerries or Bellies?"

Lowell's work rarely prevented her from having an active and enjoyable social life. Her friends were largely drawn from the same circles her professional life centered on: charity, church, politics, and reform. Her many dinner parties, which almost always were given before a protest meeting or to discuss and dissect some new strategy, often included prominent figures from the worlds of reform, politics, business, and culture: Seth Low, Felix Adler, R. R. Bowker, R. W. Gilder, and Edward Morse Shepard were just a few of her frequent guests. Naturally, her oldest friends and best advisors—Louisa Lee Schuyler, Gertrude Stevens Rice, and Ellen Collins—enjoyed an especially close relationship with Lowell and her family. The reminiscences of two of her newer friends, Charles Culp Burlingham and Jacob Riis, provided a glimpse into how her private and professional lives melded together in the 1890s.

Charles Burlingham, described as a "self-made Ivy-Leaguer," and his wife, Louise (Lou) Lawrence Burlingham, were among Lowell's closest friends outside her own family.[50] Younger than Lowell by a generation, the Harvard-educated lawyer first met her through his wife, who had gone to Miss Anna C. Brackett's school in the city with Carlotta and her cousins, May and Edith Minturn. Burlingham was carving out a brilliant career in both corporate law and municipal reform when he came under the wing of the Lowell/Shaw/Minturn/Curtis clan of New York City and Staten Island. The young and attractive couple became regulars at the Sunday night gatherings at Sarah's home on Staten Island. After Frank's death, when Sarah moved in next door to Josephine and Carlotta at 118 East 30th Street, the Burlinghams became frequent dinner guests there as well. The two brownstones, which were then connected on the first floor, served as the residence for three generations of Shaw women until Sarah's death in 1902. Their home was especially remembered for its spacious back yard, which contained a beautiful garden and a huge shade tree.[51]

In the summer, when Carlotta was visiting her father's relatives in Massachusetts or staying with her Aunt and Uncle Curtis at their country home in Ashfield, in the Berkshire hill country, the Burlinghams would take dinner almost every evening with Josephine and Sarah, and usually one of the Minturns. Burlingham recalled that they all "used to go off to the Thomas Concerts, and then down to the Bowery on the Third Avenue El to the Chinese theatre. . . . I can never forget Mrs. Lowell talking to the Chinese down there."[52] Then as now, any New Yorker who could left the city during the summer, and the elites fled in droves from June to October. Indeed, this annual flight represented a serious problem for the running of private charitable organizations, including the COS, with its dependence on volunteer district committees. At first, many offices were shut down and services curtailed, but the rising standards of professionalization made this situation more embarrassing each year, and extra staff was hired specifically to alleviate this labor shortage. Lowell herself usually stayed in town longer, went away for shorter periods, and came back earlier (almost always in early September) than most. And when away, it should be noted, the flow of letters, instructions, and admonitions from her to the COS or state board staff was steady and voluminous.

This is not to imply that Lowell did not relish her time away from the city. Among her most endearing qualities attested to by her friends and colleagues were a strong sense of humor, a charming manner, and a capacity for enjoying life. Charlie and Lou Burlingham and their children shared many pleasant visits with the Lowell/Shaw family at such beautiful spots as Keene Valley in the Adirondacks; Westport, Massachusetts; and Cornish, New Hampshire. Burlingham fondly remembered that Josephine would "let down" in the country and indulge in her passion for reading and taking long walks in the countryside. One memorable event occurred during her stay in Cornish, a favorite place for artists and literary types. Lowell decided to throw a dinner party for her summer neighbors, which that year included Henry Adams, the sculptor Augustus Saint-Gaudens (then working on the Robert Gould Shaw Memorial), and the architect Charles A. Platt (who would design Lowell's memorial fountain). Her reputation in charity had preceded her, and had evidently made her a "fearsome" presence to this jolly bunch, but they came anyway, expecting a serious, if not grim, evening. But the ice was broken and friendships formed when, serving jelly and berries for dessert, Lowell misspoke to Platt: "Will you have jerries or bellies?" His reply, "I think I'd like a few jerries on my belly," brought forth hearty laughter from the party, and all went well from then on.[53] Lowell also took occasional trips overseas, traveling to Europe in 1884, 1892, 1896, and 1899, often combining business with pleasure. These vacations allowed time for both reflection and refreshment and brought her back into the city ready to return to her demanding schedule.

"I never saw anybody that fought like she did," Charles Burlingham proclaimed.[54] Jacob Riis would have heartily concurred with this assessment of Lowell, as they shared many a battle together in the 1890s. Riis, the Danish-born journalist for the *Evening Sun*—and the author of the classic exposé, *How the Other Half Lives* (1890)—recalled his almost daily visits with Lowell: "She was never 'out,' always ready to sit down and listen and give advice and opinion."[55] Riis, who made a career out of awakening in the middle classes an empathy for slum dwellers, found in Lowell a patient and wise counselor as well as a comrade-in-arms. They worked closely together for reforms in police stations, vice control, municipal lodging houses, tenement house reform, education, the establishment of parks and recreational areas, and the establishment and support of settlement houses.

Urban political reform, women's citizenship, civil service reform, charity: the thread that bound all of Lowell's diverse activities together was her emergence as a leader among both women and men in reform circles. Lowell helped to create and sustain a network of reformers who would make significant contributions to Progressive reform long after her death in 1905. Although limited and defined by her gender and her elite status, she was nonetheless able to overcome, and occasionally to transcend, these barriers to articulate an idealistic and inclusive version of what it meant to be an American citizen. Her patriotism, however, was sorely tested when America sought an over-seas empire based on war and oppression of people of color. From 1898 to 1905 Lowell stood against America's Philippine involvement. It was her last great reform effort. Lowell's opposition brought her back to her abolitionist heritage and made her an even sharper critic of the nation's political parties.

✍ The Anti-Imperialist Movement ✍

The issues revolved around the controversy over American expansion-ism in Cuba and the Philippines. As Lowell joined forces with an anti-imperialist movement dominated by elderly abolitionists, their children, and grandchildren, she, too, returned to her roots and charged American society with abandoning its shining ideals won in the Civil War for a tawdry, racist, and undemocratic adventure. Low-ell's position placed her at odds with such great and dear friends as Jacob Riis, Joseph Choate, and Theodore Roosevelt. It left her unchar-acteristically pessimistic about the future of her country, although she believed the ultimate outcome would see justice prevail. As the pro-gression of her last illness forced her to resign or curtail most of the activities taken up in the 1890s, Lowell turned her remaining and still formidable energies to opposing America's imperialist designs.

The impulse toward an American empire had strong military, eco-nomic, religious, and intellectual underpinnings that gathered force as the 1890s progressed. The first year of the decade, in fact, was marked by the publication of Alfred Mahan's *Influence of Sea Power upon History*. Mahan, a naval strategist, advocated an imperial role for the U.S. Navy in which colonies in the Caribbean and the Pacific would be linked through a U.S.-built canal. Thus America's economic and stra-tegic interests would be served in a way that would fulfill its destiny. These ideas, enthusiastically endorsed by such ambitious politicians and thinkers as Theodore Roosevelt, Henry Cabot Lodge, and Elihu Root, were further seconded by a few influential clergymen who pro-vided a moral and religious framework. Josiah Strong, for example, put forth an imperial version of manifest destiny that advocated bringing a liberal Protestant Christianity, with its beneficial political and so-cial institutions, to the less fortunate countries of the world. The ide-ology for the rise of American imperialism was powerfully articulated by the mid-1890s, but the opportunity to actually put ideals into practice came when the conflict with Spain over Cuba erupted into war in 1898.

The narrative of the Spanish-American War is well known.[56] Spanish atrocities against its colony Cuba had been accelerating from 1895 to 1898, bringing about storms of protests from Americans. Sensationalist newspapers such as the *New York World* demanded intervention as a reluctant President William McKinley bided his time. Events overtook the president, however, when the battleship *Maine* was sunk and a state of war against Spain was declared in April 1898. Troops were sent, including Teddy Roosevelt's famous First Volunteer Cavalry, soon named the Rough Riders, and the Spanish were dispatched quickly, igniting a burst of patriotism and pride from the citizens of the United States. It was truly, in John Hay's words, a "splendid little war," causing few American deaths and little inconvenience to the country.

Josephine Shaw Lowell was only one of many former abolitionists and present Mugwumps who applauded American intervention in Cuba, which was guaranteed self-rule. But they were also uneasy, sensing potentially troublesome consequences from the ease of the victory and the mood of the people. In a letter to the editor of the *New York Daily Tribune,* she pleaded for a display of American pity for the Spanish people in not making them pay an excessive war indemnity: "Were it possible to force the Spanish Government to pay in money for its sins, it ought to be done, but we cannot be so inconsistent as to demand that the starving Spanish people shall be starved still further to pay us for the expenses of the Cuban War." Lowell's was an unpopular opinion, as evidenced by the *Tribune's* mocking and dismissive response to her plea, which included the thought that "there are some kinds of people that can only be taught by the sternest of lessons."[57]

Of even greater concern to Lowell were the rumors in 1898 of the possible Philippine annexation to the United States. Assistant Secretary of War Roosevelt had set that chain of events in motion before the Spanish hostilities had erupted when he cabled Commodore George Dewey to capture the Philippines in case of a war. Dewey's swift destruction of the Spanish fleet in Manila Bay in May 1898 brought more American troops to the vast archipelago, and the future of the Philippines was decided at the conference table in Paris, where negotiations between America and Spain were being conducted. The Paris Treaty, as it was called, gave the United States control over the 7,000 Philippine islands in return for a $20 million payment to Spain. The Senate debate over this treaty, which squeaked by on one vote more than the necessary two-thirds on February 6, 1899, was framed by a national debate over the pros and cons of annexation and the simmering discontent of the Philippine insurrection, which broke out just two days before the treaty's ratification. Unlike Cuba, the Philippines were not going to be guaranteed self-rule, and this enraged Emilio Aguinaldo and other native freedom fighters who had cooperated with the United States against Spain and now felt betrayed and abandoned by their former allies.

These were the immediate reasons for the formation and early successes of the anti-imperialist movement, which formally began on June 15, 1898, when Boston reformers held a mass meeting at Faneuil Hall to announce the formation of an Anti-Imperialist League. The leadership of the anti-imperialist movement included names familiar from the interconnected worlds of civil service reform, Mugwump politics, academia, social gospel, and settlement houses. Although many leaders—such as Erving Winslow, Moorefield Storey, George Hoar, Gamaliel Bradford, Charles Francis Adams, Charles Eliot Norton, Edward Atkinson, and William Lloyd Garrison, Jr.—were from New England, others—such as J. G. Schurman (president of Cornell), Carl Schurz, Horace White, Josephine Shaw Lowell, Andrew Carnegie, and Jane Addams—were known and respected nationally.

The goals of the league were to withdraw American troops from the Philippines, negotiate a peace settlement with Aguinaldo, and discuss the terms of compensation for American damages to life and property. To accomplish this, the league and its various branches (which were springing up around the country) sought to stir up and sway public opinion by holding meetings, publishing newsletters and pamphlets, influencing newspapers, and seeking to place the issue on the political agenda through the presidential and congressional elections, especially in 1900.

The league's membership rolls swelled in its early years to an impressive 30,000 and reflected a heterogeneity rarely found among such reform groups. Members of women's organizations, peace activists, educators, African Americans, urban reformers, labor representatives, and prominent industrialists helped to enlarge the ranks of dissenters to American foreign policy. The diversity of the membership not surprisingly embraced conflicting aims and goals. African Americans were concerned at the level of official racism that was being expressed toward the Filipino, and worried that this would make a bad situation for blacks even worse. Conversely, racist Senator Ben Tillman of South Carolina articulated the concerns of those who feared further involvement with the "colored people" that the Philippine invasion represented.

But Tillman was more the exception than the rule. The majority of anti-imperialists were women and men who "wanted to sustain an America that was prosperous but not plutocratic, internationally respected but not imperialistic."[58] Their stance was comprised of equal parts moral suasion, civic purity, and a commitment to the ideals of republicanism, most notably documented in their unceasing demand for self-rule for the Filipinos. Former abolitionists or those Mugwump anti-imperialists who were from an abolitionist background put forth the most egalitarian arguments of the lot.

Lowell is a good example of the latter. In a speech to an anti-imperialist rally, entitled "Moral Deterioration Following War," she delineated the tangled strands of an argument that wove the present into the past and presented an impassioned opposition to imperialism. She began her speech by drawing a sharp distinction between the Civil War and the Philippine War. The former, she claimed, was "fought for noble purposes," and demanded the moral and physical sacrifices of all the citizens. Thus people knew the price they were paying for waging the war. Even so, Lowell added, the moral luster of the Civil War did not last long, and the postwar era was marked by "dishonesty and recklessness" among many people. "But," she stated, "if that is unhappily true of a war in which the motives were to preserve the life of the nation and to free from slavery four million men and women, what can be said of a war in which the nation makes no sacrifice, does not even feel the weight of added taxation, goes about its own selfish business and its own selfish pleasure exactly as if not in any sense responsible for the war?"

Lowell contended that the war in the Philippine islands was based on a betrayal of the revolutionaries led by Aguinaldo, and ultimately a betrayal of America's ideals. She summed up the first part of her speech: "That is, the United States having obtained a foothold in a foreign country by professing friendship for the inhabitants, calls those inhabitants rebels because the people resist the invasion and try to defend their country. We direct our army to crush out all resistance. The Filipino people prefer death to subjugation, saying, as did Patrick

Henry, the American patriot, 'Give me liberty or give me death.'" Lowell pointed out that this kind of low moral standard infected the U.S. armed forces to such an extent that they were committing atrocities against the Philippine people.

The second part of her speech contained a call to Americans to oppose "the great wrong which has been done in their name." This was a crucial part of Lowell's and the anti-imperialists' argument, for they believed that America could not run an empire without seriously tarnishing its reputation. "No other nation," she warned, "has ever laid down the principle that all men are equal, or that governments derive their just powers from the governed or that taxation without representation is tyranny. To ignore these principles and deny them by their acts would not therefore scar the conscience of Englishmen, Frenchmen, or Germans, but it is impossible for us to do such things and preserve the moral qualities of which in past years we have been most proud." Finally, she reminded her listeners of Abraham Lincoln's wise words: "'He who would be no slave must consent to have no slave. Those who deny freedom to others deserve it not for themselves, and under a just God cannot long retain it.'"[59]

Lowell, who was already an active member of the New England Anti-Imperialist League, characteristically backed up her words with direct action. She joined with Edward L. Ordway, the secretary of the Social Reform Club (she was a member of the club's Advisory Board), who began the New York branch of the league in January 1900. What followed for her was five years of hard, unrewarding work, ending with defeat and discouragement, and with the realization that an ultimate moral victory would not be achieved in her lifetime.

Lowell's organizational labors for the anti-imperialist league bore the unmistakable imprint of years of experience working in and for public interest groups. The correspondence between Lowell and Ordway is filled with crisply worded directives from her on how to begin and sustain a protest movement. Meetings, petitions, leadership and membership recruitment, and fund-raising had filled the hours of her daily life for almost forty years. "Ask President Eliot about enclosing Professor James's letter," she wrote Ordway, "but don't send it to the Judges! They must have a very short letter and only the blank or they will throw the stuff away!"[60] Other letters show Lowell to have been in constant contact with national, state, and local leaders of the anti-imperialist movement, asking for, and dispensing, advice and information about new and better ways to influence public opinion and government policy.[61]

Lowell's illness forced her to retire (gradually) from the public eye for longer and longer periods of time, leaving much of the day-to-day work to Ordway. She appreciated his achievements in sustaining their work and tried to keep up his spirits during the many times it seemed hopeless at best: "Remember that it is always one or two men who have to bear the burden, but that finally they do open the eyes of the people and they see the truth."[62] Her letter, written in 1902, reflected the disappointment anti-imperialists felt in the lack of public support for their position. This lack was clearly demonstrated in the election of 1900, which the anti-imperialists hoped to make a referendum on the Philippines issue, but instead McKinley's overwhelming victory proved to be an unhappy portent for the future of the anti-imperialist movement.[63] They were decisively defeated not only by the general prosperity that made voters reluctant to change administrations, but also by a rousing and successful defense of imperialism by Republicans. Theodore Roosevelt, both before and after his ascension to the presidency in 1901, formulated the most effective argument. Calling the leadership of the anti-imperialist movement "unhung traitors," Roosevelt waxed eloquent on the uniquely beneficial qualities of American stewardship, calling forth images of a benign, progressive, and honorable rule over the lesser nations.[64] And once Aguinaldo's rebels were defeated, he promised, the American government would be only too eager to teach, preach, and support democracy and republicanism in the Philippines.

In the meantime, however, Roosevelt and his friends and fellow imperialists Lodge and Root thundered, anti-imperialists were giving aid and comfort to the enemy and endangering the safety of U.S. soldiers. Moreover, the anti-imperialists were not the only ones to invoke the memory of the Civil War. Republican partisans were quick to point out that the soldier fighting in the Philippines was possessed of the same courage and fortitude as his previous incarnation. The military triumphs and patriotic fervor of Civil War America proved a constant and popular reference point for the nation's imperial enthusiasts. They were supported wholeheartedly by the national northern veterans' organization, the Grand Army of the Republic, which declared the anti-imperialists to be a bunch of "aunties," "half-men," or simply "Copperheads," the last a dreaded and much used epithet against Democrats in the postwar period.[65] When not being portrayed as "sissies," the anti-imperialists were charged with treasonous actions that placed American soldiers in danger, while the expansionists proclaimed themselves the harbingers of a new and powerful American empire of progress.

This potent and virile linking of American manhood and nationhood overwhelmed the anti-imperialist cause, and after 1900 their movement never again achieved its initial promise and respect. The emphasis on defining American manhood through patriotic symbols also may explain the lack of women in leadership positions—a distinct anomaly within reform groups by the early Progressive era. Josephine Shaw Lowell and Jane Addams were among the few women to appear in national publications as opposing the war, and Lowell especially seemed hesitant to make her contributions to the movement too widely known, especially after 1902. Declining an invitation to a meeting in 1905, she wrote, "I could not possibly go to any meeting in September—and it is better for the cause I should not—the more I keep out, the more interested others will be."[66]

Still, the indefatigable Lowell wrote often to political leaders such as Roosevelt, Root, and Taft, hoping to persuade them to change their policy through reason and tact. "The great point," she insisted, "is to make people think of the subject—and if a few people only are induced to write to Congressmen and the President, it all helps. Besides, I believe in bothering the administration!"[67] The war itself ended in 1902, whereupon the goal of the anti-imperialist leagues switched to demanding complete independence for the Filipino people—a goal that the U.S. government was not ready to grant. William Howard Taft was McKinley's and later Roosevelt's appointee as the first civilian governor in the Philippines. Lowell hoped that he, Roosevelt, and Root would be more amenable to suggestions from the anti-imperialists, now that the hostilities had ended. It was in a conciliatory spirit that Lowell and Ordway formed the Filipino Progress Association early in 1905.

While this effort proved as unpopular as the earlier league, Lowell remained steadfastly optimistic. "I am sure that the anti-Imperialists should not 'disband,'" she wrote to Ordway shortly before her death. "No matter how fast public opinion or the Republican Party, or anybody else is coming round, it is necessary to have at least a few people who will keep on the watch, and be ready to point the moral and to lead the way, for it is quite impossible that the questions involved should be understood by the masses without the help of those who have kept themselves informed from the beginning."[68] Later in the same letter, she referred to a similar service the abolitionists performed for the country, especially during those years when "all feeling seemed dead," as it did in the present time. Finally, in summing up the movement as a whole, she argued, "I believe that, whatever protection they have had so far against exploiters, and whatever decency the U.S. has shown in China and elsewhere has been due to the Anti-Imperialists, and that we cannot disband without immediate loss to the cause of justice and freedom."[69]

✍ Endings ☙

In the spring of 1905 Josephine Shaw Lowell was finally bedridden from the cancer that had been slowly advancing through her body. She and Carlotta elected to spend the summer and fall months in Greenwich, Connecticut, with brief stays in Ashfield and Lenox, Massachusetts, resting and receiving a few selected visitors who came to pay their last respects. One of those invited was Jacob Riis, who found Lowell "wonderfully aged and worn, and so tired." They sat together in front of the fire, holding hands, and spoke of the people dear to both of them. "I could see in her face that she had but a little time; and she knew it," Riis later recalled. Lowell's parting message to him eased the sorrow he was obviously feeling: "'Yes, Yes; I know it. It is after all of my waiting for my husband for forty-one years.' She repeated it twice. I saw her look into the fire; and there is not one of us who would deny to her the pleasure that she found in the re-union after forty-one years waiting."[70] A few weeks later Lowell and her daughter were back in New York City, having moved into a new house on 43 East 64th Street. This move was precipitated by the tall apartment buildings that were being built across the way from Lowell's brownstone on 30th Street and blocked out the light. Lowell wanted to feel the warm sun as she lay on her sickbed.

On Thursday October 12, 1905, Josephine Shaw Lowell passed away quietly, just two months short of her sixty-second birthday. Fallen from her hands was a list of names of women she thought could contribute to the cause of the Women's Auxiliary to the Civil Service Reform Association.[71] Unlike her body, her mind never failed her. To the very end she was writing—or when that effort was too much for her, dictating to Carlotta—memoranda, letters, and reports to officials of the COS and other reform groups. She remembered them in her will, too. The COS received $75,000, while smaller sums enriched the coffers of the Consumers' League, the Woman's Municipal League, the Women's Auxiliary, the New York Infirmary for Women and Children, and Berea College in Berea, Kentucky.[72] A private memorial service was conducted in Lowell's residence the following day. Shortly thereafter, she was buried at Mount Auburn Cemetery, in Cambridge, Massachusetts, next to Charley.

Lowell's passing did not go unnoticed in her adopted city. Newspaper obituaries mourned her death and saluted her life. A memorial meeting was held in her honor in the Assembly Room of the United Charities Building on November 13, 1905, bringing together many of her closest friends and colleagues who eloquently testified to her service to New York. Later, fountains, parks, books, and even a memorial symphony concert were dedicated to her memory.[73]

Significantly absent from most of the tributes was any mention of the activity that so dominated Lowell's heart and mind in the last years of her life: the anti-imperialist movement. Perhaps this omission is easily explained—after all, her major achievements were definitely in philanthropy—and to tell the truth, anti-imperialism by 1905 seemed a trifling and noisome exception to the general approbation that greeted the American imperial state. Yet Lowell herself would have relished it if her death had brought extra attention to the movement. When the eighty-seven-year-old Sarah Blake Shaw died on New Year's Eve in 1902, Lowell was in the midst of a heated campaign to force the political parties to acknowledge the Philippine independence movement. Propriety demanded a mourning period, but Lowell brushed aside the social conventions, explaining to a friend whom she invited to a strategy meeting, "We should not ask any one to dine here so soon after my mother's death, unless in a cause so vital in its importance and so dear to her."[74]

Sarah Shaw was an indomitable supporter of the anti-imperialist movement. That fact should hardly surprise, as the movement's leadership was studded with familiar abolitionist names like Storey, Garrison, and Higginson, and its geographical center was in New England. The movement's moral center, with its emphasis on freedom for an oppressed people of color, echoed the earlier protest movement as well. Indeed, abolitionism in Sarah and Frank's day had a position on foreign policy that was not dissimilar to modern anti-imperialism. For example, their friend Lydia Maria Child had critiqued the U.S. government's refusal to recognize the black government of Haiti, and she penned impassioned pleas to halt national expansion in Texas and the Southwest. "We want an agitation like the Abolitionist movement," declared Lowell in 1901, in one of her many comments that linked the two reform traditions.[75]

Toward the end of her life, Josephine Shaw Lowell articulated a principled opposition to America's imperialist designs. Her efforts drew her ever closer to the world of her youth and to the memory of her parents' egalitarian abolitionism. "I suppose that in the course of time," Lowell mused in one of her final letters, "both the two old inconsistent parties will disappear, and we shall have a real genuine struggle between democratic Democrats and plutocrats, the former defending human rights for all races, and the latter advocating the control of 'inferior' men, white, yellow, brown or black, by the superior classes."[76] The connection proved pleasurable, too, for other memories, of Rob and Charley, also came flooding back in the last years of her life. In 1897 Augustus Saint-Gaudens's stunning Robert Gould Shaw Memorial was unveiled in its permanent resting place on the Boston Common, across from the State House. Lowell and her closest remaining family members—Sarah Blake Shaw, Anna Shaw Curtis, Susanna Shaw Minturn, and Ellen Shaw Barlow—gathered in their native city to partake of the celebrations honoring Colonel Robert Gould Shaw and the Massachusetts Fifty-fourth Regiment.[77]

Lowell was also helping Edward Emerson, the writer and Ralph Waldo's son, select Charley's letters for eventual publication in book form. In going over her husband's old photographs, letters, and other materials, she remarked to Emerson, "This reminds me that I feel very differently about war since these more wicked modern wars." She very much wanted Charley's memorial to make a strong statement against "the evil influence of military glamour cast over this [America's military engagements in Cuba and the Philippines] by the enthusiasms of the civil war."[78] Lowell, who loved poetry, would have very much appreciated T. S. Eliot's moving words: "Time present and time past / Are both perhaps present in time future / And time future contained in time past."[79]

And so, as Lowell rested on her sickbed in the days before her death, enjoying the warmth of the late autumnal sun, we might imagine her reflecting on the happier, more hopeful world of her youth, especially cherishing the memories of the short time she had with Charley as his wife and lover. She had truly become "the useful citizen" described by Charley just before his own death forty-one years earlier. She was at peace with her life in that way; she had fulfilled the duty of her generation to honor those who died in the Civil War. Just perhaps, though, we might also imagine that in her final moments of consciousness, she was not dwelling on the meaning of her public life, did not really care so much about that list of virtuous women she was compiling, but rather was recalling Charley's tender line written from wartime Virginia: "I picked a morning-glory (a white one) for you."[80]

Notes

Abbreviations

CSS   Community Service Society Records, Rare Book and Manuscript Library, Columbia University

GCRO   Thomas Barwick Lloyd Baker Records, Gloucestershire County Record Office, Gloucester, England

HL   Houghton Library, Harvard University

LC   Library of Congress

MHS   Massachusetts Historical Society

NYPL   Various Collections, Manuscript Division, New York Public Library

Introduction

1. The account of this ceremony is drawn from material, clippings, and letters found in Box 143, CSS. A sad and then a happy note: the fountain was recently for sale and in disrepair. Funds needed to restore it to its original beauty were estimated to be in the range of $175,000. Fortunately, the money was raised to restore "New York City's only fountain honoring a woman." Information from the *New York Times,* 30 March 1992 and 6 May 1990.

2. Gerda Lerner wrote in 1988, "The biographical field within women's history remains one of the most promising and challenging for the researcher." Lerner, "Priorities and Challenges in Women's History Research," *Perspectives* 26 (1988): 17–22. For the classic work on women's biography, see Carolyn Heilbrun, *Writing a Woman's Life* (New York: Norton, 1988).

3. Geoffrey Blodgett, "A New Look at the Gilded Age: Politics in a Cultural Context," in *Victorian America,* ed. Daniel Walker Howe (Philadelphia: University of Pennsylvania Press, 1976), 95–108, quote p. 95. See also Richard E. Welch, Jr., *The Presidencies of Grover Cleveland* (Lawrence: University Press of Kansas, 1988), 1–8, for a timely review of Gilded Age historiography.

4. A recent manifestation of this scholarly tendency is Amy Dru Stanley, "Beggars

Can't Be Choosers: Compulsion and Contract in Postbellum America," *Journal of American History* 78 (1992): 1265–93.

5. George M. Fredrickson, *The Inner Civil War: Northern Intellectuals and the Crisis of the Union* (New York: Harper & Row, 1965), 212.

6. Ibid., 215.

7. Paul Boyer, *Urban Masses and Moral Order in America, 1820–1926* (Cambridge, Mass.: Harvard University Press, 1978); Lori D. Ginzberg, "'Moral Suasion Is Moral Balderdash': Women, Politics, and Social Activism in the 1850s," *Journal of American History* 73 (1986): 601–22, and *Women and the Work of Benevolence: Morality, Politics, and Class in the Nineteenth-Century United States* (New Haven, Conn.: Yale University Press, 1990).

8. Scholars whose work has influenced my thinking on the writing of social welfare history include Clarke Chambers, "Toward a Redefinition of Welfare History," *Journal of American History* 74 (1986): 407–33; Linda Gordon, *Heroes of Their Own Lives: The Politics and History of Family Violence in Boston, 1880–1960* (New York: Viking Penguin, 1988); Eric H. Monkkonen, "Something Is Out of Place: The History of Welfare Reform," *Law and Society Review* 21 (1988): 889–94; Kathryn Kish Sklar, *Florence Kelley and the Nation's Work: The Rise of Women's Political Culture, 1830–1900* (New Haven, Conn., and London: Yale University Press, 1995).

9. Dorothy Becker, "Exit Lady Bountiful: The Volunteer and the Professional Social Worker," *Social Service Review* 38 (1964): 57–72, and "The Visitor to the New York City Poor, 1843–1920," *Social Service Review* 35 (1961): 382–96; Lillian Brandt, *Growth and Development of the AICP and COS* (New York: Community Service Society of New York, 1942); Frank J. Bruno, *Trends in Social Work, 1874–1956, as Reflected in the Proceedings of the National Conference of Social Work: 1874–1946* (New York: Columbia University Press, 1948); Edward T. Devine, *When Social Work Was Young* (New York: Macmillan, 1939); *Frontiers in Human Welfare: The Story of a Hundred Years of Service to the Community of New York, 1848–1948* (New York: Community Service Society of New York, 1948); Ralph E. and Muriel W. Pumphrey, eds., *The Heritage of American Social Work: Readings in Its Philosophical and Institutional Development* (New York: Columbia University Press, 1961); Margaret E. Rich, *Josephine Shaw Lowell, 1843–1905: A Volunteer in Social Work* (New York: Community Service Society, 1954); David M. Schneider and Albert Deutsch, *The History of Public Welfare in New York State, 1867–1940*, vol. 2 (Chicago: University of Chicago Press, 1938); Lloyd C. Taylor, Jr., "Josephine Shaw Lowell and American Philanthropy," *New York History* 64 (1963): 336–64; Frank D. Watson, *The Charity Organization Movement in the United States: A Study in American Philanthropy* (New York: Macmillan, 1922).

10. Josephine Shaw Lowell, "Sunday School Talk to Children," in William Rhinelander Stewart, *The Philanthropic Work of Josephine Shaw Lowell* (New York: Macmillan, 1911; rpt., Montclair, N.J.: Patterson Smith Publishing, 1974), 151.

11. Three outstanding examples of the use of the social-control theory applied to welfare history are Frances F. Piven and Richard Cloward, *Regulating the Poor: The Functions of Public Welfare* (New York: Random House, 1971), and *The New Class War* (New York: Pantheon, 1982); Michael B. Katz, *In the Shadow of the Poorhouse: A Social History of Welfare in America* (New York: Basic Books, 1986).

Other examples are Rejean Attie, "'A Swindling Concern': The United States Sanitary Commission and the Northern Female Public, 1861–1865" (Ph.D. diss., Columbia University, 1987); Barbara M. Brenzel, *Daughters of the State: A Social Portrait of the First Reform School for Girls in North America, 1856–1905* (Cambridge, Mass.: MIT Press, 1983); Willard Gaylin et al., *Doing Good: The Limits of Benevolence* (New York: Pantheon, 1978); Marvin E. Gettleman, "Philanthropy as Social Control in Late-Nineteenth-Century America: Some Hypotheses and Data on the Rise of Social Work," *Societas* 5 (1975): 49–59; Barry J. Kaplan, "Reformers and Charity: The Abolition of Public Outdoor Relief in New York City, 1870–1890," *Social Service Review* 52 (1978): 202–14; Kenneth Kusmer, "The Functions of Organized Charity in the Progressive Era: Chicago as a Case Study," *Journal of American History* 60 (1973): 657–78; Peter Mandler, ed., *The Uses of Charity: The Poor on Relief in the Nineteenth-Century Metropolis* (Philadelphia: University of Pennsylvania Press, 1990); David J. Pivar, *Purity Crusade: Sexual Morality and Social Control, 1869–1900* (Westport, Conn.: Greenwood Press, 1973); David J. Rothman, *The Discovery of the Asylum: Social Order and Disorder in the New Republic* (Boston: Little, Brown, 1971); Edward Saveth, "Patrician Philanthropy in America," *Social Service Review* 54 (1980): 76–91.

12. Ginzberg, "'Moral Suasion Is Moral Balderdash,'" 620.

13. My interpretation of women's "public culture" has been shaped by Mary P. Ryan, *Women in Public: Between Banners and Ballots, 1825–1880* (Baltimore and London: Johns Hopkins University Press, 1990), and Sklar, *Florence Kelley*. The historical literature on gender and philanthropy is a growing field: a few examples are Barbara J. Berg, *The Remembered Gate: Origins of American Feminism: The Woman and the City, 1800–1860* (New York: Oxford University Press, 1978); Ruth Bordin, *Women and Temperance: The Quest for Power and Liberty, 1873–1900* (Philadelphia: Temple University Press, 1981); Anne M. Boylan, "Women in Groups: An Analysis of Women's Benevolent Organizations in New York and Boston, 1797–1840," *Journal of American History* 71 (1984): 497–523; Ginzberg, *Women and the Work of Benevolence*; Nancy A. Hewitt, *Women's Activism and Social Change: Rochester, New York, 1822–1872* (Ithaca, N.Y.: Cornell University Press, 1984); Kathleen D. McCarthy, ed., *Lady Bountiful Revisited: Women, Philanthropy, and Power* (New Brunswick, N.J., and London: Rutgers University Press, 1990), and *Noblesse Oblige and Cultural Philanthropy in Chicago, 1849–1929* (Chicago: University of Chicago Press, 1982).

14. Describing her early days as an investigator of New York State poorhouses, Lowell wrote, "The State had been roused and shocked by the horrors depicted by Dr. Willard and Miss Dix, to the point of establishing an asylum for the chronic insane." Stewart, *The Philanthropic Work,* 78. Thomas J. Brown, *Dorothea Dix: New England Reformer* (Cambridge, Mass.: Harvard University Press, forthcoming); David Gollaher, *Voice for the Mad: The Life of Dorothea Dix* (New York: Free Press, 1995); Lawrence D. Kramer, "Dorothea Lynde Dix: A Psychobiographical Study" (Ph.D. diss., UCLA, 1997); Dorothy Clark Wilson, *Stranger and Traveler: The Story of Dorothea Dix, American Reformer* (Boston: Little, Brown, 1975).

15. I am hardly alone in critiquing the social-control theory. Besides the historians cited in note 8, I owe a debt to the following scholars whose viewpoints have

influenced my own work: Robert Bremner, *The Public Good* (New York: Knopf, 1980); Gerald Grob, *Mental Illness and American Society, 1875–1940* (Princeton, N.J.: Princeton University Press, 1983); James Leiby, "Charity Organization Reconsidered," *Social Service Review* (December 1984); Walter I. Trattner, ed., *Social Welfare or Social Control: Some Historical Reflections on Regulating the Poor* (Knoxville: University of Tennessee Press, 1983).

16. Lowell's organization is now called the Community Service Society of New York.

17. Sklar, *Florence Kelley*, 146. David C. Hammack, *Power and Society: Greater New York at the Turn of the Century* (New York: Russell Sage Foundation, 1982), 77.

18. Carlotta Russell Lowell to Edward Emerson, 8 February 1906, Edward Emerson Papers, MHS; my italics.

19. Roy Porter, "Charitable Contributions," *New Republic* 205 (1991): 34–37; quote p. 37.

1. Beginnings

1. The following sources have been useful for Brook Farm and transcendentalism: John White Chadwick, *Theodore Parker: Preacher and Reformer* (Boston and New York: Houghton Mifflin, 1900); Bell Gale Chevigny, *The Woman and the Myth, Margaret Fuller Ossoli* (New York: Feminist Press, 1976); Henry Steele Commager, *Theodore Parker* (Boston: Little, Brown, 1936); Mary Caroline Crawford, *Romantic Days in Old Boston* (Boston: Little, Brown, 1910); Sterling F. Delano, *"The Harbinger" and New England Transcendentalism: A Portrait of Associationism in America* (London and Toronto: Associated University Presses, 1983); Martin Duberman, *James Russell Lowell* (Boston: Houghton Mifflin, 1966); Carl J. Guarneri, *The Utopian Alternative: Fourierism in Nineteenth-Century America* (Ithaca, N.Y., and London: Cornell University Press, 1991); Zoltan Haraszti, *The Idyll of Brook Farm as Revealed by Unpublished Letters in the Boston Public Library* (Boston: Trustees of the Public Library, 1937); Joel Myerson, "James Burrill Curtis and Brook Farm," *New England Quarterly* 51 (1978): 396–423; Joel Myerson, *The New England Transcendentalists and The Dial* (London and Toronto: Associated University Presses, 1980); Joel Myerson, "Rebecca Codman Butterfield's Reminiscences of Brook Farm," *New England Quarterly* 65 (1992): 603–30; Anne C. Rose, *Transcendentalism as a Social Movement, 1830–1850* (New Haven, Conn., and London: Yale University Press, 1981); Lindsay Swift, *Brook Farm: Its Members, Scholars, and Visitors* (New York: Macmillan, 1900); J. B. Wilson, "The Antecedents of Brook Farm," *New England Quarterly* 15 (1942).

2. Swift, *Brook Farm*, 20–23.

3. Crawford, *Romantic Days in Old Boston*, 51; Commager, *Theodore Parker*, 4; Swift, *Brook Farm*, 205.

4. My description of Staten Island and the Shaws' life there is based on the following sources: Richard Mather Bayles, ed., *History of Richmond County, Staten Island New York, from Its Discovery to the Present Time* (New York: L. E. Preston, 1887); Charles Gilbert Hine and William T. Davis, *Legends, Stories, and Folklore of Old Staten Island* (Staten Island, N.Y.: Staten Island Historical Society, 1925), 37, 64; Vernon B. Hampton, *Staten Island's Claim to Fame* (Staten Island, N.Y.: Richmond

Borough, 1925), 165; Charles William Leng and William Thompson David, *Staten Island and Its People, a History, 1609–1929*, vol. 2 (New York: Lewis Historical Publishing, 1930), 573, 810; Charles L. Sack, "Staten Island," in Kenneth T. Jackson, ed., *The Encyclopedia of New York City* (New Haven, Conn., and London: Yale University Press, 1995), 1112–18.

5. Sarah's sister Harriet Tilden Sturgis married William A. White, Maria's brother. Robert Faxton Sturgis, *Edward Sturgis of Yarmouth, Massachusetts, 1613–1675, and His Descendants* (Boston: Stanhope, 1914), 53. Both Harriet and her husband died early, and the Shaws adopted their son, William Howard White.

6. Robert N. Hudspeth, ed., *The Letters of Margaret Fuller*, vol. 4 (Ithaca, N.Y.: Cornell University Press, 1988), 127.

7. Hine and Davis, *Legends*, 45–47.

8. Hampton, *Staten Island's Claim to Fame*, 38–39.

9. Lydia Maria Child to Louisa Gilman Loring, 24 June 1849, and Child to Ellis Gray Loring, 3 December 1849, in Patricia G. Holland and Milton Meltzer, eds., *The Collected Correspondence of Lydia Maria Child 1817–1880*, microfiche edition (Millwood, N.Y.: Kraus Microform, Kraus-Thomson Organization, 1982), 27/753, 27/766; hereafter cited as *Collected Correspondence*.

10. Bayles, *History of Richmond County*, 573.

11. Peter Burchard, *One Gallant Rush: Robert Gould Shaw and His Brave Black Regiment* (New York: St. Martin's Press, 1965), 6–7.

12. Walter Meagher, ed., *A Proper Bostonian, Priest, Jesuit: Diary of Fr. Joseph Coolidge Shaw, S.J.* (Boston: published by the author, 1965), 76. See also Lydia Maria Child to Francis Shaw, 5 September 1852, Shaw Family Papers, HL.

13. Hudspeth, ed., *Letters*, 4:306.

14. By the time the Shaws traveled to Europe, the number of transatlantic passengers had increased from 5,000 a year to approximately 30,000. This was at a time when a first-class passage on a luxury ocean liner cost $160 one way. Foster Rhea Dulles, *Americans Abroad: Two Centuries of European Travel* (Ann Arbor: University of Michigan Press, 1964), 44–47.

15. William Rhinelander Stewart, *The Philanthropic Work of Josephine Shaw Lowell* (New York: Macmillan, 1911; rpt., Montclair, N.J.: Patterson Smith Publishing, 1974), 6.

16. Robert Gould Shaw to Francis Shaw, 7 November 1855, *Letters: Robert Gould Shaw* (New York: Collins & Brother, 1876), HL, shelf mark bMS Am 1910 (59)–(73). Reprinted by permission of the Houghton Library, Harvard University.

17. Stewart, *Philanthropic Work*, 68. Several references to "the four" can be found in *Letters: Robert Gould Shaw*, HL, shelf mark bMS Am 1910 (59)–(73). Reprinted by permission of the Houghton Library, Harvard University.

18. Meagher, *A Proper Bostonian*, 77.

19. Louisa Lee Schuyler, "Mrs. Lowell's Early Life and Her Connection with the State Charities Aid Association," *Woman's Municipal League Bulletin* 4 (1906): 4.

20. Autograph File, Letters of Elizabeth Barrett Browning to Sarah Blake Shaw, HL, shelf mark bMS Am 108 (6546)–(6550). Reprinted by permission of the Houghton Library, Harvard University.

21. Burchard, *One Gallant Rush*, 10.

22. Robert Gould Shaw to Sarah Blake Shaw, 14 December 1859, *Letters: Robert Gould Shaw*, HL, shelf mark bMS Am 1910 (59)–(73). Reprinted by permission of the Houghton Library, Harvard University.

23. Hudspeth, ed., *Letters*, 3:168.

24. Information on the Sturgis family is taken from Mary Caroline Crawford, *Famous Families of Massachusetts*, vol. 1 (Boston: Little, Brown, 1930), 319–26; Roger Faxton Sturgis, *Edward Sturgis of Yarmouth, Massachusetts, 1613–1675, and His Descendants* (Boston: Stanhope, 1914), 50–54.

25. Francis George Shaw, "Robert Gould Shaw," in *Memorial Biographies of the New England Historic Genealogical Society*, vol. 2 (Boston: New England Historic Genealogical Society, 1881), 38–61, quote p. 53. Other information on the Shaw family can be found in Crawford, *Famous Families of Massachusetts*, 1:233–53, and Bradford Adams Whittemore, *Memorials of the Massachusetts Society of the Cincinnati* (Boston: Massachusetts Society of the Cincinnati, 1964), 545–46.

26. Shaw, *Memorial Biographies*, 2:54–55.

27. Ibid., 2:55.

28. Peter Dobkin Hall, *The Organization of American Culture, 1700–1900: Private Institutions, Elites, and the Origins of American Nationality* (New York: New York University Press, 1982). In addition to the above, my background on the Boston upper class is based on E. Digby Baltzell, *Puritan Boston and Quaker Philadelphia: Two Protestant Ethics and the Spirit of Class Authority and Leadership* (New York: Free Press, 1979); Robert Dalzell, *Enterprising Elite* (Cambridge, Mass.: Harvard University Press, 1987); Frederic Cople Jaher, *The Urban Establishment: Upper Strata in Boston, New York, Charleston, Chicago, and Los Angeles* (Urbana: University of Illinois Press, 1982); Ronald Story, *The Forging of an Aristocracy: Harvard and the Boston Upper Class, 1800–1870* (Middletown, Conn.: Wesleyan University Press, 1980).

29. The children of Robert Gould Shaw and Elizabeth Willard Parkman are: Francis George Shaw, b. 1809, m. Sarah Blake Sturgis; Sarah Parkman Shaw, b. 1811, m. George Robert Russell; Samuel Parkman Shaw, b. 1813, m. Hannah Buck; Robert Gould Shaw, b. 1815, m. Mary Louisa Sturgis; Anna Blake Shaw, b. 1817, m. William Batchelder Greene; Gardner Howland Shaw, b. 1819, m. Cora Lyman; Joseph Coolidge, b. 1821; Elizabeth Willard Shaw, b. 1823, m. Daniel Augustus Oliver; Quincy Adams Shaw, b. 1825, m. Pauline Agassiz; William Henry Shaw, b. 1827, d. 1828; Marian Shaw, b. 1828, m. Frederick Richard Sears.

30. Abner Forbes and J. W. Greene, *The Rich Men of Massachusetts* (Boston: Fetridge, 1852), 8.

31. Shaw, *Memorial Biographies*, 2:54, 58–59.

32. As quoted in Burchard, *One Gallant Rush*, 5. I have found no evidence that Rob, in Europe at the time of his grandfather's death, was present at this scene. A letter to his mother written from Neuchâtel indicated the opposite: "The reason I didn't say anything about grandfather's death was because I didn't know what to say." Rob goes on to mention his father's visit to America. Robert Gould Shaw to Sarah Blake Shaw, 24 June 1853, *Letters: Robert Gould Shaw*, HL. Other correspondence shows that Frank, and maybe one or more member of the Shaw family, crossed the

Atlantic several times during their stay in Europe. Lydia Maria Child to Francis George Shaw, 12 April 1855, *Collected Correspondence*, 31/880.

33. The following books cover the political, social, and economic changes in Jacksonian America: Ronald P. Formisano, *The Transformation of Political Culture: Massachusetts Parties, 1790s–1840s* (New York: Oxford University Press, 1983); Daniel Walker Howe, *The Political Culture of the American Whigs* (Chicago: University of Chicago Press, 1979); Charles P. Sellars, *The Market Revolution: Jacksonian America, 1815–1846* (New York and Oxford: Oxford University Press, 1991); Harry L. Watson, *Liberty and Power* (New York: Hill & Wang, 1990).

34. Alice Felt Tyler, *Freedom's Ferment: Phases of American Social History from the Colonial Period to the Outbreak of the Civil War* (New York: Harper & Row, 1962, 1944). For good accounts of the religious ferment, in particular, see Whitney R. Cross, *The Burned-Over District: The Social and Intellectual History of Enthusiastic Religion in Western New York, 1800–1850* (New York: Harper & Row, 1965, 1950), and Kathryn Kish Sklar, *Catharine Beecher, a Study in American Domesticity* (New York: Norton, 1976).

35. Lowell to Thomas Baker, 17 September 1879, Baker Records, GCRO. For Frank and Sarah's religious background, see Bayles, *History of Richmond County*, 573. Scholarship on the role of the Unitarians in the evangelical movement includes Daniel W. Howe, *The Unitarian Conscience* (Cambridge, Mass.: Harvard University Press, 1970), and Rose, *Transcendentalism as a Social Movement*.

36. Shaw, *Memorial Biographies*, 2:57.

37. Whittemore, *Memorials of the Massachusetts Society*, 545.

38. As quoted in Delano, *"The Harbinger" and New England Transcendentalism*, 36. Frank Shaw's contributions can be found in the first, second, third, fourth, and sixth volumes of *The Harbinger*.

39. Francis George Shaw, "Political Economy," in *The Harbinger*, vol. 2 (New York: Burgess, Stringer; Boston: Redding, 1846), 284–86.

40. Rose, *Transcendentalism as a Social Movement*, 146.

41. Guarneri, *The Utopian Alternative*, 9.

42. Hudspeth, ed., *Letters*, 4:51–52.

43. Delano, *"The Harbinger" and New England Transcendentalism*.

44. Francis George Shaw, "To the Women of the Boston Anti-Slavery Fair," *The Harbinger*, 2:269. Excellent studies on women and abolitionism are Blanche Glassman Hersh, *The Slavery of Sex: Feminist-Abolitionists in America* (Urbana: University of Illinois Press, 1978), and Deborah Gold Hansen, *Strained Sisterhood: Gender and Class in the Boston Female Anti-Slavery Society* (Amherst: University of Massachusetts Press, 1993).

45. Sarah B. Shaw to Charles E. Norton, 27 September 1899, Norton Papers, HL, shelf mark bMS Am 1088 (6546)–(6550). Published by permission of the Houghton Library, Harvard University.

46. Hersh explores this aspect of feminist marriages. See also Jane H. Pease and William H. Pease, *Ladies, Women, and Wenches: Choice and Constraint in Antebellum Charleston and Boston* (Chapel Hill: University of North Carolina Press, 1990). For a comparative look at English "gentlewomen" and their lives, see M.

Jeanne Petersen, *Family, Love, and Work in the Lives of Victorian Gentlewomen* (Bloomington and Indianapolis: Indiana University Press, 1989).

47. Evidence of Sarah's largesse can be found in John G. Whittier, ed., *Letters of Lydia Maria Child* (Boston: Houghton Mifflin, 1883).

48. Thomas Woodson, Neal Smith, and Norman H. Pearson, eds., *Nathaniel Hawthorne: The Letters, 1843–1853* (Columbus: Ohio State University Press, 1985), 157.

49. Schuyler, "Mrs. Lowell's Early Life," 5.

50. As quoted in Russell Duncan, ed., *Blue-Eyed Child of Fortune: The Civil War Letters of Colonel Robert Gould Shaw* (Athens and London: University of Georgia Press, 1992), 261.

51. Ralph Waldo Emerson, William Henry Channing, and James Freeman Clark, eds., *Memoirs of Margaret Fuller Ossoli*, vol. 1 (Boston: Phillips, Sampson, 1852), 325. Charles Capper, *Margaret Fuller: An American Romantic Life*, vol. 1, *The Private Years* (New York: Oxford University Press, 1992).

52. Emerson et al., *Memoirs of Margaret Fuller Ossoli*, 325, 338. Myerson, *New England Transcendentalist and "The Dial*," 155–56, 166, 207. Caroline Healy Dall, *Margaret and Her Friends* (Boston: Roberts, 1895). Sarah met Fuller as a child; Margaret was a longtime friend of Sarah's brother Nathaniel Russell Sturgis (1805–87). Hudspeth, ed., *Letters*, 4:169.

53. Burchard, *One Gallant Rush*, 6; Stewart, *Philanthropic Work*, 5. One of the earliest indications of Sarah's health problems comes from a letter written by Child, who noted that "Mrs. Shaw seems quite well, except for her eyes." Child to John Parkman, 11 July 1839, *Collected Correspondence*, 7/183.

54. Hudspeth, ed., *Letters*, 3:225–26.

55. Ibid., 3:246.

56. Joseph H. Choate, "A Memorial Number: Josephine Shaw Lowell," *Charities and the Commons* 15 (1905): 313–16, quote p. 315.

57. James M. McPherson, *The Abolitionist Legacy: From Reconstruction to the NAACP* (Princeton, N.J.: Princeton University Press, 1975).

2. First Heroes

1. "A Young Girl's Wartime Diary," hereafter cited as "Diary," in William Rhinelander Stewart, *The Philanthropic Work of Josephine Shaw Lowell* (New York: Macmillan, 1911; rpt., Montclair, N.J.: Patterson Smith Publishing, 1974), 26–27.

2. As quoted in George M. Fredrickson, *The Inner Civil War: Northern Intellectuals and the Crisis of the Union* (New York: Harper & Row, 1965), 212.

3. Thomas Bender, *New York Intellect: A History of Intellectual Life in New York City, from 1750 to the Beginnings of Our Own Time* (New York: Knopf, 1987).

4. Gordon Milne, *George William Curtis and the Genteel Tradition* (Bloomington: Indiana University Press, 1956); Joel Myerson, "James Burrill Curtis and Brook Farm," *New England Quarterly* 51 (1978): 396–423.

5. George William Curtis, *From the Easy Chair*, vol. 3 (New York: Harper & Brothers, 1894), 15.

6. Lowell to Parke Godwin, 11 October 1892, Bryant-Godwin Papers, Manuscripts and Archives Division, NYPL, Astor, Lenox, and Tilden Foundations; and Milne, *George William Curtis*, 84–85.

7. Milne, *George William Curtis*, 84.

8. Ibid.

9. Lydia Maria Child to Sarah Shaw, 25 October 1856, Patricia G. Holland and Milton Meltzer, eds., *The Collected Correspondence of Lydia Maria Child 1817–1880*, microfiche edition (Millwood, N.Y.: Kraus Microfilm, Kraus-Thomson Organization, 1982), 34/952; hereafter cited as *Collected Correspondence*.

10. Charles Eliot Norton, ed., *Orations and Addresses of George William Curtis*, vol. 1 (New York: Harper & Brothers, 1894), 15–16.

11. Milne, *George William Curtis*, 112.

12. James M. McPherson, *The Abolitionist Legacy: From Reconstruction to the NAACP* (Princeton, N.J.: Princeton University Press, 1975), 3.

13. Child to Sarah Shaw, 14 September 1856, *Collected Correspondence*, 34/941.

14. Ibid.

15. John G. Whittier, ed., *The Letters of Lydia Maria Child* (Boston: Houghton Mifflin, 1883), 85.

16. For accounts of the switch from moral to political abolitionism, see Fredrickson, *The Inner Civil War*, and Lori D. Ginzberg, "'Moral Suasion Is Moral Balderdash': Women, Politics, and Social Activism in the 1850s," *Journal of American History* 73 (1986): 601–22. Two scholars who have analyzed the relationship among gender, religion, and American political culture are Norma Basch, "Marriage, Morals, and Politics in the Election of 1828," *Journal of American History* 80 (1993): 890–918, and Daniel W. Howe, "The Evangelical Movement and Political Culture in the North during the Second Party System," *Journal of American History* 77 (1991): 1216–39.

17. Quoted in Paul C. Nagel, *This Sacred Trust: American Nationality, 1798–1898* (New York: Oxford University Press, 1971), 152–53.

18. Quoted in Adelaide Weinberg, *John Elliot Cairnes and the American Civil War: A Study in Anglo-American Relations* (London: Kingswood Press, 1969), 142–43. In the summer of 1862, Sarah initiated a correspondence with the British political economist J. E. Cairnes. Cairnes, a friend and follower of John Stuart Mill, had just written his masterpiece, *The Slave Power*, which, among other things, urged the English to heed their abolitionist tradition and support the American North in the Civil War. Their correspondence quickly ripened into friendship and extended to their families as well.

19. Ibid., 147.

20. From the 1860s to World War I, "the established eastern elites—Boston Brahmins, Philadelphia Main Liners, and the Hudson Valley New Yorkers—preferred to educate daughters privately at home, in boarding school, and through travel abroad." Barbara Miller Solomon, *In the Company of Educated Women: A History of Women and Higher Education in America* (New Haven, Conn.: Yale University Press, 1985), 64.

21. Norton, ed., *Orations and Addresses*, 1:230–31.

22. Quoted in Russell Duncan, ed., *Blue-Eyed Child of Fortune: The Civil War Letters of Robert Gould Shaw* (Athens and London: University of Georgia Press, 1992), 198.

23. Robert Gould Shaw to Sarah Blake Shaw, 4 February 1856, *Letters: Robert Gould*

Shaw (New York: Collins & Brother, 1876), HL, shelf mark bMS Am 1910 (59)–(73). Reprinted by permission of the Houghton Library, Harvard University.

24. Louisa Lee Schuyler, "Mrs. Lowell's Early Life and Her Connection with the State Charities Aid Association," *Woman's Municipal League Bulletin* 4 (1906): 4.

25. "Diary," 18–19.

26. Robert Gould Shaw to Josephine Shaw, 11 September 1861, Robert Gould Shaw Papers, HL, shelf mark bMS Am 1910 (59)–(73). Reprinted by permission of the Houghton Library, Harvard University.

27. "I am very sorry that Father is losing so much. His income won't be reduced more than half, will it?" wrote a worried Rob to his mother after the crash of 1858. Robert Gould Shaw to Sarah Blake Shaw, 22 June 1857, *Letters: Robert Gould Shaw,* HL, shelf mark bMS Am 1910 (59)–(73). Reprinted by permission of the Houghton Library, Harvard University. See also Peter Burchard, *One Gallant Rush: Robert Gould Shaw and His Brave Black Regiment* (New York: St. Martin's Press, 1965), 19–20.

28. Burchard, *One Gallant Rush,* 24.

29. Thomas Wentworth Higginson, ed., *Harvard Memorial Biographies,* vol. 1 (Cambridge, Mass.: Sever & Francis, 1867), iii.

30. Duncan, ed., *Blue-Eyed Child of Fortune,* 73.

31. Robert Gould Shaw to Josephine Shaw, 30 April 1861, Shaw Papers, HL, shelf mark bMS Am 1910 (59)–(73). Reprinted by permission of the Houghton Library, Harvard University.

32. Robert Gould Shaw, "Letters from Camp Written by Robert Gould Shaw," *Magazine of History* 18 (1914): 104–10, quote p. 104.

33. Burchard, *One Gallant Rush,* 38–39.

34. "Diary," 10.

35. See James M. McPherson, *Battle Cry of Freedom* (New York: Oxford University Press, 1988), 490–510, and *The Struggle for Equality: Abolitionists and the Negro in the Civil War and Reconstruction* (Princeton, N.J.: Princeton University Press, 1964).

36. "Diary," 10–11.

37. Duncan, ed., *Blue-Eyed Child of Fortune,* 137.

38. "Letters from Camp," 107.

39. "Diary," 22.

40. Ibid., 18–19.

41. Ibid., 16, 28, 36.

42. Ibid., 17, 36.

43. Linda K. Kerber, *Women of the Republic: Intellect and Ideology in Revolutionary America* (Chapel Hill: University of North Carolina Press, 1980); Mary Beth Norton, *Liberty's Daughters: The Revolutionary Experience of American Women, 1750–1800* (Boston: Little, Brown, 1980).

44. My account of the Woman's Central and the U.S. Sanitary Commission is based on the following works: Robert H. Bremner, *The Public Good* (New York: Knopf, 1980); Fredrickson, *The Inner Civil War;* Lori D. Ginzberg, *Women and the Work of Benevolence: Morality and Politics in the Nineteenth-Century United States* (New Haven, Conn.: Yale University Press, 1990); Marjorie Barstow Greenbie,

Lincoln's Daughters of Mercy (New York: Putnam, 1944); Mary Elizabeth Massey, *Bonnet Brigades* (New York: Knopf, 1966); William Quentin Maxwell, *Lincoln's Fifth Wheel: The Political History of the United States Sanitary Commission* (New York: Longmans, Green, 1956); Agatha Young, *The Women and the Crisis: Women of the North in the Civil War* (New York: McDowell, Obolensky, 1959). For a comprehensive and very negative evaluation of the commission's work, see Rejean Attie, "'A Swindling Concern': The United States Sanitary Commission and the Northern Female Public, 1861–1865" (Ph.D. diss., Columbia University, 1987). Other scholarly works about women in the Civil War are Catherine Clinton and Nina Silber, eds., *Divided Houses: Gender and the Civil War* (New York: Oxford University Press, 1992); Marilyn Mayter Culpepper, *Trial and Triumphs: The Women of the American Civil War* (New York: Hill & Wang, 1991).

45. "Diary," 13; Robert D. Cross, "Louisa Lee Schuyler," in *Notable American Women, 1607–1950: A Biographical Dictionary,* vol. 3, ed. Edward T. James and Janet Wilson James (Cambridge, Mass.: Belknap Press of Harvard University Press, 1971), 244–46.

46. "Diary," 22.

47. Duncan, ed., *Blue-Eyed Child of Fortune,* 169.

48. "Diary," 25–26.

49. Ibid., 31.

50. Her most recent biographer is Stephen B. Oates, *A Woman of Valor: Clara Barton and the Civil War* (New York: Free Press, 1994).

51. "Big Three," from a remark made by Homer Folks, in "100th Anniversary Celebration of the Birth of Josephine Shaw Lowell," 16 December 1943, Box 143, CSS.

52. See Fredrickson, *The Inner Civil War,* 98–112, for an excellent discussion of the ideology of the Sanitary Commission.

53. Reid Mitchell, *The Vacant Chair: The Northern Soldier Leaves Home* (New York: Oxford University Press, 1993), 37.

54. "Diary," 13.

55. Robert Gould Shaw to Josephine Shaw, undated fragment, Shaw Papers, HL, shelf mark bMS Am 1910 (59)–(73). Reprinted by permission of the Houghton Library, Harvard University.

56. Robert Gould Shaw to Josephine Shaw, 11 November 1861, Shaw Papers, HL, shelf mark bMS Am 1910 (59)–(73). Reprinted by permission of the Houghton Library, Harvard University.

57. Duncan, ed., *Blue-Eyed Child of Fortune,* 306.

58. Weinberg, *John Elliot Cairnes,* 167.

59. Quote by Henry Lee Higginson in Bliss Perry, *The Life and Letters of Henry Lee Higginson* (Boston: Atlantic Monthly Press, 1921), 531.

60. Burchard, *One Gallant Rush,* 21.

61. Weinberg, *John Elliot Cairnes,* 167.

62. Burchard, *One Gallant Rush,* 20.

63. Duncan, ed., *Blue-Eyed Child of Fortune,* 35.

64. Burchard, *One Gallant Rush,* 28.

65. Ibid., 39.

66. Ibid., 64; McPherson, *Battle Cry of Freedom,* 544.

67. "Diary," 34–35.
68. Henry Greenleaf Pearson, *The Life of John A. Andrew: Governor of Massachusetts, 1861–1865* (Boston and New York: Houghton Mifflin, 1904), 74.
69. Ibid., 75.
70. Ibid.; see McPherson, *The Struggle for Equality*, for the best account of the abolitionists' role during the war and their efforts to raise black units. The story of the Union's efforts to raise African-American regiments can be found in Joseph T. Glatthaar, *Forged in Battle: The Civil War Alliance of Black Soldiers and White Officers* (New York: Penguin Books, 1991).
71. William James, *Memories and Studies* (London: Longmans, Green, 1911), 45.
72. Burchard, *One Gallant Rush*, 74.
73. Ibid.
74. Stewart, *Philanthropic Work*, 37.
75. Burchard, *One Gallant Rush*, 87; Stewart, *Philanthropic Work*, 45.
76. Massey, *Bonnet Brigades*, 256.

3. Lights and Shadows

1. William Rhinelander Stewart, *The Philanthropic Work of Josephine Shaw Lowell* (New York: Macmillan, 1911; rpt., Montclair, N.J.: Patterson Smith Publishing, 1974), 45.
2. M. A. DeWolfe Howe, ed., *New Letters of James Russell Lowell* (New York: Harper & Brothers, 1932), 113.
3. Russell Duncan, ed., *Blue-Eyed Child of Fortune: The Civil War Letters of Colonel Robert Gould Shaw* (Athens and London: University of Georgia Press, 1992), 280.
4. Lowell to Jacob A. Riis, 7 March 1901, Container 4, Jacob Riis Papers, Manuscript Division, LC.
5. Stewart, *Philanthropic Work*, 38.
6. Louisa Lee Schuyler, "Mrs. Lowell's Early Life and Her Connection with the State Charities Aid Association," *Woman's Municipal League Bulletin* 4 (1906): 4–6; quote p. 4. There are a few references to romantic interests in the sources. See Stewart, *Philanthropic Work*, 30, 37. Rob wrote this to Effie: "Your treatment of James Jackson struck me as being very brutal—I can imagine the poor devil's feelings, while a lot of girls were laughing at him." Robert Gould Shaw to Josephine Shaw, 9 February 1862, Shaw Papers, HL, shelf mark bMS Am 1910 (59)–(73). Reprinted by permission of the Houghton Library, Harvard University.
7. Ellen Jackson to Edward Emerson, June 3 [?], Edward Emerson Papers, MHS.
8. Stewart, *Philanthropic Work*, 534.
9. Edward Waldo Emerson, *The Life and Letters of Charles Russell Lowell* (Boston and New York: Houghton Mifflin, 1907), 244.
10. Howe, ed., *New Letters*, 113–14.
11. Bliss Perry, *The Life and Letters of Henry Lee Higginson* (Boston: Atlantic Monthly Press, 1921), 192.
12. Robert Gould Shaw to Charles Russell Lowell, 20 June 1863, Shaw Family Papers, Manuscripts and Archives Division, NYPL, Astor, Lenox, and Tilden Foundations.

13. Sarah Blake Shaw to James Russell Lowell, 19 March 1863, James Russell Lowell Papers, MHS.

14. Lowell to Lida Perry, 2 July 1889, Huntington Library, Annie Adams Fields Collection, San Marino, Calif.

15. Gary Collison, "Anti-Slavery, Blacks, and the Boston Elite: Notes on the Reverend Charles Lowell and the West Church," *New England Quarterly* 61 (1988): 419–29.

16. My account of the Lowell family is drawn from the following sources: Mary Caroline Crawford, *Famous First Families of Massachusetts*, vol. 2 (Boston: Little, Brown, 1930), 37–39, 44–45; Robert F. Dalzell, Jr., *Enterprising Elite: The Boston Associates and the World They Made* (Cambridge, Mass.: Harvard University Press, 1987); Martin Duberman, *James Russell Lowell* (Boston: Houghton Mifflin, 1966); Emerson, *Life and Letters*; Abner Forbes and J. W. Greene, *The Rich Men of Massachusetts* (Boston: Fetridge, 1852); Ferris Greenslet, *The Lowells and Their Seven Worlds* (Boston: Houghton Mifflin, 1946); Leon Harris, *Only to God: The Extraordinary Life of Godfrey Cabot Lowell* (New York: Athenaeum, 1967); Frederic Cople Jaher, *The Urban Establishment: Upper Strata in Boston, New York, Charleston, Chicago, and Los Angeles* (Urbana: University of Illinois Press, 1982).

17. Lowell to Edward Waldo Emerson, 3 October 1904, Emerson Papers, MHS. An account of Anna Lowell's school can be found in Greenslet, *The Lowells and Their Seven Worlds*, 239, 288.

18. Emerson, *Life and Letters*, 10.

19. Ibid., 86.

20. Henry Lee Higginson was Charley's cousin, neighbor, and closest friend; Savage and Perkins were his Harvard classmates and intellectual soulmates; William James Potter, another classmate, became a teacher and a minister; John C. Bancroft was an artist and the son of the historian George Bancroft; Franklin B. Sanborn, a year behind Lowell in college, opened a private school in Concord, Massachusetts, which flourished despite his radical stance on politics and religion.

21. Emerson, *Life and Letters*, 398–99. For further details of Forbes's relationship with Charles Russell Lowell, see Sarah Forbes Hughes, ed., *The Letters and Recollections of John Murray Forbes*, vol. 2 (Boston and New York: Houghton Mifflin, 1899), 115.

22. Emerson, *Life and Letters*, 169.

23. Ibid., 184.

24. Ibid., 187.

25. Ibid., 188.

26. Ibid., 29.

27. Duncan, ed., *Blue-Eyed Child of Fortune*, 252.

28. "Diary," 34.

29. Emerson, *Life and Letters*, 234.

30. Duncan, ed., *Blue-Eyed Child of Fortune*, 311, 313.

31. Henry L. Higginson to Josephine Shaw, 15 March, 1863, James Russell Lowell Papers, MHS.

32. Duncan, ed., *Blue-Eyed Child of Fortune*, 311.

33. Ibid., 328.

34. Quotes from Peter Burchard, *One Gallant Rush: Robert Gould Shaw and His Brave Black Regiment* (New York: St. Martin's Press, 1965), 91.

35. Ibid., 74.

36. Greenslet, *The Lowells and Their Seven Worlds*, 289.

37. Emerson, *Life and Letters*, 278.

38. As quoted in James M. McPherson, *Battle Cry of Freedom* (New York: Oxford University Press), 574.

39. Ibid., 591–625.

40. I have used the following works on the draft riots: Iver Bernstein, *The New York City Draft Riots: Their Significance for American Society and Politics in the Age of the Civil War* (New York: Oxford University Press, 1990), and Adrian Cook, *The Armies of the Streets: The New York City Draft Riots of 1863* (Lexington: University Press of Kentucky, 1974).

41. Charles Gilbert Hine and William T. Davis, *Legends, Stories, and Folklore of Old Staten Island* (Staten Island, N.Y.: Staten Island Historical Society, 1925), 69–79, quote p. 7–8. For another source on the Staten Island riots, see "The Riot in Staten Island," *New York Tribune*, 17 July 1863.

42. Hughes, ed., *Letters and Recollections of John Murray Forbes*, 2:50.

43. Hine and Davis, *Legends*, 72.

44. Burchard, *One Gallant Rush*, 133.

45. My account of Shaw's and the Fifty-fourth's military experiences is based on the following: Burchard, *One Gallant Rush*; Duncan, ed., *Blue-Eyed Child of Fortune*; George M. Fredrickson, *The Inner Civil War: Northern Intellectuals and the Crisis of the Union* (New York: Harper & Row, 1965); Joseph T. Glatthaar, *The Civil War Alliance of Black Soldiers and White Officers* (New York: Free Press; London: Collier Macmillan, 1990); Lawrence Lader, *The Bold Brahmins: New England's War against Slavery, 1821–1863* (New York: Dutton, 1961); James M. McPherson, *The Negroes' Civil War* (New York: Pantheon, 1963); Gary Scharnhorst, "From Soldier to Saint: Robert Gould Shaw and the Rhetoric of Racial Justice," *Civil War History* 34 (1988): 308–22.

46. James Russell Lowell, 1863, "Memoriae Positum R.G. Shaw." The lines are inscribed on the Robert Gould Shaw Memorial on Beacon Street in Boston.

47. Quotes from Burchard, *One Gallant Rush*, 143.

48. Robert Lowell, "For the Union Dead" (1964). Lowell, one of America's greatest twentieth-century poets, was the great-grandnephew of James Russell Lowell and, by the marriage of Charles Russell Lowell to Josephine Shaw, related to Robert Gould Shaw. Steven Gould Axelrod, *Robert Lowell: Life and Art* (Princeton, N.J.: Princeton University Press, 1978).

49. Adelaide Weinberg, *John Elliot Cairnes and the American Civil War: A Study in Anglo-American Relations* (London: Kingswood Press, 1969), 167. For the effect of the sacrifices of the Fifty-fourth, see McPherson, *The Negroes' Civil War*, 191–92.

50. Robert Gould Shaw to Charles Russell Lowell, 20 June 1863, Shaw Family Papers, Manuscripts and Archives Division, NYPL, Astor, Lenox, and Tilden Foundations.

51. Quotes from Emerson, *Life and Letters*, 286–87.

52. Quotes from ibid., 308, 309, 310, 311. Charley's mother, Anna, had given him $1,000 to help out in their first year of marriage. His pay was $2,400 annually. At her death, Josephine's cash assets were over $250,000 (not including property and other assets). "Will of Josephine Shaw Lowell," signed and dated 15 February 1905, probated, New York City, 9 November 1905, Surrogate Court, New York County.

53. Description by Lydia Maria Child. Child to Emily F. Damon, 22 December 1874, in Patricia G. Holland and Milton Meltzer, eds., *The Collected Correspondence of Lydia Maria Child, 1817–1880*, microfiche edition (Millwood, N.Y.: Kraus Microfilm, Kraus-Thomson Organization, 1982).

54. Burchard, *One Gallant Rush*, 87. For the social life of Civil War army camps, see Mary Elizabeth Massey, *Bonnet Brigades* (New York: Knopf, 1966), 64–72.

55. Emerson, *Life and Letters*, 315.

56. W. R. Crampton to Lowell, 26 March 1899, Josephine Shaw Lowell Papers, Manuscripts and Archives Division, NYPL, Astor, Lenox, and Tilden Foundations.

57. Emerson, *Life and Letters*, 445.

58. Bliss Perry, *The Life and Letters of Henry Lee Higginson* (Boston: Atlantic Monthly Press, 1921), 226.

59. Emerson, *Life and Letters*, 241, 249–50.

60. Unidentified correspondent to Lizzie, 27 October 1864, Lowell Papers, MHS.

61. Greenslet, *The Lowells and Their Seven Worlds*, 292. My account of Charley's military career is based on the following sources: Emerson, *Life and Letters*; Fredrickson, *The Inner Civil War*; Greenslet, *The Lowells and Their Seven Worlds*; Pierce, "Charles Russell Lowell," *Harvard Memorial Biographies*, 2:275–304; Howe, ed., *New Letters of James Russell Lowell*; Hughes, ed., *Letters and Recollections of John Murray Forbes*; Thomas A. Lewis, *The Guns of Cedar Creek* (New York: Harper & Row, 1988); Perry, *Life and Letters of Henry Lee Higginson*; Jeffrey Wert, *From Winchester to Cedar Creek: The Shenandoah Campaign of 1864* (New York: Simon & Schuster, 1989).

62. Emerson, *Life and Letters*, 61.

63. Ibid., 482. Three excellent studies that examine the concept of courage during the Civil War are Gerald F. Linderman, *Embattled Courage: The Experience of Combat in the American Civil War* (New York: Free Press, 1987); James M. McPherson, *For Cause and Comrades: Why Men Fought in the Civil War* (New York: Oxford University Press, 1997); Reid Mitchell, *The Vacant Chair: The Northern Soldier Leaves Home* (New York and Oxford: Oxford University Press, 1993).

64. Emerson, *Life and Letters*, 357–58.

65. Extracts from letter of Dr. Oscar DeWolf, 21 October 1864, James Russell Lowell Papers, MHS.

66. Unidentified correspondent to Lizzie, 27 October 1864, James Russell Lowell Papers, MHS.

67. Emerson, *Life and Letters*, 365. The poem was written by George Lunt.

68. Quote by Charles Culp Burlingham to Clare Tousley, 30 November 1943, Box 2 Correspondence, CSS.

69. Otto Friedrich, *Clover* (New York: Simon & Schuster, 1979), 81.

70. Stewart, *Philanthropic Work*, 48.

71. Friedrich, *Clover*, 81.

72. Emerson, *Life and Letters,* 340–41.

73. Stewart, *Philanthropic Work,* 50–51.

74. Samuel Macauley Jackson to Edward T. Devine, 12 November 1905, "Josephine Shaw Lowell Memorial Meeting, 1905," Box 143, CSS.

75. Emerson, *Life and Letters,* 314.

76. Friedrich, *Clover,* 81–82; Stewart, *Philanthropic Work,* 48.

77. Lowell to Frederick William Holls, 2 January 1894, Frederick William Holls Papers, Columbia University Special Collections. Information on suffrage meeting from Friedrich, *Clover,* 81–82. For the elder Shaw's support of suffrage, see Elizabeth Cady Stanton, Susan B. Anthony, and Matilda Joslyn Gage, eds., *History of Woman Suffrage, 1861–1876,* vol. 2 (New York: Fowler & Wells, 1882), 239–40.

78. James M. McPherson, *The Struggle for Equality: Abolitionists and the Negro in the Civil War and Reconstruction* (Princeton, N.J.: Princeton University Press, 1964), 386.

79. I have relied on the following works for information about the Freedmen's Aid movement: Ronald E. Butchart, *Northern Schools, Southern Blacks, and Reconstruction* (Westport, Conn.: Greenwood Press, 1980); McPherson, *The Struggle for Equality;* Henry Lee Swint, *The Northern Teacher in the South, 1862–1870* (New York: Octagon Books, 1967).

80. Information about Lowell's involvement with freedmen's schools can be found in "Freedmen's Aid Society Daily Journal," 1 October 1869–17 May 1871 (unidentified hand), HL, Harvard University. See also Stewart, *Philanthropic Work,* 49.

81. The link among abolitionists, their experiences in the immediate postwar South, and the rise of vagrancy legislation in the eastern states is explored in Amy Dru Stanley, "Beggars Can't Be Choosers: Compulsion and Contract in Postbellum America," *Journal of American History* 78 (1992): 1265–93.

82. Paul Boyer, *Urban Masses and Moral Order in America, 1820–1926* (Cambridge, Mass.: Harvard University Press, 1978); Fredrickson, *The Inner Civil War;* Lori D. Ginzberg, "'Moral Suasion Is Moral Balderdash': Women, Politics, and Social Activism in the 1850s," *Journal of American History* 73 (1986): 601–22, and *Women and the Work of Benevolence: Morality, Politics, and Class in the Nineteenth-Century United States* (New Haven, Conn.: Yale University Press, 1990); Barbara Randall Joseph, "The Discovery of Need 1880–1914: A Case Study of the Development of an Idea in Social Welfare Thought" (Ph.D. diss., Columbia University, 1986); Michael B. Katz, *In the Shadow of the Poorhouse: A Social History of Welfare in America* (New York: Basic Books, 1986); Stanley, "Beggars Can't Be Choosers."

83. Boyer, *Urban Masses,* 148.

84. Hines and Davis, *Legends,* 73.

85. Lowell to Thomas Baker, 5 August 1883, Baker Records, GCRO.

86. Duncan, ed., *Blue-Eyed Child of Fortune,* 17.

87. Weinberg, *John Elliot Cairnes,* 152.

88. Ralph Waldo Emerson, "Man the Reformer," in *The Collected Works of Ralph Waldo Emerson,* vol. 2, ed. Alfred R. Ferguson and Jean Ferguson Carr (Cambridge, Mass., and London: Belknap Press of Harvard University Press, 1971), 145–60; quote p. 156.

89. Lowell to Thomas Baker, 16 July 1879, Baker Records, GCRO.

4. *Charity Is Our Science*

1. "A Dead Child," *New York Daily Tribune*, 20 December 1876. Information on Davis can be found in Margaret Wyman Langworthy, "Rebecca Harding Davis," *Notable American Women, 1607–1950*, vol. 1, ed. Edward T. James and Janet Wilson James (Cambridge, Mass.: Belknap Press of Harvard University Press, 1971), 445–47.

2. Holland's and Lowell's letters appeared in the *New York Daily Tribune*, 23 December 1876.

3. "That Mother's Dead Child," *New York Daily Tribune*, 2 January 1877.

4. "Charity," *New York Daily Tribune*, 4 January 1877.

5. "Organized Charity," *New York Daily Tribune*, 11 January 1880.

6. Similar to Deems's is "The Case of Lizzy Aaronnsen," *New York Daily Tribune*, 1 June 1881. See also Charles O. Burgess, "The Newspaper as Charity Worker: Poor Relief in New York City, 1893–1894," *New York History* 43 (1962): 249–68.

7. Lowell to James Russell Lowell, 26 July 1871, James Russell Lowell Collection, HL.

8. William Rhinelander Stewart, *The Philanthropic Work of Josephine Shaw Lowell* (New York: Macmillan, 1911; rpt., Montclair, N.J.: Patterson Smith Publishing, 1974), 50.

9. For background, see Peter d'Alroy Jones, *The Christian Socialist Revival, 1877–1914: Religion, Class, and Social Conscience in Late-Victorian England* (Princeton, N.J.: Princeton University Press, 1968).

10. Stewart, *Philanthropic Work*, 157. For religious motivations of elite reformers, see Edward Saveth, "Patrician Philanthropy in America," *Social Service Review* 54 (1980): 76–91.

11. The preceding account of liberal philanthropy is based on Peter Clarke, *Liberals and Social Democrats* (Cambridge: Cambridge University Press), 9–27; Jonathan Riley, "Philanthropy under Capitalism," in *The Responsibilities of Wealth*, ed. Dwight F. Burlingame (Bloomington and Indianapolis: Indiana University Press, 1992), 68–93; Robert Kelley, *The Transatlantic Persuasion: The Liberal-Democratic Mind in the Age of Gladstone* (New York: Knopf, 1969).

12. Three books that offer excellent overviews of the English experience are Derek Fraser, *The Evolution of the British Welfare State: A History of Social Policy* (London: Macmillan, 1984); Gertrude Himmelfarb, *Poverty and Compassion: The Moral Imagination of the Late Victorians* (New York: Knopf, 1991); Michael Rose, *The Relief of Poverty, 1834–1914* (London: Macmillan, 1972).

13. My discussion of nineteenth-century social science and its practitioners is based on the following works: William R. Brock, *Investigation and Responsibility: Public Responsibility in the United States, 1865–1900* (New York: Cambridge University Press, 1984); Ellen Fitzpatrick, *Endless Crusade: Women Social Scientists and Progressive Reform* (New York and Oxford: Oxford University Press, 1990); Mary O. Furner, *Advocacy and Objectivity: A Crisis in the Professionalization of American Social Science, 1865–1905* (Lexington: University of Kentucky Press, 1975); Thomas Haskell, *The Emergence of Professional Social Science: The American Social Science Association and the Nineteenth-Century Crisis of Authority* (Urbana: University of Illinois Press, 1977); William Leach, *True Love and Perfect Union: The Feminist Reform of Sex and Society* (New York: Basic Books, 1980); Dorothy Ross,

The Origins of American Social Science (Cambridge: Cambridge University Press, 1991); Stephen Skowronek, *Building a New American State: The Expansion of National Administrative Capacities, 1877–1920* (Cambridge: Cambridge University Press, 1982).

14. Josephine Shaw Lowell, *Public Relief and Private Charity* (New York: Putnam, 1884), preface.

15. The overview of pauperism and tramps is based on two works: Eric H. Monkkonen, ed., *Walking to Work: Tramps in America, 1790–1935* (Lincoln and London: University of Nebraska Press, 1984), and Paul T. Ringenbach, *Tramps and Reformers, 1873–1916: The Discovery of Unemployment in New York* (Westport, Conn.: Greenwood Press, 1973). See also Barry J. Kaplan, "Reformers and Charity: The Abolition of Public Outdoor Relief in New York City, 1870–1890," *Social Service Review* 52 (1978): 202–14; Samuel Rezneck, "Distress, Relief, and Discontent in the United States during the Depression of 1873–1878," *Journal of Political Economy* 58 (1950): 494–512.

16. David M. Schneider and Albert Deutsch, *The History of Public Welfare in New York State, 1867–1940*, vol. 2 (Chicago: University of Chicago Press, 1938), 13.

17. Two excellent books discuss a different kind of welfare benefit to emerge from the Civil War era: that of pensions for Civil War veterans and their dependents. Stuart McConnell, *Glorious Contentment: The Grand Army of the Republic, 1865–1900* (Chapel Hill and London: University of North Carolina Press, 1992), and Theda Skocpol, *Protecting Soldiers and Mothers: The Political Origins of Social Policy in the United States* (Cambridge, Mass.: Harvard University Press, 1992).

18. The preceding description of social dislocation following the war is based on: Robert H. Bremner, *From the Depths: The Discovery of Poverty in the United States* (New York: New York University Press, 1956), 10, 19, and *The Public Good* (New York: Knopf, 1981), 144.

19. John W. Pratt, "Boss Tweed's Public Welfare Program," *New York Historical Society Quarterly* 4 (1961): 396–411.

20. My ideas on the development of government and the state in the Gilded Age are based on the following sources: Brock, *Investigation and Responsibility*; L. Ray Gunn, *The Decline of Authority, 1800–1860* (Ithaca, N.Y.: Cornell University Press, 1988); Morton Keller, *Affairs of State: Public Life in Late Nineteenth Century America* (Cambridge, Mass.: Belknap Press of Harvard University Press, 1977); James C. Mohr, *The Radical Republicans in New York during Reconstruction* (Ithaca, N.Y.: Cornell University Press, 1973); Skowronek, *Building a New American State*.

21. Steven P. Erie, *Rainbow's End: Irish-Americans and the Dilemmas of Urban Machine Politics, 1840–1985* (Berkeley: University of California Press, 1988); Ari Hoogenboom, *Outlawing the Spoils: A History of the Civil Service Reform Movement, 1865–1883* (Urbana: University of Illinois Press, 1961); Michael McGerr, *The Decline of Popular Politics: The American North, 1865–1928* (New York: Oxford University Press, 1986).

22. Quoted in Sean Dennis Cashman, *America in the Gilded Age*, 3d ed. (New York and London: New York University Press, 1993), 156–57. For a sympathetic look at the Tweed ring, see Leo Hershkowitz, *Tweed's New York: Another Look* (Garden City, N.Y.: Anchor/Doubleday, 1977).

23. Allen Johnson, ed., *Dictionary of American Biography*, vol. 1 (New York: Scribners, 1964), 608.

24. Kaplan, "Reformers and Charity: The Abolition of Public Outdoor Relief in New York City, 1870–1890," 202–14; Ringenbach, *Tramps and Reformers, 1873–1916*, 12–13; Schneider and Deutsch, *The History of Public Welfare in New York State, 1867–1940*, 2:45–46.

25. Michael McGerr, "Political Style and Women's Power, 1830–1930," *Journal of American History* 77 (1990): 864–85; S. Sara Monoson, "The Lady and the Tiger: Women's Electoral Activism in New York City before Suffrage," *Journal of Women's History* 2 (Fall 1990): 100–135.

26. Louisa Lee Schuyler, "Forty-Three Years Ago or the Early Days of the SCAA, 1872–1875," Box 5, Homer Folks Collection, Rare Book and Manuscript Library, Columbia University.

27. Brock, *Investigation and Responsibility*, 88–115, offers comprehensive analysis of charity boards.

28. For good descriptions of the early years of the SCAA, see Peter Romanofsky, "Saving the Lives of the City's Foundlings: The Joint Committee and New York City Child Care Methods, 1860–1907," *New York Historical Society Quarterly* 61 (1977): 49–68; Walter I. Trattner, "Louisa Lee Schuyler and the Founding of the State Charities Aid Association," *New York Historical Association Quarterly* 51 (1967): 233–48.

29. "1873 Annual Report of the Local Visiting Committee for Richmond County Institutions," in SBC, *First Annual Report* (1874). See also Lloyd C. Taylor, Jr., "Josephine Shaw Lowell and American Philanthropy," *New York History* 44 (1963): 336–64.

30. Ibid., 338.

31. Michael B. Katz, *In the Shadow of the Poorhouse: A Social History of Welfare in America* (New York: Basic Books, 1986); Schneider and Deutsch, *The History of Public Welfare in New York State*.

32. Stewart, *Philanthropic Work*, 78.

33. Schneider and Deutsch, *The History of Public Welfare in New York State*, 15.

34. This law originated in the reluctance of some local officials to allow the SCAA visitors access to the county poorhouses. In the late 1870s, disagreements over the extent of the authority of the SCAA's visitors led to a widely publicized break between the board and the association. This was resolved with the passage of the 1881 legislative bill that clarified their respective roles. For details, see Schneider and Deutsch, *The History of Public Welfare in New York State*, 24.

35. SCAA, *First Annual Report* (1873), 10. Saveth, "Patrician Philanthropy in America," also explores this group of elite philanthropists.

36. SCAA, *First Annual Report*, 2.

37. For an excellent analysis of the relations between the private and public charity sector, see Katz, *In the Shadow of the Poorhouse*.

38. Stewart, *Philanthropic Work*, 296.

39. Trattner, "Louisa Lee Schuyler and the Founding of the State Charities Aid Association," 243. The removal of children from poorhouses had the unintended consequence of swelling the number of orphanages—a development Lowell vigorously

opposed. See Romanofsky, "Saving the Lives of the City's Foundlings," and Elizabeth Kennedy Hartley, "Social Work and Social Reform: Selected Women Social Workers and Child Welfare Reforms, 1877–1932" (D.S.W., University of Pennsylvania, 1985), 103–23, for good accounts of Lowell's and the SCAA's work in this area.

40. SCAA, *Fourth Annual Report* (1876), 27.
41. Cynthia Eagel Russett, *Darwin in America: The Intellectual Response, 1865–1912* (San Francisco: W. H. Freeman, 1976).
42. Ibid., 87; Fredrickson portrays the effect of Darwin on reform in *The Inner Civil War*, 183–98.
43. John G. Whittier, ed., *The Letters of Lydia Maria Child* (Boston: Houghton Mifflin, 1882), 253.
44. From the Saratoga paper came a book, first published in 1875. R. L. Dugdale, *"The Jukes": A Study in Crime, Pauperism, Disease, and Heredity* (New York and London: Putnam, 1895). See Ringenbach, *Tramps and Reformers*, 18–19, for Dugdale's influence on reformers.
45. Nicole H. Rafter, "Claims-Making and Socio-Cultural Context in the First U.S. Eugenics Campaign," *Social Problems* 39 (1992): 17–34.
46. Stewart, *Philanthropic Work*, 454. See also Ringenbach, *Tramps and Reformers*, 23. For an extremely negative evaluation of Lowell's and the SCAA's role in promoting vagrancy legislation, see Stanley, "Beggars Can't Be Choosers," 1265–93.
47. SCAA, *Fourth Annual Report*, 42.
48. Brock, *Investigation and Responsibility*, 32.
49. Russett, *Darwin in America*, 18.
50. Lowell, "The Bitter Cry of the Poor in New York: Some of Its Causes and Some of Its Remedies," *Christian Union* 31 (1885): 6–7.

5. *The Commissioner*

1. As quoted from the SCAA, *Fourth Annual Report* (1876), 92.
2. Ibid., 101–2.
3. Charles H. Marshall declined Governor Tilden's offer. Certificate of Appointment as Commissioner of the State Board of Charities, April 29, 1876, oversized file, James Russell Lowell Papers, MHS.
4. Louisa Lee Schuyler, "Mrs. Lowell's Early Life and Her Connection with the State Charities Aid Association," *Woman's Municipal League Bulletin* 4 (1906): 4–6; quote p. 6.
5. Robert W. de Forest described Lowell as "every inch a woman" in "A Memorial Number: Josephine Shaw Lowell," *Charities and the Commons* (1905): 309–35; quote p. 6.
6. Lydia Maria Child to Sarah Blake Shaw, 18 June 1876, in Patricia G. Holland and Milton Meltzer, eds., *The Collected Correspondence of Lydia Maria Child, 1817–1880*, microfiche edition (Millwood, N.Y.: Kraus Microfilm, Kraus-Thomson Organization, 1982), 87/2276; hereafter cited as *Collected Correspondence*.
7. The preceding information is from the SCAA's *First Annual Report* (1873), *Second Annual Report* (1874), and *Third Annual Report* (1875).
8. The description of the Shaws' house is from Stewart, *Philanthropic Work*, 49–51.

The quotation is from John G. Whittier, ed., *The Letters of Lydia Maria Child* (Boston: Houghton Mifflin, 1882), 231.

9. Child to John B. Wight, 12 December 1874, *Collected Correspondence*, 84/2204.

10. Child to Sarah Shaw, 8 June 1875 and 13 May 1875, *Collected Correspondence*, 85/2236, 85/2232.

11. Child to Martha Wight, 24 February 1875, *Collected Correspondence*, 85/2223.

12. Child to Sarah Blake Shaw, 13 May 1875, *Collected Correspondence*, 85/2232.

13. Lowell's description of her daughter is from Josephine Shaw Lowell to James Russell, 2 November 1879, James Russell Lowell Collection, HL. Child's description of the horse is in a letter from Child to Martha Wight, 24 February 1875, *Collected Correspondence*, 85/2223.

14. *New York Daily Tribune*, 2 May 1876.

15. Information on the commissioners' duties is from the SBC, *Eighth Annual Report* (1875), 10. Lowell's attendance at board meetings in 1880 is found in the SBC's *Thirteenth Annual Report* (1880). Her committee assignments and other examples of her service can be found in the SBC's *Annual Report* for 1884, 1885, and 1886.

16. William Rhinelander Stewart, *The Philanthropic Work of Josephine Shaw Lowell* (New York: Macmillan, 1911; rpt., Montclair, N.J.: Patterson Smith Publishing, 1974), 233. Lowell remained close with her widowed sister-in-law through frequent letters and occasional visits to Annie in Paris and Geneva, where she lived an invalid's existence, returning to Boston three years before her death in 1907. Information on Annie Shaw is from a questionnaire prepared by Stewart for Mrs. Anna Shaw Curtis, William Rhinelander Stewart Papers, Manuscripts and Archives Division, NYPL, Astor, Lenox, and Tilden Foundations.

17. J. N. Larned, *The Life and Work of William Pryor Letchworth* (Boston and New York: Houghton Mifflin, 1912); Jim Stafford, "William Pryor Letchworth," in *Biographical Dictionary of Social Welfare in America*, ed. Walter I. Trattner (Westport, Conn.: Greenwood Press, 1986), 491–93.

18. Her negative assessment of Letchworth can be found in Lowell to Thomas Baker, 21 February 1881, Baker Records, GCRO.

19. Lowell to Thomas Baker, 11 December 1879, Baker Records, GCRO. For information on Roosevelt Senior, see Kathleen M. Dalton, "Theodore Roosevelt, Knickerbocker Aristocrat," *New York History* 84 (1986): 39–65; David McCulloch, *Mornings on Horseback* (New York: Simon & Schuster, 1981); Edmund Morris, *The Rise of Theodore Roosevelt* (New York: Coward, McCann & Geoghegan, 1979).

20. In 1880, Sarah M. Carpenter became the second woman to be appointed to the SBC.

21. "Schedule Number Three, Showing the Principal visitations made by members and officers of the board since the last annual report," SBC, *Twelfth Annual Report* (1879). For the number of visits and reports for the next year, see SBC, *Thirteenth Annual Report* (1880), 183–93.

22. Stewart, *Philanthropic Work*, 62–63.

23. Quoted in Elizabeth Kennedy Hartley, "Social Work and Social Reform," 130.

24. For the classic statement on female networks, see Carroll Smith-Rosenberg, "The Female World of Love and Ritual: Relations between Women in Nineteenth-Century America," *Signs* 1 (1975): 1–29. See also Estelle Freedman, "Separatism as

Strategy: Female Institution Building and American Feminism, 1870–1930," *Feminist Studies* 5 (Fall 1979): 512–29. Nancy Cott has called attention to the problems with separatism in "What's in a Name? The Limits of 'Social Feminism,' or, Expanding the Vocabulary of Women's History," *Journal of American History* 76 (1989): 809–29.

25. Robert H. Bremner, "Ellen Collins," in *Notable American Women, 1607–1950*, vol. 1, ed. Edward T. James and Janet Wilson James (Cambridge, Mass.: Belknap Press of Harvard University Press, 1971), 360–63.

26. Merton L. Dillon, "Abigail Hopper Gibbons," in *Notable American Women*, 2:29. The joint effort of Lowell and Gibbons toward prison reform is documented in Stewart, *Philanthropic Work*, 306–10.

27. Quotes from Stewart, *Philanthropic Work*, 96–98. See also Josephine Shaw Lowell, "One Means of Preventing Pauperism," *Proceedings of the Sixth Annual Conference of Charities and Correction* (1879), and "Reformatories for Women," SBC, *Thirteenth Annual Report* (1880), 173–80. Two excellent works of scholarship on women's prisons are Estelle B. Freedman, *Their Sisters' Keepers: Women's Prison Reform in America, 1830–1870* (New York: Cambridge University Press, 1982), and Nicole Hahn Rafter, *Partial Justice: Women in State Prisons, 1800–1935* (Boston: Northeastern University Press, 1985).

28. Stewart, *Philanthropic Work*, 99–100.

29. John Phillips Resch, "Anglo-American Efforts in Prison Reform, 1850–1900: The Work of Thomas Barwick Lloyd Baker" (Ph.D. diss., Ohio State University, 1969); Larry E. Sullivan, *The Prison Reform Movement: Forlorn Hope* (Boston: Twayne Publishers, 1990).

30. Lowell to William Rhinelander Stewart, 14 March 1891, Box 2, William Rhinelander Stewart Papers, Manuscripts and Archives Division, NYPL, Astor, Lenox, and Tilden Foundations.

31. Stewart, *Philanthropic Work*, 110. Background on New York State asylums is found in Ellen Dwyer, *Homes for the Mad: Life Inside Two Nineteenth-Century Asylums* (New Brunswick, N.J.: Rutgers University Press, 1987).

32. Examples of her continuing involvement are found in letters from Lowell to Stewart, 30 November 1886, 16 December 1890, and 14 March 1891, Box 2, William Rhinelander Stewart Papers, Manuscripts and Archives Division, NYPL, Astor, Lenox, and Tilden Foundations.

33. Scholars of women's history have described exactly how women participated in affecting American public and political life. A selected sample of these works include Paula Baker, "The Domestication of Politics: Women and American Political Society, 1780–1920," *American Historical Review* 89 (1984): 620–47; Karen J. Blair, *The Clubwoman as Feminist: True Womanhood Redefined, 1868–1914* (New York: Holmes & Meier Publishers, 1980); Nancy F. Cott, *The Grounding of Modern Feminism* (New Haven, Conn., and London: Yale University Press, 1987); Ellen Carol DuBois, "Working Women, Class Relations, and Suffrage Militance: Harriot Stanton Blatch and the New York Suffrage Movement, 1894–1909," *Journal of American History* 74 (1987): 34–58; Lori D. Ginzberg, *Women and the Work of Benevolence: Morality, Politics, and Class in the Nineteenth-Century United States*

(New Haven, Conn.: Yale University Press, 1990); Robyn Muncy, *Creating a Female Dominion in American Reform, 1890–1935* (New York: Oxford University Press, 1991); Mary P. Ryan, *Women in Public: Between Banners and Ballots, 1825–1880* (Baltimore and London: Johns Hopkins University Press, 1990); Kathryn Kish Sklar, *Florence Kelley and the Nation's Work* (New Haven, Conn., and London: Yale University Press, 1995).

34. Sonya Michel and Seth Koven, "Womanly Duties: Maternalist Politics and the Origins of Welfare States in France, Germany, Great Britain, and the United States, 1880–1920," *American Historical Review* 95 (1990): 1076–1108.

35. Stewart, *Philanthropic Work,* 443.

36. Lowell to William Rhinelander Stewart, 16 December 1890, Box 2, William Rhinelander Stewart Papers, Manuscripts and Archives Division, NYPL, Astor, Lenox, and Tilden Foundations.

37. Rafter, *Partial Justice,* xxii; Freedman, *Their Sisters' Keepers,* 14.

38. Michel Foucault, *Madness and Civilization* (New York: Vintage Press, 1988). Foucault's brilliant insight into the rise of capitalism and the concomitant desire to identify and isolate the abnormal from the normal is applied to the United States in David J. Rothman, *The Discovery of the Asylum: Social Order and Disorder in the New Republic* (Boston: Little, Brown, 1971). Two scholars who use Foucault and Rothman's analysis but cast a more appreciative glance at the achievements and accomplishments of reformers and institutions are Dwyer, *Homes for the Mad,* and Gerald N. Grob, *Mental Institutions in America: Social Policy to 1875* (New York: Free Press, 1973), and *Mental Illness and American Society, 1875–1940* (Princeton, N.J.: Princeton University Press, 1983).

39. Lowell's fullest statement on the need for work is in *Public Relief and Private Charity* (New York: Putnam, 1884). For the economic expectations of Irish immigrant women, see Hasia R. Diner, *Erin's Daughters in America: Irish Immigrant Women in the Nineteenth Century* (Baltimore and London: Johns Hopkins University Press, 1983), 89.

40. Freedman, *Their Sisters' Keepers,* 100.

41. Stewart, *Philanthropic Work,* 104. For some examples of Lowell's persistence in securing positions for women, see Stewart, *Philanthropic Work,* 320–22, 330.

42. Stewart, *Philanthropic Work,* 273. Lowell's position on aid to mothers is in Stewart, 473–74.

43. Quotes from Lowell to Thomas Baker, 25 April 1885 and 1 May 1885, Baker Records, GCRO.

44. Examples of Lowell's battles over city charities can be found in the following sources: "Communication to the Board of Estimate and Apportionment, City of New York, December 24, 1877," in SBC, *Eleventh Annual Report* (1878), 231–34; "Bad State of Public Charities," *New York Times,* 31 October 1877; "Aid to Local Charities, What Mrs. Lowell Says," *New York Times,* 31 March 1880; "The City Charities: Discussing the Per Capita Allowance—A Meeting without Results," *New York Times,* 25 May 1880.

45. Stewart, *Philanthropic Work,* 495.

46. Quotes from SBC, *Fifteenth Annual Report* (1882), 289–90.

47. Ibid., 289.
48. Nathan Huggins, *Protestants against Poverty: Boston's Charities, 1870–1900* (Westport, Conn.: Greenwood Press, 1971), 10.
49. Quotes from Lowell to Thomas Baker, 21 February 1881, Baker Records, GCRO.
50. Lowell, *Public Relief and Private Charity*. For a discussion of Lowell's importance in scientific charity, see Verl S. Lewis, "The Development of the Charity Organization Movement in the United States, 1875–1900: Its Principles and Methods" (Ph.D. diss., Case Western Reserve University, 1954), 56–77.
51. Lowell, *Public Relief and Private Charity*, 1–2.
52. Quotes from ibid., 62, 70.
53. Quotes from ibid., 89, 59.
54. Quotes from Stewart, *Philanthropic Work*, 214, 217; Lowell, *Public Relief and Private Charity*, 94.
55. Lowell to Charles Fairchild, 28 November 1881, Fairchild Papers, Manuscript Division, NYHS.

6. Charity Organization

1. For a comprehensive examination of the spread of "gentility" and the elaboration of proper behavior for men and women, see Richard L. Bushman, *The Refinement of America: Persons, Houses, Cities* (New York: Vintage Books, 1993), and John F. Kasson, *Rudeness and Civility: Manners in Nineteenth-Century Urban America* (New York: Hill & Wang, 1990).
2. The above sketch was largely drawn from Alice Decker, an agent who worked with Lowell for many years in the Third District Office. Decker, "Lowell, Josephine Shaw, Memorial Meeting, 1905," Box 143, CSS. Physical descriptions of Lowell in her middle age are found in William Rhinelander Stewart, *The Philanthropic Work of Josephine Shaw Lowell* (New York: Macmillan, 1911; rpt., Montclair, N.J.: Patterson Smith Publishing, 1974), 56–59. Lowell's hectic schedule and modest style freed her from undue concern about her appearance, but she always exuded a feminine graciousness and was dismayed when her appearance sometimes contradicted her self-image. "My dear Mr. Stewart," Lowell wrote, "I was fatigued yesterday . . . and when I got home, shocked to see how evident it was that I had not washed my face! I could not rush out among all those men, however, so you and General Milhau made allowance, I hope." Lowell to William Rhinelander Stewart, 12 April 1889, William Rhinelander Stewart Papers, Box 2, Manuscripts and Archives Division, NYPL, Astor, Lenox, and Tilden Foundations. From an unlikely source comes this description: "I remember vividly her distinctly striking appearance. She was a matronly woman who always wore a little bonnet tied under her chin and an old-fashioned shawl." Samuel Gompers, *Seventy Years of Life and Labour*, vol. 1 (London: Hurst & Blacketts, 1925), 482.
3. Verl S. Lewis, "The Development of the Charity Organization Movement in the United States, 1875–1900: Its Principles and Methods" (Ph.D. diss., Case Western Reserve University, 1954). Two other works devoted to the charity organization movement in the United States are Lillian Brandt, *Growth and Development of the AICP and COS New York* (New York: Community Service Society of New York,

1942), and Frank D. Watson, *The Charity Organization Movement in the United States: A Study in American Philanthropy* (New York: Macmillan, 1922). See also John T. Cumbler, "The Politics of Charity: Gender and Class in Late Nineteenth-Century Charity Policy," *Journal of Social History* 14 (1980): 99–112; Marvin E. Gettleman, "Philanthropy as Social Control in Late Nineteenth-Century America: Some Hypotheses and Data on the Rise of Social Work," *Societas* 5 (1975): 49–59; Alvin B. Kogut, "The Negro and the Charity Organization Society in the Progressive Era," *Social Service Review* 44 (1970): 11–21; Kenneth Kusmer, "The Functions of Organized Charity in the Progressive Era: Chicago as a Case Study," *Journal of American History* 60 (1973): 657–78. Numerous other scholarly articles and books discuss the American COS movement and are cited when appropriate.

4. Information on these leaders can be found in Lewis, "The Development of the Charity Organization Movement," 60–91.

5. Stephen Humphreys Gurteen, *Handbook of Charity Organization* (Buffalo: privately printed, 1882). Gurteen appeared at one of the earliest meetings to offer Lowell advice on how to run a charity organization society. COS *Central Minutes, 1882–1893,* vol. 1, January 1882–May 1884, Box 205, CSS.

6. Lowell to Thomas Baker, 18 May 1881, Baker Records, GCRO.

7. Lowell to Annie Adams Fields, 19 May 1882 and 31 March 1883, Annie Adams Fields Papers, Huntington Library, San Marino, California. See also W. S. Tryon, "Annie Adams Fields," in *Notable American Women, 1607–1950: A Biographical Dictionary,* vol. 1, ed. Edward T. James and Janet Wilson James (Cambridge, Mass.: Belknap Press of Harvard University Press, 1971), 615–17; Roy Lubove, "Zilpha Drew Smith," in *Notable American Women,* 3:321–23.

8. J. S. Lowell to Charles Fairchild, 28 November 1881, Fairchild Papers, Box I, #122, The New-York Historical Society.

9. J. S. Lowell to Charles Fairchild, 23 December 1881, Fairchild Papers, Box I, #124, The New-York Historical Society.

10. For a brief discussion of male dominance in the charity organization movement, see Michael B. Katz, *In the Shadow of the Poorhouse: A Social History of Welfare in America* (New York: Basic Books, 1986), 78–79.

11. Stewart, *Philanthropic Work,* 379.

12. Phrase used in Lowell to Edward W. Ordway, 10 January 1902, Edward W. Ordway Papers, Manuscripts and Archives Division, NYPL, Astor, Lenox, and Tilden Foundations.

13. Lowell to Annie Shaw, 23 May 1882, in Stewart, *Philanthropic Work,* 129.

14. Kennedy left the COS $1 million at his death, which the society received in 1912. Edward T. Devine, *When Social Work Was Young* (New York: Macmillan, 1939), 30.

15. Johnston de Forest to Stanley P. Davies, 7 December 1943, "Lowell, J.S., 100th Anniversary Plaque Memorial," Box 143, CSS.

16. Henry C. Potter to Charles Kellogg, 11 March 1882, Frederick William Holls Papers, Rare Book and Manuscript Library, Columbia University.

17. Information on Robert de Forest, anecdote, and $7 million figure from "COS Personalities," Box 153, CSS. Current endowment figure from oral interview, conducted by Joan Waugh with Carol Brownell, assistant general director, Community Service Society of New York (New York City, 22 August 1988). On 12 April 1939, the COS

and the AICP were consolidated into the Community Service Society. *Frontiers in Human Welfare: The Story of a Hundred Years of Service to the Community of New York, 1848–1948* (New York: Community Service Society of New York, 1948).

18. Information on Bannard from "COS Personalities," Box 152, CSS; *Who's Who in New York City and State,* 4th ed., ed. John W. Leonard (New York: L. R. Hammersly, 1909), 67. An item of interest: both de Forest and Bannard were students of William Graham Sumner while at Yale. Devine, *When Social Work Was Young,* 38.

19. Remarks of Charles C. Burlingham in "100th Anniversary Celebration of the Birth of Josephine Shaw Lowell," 16 December 1943, Box 143, CSS.

20. "Fairchild, Charles Stebbins," in *Dictionary of American Biography,* vol. 3, ed. Allen Johnson and Dumas Malone (New York: Scribners, 1930), 251–52.

21. Lowell to Mrs. Charles Fairchild, 17 July 1886, Fairchild Papers, NYHS.

22. For an account of Curtis's activities during these years, see John M. Dobson, "George William Curtis and the Election of 1884: The Dilemma of the New York Mugwumps," *New York Historical Society Quarterly* 52 (1968), 215–34; see also Robert Charles Kennedy, "Crisis and Progress: The Rhetoric and Ideals of a Nineteenth-Century Reformer, George William Curtis (1824–1892)" (Ph.D. diss., University of Illinois at Urbana, 1993).

23. "Stewart, William Rhinelander," in *Dictionary of American Biography,* vol. 4, ed. Dumas Malone (New York: Scribners, 1935), 15.

24. Lowell to Annie Shaw, 27 October 1881, in Stewart, *Philanthropic Work,* 127.

25. COS, *Eleventh Annual Report* (1892), 2.

26. COS, *Fourth Annual Report* (1886).

27. Remarks of Homer Folks, "100th Anniversary Celebration of the Birth of Josephine Shaw Lowell," 16 December 1943, Box 143, CSS.

28. David C. Hammack, *Power and Society: Greater New York at the Turn of the Century* (New York: Russell Sage Foundation, 1982), 77.

29. Stewart, *Philanthropic Work,* 64–65.

30. Quoted in ibid., 53.

31. Remarks of Burlingham, "100th Anniversary Celebration," Box 143, CSS.

32. Jacob Riis in "A Memorial Number: Josephine Shaw Lowell," *Charities and the Commons* (1905): 309–15; quote pp. 316–17.

33. Ibid.

34. Devine, *When Social Work Was Young,* 23.

35. Stewart, *Philanthropic Work,* 55, 371.

36. Some of these early activities are recorded in COS *Central Council Minutes, 1882–1893,* vol. 1, January 1882–May 1884, Box 205, CSS.

37. The organizational structure is found in the COS constitution, *Second Annual Report* (1884), 37. Examples of Lowell's leadership can be found in the COS *Seventh Annual Report* (1889), 18, and *Eighth Annual Report* (1890), 19.

38. Lowell to Charles Kellogg, memo dated 19 March 1882, No. 5, Manuscript Collection, CSS. The position of general secretary was initially offered to Gurteen, who agreed to accept it conditionally at $6,000 per annum. This was "utterly beyond what the Society can or ought to give," and they hired Kellogg at $4,300. He later took a cut in pay so that he could hire a Miss Frances A. Smith of Boston as his assistant for $1,200. Quote and information from COS *Central Council Minutes,*

1882–1893, vol. 1, January 1882–May 1884, 23 February 1882, Box 205, CSS. Information on Frances A. Smith from COS *Executive Committee Minutes, July 11, 1882–March 7, 1887,* 27 December 1886, vols. 1–3, Box 212, CSS.

39. Stewart, *Philanthropic Work,* 131. Kellogg wrote, "The principles laid down at the outset were so wise as to require but trifling new adaptation for many years, and the high character and thoroughly representative capacity of the citizens who worked with Mrs. Lowell to found the Charity Organization Society, and their unity of purpose, were such that the inauguration of the society was accompanied by far less distrust and jealousy than was encountered in other of the large cities."

40. Quote from "Mr. Peters Attacks Charity: He Sees No Merit in the Work of Prominent Citizens," *New York Times,* 19 September 1893. Peters, the pastor of the Bloomingdale Reformed Church, went on to say, "I have no respect for the institution, and I think that it is a mistake and a delusion . . . If it spends as many cents in actual charity as it does in 'organization' and investigation, I will become its warm defender."

41. Lewis, "The Development of the Charity Organization Movement," 109.

42. Josephine Shaw Lowell, "The Influence of Cheap Lodging Houses on City Pauperism," written for the Baltimore, Maryland, COS, February 1897, in Stewart, *Philanthropic Work,* 453–59; quote p. 455. See also "A Timely Warning to the Public: Mrs. Lowell Approves the *Times*'s Views on Lodging Homeless Men," *New York Times,* 18 March 1896; "Floating Lodging-House Work: Mrs. Josephine Shaw Lowell's Report Shows Results," *New York Times,* 20 May 1896; "Mrs. Lowell on Vagrancy: Advocates Vigorous Action against Shiftless Persons," *New York Times,* 17 February 1897.

43. Stewart, *Philanthropic Work,* 458.

44. Ibid., 450.

45. See, for example, Ellen Fitzpatrick, *Endless Crusade: Women Social Scientists and Progressive Reform* (New York and Oxford: Oxford University Press, 1990), 185, 191–92; Linda Gordon, "Black and White Visions of Welfare: Women's Welfare Activism, 1890–1945," *Journal of American History* 78 (1991): 559–90, 577–78; Lewis, "The Development of the Charity Organization Movement," 111–12.

46. Robert M. Muccigrosso, "The City Reform Club: A Study in Late Nineteenth-Century Reform," *New York Historical Society Quarterly* 52 (1968): 235–54; Jeremy P. Felt, "Vice Reform as a Political Technique: The Committee of Fifteen in New York, 1900–1901," *New York History* 54 (1973): 24–51.

47. COS, *Eighth Annual Report* (1890), 40. For examples of the society's campaign against street beggars, see also *Second Annual Report* (1884), 46–48; *Fourth Annual Report* (1886), 16–17; *Seventh Annual Report* (1889), 37.

48. Timothy J. Gilfoyle criticized vice-control societies that, he argued, "undermined the authority of municipal government, privatized 'moral' law enforcement in regulating sexual and leisure activity in the city, and set the stage for their successors to move from moral to political surveillance of the citizenry." Gilfoyle, "The Moral Origins of Political Surveillance: The Preventive Society in New York City, 1867–1918," *American Quarterly* 38 (1986): 637–52, quote p. 637. Of course, Lowell and other municipal reformers would question how much "authority" there was to

undermine, for the city municipal government had a distinctly laissez-faire cast to it, which, according to reformers, was precisely the source of its problems.

49. "When the Committee for the Advancement of Public Morality was being organized," wrote the Reverend Robert L. Paddock, "Mrs. Lowell was one of the most trusted advisers and her sense of shame at what was being permitted in this great city did much to inspire the other members to renewed efforts for the saving of the poor girls in what was known as the 'Red Light District.'" From Paddock, "A Memorial Number," 329; Stewart, *Philanthropic Work,* 416.

50. The account of Lowell's campaign to install female matrons in New York City police stations can be found in Stewart, *Philanthropic Work,* 320–33. An approving account of Lowell's efforts can be found in Elizabeth Cady Stanton, Susan B. Anthony, and Matilda Joslyn Gage, eds., *History of Woman Suffrage, 1876–1885,* vol. 3 (New York: Fowler & Wells, 1882), 431–33. Other of Lowell's recorded vice control efforts include "Inquiry Made of Police Matrons Concerning Women Arrested for Prostitution," and "First Step to Protect Children," in William Rhinelander Stewart Papers, Manuscripts and Archives Division, NYPL. Lowell was also active in vice suppression in the Philippines. Materials relating to this can be found in the Edward W. Ordway Papers, Manuscripts and Archives Division, NYPL, and in letters to Governor Theodore Roosevelt, 17 December 1900 and 20 December 1900, in the Roosevelt Papers, microfilm edition, series 1, Huntington Library, San Marino, Calif. For a broad perspective, see David J. Pivar, *Purity Crusade: Sexual Morality and Social Control, 1869–1900* (Westport, Conn.: Greenwood Press, 1973), esp. 103–11.

51. Quote from COS, *Fifth Annual Report* (1887), 31. Relations between the COS and Jewish philanthropy are examined in Moses Rischin, *The Promised City: New York's Jews, 1870–1914* (Cambridge, Mass.: Harvard University Press, 1962).

52. COS, *Fifth Annual Report* (1887), 33.

53. COS, *Ninth Annual Report* (1891), 22.

54. Quoted in Lewis, "The Development of the Charity Organization Movement," 137.

55. This fascinating aspect of the COS is explored in Dawn M. Greeley, "Beyond Benevolence: Gender, Class and the Development of Scientific Charity in New York City, 1882–1935" (Ph.D. diss., State University of New York at Stony Brook, 1995).

56. The preceding account of COS district office practice is based on an examination of "COS: Committee on District Work, 1887–1909," Box 117, CSS; selected case files from the records of the Community Service Society, Boxes 240A, 240, 241, CSS.

57. Remarks of Burlingham, "100th Anniversary Celebration," Box 143, CSS.

58. "Harmonizer of the ideal and the realistic," from Felix Adler, in "Lowell, Josephine Shaw, Memorial Meeting, 1905," Box 143, CSS. "Intellectual honesty," from remarks of Homer Folks, in "100th Anniversary Celebration," Box 143, CSS. Robert Hebbard, who worked for both the COS and the SBC, wrote of Lowell, "While always more or less tenacious of her opinions she was quite willing to be convinced that her views were incorrect and to change them accordingly." Robert W. Hebberd to Mary Forbes, 6 November 1905, "Memorial Meeting," 1905, Box 143, CSS.

59. Remarks of Homer Folks, "100th Anniversary Celebration," Box 143, CSS.

60. Stewart, *Philanthropic Work,* 216.

61. Quote from Alice Decker, "Memorial Meeting," 1905, Box 143, CSS. "She always opposed, in principle, the giving of any material relief. . . . But when it came to giving, herself, there was none I know of who was so lavish," wrote Robert W. de Forest, "Memorial Meeting," 1905, Box 143, CSS.

62. Stewart to Lowell, 1 August 1902, Letterbook No. 13, 1901–1902, Box 19, William Rhinelander Stewart Papers, Manuscripts and Archives Division, NYPL, Astor, Lenox, and Tilden Foundations.

63. Quotes from de Forest, "A Memorial Number," 310; Stewart, *Philanthropic Work,* 139; Father Huntington, "A Memorial Number," 313.

64. Quote from Stewart, *Philanthropic Work,* 137; Lowell to Annie Adams Fields, 18 October 1887, Annie Adams Fields Papers, Huntington Library, San Marino, Calif.

65. See Roy Lubove, *The Professional Altruist: The Emergence of Social Work as a Career, 1880–1930* (Cambridge, Mass.: Harvard University Press, 1965).

66. Lowell, memo dated 15 February 1887, No. 6, Manuscript Collection, CSS, and memo dated 24 March 1887, No. 7, Manuscript Collection, CSS.

67. George Rowell, Internal Memo, 6 January 1890, Box 212, CSS.

68. Lowell to Henry B. Anderson, undated draft, COS: Committee on District Work, 1887–1909, Box 117, CSS.

69. Henry B. Anderson to Robert de Forest, COS: Committee on District Work, 1887–1909, Box 117, CSS.

70. Lowell to Henry B. Anderson, undated draft, Box 117, CSS.

71. Lewis, "The Development of the Charity Organization Movement," 123. See also Dorothy Becker, "Exit Lady Bountiful: The Volunteer and the Professional Social Worker," *Social Service Review* 30 (1964): 57–72, and "The Visitor to the New York City Poor, 1843–1920," *Social Service Review* 35 (1961): 382–96, for excellent overviews on friendly visiting.

72. COS, *Tenth Annual Report* (1891), 8.

73. Lowell, "Duties of Friendly Visitors," in Stewart, *Philanthropic Work,* 142–50; quote p. 143. See also COS of the City of New York, *Handbook for Friendly Visitors among the Poor* (New York: Putnam, 1883).

74. See COS, *Twelfth Annual Report* (1893); *Thirteenth Annual Report* (1894), 40; *Fourteenth Annual Report* (1895), 73. An example of family participation can be found in the *Thirteenth Annual Report,* 69, where Mr. and Mrs. Henry L. Stimson and their daughter Miss Candace Stimson are listed as being members of District Committee No. 2. Joining them on the same committee are Mr. and Mrs. Edward C. Henderson and Mr. and Mrs. Charles S. Brown.

75. "Report of District Committee No. 5," COS, *Seventh Annual Report* (1888), 60.

76. Lowell to F. N. Goddard, 25 May 1889, Bryant-Godwin Papers, Manuscripts and Archives Division, NYPL, Astor, Lenox, and Tilden Foundations.

77. A COS and AICP joint fund-raising committee had collected $50,000 of the estimated $200,000 when Kennedy's contribution was made. COS, *Twenty-fifth Annual Report* (1907), 19–20.

78. "A Building for Charity," *New York Times,* 10 March 1891. From 1882, the COS

moved four times, from 67 Madison Avenue to across the street to number 54, until expansion forced a move to 79 Fourth Avenue (sharing quarters with the AICP) and then to 21 University Place. COS, *Twenty-fifth Annual Report*, 19. The headquarters of the combined organizations (COS and AICP, renamed the Community Service Society) remain to this day in the United Charities Building.

79. Quotes from Peter Mandler, ed., *The Uses of Charity: The Poor on Relief in the Nineteenth-Century Metropolis* (Philadelphia: University of Pennsylvania Press, 1990), 21, and Astrida Ilga Butners, "Institutionalized Altruism and the Aged: Charitable Provisions for the Aged in New York City, 1865–1930" (Ph.D. diss., Columbia University, 1980), 279.

80. Lowell's position on public relief is succinctly put in "The Economic and Moral Effects of Public Outdoor Relief," NCCC *Proceedings* (Boston: Press of Geo. H. Ellis, 1890), 81–91. Contemporary critics of her position included an old friend of Charley's, Franklin B. Sanborn, now the Massachusetts state inspector of charities. Sanborn, like Josephine Lowell, was one of America's first social scientists, and he founded the American Social Science Association in 1865. He believed that outdoor relief was more humane as well as less expensive than indoor, or institutional relief, and said so in a paper presented at the 1890 National Conference of Charities and Correction. Lowell disagreed vigorously, restating her polished argument that public relief must be limited to the chronically dependent. Contemporary scholars have disagreed over the number of people harmfully affected by the abolition of public relief. Paul T. Ringenbach in *Tramps and Reformers* states that it is impossible to estimate how many unemployed people needed aid in New York City during the late nineteenth century. Barry J. Kaplan, on the other hand, asserts that 60,000 people suffered when public aid was cut off. Kaplan, "Reformers and Charity: The Abolition of Public Outdoor Relief in New York City, 1870–1890," *Social Service Review* 52 (1978): 202–14, figure from p. 210.

81. Two of many such examples are "Charity for Women," *New York Times,* 22 September 1893, and "Charity for Homeless Women," *New York Times,* 24 September 1893.

82. Quote from COS *Fifth Annual Report* (1887), 33–34. For other examples of the shift, see COS *Sixth Annual Report* (1888), 38, and *Seventh Annual Report* (1889), 45–46.

83. The review of the COS's new programs, beginning in the late 1880s, is based on COS, *Twenty-fifth Annual Report* (1907).

84. COS, *Twenty-fifth Annual Report* (1907), 30.

85. Ruth H. Crocker, *Social Work and Social Order: The Settlement House Movement in Two Industrial Cities, 1889–1930* (Urbana: University of Illinois Press, 1992); Allen F. Davis, *Spearheads for Reform: The Social Settlements and the Progressive Movement, 1890–1914* (New York: Oxford University Press, 1967).

86. Quotes from Stewart, *Philanthropic Work,* 365, and Lowell, "Poverty and Its Relief: The Methods Possible in the City of New York," NCCC *Proceedings* (Boston: Press of Geo. H. Ellis, 1895), 44–54. Stanton Coit and Charles B. Stover served on the Third District Committee with Lowell. COS, *Eleventh Annual Report* (1892), 54. Coit served in 1888 and from 1893 to 1894; Stover served from 1888 through 1894. COS, *Twenty-fifth Annual Report* (1907), 178.

87. Quote from Lowell, undated memo, included in minutes of the 15 February 1887 Executive Committee Meeting, COS *Executive Committee Minutes,* March 1887–November 1891, vol. 2, Box 212, CSS.

88. Quote from Lowell, 25 November 1889 Executive Committee Meeting, Box 212, CSS.

89. Devine, *When Social Work Was Young,* 33.

90. The COS Executive Committee and Central Committee minutes are filled with references to personnel actions regarding the hiring, firing, and disciplining of agents. Occasionally agents were involved in serious infractions of the rules. Lowell was closely involved in a distressing case involving a COS agent named Ada Craig, who was accused of bilking money from grieving parents. She was eventually exonerated, after some painstaking detective work by Lowell. Case of Craig/Atherton, 1887 in "COS: Administration: Criticism of Staff, 1898–1907," CSS.

91. Robert de Forest, "Memorial Meeting," 1905, Box 143, CSS. Lowell also consistently supported higher wages for state employees.

92. Lowell, "To the Executive Committee of the Central Council, C.O.S.," recorded in the Executive Committee Meeting 11 December 1894, COS *Executive Committee Minutes,* vol. 3, Box 212, CSS.

93. Quoted in *Charities Review* 4 (1895): 465–92, 465.

7. The Labor Question

1. Lowell, "The Bitter Cry of the Poor in New York: Some of Its Causes and Some of Its Remedies," *Christian Union* 31 (March 1885): 6–7.

2. William Rhinelander Stewart, *The Philanthropic Work of Josephine Shaw Lowell* (New York: Macmillan, 1911; rpt., Montclair, N.J.: Patterson Smith Publishing, 1974), 358–59.

3. Thomas Bender, *New York Intellect: A History of Intellectual Life in New York City from 1750 to the Beginnings of Our Own Time* (New York: Knopf, 1987), 203.

4. Edward T. Devine, *When Social Work Was Young* (New York: Macmillan, 1939), 24.

5. Lowell to Thomas Baker, 24 January 1883, Baker Records, GCRO. Frank's death was reported in the *New York Times,* 9 November 1882. A local history of Staten Island reported the day of his death as 4 November. He was buried in the Moravian cemetery on the island. Richard Mather Bayles, ed., *History of Richmond County, (Staten Island) New York, from Its Discovery to the Present Time* (New York: L. E. Preston, 1887), 574.

6. Ibid., 574–81. The postwar fortune of Fourierism in American social reform circles is discussed in Carl J. Guarneri, *The Utopian Alternative: Fourierism in Nineteenth-Century America* (Ithaca, N.Y.: Cornell University Press, 1991), 385.

7. My discussion of Henry George is drawn from Charles Albro Barker, *Henry George* (New York: Oxford University Press, 1955); Anna George de Mille, *Henry George: Citizen of the World,* ed. Don C. Shoemaker (Chapel Hill: University of North Carolina Press, 1950); Henry George, Jr., *The Life of Henry George* (New York: Doubleday, Page, 1911); Steven J. Ross, "Political Economy for the Masses: Henry

George," *Democracy* 2 (1982): 125–34; John L. Thomas, *Alternative America: Henry George, Edward Bellamy, Henry Demarest Lloyd and the Adversary Tradition* (Cambridge: Mass.: Belknap Press of Harvard University Press, 1983).

8. Henry George, *Progress and Poverty* (New York: Robert Schalkenbach Foundation, 1946), 10.

9. As quoted in Barker, *Henry George,* 337.

10. Francis Shaw to Henry George, 12 June 1882, Henry George Papers, Manuscripts and Archives Division, NYPL, Astor, Lenox, and Tilden Foundations. Shaw gave George $500, along with the above letter. He also persuaded his brother-in-law of Boston, Quincy Shaw, to contribute $5,000 to George's movement. De Mille, *Citizen of the World,* 111. Shaw also remembered George in his will with a small legacy of $1,000. De Mille, 119. Shaw told George the money would "strengthen his hands" for the work that lay ahead. Henry George to Sarah Shaw, Shaw Family Letters, Boston Athenaeum, Boston, Mass.

11. Henry George to Lowell, 8 January 1883, Henry George Papers, Manuscripts and Archives Division, NYPL, Astor, Lenox, and Tilden Foundations. An example of the extraordinary closeness that the Shaw family felt for George can be found in a letter from Lowell to George in which she told him that his "cross of flowers" was the only arrangement (among many) placed on her father's grave. Lowell to Henry George, 11 November 1882, Henry George Papers, Manuscripts and Archives Division, NYPL, Astor, Lenox, and Tilden Foundations.

12. Henry George to Lowell, 23 October 1883, Henry George Papers, Manuscripts and Archives Division, NYPL, Astor, Lenox, and Tilden Foundations.

13. De Mille, *Citizen of the World,* 188.

14. Richard L. McCormick, *From Realignment to Reform: Political Change in New York State, 1893–1910* (Ithaca, N.Y.: Cornell University Press, 1981), 32; see also Howard Lawrence Hurwitz, *Theodore Roosevelt and Labor in New York State, 1880–1900* (New York: Columbia University Press, 1943).

15. Melvyn Dubofsky, *When Workers Organize: New York City in the Progressive Era* (Amherst: University of Massachusetts Press, 1968), 1.

16. See letters from Henry George to Lowell, 5 October 1883, 23 October 1883, 15 November 1884, Henry George Papers, Manuscripts and Archives Division, NYPL, Astor, Lenox, and Tilden Foundations.

17. Lowell to Annie Shaw, 18 February 1883, in Stewart, *Philanthropic Work,* 130. Two scholars of philanthropy who have noted the importance of George's influence on charity workers in the late nineteenth century are Robert H. Bremner, *From the Depths: The Discovery of Poverty in the United States* (New York: New York University Press, 1956), 23–24, and Paul T. Ringenbach, *Tramps and Reformers, 1873–1916: The Discovery of Unemployment in New York* (Westport, Conn.: Greenwood Press, 1973), 36–37.

18. For Lowell's study of labor, see Stewart, *Philanthropic Work,* 357–62. Several of Lowell's articles were published in the house journal of the COS: "Labor Organization as Affected by Law," *Charities Review* 1 (1891): 6–11; "Felix qui causam rerum cognovit," *Charities Review* 2 (1893): 420–26; "Industrial Peace," *Charities Review* 2 (1893): 153–59; "A Chapter of Industrial History," *Charities Review* 3 (1893): 365–70; "The Great Coal Strike of 1894," *Charities Review* 4 (1894): 41–45.

19. Quotes from Stewart, *Philanthropic Work,* 381, 319.

20. Ibid., 390.

21. Ibid., 392.

22. Ibid., 394–400; quote p. 396. Lowell's position on the right of striking workers to retain their jobs and their respect echoed that of the owner of the Homestead Works, Andrew Carnegie, before the famous strike of 1892. Two excellent works on the industrialist are Joseph Frazier Wall, *Andrew Carnegie* (Pittsburgh: University of Pittsburgh Press, 1989) and Harold Livesay, *Andrew Carnegie and the Rise of Big Business* (Boston: Little, Brown, 1975).

23. Stewart, *Philanthropic Work,* 396.

24. Charles DeBenedetti, *The Peace Reform in American History* (Bloomington: Indiana University Press, 1980), 63; Jacob Henry Dorn, *Washington Gladden, Prophet of the Social Gospel* (Columbus: Ohio State University Press, 1966); Harriette A. Keyser, *Bishop Potter: The People's Friend* (New York: Thomas Whittaker, 1910), 21–26.

25. Samuel Gompers, *Seventy Years of Life and Labour,* vol. 1 (London: Hurst & Blacketts, 1925), 133.

26. My discussion of CAIL is based on "Bishop Potter as an Arbitrator," in *Gunton's Magazine* 10 (1896): 399–404; Clyde Griffin, "Christian Socialism Instructed by Gompers," *Labor History* 12 (1971): 195–214; and "Rich Laymen and Early Social Christianity," *Church History* 36 (1967): 3–23; Keyser, *The People's Friend;* Vida Dutton Scudder, *Father Huntington: Founder of the Order of the Holy Cross* (New York: Dutton, 1940).

27. As quoted in Griffin, "Christian Socialism," 201. The full account of De Costa's grudge against the COS can be found in "Press and Social Work: Lawsuit 1888 De Costa-Howell," Box 156, CSS, and the *New York Times,* 20 February 1888, and the *New York Daily Tribune,* 21 February 1888.

28. Keyser, *The People's Friend,* 51. Lowell used whatever resources made available to her to publicize the principles of arbitration. See "How to Help Working People: Mrs. Lowell Gives Her Views in Answer to Miss Willard's Request," *New York Times,* 12 November 1894.

29. Griffin, "Christian Socialism," 204.

30. Other board members who also served as individual arbitrators were Bishop Potter and Seth Low, president of Columbia University. Griffin, "Christian Socialism," 204. Accounts of Lowell's work as an arbitrator can be found in "The Big Fight Is On: Building Trades Will Support the Electrical Contractors: Each Side Watching the Other: Josephine Shaw Lowell Appeals for Arbitration—More Men Likely to Be Called Out Today," *New York Daily Tribune,* 26 February 1895. For her efforts in resolving the cloakmakers' strike of 1899, see Lowell to Seth Low, 13 January 1899, Seth Low Papers, Manuscripts and Archives Division, NYPL, Astor, Lenox, and Tilden Foundations.

31. Stewart, *Philanthropic Work,* 366–67.

32. Ibid., 368–69.

33. Ibid.

34. Ibid., 368.

35. Ibid.

36. Ibid., 369.

37. See Barker, *Henry George,* 478, for the effect of the 1886 election in the forma-tion of the Social Reform Club. Other accounts of the Social Reform Club, its membership, and its accomplishments can be found in E. McClung Fleming, *R. R. Bowker: Militant Liberal* (Norman: University of Oklahoma Press, 1952); J. K. Paulding, *Charles B. Stover: His Life and Personality* (New York: International Press, 1938); Gregory Weinstein, *The Ardent Eighties* (New York: International Press, 1928).

38. Gompers, *Seventy Years of Life and Labour,* 1:481. Quote from Stewart, *Philan-thropic Work,* 371.

39. For CAIL's involvement in the founding of the Consumers' League, see Griffin, "Christian Socialism," 201–2. The consumer revolution is covered by William R. Leach, "Transformations in a Culture of Consumption: Women and Department Stores, 1890–1925," *Journal of American History* 71 (September 1984): 319–42, and *Land of Desire: Merchants, Power, and the Rise of a New American Culture* (New York: Pantheon, 1993).

40. Louise Perkins to Leonora O'Reilly, 4 November 1905, Leonora O'Reilly Papers, *Papers of the Women's Trade Union League and Its Principal Leaders,* ed. Edward T. James (Woodbridge, Conn.: Research Publications, 1979), reel 4. Perkins, Lowell, Lillian Wald, and others formed a support group for O'Reilly that included finan-cial aid so that she could quit her factory job and devote herself full time to social reform work. See letters 12 March 1896, 30 September 1897, and 21 December 1897 on reel 4. Charles Shively, "Leonora O'Reilly," in *Notable American Women, 1607–1950,* vol. 2, ed. Edward T. James and Janet Wilson James (Cambridge, Mass.: Belknap Press of Harvard University Press, 1971), 651–53.

41. There seems to be some confusion over the exact origins of the Working Women's Society. While most accounts agree that Leonora O'Reilly was its guiding spirit, Maude Nathan gives the credit to Alice Woolbridge, and Harriette Keyser and Clyde Griffin name Ida Van Etten as the society's "moving spirit." See Shively, *Notable American Women;* Griffin, "Christian Socialism," 201–2; and Maude Nathan, *The Story of an Epoch-Making Movement* (New York: Doubleday, Page, 1926), 15–19.

42. "No Pity for Salesgirls: Josephine Shaw Lowell and Others Testify—The Law Providing for Seats Too Indefinite—Not Allowed to Sit," *New York Times,* 24 March 1895.

43. Stewart, *Philanthropic Work,* 335; *Papers of the Women's Trade Union League,* 1.

44. Philip S. Foner, *Women and the American Labor Movement: From the First Trade Unions to the Present* (New York: Free Press, 1979, 1982), 103–9; Stewart, *Philan-thropic Work,* 334–56; Nathan, *The Story of an Epoch-Making Movement,* 15–19.

45. Nathan, *The Story of an Epoch-Making Movement,* 131–33.

46. Stewart, *Philanthropic Work,* 340; Consumers' League of the City of New York, *Sixth Annual Report* (1896), 2.

47. The story of the passage of the Mercantile Inspection Act can be found in Nathan, *The Story of an Epoch-Making Movement,* 50; *New York Times,* 24 March 1895; "Too Much Inspection," *New York Times,* 21 March 1895, and Lowell's reply, *New York*

Times, 22 March 1895. For the definitive study of Florence Kelley and the National Consumers' League, see Kathryn Kish Sklar, *Florence Kelley and the Nation's Work: The Rise of Women's Political Culture, 1830–1900* (New Haven, Conn.: Yale University Press, 1995). See also Louis L. Athey, "The Consumers' Leagues and Social Reform, 1890–1923" (Ph.D. diss., University of Delaware, 1965).

48. *New York Times,* 22 March 1895.

49. Lowell, "Consumers' Leagues," in Stewart, *Philanthropic Work,* 337–43; quote p. 338. For her reading of Rogers, see Stewart, 415.

50. Stewart, *Philanthropic Work,* 409–15, quote p. 412. Lowell's vision of working-class culture had a decidedly genteel cast to it. For a sharply contrasting view of politics and culture during this period, see Daniel Czitrom, "Underworlds and Underdogs: Big Tim Sullivan and Metropolitan Politics in New York, 1889–1913," *Journal of American History* 78 (1991): 536–58.

51. Stewart, *Philanthropic Work,* 338.

52. *The Heritage of American Social Work: Readings in Its Philosophical and Institutional Development,* ed. Ralph E. Pumphrey and Muriel W. Pumphrey (New York: Columbia University Press, 1961), 139.

53. Quoted in Stewart, *Philanthropic Work,* 363.

54. The preceding portrayal of the faltering economy and its social consequences is based on Michael B. Katz, *In the Shadow of the Poorhouse: A Social History of Welfare in America* (New York: Basic Books, 1986); Nell Irvin Painter, *Standing at Armageddon: The United States, 1877–1919* (New York: Norton, 1987); Ringenbach, *Tramps and Reformers, 1873–1916.*

55. COS, *Twelfth Annual Report* (1893), 25–27.

56. Charles O. Burgess, "The Newspaper as Charity Worker: Poor Relief in New York City, 1893–1894," *New York History* 43 (1962): 249–68.

57. Quotes from "For System in Giving Alms," *New York Times,* 22 March 1894.

58. COS, *Twelfth Annual Report* (1893), 11.

59. Lowell, "Five Months' Work for the Unemployed in New York City," *Charities Review* 3 (1894): 323–42; quote p. 323. See also John Bancroft Devins, D.D., "Mrs. Lowell and the Unemployed: Organizing the East Side Relief Work Committee," in "A Memorial Number," 322–24. For Lowell's work with Seth Low, see Lowell to Seth Low, 11 and 12 December 1893, Seth Low Papers, Manuscripts and Archives Division, NYPL, Astor, Lenox, and Tilden Foundations.

60. Josephine Shaw Lowell, letter to the editor, *New York Times,* 25 December 1894.

61. Devins, "Mrs. Lowell and the Unemployed," 322.

62. Quotes and figures from ibid., 323; quote on Sea Island from Stewart, *Philanthropic Work,* 364.

63. Stewart, *Philanthropic Work,* 365.

64. Lowell, "Five Months' Work for the Unemployed in New York City," 332–38; quote pp. 332–33. Lowell herself contributed $2,162.75 to the effort, and the Fund-Raising Committee collected $102,269.99.

65. Ibid., 336.

66. Lowell to Annie Adams Fields, 11 April 1894, Annie Adams Fields Papers, Huntington Library, San Marino, Calif.

67. Burgess, "The Newspaper as Charity Worker," 252; Peter Sexias, "'Shifting Sands beneath the State': Unemployment, the Labor Market, and the Local Community, 1893–1922" (Ph.D. diss., University of California at Los Angeles, 1988), 35–36.

68. For an elaboration of the process of professionalization, see Mary O. Furner, *Advocacy and Objectivity: A Crisis in the Professionalization of American Social Science, 1865–1905* (Lexington: University of Kentucky Press, 1975), and Dawn M. Greeley, "Beyond Benevolence: Gender, Class, and the Development of Scientific Charity in New York City, 1882–1935" (Ph.D. diss., State University of New York at Stony Brook, 1995).

69. Stewart, *Philanthropic Work,* 358.

70. Ibid., 359. For a good discussion of the concept of "need," see Barbara Randall Joseph, "The Discovery of Need, 1880–1914: A Case Study of the Development of an Idea in Social Welfare Thought" (Ph.D. diss., Columbia University, 1975).

8. *The Useful Citizen*

1. Edward Waldo Emerson, *Life and Letters of Charles Russell Lowell* (Boston and New York: Houghton Mifflin, 1907), 357.

2. As quoted in Paul C. Nagel, *This Sacred Trust: American Nationality, 1798–1898* (New York: Oxford University Press, 1971), 221. The connection between the Civil War and a new sense of nationalism and citizenship is explored in Stuart McConnell, *Glorious Contentment: The Grand Army of the Republic, 1865–1900* (Chapel Hill and London: University of North Carolina Press, 1992).

3. William Rhinelander Stewart, *The Philanthropic Work of Josephine Shaw Lowell* (New York: Macmillan, 1911; rpt., Montclair, N.J.: Patterson Smith Publishing, 1974), 431–33.

4. Ibid., 481.

5. Quotes from ibid., 342–43. Class relations between poor and middle-class women are explored in Ruth Bordin, *Women and Temperance: The Quest for Power and Liberty, 1873–1900* (Philadelphia: Temple University Press, 1981); Peggy Pascoe, "Gender Systems in Conflict: The Marriage of Mission-Educated Chinese American Women, 1874–1939," in *Unequal Sisters: A Multi-Cultural Reader in U.S. Women's History,* ed. Ellen Carol DuBois and Vicki L. Ruiz (New York and London: Routledge, 1990), 123–40; Christine Stansell, *City of Women: Sex and Class in New York, 1789–1860* (Urbana and Chicago: University of Illinois Press, 1987).

6. Stewart, *Philanthropic Work,* 343.

7. Margaret Marsh, "From Separation to Togetherness: The Social Construction of Domestic Space in American Suburbs, 1840–1915," *Journal of American History* 76 (1989): 506–27; quote p. 512.

8. Stewart, *Philanthropic Work,* 377.

9. Two works that address Lowell's leadership are Betty Boyd Caroli, "Women Speak Out for Reform," in *The Rhetoric of Protest and Reform,* ed. Paul H. Boase (Athens: Ohio University Press, 1980), and Ellen Condliffe Lagemann, *A Generation of Women: Education in the Lives of Progressive Reformers* (Cambridge, Mass.: Harvard University Press, 1979).

10. Stewart, *Philanthropic Work,* 142.

11. Carlotta Russell Lowell's obituary was published in the *New York Times,* 20 September, 1924. Other information obtained from the "Will of Carlotta Russell Lowell," signed and dated 14 June 1920, probated New York City, 13 November 1924, Surrogate Court, New York County. She is buried next to her parents at Mount Auburn Cemetery in Cambridge, Massachusetts.

12. As quoted in Ellen Fitzpatrick, *Endless Crusade: Women Social Scientists and Progressive Reform* (New York: Oxford University Press, 1990), 77. Particular examples of Lowell helping women achieve their leadership potential can be found in Maude Nathan, *The Story of an Epoch-Making Movement* (New York: Doubleday, Page, 1926); Louise Perkins to Leonora O'Reilly, 12 March 1896, 30 September 1897, and 21 December 1897, "Leonora O'Reilly Papers," *Papers of the Women's Trade Union League and Its Principal Leaders,* ed. Edward T. James (Woodbridge, Conn.: Research Publications, 1979), reel 4.

13. *History of Woman Suffrage,* ed. Susan B. Anthony and Ida Husted Harper, vol. 4 (New York: Arno and the *New York Times,* 1968), 257–58. Information on the Sherry Committee is from the *New York Times,* 6 October 1894.

14. Quotes from Stewart, *Philanthropic Work,* 441, and Lowell to Frederick William Holls, 2 January 1894, Frederick William Holls Papers, Special Collections, Columbia University. Ellen Carol DuBois, "Working Women, Class Relations, and Suffrage Militance: Harriot Stanton Blatch and the New York Woman Suffrage Movement, 1894–1909," *Journal of American History* 74 (1987): 34–58.

15. "Mrs. C. R. Lowell on Reform," *New York Daily Tribune,* 12 November 1896; "Women's Part in Politics: Mrs. Lowell Says They May Aid Good Government," *New York Times,* 31 December 1896.

16. The organizations and their membership are the subject of the following works: Karen J. Blair, *The Clubwoman as Feminist: True Womanhood Redefined, 1868–1914* (New York: Holmes & Meier, 1980); Ruth Bordin, *Frances Willard: A Biography* (Chapel Hill: University of North Carolina Press, 1986), and *Women and Temperance;* Barbara Leslie Epstein, *The Politics of Domesticity: Women, Evangelism, and Temperance in Nineteenth-Century America* (Middletown, Conn.: Wesleyan University Press, 1981).

17. Mari Jo Buhle, *Women and American Socialism, 1870–1920* (Urbana: University of Illinois Press, 1981), xv.

18. Stewart, *Philanthropic Work,* 481. An example of a letter sent out under Lowell's signature to all New York State clubs is as follows: "Dear Madam President, The Standing Committee on Civil Service Reform of the New York State Federation desires to urge your Club to devote one meeting at least, during the coming year, to the question of the Merit System, which so vitally affects the welfare both of the State and the nation." Lowell, Chairman, Letter of Standing Committee, 25 November 1904, Box 14, William Rhinelander Stewart Papers, Manuscripts and Archives Division, NYPL, Astor, Lenox, and Tilden Foundations.

19. My discussion of political reform in New York City is based on the following sources: Steven P. Erie, *Rainbow's End: Irish-Americans and the Dilemmas of Urban Machine Politics, 1840–1985* (Berkeley: University of California Press, 1988); Jeremy P. Felt, "Vice Reform as a Political Technique: The Committee of Fifteen in New York, 1900–1901," *New York History* 54 (1973): 24–51; David C. Hammack,

Power and Society: Greater New York at the Turn of the Century (New York: Russell Sage Foundation, 1982); Richard L. McCormick, *From Realignment to Reform: Political Change in New York State, 1893–1910* (Ithaca, N.Y.: Cornell University Press, 1981); Terrence J. McDonald, Introduction, *Plunkitt of Tammany Hall* (New York: Bedford Books of St. Martin's Press, 1993); Michael McGerr, *The Decline of Popular Politics: The American North, 1865–1928* (New York: Oxford University Press, 1986); Robert M. Muccigrosso, "The City Reform Club: A Study in Late Nineteenth Century Reform," *New York Historical Society Quarterly* 52 (1968): 235–54; Richard Skolnik, "Civic Group Progressivism in New York City," *New York History* 51 (1970): 411–39, and "The Crystallization of Reform in New York City, 1890–1917" (Ph.D. diss., Yale University, 1964).

20. Skolnik, "Civic Group Progressivism in New York City," 423.

21. Quoted in Muccigrosso, "The City Reform Club," 118.

22. One scholar has recently drawn attention to this aspect of women's organizations in Boston: "Indeed, women's reform groups tended to sound more like machine politicians than like efficient reformers, because they spoke of their desire to humanize the city and their extensive social welfare networks that could provide, as the machine did, jobs, food, coal, child care, and nursing. Women had, in this sense, created their own machine, and their behavior reflected their knowledge of what potential power this 'machine' give them." Sarah Deutsch, "Learning to Talk More Like a Man: Boston Women's Class-Bridging Organizations, 1870–1940," *American Historical Review* 97 (1992): 379–404; quote p. 391.

23. "The churches and charities possessed eloquent spokesmen as well as wealthy backers who commanded attention and respect and who were able to influence many voters." Hammack, *Power and Society*, 142. I wish to acknowledge here the debt I owe to the scholarship of David Hammack and Richard Skolnik in the formulation of my argument on charity, politics, and reform in 1890s New York City. See also David Paul Nord, *Newspapers and New Politics: Municipal Reform, 1890–1900* (Ann Arbor, Mich.: UMI Research Press, 1981).

24. Hammack, *Power and Society*, 119–29.

25. Erie, *Rainbow's End*, 2.

26. This election is covered in Hammack, *Power and Society*, 173–78, and Steven Ross, "Political Economy for the Masses: Henry George," *Democracy* 2 (1982): 125–34.

27. Erie, *Rainbow's End*, 11.

28. Quoted in Hammack, *Power and Society*, 176.

29. Figures from Felt, "Vice Reform as a Political Technique," 25.

30. Edith Patterson Meyer, *"Not Charity but Justice": The Story of Jacob A. Riis* (New York: Vanguard Press, 1974), 79.

31. Remarks of Charles C. Burlingham, "100th Anniversary Celebration of the Birth of Josephine Shaw Lowell," 16 December 1943, Box 143, CSS.

32. "Dr. Parkhurst to Women," *New York Times*, 13 October 1894. An account of Lowell's early political involvement is found in "An Appeal from Women: Vote Against Tammany Hall," *New York Daily Tribune*, 29 October 1890.

33. *New York Daily Tribune*, 7 October 1894. WCTU quote from "Mrs. Grannis on Dr. Parkhurst's Municipal Campaign," *New York Times*, 6 October 1894.

34. *New York Daily Tribune,* 7 October 1894.
35. A partial list is as follows: Mrs. R. W. Gilder, Mrs. George Haven Putnam, Miss Kate Bond, Dr. Emily Blackwell, Mrs. James A. Scrymser, Mrs. C. A. Runkle, Mrs. William Rhinelander Stewart, Mrs. William Jay Schieffelin, Mrs. Robert Fulton Cutting, Mrs. E. L. Godkin, Mrs. Robert Abbe, Maude (Mrs. Frederick) Nathan. From the *New York Times,* 13 October 1894.
36. A study of the brief but important existence of the Woman's Municipal League, including Lowell's period of leadership, is S. Sara Monoson, "The Lady and the Tiger: Women's Electoral Activism in New York City Before Suffrage," *Journal of Women's History* 2 (1990): 100–35. The pamphlet is discussed on p. 111.
37. See "Women Have a Big Rally," *New York Times,* 3 November 1894, and Stewart, *Philanthropic Work,* 416–17, for accounts of the league's activities in this campaign.
38. "Women's Work to Go On," *New York Daily Tribune,* 12 November 1894.
39. "Its Mothers' Meetings: Woman's Municipal League Has Promoted Political Education All Summer," *New York Daily Tribune,* 24 September 1903.
40. Robert F. de Forest, in "Josephine Shaw Lowell, Memorial Meeting," 1905, Box 143, CSS.
41. Stewart, *Philanthropic Work,* 480.
42. The preceding two quotes are from Josephine Shaw Lowell, "Relation of Women to Good Government," in Stewart, *Philanthropic Work,* 435–36.
43. Above quotes from ibid., 444–45.
44. In 1900 Lowell served as secretary of the league, which sponsored lectures to keep the public appraised of their continuing work. "Work of the Municipal League: Members Take Active Part for or against Public Measures," *New York Daily Tribune,* 19 May 1900; "Politics in the Fall: The Woman's Municipal League Pledges Itself to Support the Work of the Citizens' Union," *New York Daily Tribune,* 10 May 1901. See Monoson, "The Lady and the Tiger," 109–11.
45. Hammack, *Power and Society,* 151–54.
46. Woman's Municipal League, *Facts for Fathers and Mothers* (New York: City Club, 1901).
47. Lowell to Everett P. Wheeler, 24 April 1901, Shepard-Low 1901 Campaign Scrapbook, Citizens' Union Papers, NYPL.
48. "Wrongs of the Poor: Lack of Room in Schools, Unclean Streets, and Crowded Tenements Due to Tammany's Misrule, Says Mrs. Lowell," *New York Daily Tribune,* 17 October 1901.
49. Stewart, *Philanthropic Work,* 419–20.
50. Background information on C. C. Burlingham is from Michael John Burlingham, *The Last Tiffany: A Biography of Dorothy Tiffany Burlingham* (New York: Athenaeum, 1989), esp. 138–40.
51. The preceding information is from the following sources: Remarks of Charles Culp Burlingham, "100th Anniversary Celebration of the Birth of Josephine Shaw Lowell," 16 December 1943, Box 143, CSS; Stewart, *Philanthropic Work,* 54. Lowell and Carlotta lived in their brownstone from 1874 to 1905, when, just before Lowell died, she moved into another brownstone.
52. Remarks of Burlingham, "100th Anniversary Celebration," Box 143, CSS.

53. Ibid., and Burke Wilkinson, *Uncommon Clay: The Life and Works of Augustus Saint-Gaudens* (New York: Harcourt Brace Jovanovich, 1985).

54. Remarks of Burlingham, "100th Anniversary Celebration," Box 143, CSS.

55. Stewart, *Philanthropic Work*, 527.

56. I have relied on the following works for my discussion of the events leading up to the anti-imperialist movement as well as the dynamics of the movement itself: Robert L. Beisner, *Twelve against Empire: The Anti-Imperialists, 1898–1900* (New York: McGraw-Hill, 1968); Edward P. Crapol, *Women and American Foreign Policy* (Westport, Conn.: Greenwood Press, 1987); Charles DeBenedetti, *The Peace Reform in American History* (Bloomington: Indiana University Press, 1980); Philip S. Foner and Richard C. Winchester, eds., *The Anti-Imperialist Reader*, 2 vols. (New York: Holmes & Meier, 1984); Gerald I. Linderman, *The Mirror of War: American Society and the Spanish-American War* (Ann Arbor: University of Michigan Press, 1974); C. Roland Marchand, *The American Peace Movement and Social Reform, 1898–1918* (Princeton, N.J.: Princeton University Press, 1972); James M. McPherson, *The Abolitionist Legacy: From Reconstruction to the NAACP* (Princeton, N.J.: Princeton University Press, 1975); David S. Patterson, "An Interpretation of the American Peace Movement, 1898–1914," in *Peace Movements in America*, ed. Charles Chatfield (New York: Schocken Books, 1973), 20–38; Daniel B. Schirmer, *Republic or Empire: American Resistance to the Philippine War* (Cambridge, Mass.: Schenkman Publishing, 1972); Richard E. Welch, Jr., *Response to Imperialism: The United States and the Philippine-American War, 1899–1902* (Chapel Hill: University of North Carolina Press, 1979).

57. Lowell's letter is entitled "Sympathy in the War," *New York Daily Tribune*, 19 July 1898; the *Tribune's* response is "Shall We Owe It First and Most to Spaniards or to Americans?" Earlier, Lowell had written another letter to the *Tribune*, protesting the volunteering of married men for the war. "The Duty of Married Men: It Is First to Their Wives and Families, Says Mrs. Lowell, and They Should Stay at Home," *New York Daily Tribune*, 25 April 1898.

58. DeBenedetti, *The Peace Reform in American History*, 72.

59. Preceding quotes from Stewart, *Philanthropic Work*, 466–70.

60. Lowell to Edward W. Ordway, 8 May 1904, Edward W. Ordway Papers, Manuscripts and Archives Division, NYPL, Astor, Lenox, and Tilden Foundations. See also Lowell to Ordway, 3 and 4 June 1904, Edward W. Ordway Papers, Manuscripts and Archives Division, NYPL, Astor, Lenox, and Tilden Foundations, which are two of many letters that demonstrated Lowell's instructive capabilities.

61. Among the figures Lowell corresponded with are Edwin Burrit Smith, Charles Eliot Norton, Carl Schurz, Erving Winslow, Andrew Carnegie, and Felix Adler. All of this correspondence can be found in the Edward W. Ordway Papers, Manuscripts and Archives Division, NYPL, Astor, Lenox, and Tilden Foundations.

62. Lowell to Edward W. Ordway, 4 October 1902, Edward W. Ordway Papers, Manuscripts and Archives Division, NYPL, Astor, Lenox, and Tilden Foundations.

63. Josephine Shaw Lowell, "To the Editor of *City and State*," 13 September 1900, reprinted in *The Anti-Imperialist Reader*, 1:472–73.

64. Welch, *Response to Imperialism*, 52.

65. Ibid. For a good account of the GAR's role in the pro-war movement, see McConnell, *Glorious Contentment.*

66. Lowell to Edward W. Ordway, 24 August 1905, Edward W. Ordway Papers, Manuscripts and Archives Division, NYPL, Astor, Lenox, and Tilden Foundations.

67. Lowell to Edward W. Ordway, 24 December 1904, Edward W. Ordway Papers, Manuscripts and Archives Division, NYPL, Astor, Lenox, and Tilden Foundations.

68. Lowell to Edward W. Ordway, 22 September 1905, Edward W. Ordway Papers, Manuscripts and Archives Division, NYPL, Astor, Lenox, and Tilden Foundations.

69. Ibid. One historian agreed with Lowell: "Though they failed to prevent the United States from becoming a colonial power, the anti-imperialists did put their opponents on the defensive, they helped bring about relatively restrained rule in the Philippines looking toward early independence, and after 1904 they focused glaring publicity on America's noncolonial imperialism in the Caribbean." McPherson, *The Abolitionist Legacy,* 325–26.

70. Jacob Riis in "Memorial Meeting," 1905, Box 143, CSS.

71. Stewart, *Philanthropic Work,* 483.

72. "Will of Josephine Shaw Lowell," signed and dated 15 February 1905, probated 9 November 1905; author obtained copy of it 15 December 1987. Of the $75,000 left to the COS, $25,000 was to cover general expenses and $50,000 was to be used to establish a pension fund for employees. Lowell also left small legacies to several COS agents, as well as to a police matron.

73. "Her Public Spirit," *New York Daily Tribune,* 14 October 1905; "Josephine Shaw Lowell Dead," *New York Times,* 13 October 1905. For accounts of many of the tributes to Lowell immediately following her death, see "A Memorial Number: Josephine Shaw Lowell," *Charities and the Commons* 15 (1905): 309–35. The Community Service Society honored Lowell's one-hundredth birthday with a ceremony at the United Charities Building on 16 December 1943. CSS officials managed to get a *Liberty Ship* named after Lowell as part of the anniversary celebration. The dedication of the ship was held 7 March 1944 in Panama City, Florida, and was attended by Lowell's great-niece, Lieutenant Frances Jay of the U.S. Navy. For details of both ceremonies, see "100th Anniversary Celebration of the Birth of Josephine Shaw Lowell," 16 December 1943, Box 143, CSS, and "Lowell, Josephine Shaw, Launching of *Liberty Ship,*" Box 143, CSS.

74. Lowell to Edward M. Shepard, 24 January 1903, No. 13, Edward M. Shepard Papers, Rare Book and Manuscript Library, Columbia University.

75. Lowell to Edward W. Ordway, 27 November 1901, Edward W. Ordway Papers, Manuscripts and Archives Division, NYPL, Astor, Lenox, and Tilden Foundations. Edward P. Crapol, "Lydia Maria Child," in Crapol, ed., *Women and American Foreign Policy* (Westport, Conn.: Greenwood Press, 1987), 1–18.

76. Lowell to Edward W. Ordway, 22 September 1905, Edward W. Ordway Papers, Manuscripts and Archives Division, NYPL, Astor, Lenox, and Tilden Foundations.

77. *The Monument to Robert Gould Shaw: Its Inception, Completion, and Unveiling* (Boston and New York: Houghton Mifflin, 1897); Thomas W. Higginson et al., "The Shaw Memorial and the Sculptor St.-Gaudens," *Century Magazine* 54 (1897): 176–200; Ludwig Lauerhass, Jr., "Beyond Glory: The Continuing March of an American

Epic," unpublished paper in author's possession; Stephen J. Whitfield, "'Sacred in History and Art': The Shaw Memorial," *New England Quarterly* 60 (1987): 3–37; Burke Wilkinson, *Uncommon Clay: The Life and Works of Augustus Saint-Gaudens* (New York: Harcourt Brace Jovanovich, 1985).

78. First quote, Lowell to Edward W. Emerson, 24 August 1904; second quote, Lowell to Edward W. Emerson, 3 October 1904, Emerson Papers, MHS. The book was published two years after Lowell's death. Edward Waldo Emerson, *The Life and Letters of Charles Russell Lowell* (Boston and New York: Houghton Mifflin, 1907).

79. T. S. Eliot, "Burnt Norton," in *Four Quartets* (New York: Harcourt, Brace & World, 1943).

80. Emerson, *Life and Letters,* 278.

Bibliography

Manuscript Collections

Boston Athenaeum Shaw Family Letters
Columbia University, Butler Library, Rare Book and Manuscript Collection
Felix Adler Papers
Community Service Society Records
Homer Folks Collection
Frederick William Holls Papers
Robert Underwood Johnson Papers
Seth Low Manuscript Collection
Edward Morse Shepard Papers

Gloucestershire County Record Office
Thomas Barwick Lloyd Baker Papers

Houghton Library, Harvard University
Freedmen's Aid Society Journal
John Jay Chapman Papers
Henry Lee Higginson Papers
Thomas Wentworth Higginson Papers
James Family Papers
James Russell Lowell Collection
Charles Eliot Norton Papers
Louise Schiefflin Papers
Robert Gould Shaw Papers

Huntington Library
Annie Adams Fields Papers
Miscellaneous Collections

Bibliography

Library of Congress, Manuscript Division
Andrew Carnegie Papers
National Women's Trade Union League
The Reid Family Papers
Jacob Riis Papers
Theodore Roosevelt Papers

Massachusetts Historical Society
Edward Emerson Papers
James Russell Lowell Papers

New York County, Surrogate Court
Will of Carlotta Russell Lowell, signed and dated 14 June 1920,
probated New York City, 13 November 1924
Will of Josephine Shaw Lowell, signed and dated 15 February 1905,
probated New York City, 9 November 1905

New-York Historical Society, Manuscripts Division
Charles S. Fairchild Collection
Louisa Lee Schuyler Correspondence

New York Public Library, Manuscripts Division
Thomas Barwick Lloyd Baker Papers
R. R. Bowker Collection
Bryant-Godwin Collection
Century Collection
Henry George Papers
R. W. Gilder Papers
Josephine Shaw Lowell Miscellaneous Papers
Edward W. Ordway Papers
Shaw Family Papers
William Rhinelander Stewart Papers

Radcliffe College, Arthur and Elizabeth Schlesinger Library
Almy Family Papers
Elizabeth Glendower Evans Papers
Leonora O'Reilly Papers

Microfilm Collections

The Collected Correspondence of Lydia Maria Child, 1817–1880. Edited by Patricia G. Holland and Milton Meltzer. Microfiche edition. Millwood, N.Y.: Kraus Microfilm, Kraus-Thomson Organization, 1982.
Papers of the Women's Trade Union League and Its Principal Leaders. Edited by Edward T. James. Woodbridge: Conn.: Research Publications, 1979.

Bibliography

Oral Interviews

Carol Brownell, Assistant General Director, Community Service Society of New York

Private Collection

Faith Knapp Collection, Cazenovia, New York

Selected Works by Josephine Shaw Lowell

"A Young Girl's Wartime Diary," 23 July 1861–9 November 1862. In William Rhinelander Stewart. *The Philanthropic Work of Josephine Shaw Lowell.* New York: Macmillan, 1911; rpt., Montclair, N.J.: Patterson Smith Publishing, 1974, 10–37. Hereafter cited as Stewart.

"Bad State of Public Charities." *New York Times,* 31 October 1877.

With Theodore Roosevelt. "Communication to the Board of Estimate and Apportionment, City of New York, December 24, 1877." New York State Board of Charities [hereafter cited as SBC]. *Eleventh Annual Report* (1878), 231–34.

With Theodore Roosevelt and Henry Hoguet. "Report Relating to the New York Juvenile Guardian Society of the City of New York." SBC. *Eleventh Annual Report* (1878), 99–102.

"One Means of Preventing Pauperism." National Conference of Charities and Correction. *Proceedings* (1879), 189–200. Hereafter cited as NCCC *Proceedings.*

With Riley Ropes. "Report of the Committee on a Reformatory for Women." SBC. *Twelfth Annual Report* (1879), 289–92.

"A Paper Read before the New York Association of Teachers, 1880." In Stewart, 257–67.

"Public Charities of New York City." SBC. *Thirteenth Annual Report* (1880), 137–69.

"Reformatories for Women." SBC. *Thirteenth Annual Report* (1880), 173–80.

"Considerations upon a Better System of Public Charities and Correction for Cities." NCCC *Proceedings* (1881), 168–83.

"Report upon the Condition and Needs of the Insane of New York City." SBC. *Fourteenth Annual Report* (1881), 177–93.

"Report on the Public Charities of New York City." SBC. *Fifteenth Annual Report* (1882), 289–317.

"Report in Relation to Out-door Relief Societies in New York City." SBC. *Fifteenth Annual Report* (1882), 321–31.

"Report on the State Institutions for the Deaf and Dumb, and the Asylum for Idiots." SBC. *Fifteenth Annual Report* (1882), 117–51.

"Duties of Friendly Visitors." *Charity Organization Society Papers,* no. 11. New York, 1883. Also in Stewart, 142–50.

Public Relief and Private Charity. New York: Putnam, 1884.

With Ripley Ropes. "Report of the Standing Committee on Outdoor Relief." SBC. *Seventeenth Annual Report* (1884), 141–61.

"The Bitter Cry of the Poor in New York: Some of Its Causes and Some of Its Remedies." *Christian Union* 31 (1885): 6–7.

"Report on the Institution for the Care of Destitute Children of the City of New York." SBC. *Nineteenth Annual Report* (1886), 165–243.

"Report on the Public Charities of New York City for the Year 1886." SBC. *Twentieth Annual Report* (1887), 216–79.

"How to Adapt Charity Organization Methods to Small Communities." NCCC *Proceedings* (1887), 135–43.

"Sunday School Talks to Children." Five papers read before the Sunday School of the Lenox Avenue Unitarian Church, New York City, 1888. In Stewart, 150–58.

"Paper Read at the First Public Meeting of the Working Women's Society." 2 February 1888. In Stewart, 372–80.

"Report upon the Care of Dependent Children in the City of New York and Elsewhere." SBC. *Twenty-third Annual Report* (1890), 175–249.

"The Economic and Moral Effects of Public Outdoor Relief." NCCC *Proceedings* (1890), 81–91.

"Letter in Support of the Opening of the Johns Hopkins Medical School to Women." *Century Magazine* 41 (February 1891): 634–35.

Review of *In Darkest England and the Way Out,* by General William Booth. *Magazine for Christian Literature* 3 (1891): 440–42.

"Labor Organization as Affected by Law." *Charities Review* 1 (1891): 6–11.

"On Labor." Letter to the *New York Times,* 2 December 1892. In Stewart, 361.

"Workingmen's Rights in Property Created by Them." Letter to the *New York Tribune,* 15 July 1892. In Stewart, 390–94.

"A Chapter of Industrial History." *Charities Review* 2 (1893): 365–70.

"Felix qui causam rerum cognovit." *Charities Review* 2 (1893): 420–26.

Industrial Arbitration and Conciliation. New York: Putnam, 1893.

"Industrial Peace." *Charities Review* 2 (1893): 153–59.

"A Chapter of Industrial History." *Charities Review* 3 (1893): 365–70.

"Methods of Relief for the Unemployed." *Forum* (1894): 655–62.

"Five Months' Work for the Unemployed in New York City." *Charities Review* 3 (1894): 323–42.

"The Great Coal Strike of 1894." *Charities Review* 4 (1894): 41–45.

"Poverty and Its Relief: The Methods Possible in the City of New York." NCCC *Proceedings* (May 1895), 45–55.

"County Visiting Committees." Paper dated 15 November 1895. In Stewart, 77–85.

"Report of the Governing Board for 1895." Consumers' League. In Stewart, 343–56.

"The True Aim of Charity Organization Societies." 1895. In Stewart, 196–204.

"Charity Problems." *Charities Review* 5 (1896): 123–27.

"Industrial Conciliation." Paper prepared for the Live Question Bureau, January 1896. In Stewart, 394–400.

"Homeless Men and Women." A letter to Commander Booth Tucker, Salvation Army. Written by Lowell for a committee on 30 September 1896. In Stewart, 446–53.

"The Reform of the Civil Service and the Spoils System." Paper given at a meeting of the Women's Auxiliary of the Civil Service Reform Association and the League for Political Education, 30 December 1896. In Stewart, 483–96.

"The Influence of Cheap Lodging Houses on City Pauperism." Paper written 16 February 1897 for the Baltimore Charity Organization Society. In Stewart, 453–59.

"The Rights of Capital and Labor and Industrial Conciliation." Pamphlet published by the Church Social Union, Boston, 15 June 1897. In Stewart, 400–408.

"Civil Service Reform and Public Charity." Paper sent 29 June 1897 to the Convention of the Superintendents of the Poor in New York State. In Stewart, 496–500.

"Consumers' Leagues." Written in February 1898. In Stewart, 337–43.

"What Can Young Men Do for the City?" Dated 28 March 1898. In Stewart, 422–35.

"The Evils of Investigation and Relief." A paper read before the training class in Practical Philanthropic Work, 21 June 1898. Later published in *Charities* 1 (1898): 8–10. Also in Stewart, 207–17.

"The Living Wage." Paper delivered at Cooper Union, 1 June 1898. In Stewart, 409–15.

"Sympathy in the War." *New York Daily Tribune,* 19 July 1898.

"Woman's Municipal League." *Municipal Affairs* 2 (1898): 465–66.

"Children." A speech for volunteer workers of the Charity Organization Society, 18 November 1898. In Stewart, 267–76.

With others. "City Coal." Letter to *Charities* 2 (1898): 11.

"Civil Service Reform." NCCC *Proceedings* (1898), 256–61.

"The Ethics of Civil Service Reform." Speech delivered at the Broadway Tabernacle, 1898. In Stewart, 500–506.

"Relation of Women to Good Government." Speech delivered to the Young Women's Christian Association, 6 February 1899. In Stewart, 435–44.

With others. "Report of Committee on Dependent Children." *Charities* 2 (1899): 2–5.

"Report of Committee on District Work for the Year ending July 1, 1899." *Charities* 3 (1899): 4–5.

"Inspection of Charities." *New York Daily Tribune,* 4 February 1900.

"To the Editor of *City and State.*" Letter published 13 September 1900. Reprinted in *The Anti-Imperialist Reader: A Documentary History of Anti-Imperialism in the United States,* vol. 1, 472–73, edited by Philip S. Foner and Richard C. Winchester. New York and London: Holmes & Meier, 1984.

"Moral Deterioration Following War." Ca. 1900. In Stewart, 466–70.

"The Peril in the Charities." *New York Times,* 17 January 1901.

Letter to *Charities* (3 May 1902). In Stewart, 473–74.

"Booker T. Washington." An address delivered 20 August 1903. In Stewart, 471–73.

Index